The Translational Design of Universities

# Advances in Learning Environments Research

*Series Editors*

Barry J. Fraser (*Curtin University, Australia*)
David B. Zandvliet (*Simon Fraser University, Canada*)

*Editorial Board*

Perry den Brok (*Wageningen University, The Netherlands*)
Bruce Johnson (*University of Arizona, USA*)
Celia Johnson (*Bradley University, USA*)
Rosalyn Anstine Templeton (*Montana State University-Northern, USA*)

VOLUME 12

The titles published in this series are listed at *brill.com/aler*

# The Translational Design of Universities

*An Evidence-Based Approach*

Edited by

Kenn Fisher

BRILL
SENSE

LEIDEN | BOSTON

Cover illustration: The University of Sydney Business School, photograph by Woods Bagot

All chapters in this book have undergone peer review.

Library of Congress Cataloging-in-Publication Data

Names: Fisher, Kenn, editor.
Title: The translational design of universities : an evidence-based approach / edited by Kenn Fisher.
Description: Leiden ; Boston : Brill Sense, [2019] | Series: Advances in learning environments research, ISSN 2542-9035 ; volume 12 | Includes bibliographical references.
Identifiers: LCCN 2019010129 (print) | LCCN 2019016809 (ebook) | ISBN 9789004391598 (Ebook) | ISBN 9789004391581 (hardback : alk. paper) | ISBN 9789004391574 (pbk. : alk. paper)
Subjects: LCSH: Campus planning. | College facilities--Planning. | Internet in higher education. | Education, Higher--Effect of technological innovations on.
Classification: LCC LB3223 (ebook) | LCC LB3223 .T73 2019 (print) | DDC 727/.3--dc23
LC record available at https://lccn.loc.gov/2019010129

ISSN 2542-9035
ISBN 978-90-04-39157-4 (paperback)
ISBN 978-90-04-39158-1 (hardback)
ISBN 978-90-04-39159-8 (e-book)

Copyright 2019 by Koninklijke Brill NV, Leiden, The Netherlands, except where stated otherwise.
Koninklijke Brill NV incorporates the imprints Brill, Brill Hes & De Graaf, Brill Nijhoff, Brill Rodopi, Brill Sense, Hotei Publishing, mentis Verlag, Verlag Ferdinand Schöningh and Wilhelm Fink Verlag.
All rights reserved. No part of this publication may be reproduced, translated, stored in a retrieval system, or transmitted in any form or by any means, electronic, mechanical, photocopying, recording or otherwise, without prior written permission from the publisher.
Authorization to photocopy items for internal or personal use is granted by Koninklijke Brill NV provided that the appropriate fees are paid directly to The Copyright Clearance Center, 222 Rosewood Drive, Suite 910, Danvers, MA 01923, USA. Fees are subject to change.

This book is printed on acid-free paper and produced in a sustainable manner.

# CONTENTS

Foreword      vii
*Robert A. Ellis*

Preface      ix

List of Figures and Tables      xi

Notes on Contributors      xvii

**Part 1: Emerging Trends in Higher Education and Their Impact on the Physical Campus**

Introduction to Part 1      3
*Kenn Fisher*

1. The Translational Design of Universities: From Campus to Classroom      5
   *Kenn Fisher*

2. Scoping the Future of the Higher Education Campus      23
   *Kenn Fisher*

3. Designing the University of the Future      51
   *Rifca Hashimshony and Jacov Haina*

4. The Relationship between Innovation, Campuses and Cities: Lessons about Synergy from the Development of the MIT in Cambridge      71
   *Flavia Curvelo Magdaniel*

5. "The Third Teacher" of the XXI Century: Educational Infrastructure, Its Problems and Challenges      93
   *Alejandra Torres-Landa Lopez*

**Part 2: The Socio-Cultural Implications in Aligning Virtual and Physical Learning Spaces**

Introduction to Part 2      105
*Kenn Fisher*

6. Virtual Worlds in Higher Education: Embodied Experiences of Academics      107
   *Leah Irving*

CONTENTS

7. The Assessment of the Psychosocial Learning Environment of
   University Statistics Classrooms    131
   *Panayiotis Skordi and Barry J. Fraser*

8. Learning Space Design in Higher Education    149
   *Ronald Beckers*

9. Implementing Grounded Theory in Research on Blended Learning
   Environments    177
   *Mahmoud Reza Saghafi*

10. Modelling Learning Space and Student Learning in Higher Education:
    An Evidence-Based Exploration    205
    *Ji Yu*

11. Mind the Gap: Co-Created Learning Spaces in Higher Education    221
    *Marian Mahat and Mollie Dollinger*

**Part 3: Evaluating Learning Space/Place Planning and Design, and the
Implications for Future Campus Planning and Design**

Introduction to Part 3    239
  *Kenn Fisher*

12. A Critical Review of Post 2012 Scholarly Literature on the
    Evidence-Based Design and Evaluation of New Generation
    Active Learning Environments    241
    *Kenn Fisher and Robert A. Ellis*

13. Designing for the Future: A Post-Occupancy Evaluation of the
    Peter Jones Learning Centre    259
    *Jacqueline Pizzuti-Ashby*

14. Defining Quality in Academic Library Spaces: Criteria to Guide Space
    Planning and Ongoing Evaluation    287
    *Neda Abbasi and Kenn Fisher*

15. At-scale Innovative University Learning Spaces of the Future:
    An Approach to Evidencing and Evaluating What Works    315
    *Leanne Rose-Munro and Saadia Majeed*

16. Afterword: 21st C Learner Modalities    327
    *Kenn Fisher*

ROBERT A. ELLIS

# FOREWORD

There is much debate about the role of higher education at present. Learning, innovation and quality are themes which dominate much of discourse and there is genuine concern about how these intersect for the benefit of students, researchers and universities. Within this debate, higher education as a sector has recognised its responsibility to demonstrate how its outcomes can contribute to a better society and thereby emphasising the nature of the role of universities. This recognition has stimulated a theme of *translational research*, the idea that there is still much work to be done once research has been completed, in disseminating discovery through a reconstrual of the outcomes for different audiences in order to pass on knowledge in understandable ways. Without attending to the effective dissemination of research, half the job of researchers is left undone.

In this volume, there is a concerted effort to pass on the findings of the research of experienced and new researchers alike, those who have been investigating universities, learning and space for many years, and those who have just begun the challenge. In all cases, the goal has been to reveal the outcomes in such a way as to push the field on, to reduce ambiguity in shared terms and concepts, to canvass different methodologies which tilt the lens of analysis on learning space. These different approaches to researching university design and learning space reveal different aspects of the phenomenon, and to aim to deal with the complexities of the variables involved, which seem to grow with every new innovation in pedagogy and technology.

The concept of universities as 'learning spaces' that underpins this volume, comes at a tipping point in the international higher education sector. New pedagogies, new technologies, new partners in the provision of higher education and new drivers for the outcomes of higher education to deal with the workplace and third place, those places supporting informal learning, have meant that learners and teachers are finding themselves in new configurations of physical and virtual learning space, both on and off campus, in social and professional contexts and in rural and international areas. This growing variation in the structure of the learning space has meant that teachers find their approaches to design having to mature and become more sensitive to the affordances of the learners' context in order to leverage learning benefit where possible, and avoid impediments that it might create. This is no easy matter. Consequently, the more that studies reveal these complexities and their solutions, the better informed educators and those concerned about the quality of higher education will be.

FOREWORD

One of the challenges for the field of learning space research at present is the separation of the physical and virtual. The field has tended to be divided into two foci: those focussing mostly on the built environment, and those focusing mostly on the online environment. The problem with this division is that from a learner's perspective at university, students are often required to pursue learning tasks across in-class and online spaces, repeatedly back and forth, both on and off campus, until they understand the purpose of, and have demonstrated their understanding of, the activity in which they have been engaging. This volume addressess this weakness in the field by including research studies into both the built environment as well as the online environment and how activity design that traverses both spaces can contribute to learning outcomes.

Another key challenge for learning space research that this volume addresses is evaluation. One of the difficulties of evaluating learning space for its contribution to learning lies in the observation that it is unlikely to have a *direct* impact on learning. Rather, it is the way students engage with aspects and configurations of tools and people within and across physical and virtual learning space that is likely to have an indirect impact on their outcomes. Consequently, discovering new ways of evaluating the contribution of learning space to the outcomes sought by students and teachers remains an ongoing objective in the field, an objective on which this volume brings some sustained reflection to bear.

The thread that ties this volume together across all the reported research studies is a desire to put into practice a translational cycle that will move the field onwards. By considering university futures in the first part, arguing for an evidence-based model in the second, and then seeking to uncover knowledge which can be acted upon to improve learning space design in the third, this volume provides a useful and helpful approach to addressing many of the pedagogical and material challenges in the design of universities as places of learning.

*Robert A. Ellis*
*AEL Group*
*Griffith University*

# PREFACE

This book – which hinges on the idea of the translational design of learning environments – is the second in the series, with the first volume focussing on schools. Whilst the schools are transforming at a relatively glacial pace in most countries across the globe, universities are under extreme pressure to adapt to the rapid emergence of the virtual campus. Competition for students from online courses is increasing, although the certification and graduation rates from these modes is in its early stages. But there is clearly an emerging impact on what the nature of the traditional campus will look like in the 21st C.

In this context, technology enabled active blended learning environments are now integrating the face-to-face and online virtual experience synchronously and asynchronously. Local branch campuses are emerging in city and town centres, and international branch campuses are growing at a rapid rate:

> International branch campuses (IBCs) continue to be a sought-after form of transnational education (TNE): at last count, there were 263 campuses open in 77 countries around the world. Around half (130) of these campuses are more than 10 years old. At least 15 new IBCs are under development. Year after year, waves of students choose to study at these campuses with the belief that the IBC will provide the same opportunities to succeed as the home campus. (Merola, 2018)

So, there is increasing pressure at the city level, the campus level, the formal and informal learning space level and the library and social or third-space level.

This book attempts to cover the city to the classroom and those elements in between. It uses an evidence-based approach which is based on doctoral dissertations to evaluate what drivers of change are emerging and how affective those changes are. It also seeks to fathom what the future might look like as judgements are made about what does work.

As this preface is being written, an academic colleague sent a little diagram about this evolution. Chapter 1 ended talking about Universities 2.0. This book could already be out of date as we move into the Universities 3.0 generation.

Nevertheless, we must document and evaluate current practice, so we can 'place a peg in the ground' and know on what basis we are moving forward from. As you read extracts in this book, please remember the majority of the material comes from significant scholarly pieces of work primarily, namely that of doctoral dissertations. I encourage you to seek out those original longitudinal research projects to develop a deeper understanding of the summaries which appear herein.

# PREFACE

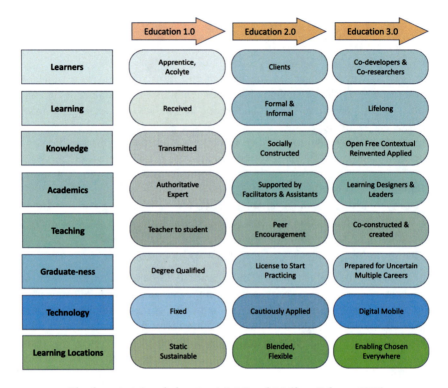

*The characteristics of education 1.0, 2.0 and 3.0 (from Salmon, 2018)*

## REFERENCES

Merola, R. (2018). *Tracking down student outcomes at international branch campuses*. The Observatory on Borderless Higher Education.

Salmon, G. (2019). *Higher education 1.0 to 3.0 and beyond* [Blog]. Retrieved from https://www.gillysalmon.com/blog/higher-education-3-0-and-beyond

# FIGURES AND TABLES

FIGURES

| | | |
|---|---|---|
| 1.1. | Tacit: Explicit knowledge interchange (Nonaka, 1991) | 8 |
| 1.2. | Strengths and weaknesses of qualitative vs quantitative (Looi, 2014) | 14 |
| 2.1. | Complex adaptive assemblage drivers (adapted from Deleuze & Guattari, 1987, in Dovey, 2016, p. 269) | 25 |
| 2.2. | Four future university scenarios (OECD, 2006) | 40 |
| 2.3. | Forces for change determining the size of the university (from Hashimshony & Haina, 2014) | 41 |
| 2.4. | The new American university and its origins (adapted from Crow & Dabars, 2014) | 42 |
| 2.5. | The emergence of the branch campus model (Garrett & Gallagher, 2014) | 42 |
| 2.6. | Four possible evolutionary scenarios for universities (Ernst & Young, 2014) | 43 |
| 2.7. | Research intensive vs teaching; professional training vs higher education | 45 |
| 3.1. | Main layout prototypes: Schematic presentation of examples | 53 |
| 3.2. | Schematic description of changes in the organisational structure of the university | 58 |
| 3.3. | Forces for change determining the size of the university | 59 |
| 3.4. | Graphic presentation of alternative values for each spatial variable | 61 |
| 3.5. | Values applied to the three main uncertainties to generate the four scenarios | 62 |
| 3.6. | Graphic presentation of the spatial characteristics of each of the four scenarios | 64 |
| 4.1. | Input conditions (left) in the conceptual model explaining the proposition of the built environment as catalyst for innovation. These interdependent conditions are required to create and apply knowledge (innovation as a process in the middle) conducting to different outputs (right) (from Curvelo Magdaniel, 2016, p. 326) | 74 |
| 4.2. | Overview of the main stakeholders influencing the demand for developing tech-campuses framed into the Triple Helix model (Etzkowitz, 2008) (from Curvelo Magdaniel, 2016, p. 108) | 76 |
| 4.3. | Data collection plan (from Curvelo Magdaniel, 2016, p. 463) | 78 |
| 4.4. | Location of urban areas developed by the MIT in collaboration with public and private partners since 1959. Green: Urban area developments. Grey: The MIT's owned land. Black: The MIT's owned/leased buildings (Curvelo Magdaniel, 2016, p. 256) | 80 |

FIGURES AND TABLES

| | | |
|---|---|---|
| 4.5. | Technology Square in 2014 | 81 |
| 4.6. | Kendall Square in 2014 | 84 |
| 4.7. | University Park @MIT in 2014 | 85 |
| 5.1. | The cause and effects of a postmodern world (based on Ishikawa Diagram) | 95 |
| 5.2. | Educational trends | 100 |
| 8.1. | The purpose-process-place framework (visualised after Duffy et al., 2011, in Beckers, Van der Voordt and Dewulf, 2015, p. 3) | 154 |
| 8.2. | Purpose of education (derived from Beckers et al., 2015) | 156 |
| 8.3. | Education processes (derived from Beckers et al., 2015) | 158 |
| 8.4. | Framework for aligning learning space with educational purpose and process (Beckers, 2016a, p. 40) | 159 |
| 8.5. | Impression of learning settings in the Nijmegen building (Beckers, 2016b) | 163 |
| 8.6. | Mean values regarding the importance of characteristics of the physical study environment in higher education buildings (N=697) (Beckers, 2016b) | 164 |
| 8.7. | Higher education learning space framework (adapted from Beckers et al., 2015) | 165 |
| 8.8. | Mean values regarding the learning space preferences (N=697) (adapted from Beckers, 2016b) | 165 |
| 8.9. | Settings for an activity based learning environment (classrooms excluded) (Beckers, 2016, p. 163) | 167 |
| 9.1. | Philosophical position of the grounded theory (philosophical triangle, based on Candy, 1993) | 180 |
| 9.2. | The interrelationship of the components of the research approach | 181 |
| 9.3. | The ten-step process of the research approach in the main study | 183 |
| 9.4. | The six step process: Archiving, coding, and analysing data in the pilot study | 186 |
| 9.5. | An example of mapping an individual perception of one student | 187 |
| 9.6. | Tree codes: Presenting the hierarchical structure of codes in MAXQDA | 188 |
| 9.7. | Selected codes for technology as an element of the tree codes | 190 |
| 9.8. | Planning the element based model: Positioning each code to realise its attribute, element, and environment | 191 |
| 9.9. | The fourth step of coding: Selected codes of nine elements | 191 |
| 9.10. | The fifth step of coding: Each code positioned according to its environment and its value | 192 |
| 9.11. | The main attributes of the place-time environments | 193 |
| 9.12. | The HBDS model and its attributes | 194 |
| 9.13. | The summarised HBDS model complemented by Face-to-Face and web-based education | 194 |
| 9.14. | Elements in design studio education: The final conceptual framework | 199 |
| 10.1. | Space 1 | 209 |

xii

FIGURES AND TABLES

10.2.   Space 2 (Photo: Sino-Finnish Centre, 2016)                                              209
10.3.   An integrated model of learning space and student learning in higher
        education based on an empirical study in China                                          210
11.1.   Social construction of knowledge (from Nonaka & Konno, 1998)        224
12.1.   Schematic diagram of an active learning classroom
        (from Brooks, 2013)                                                                     246
12.2.   Steelcase 'solutions' for active learning classrooms
        (from Scott Webber et al., 2013)                                                        250
12.3.   Emergent relational model linking pedagogy, learning environment
        and student wellbeing (from Waldrip, Cox, & Jin Yu, 2014)             251
13.1.   Peter Jones Learning Commons. Exterior view of west entrance         266
13.2.   Library first floor (G170). Entrance of library                                        267
14.1.   Six key qualities of academic library spaces                                           291
14.2.   *Barry Street Library of the University of Melbourne, Australia*:
        The library showcases some good example of the use of artificial
        lighting in study areas with the feature of students' ability to control
        the desired level lighting                                                              293
14.3.   In order to control the noise created from student groups
        working together, in *La Trobe University Library at Bundoora Campus,
        Melbourne*, sound absorbing materials were used for the screens
        dividing the space and defining the group study areas                        293
14.4.   Study spaces created along two sides of an internal garden
        in *University of Queensland Ipswich Library, Ipswich*, accommodate
        quiet individual study, offer a pleasant well-lit ambient and view of the
        rainforest garden and water features, and are not completely secluded
        or isolated                                                                             296
14.5.   In *Deakin University Library at Waurn Ponds Campus, Geelong*, project
        and study rooms are defined as separate enclosed spaces while maintaining
        visual connections. These spaces are also equipped with technologies
        and furniture to support students' collaborative learning needs          297
14.6.   Refurbishment of *Brownless Biomedical Library of University of
        Melbourne* showcases some good examples of using furniture
        and colours to define a range of spaces where a formerly dull
        rectangular space was broken down into a number of smaller spaces
        that accommodate a variety of functions. Built-in furniture helps
        in defining areas for small group collaboration and study                   298
14.7.   In *Queensland University of Technology at Kelvin Grove Campus,
        Brisbane*, a range of colour palettes are used in different library spaces
        corresponding to specific activities that students are engaged in          299
14.8.   A variety of learning spaces is created in *Biological Science
        Library of University of Queensland, Brisbane*, to accommodate a range
        of individual and group activities. Sliding panels also installed to open
        up adjacent spaces and create bigger space when necessary                 300

xiii

FIGURES AND TABLES

14.9. Dividing elements adjusted on the tables in *Macquarie University Library at Macquarie Park Campus, Sydney*, have the flexibility to be taken out and create different learning settings     301

14.10. *Macquarie University Library, Sydney*, showcases efforts to create a sustainable learning environment by implementing a range of sustainable design solutions i.e. reusing and recycling demolition and construction wastes, using recycled materials, maximising the use of natural light from courtyards and skylights and controlling glare by shading and double facades, and using Automated Storage & Retrieval System (ASRS)     302

14.11. In *La Trobe University Library at Bundoora Campus, Melbourne*, one of the main entrances is located along one side of the Agora, the central hub of the campus accommodating a range of student services and amenities i.e. ATM, coffee shops, and stores; a strategy that highlights the role of library as the 'focal point' of the university campus     303

14.12. A number of design features is included in *Deakin University Library at Waurn Ponds Campus, Geelong,* to turn the library into the heart of the campus. An outdoor area is being designed in front of the library. The library is also in close proximity to student centre building and a natural open area including a pond     304

14.13. Inside *Deakin University Library at Waurn Ponds Campus, Geelong,* the design creatively incorporates some of the carrels of the old library in the ceiling defining a space below and adding a style to the interior architecture. Staircase walls were also made using old and outdated books from the old library which contributes to the identity and historical backgrounds of the library     304

14.14. *Deakin University Library at Burwood Campus, Melbourne,* presents some good examples of providing opportunities for students to not only find their spaces in the library but also to create their "own" places among the library spaces     305

14.15. In the refurbishment of level 2 of *Walter Harrison Law Library of University of Queensland, Brisbane*, design solutions were incorporated to address requirements of technology use i.e. provision of power points on the partitions next to desks and creating a range of spaces to accommodate different functions and activities     306

14.16. Refurbishment of *Baillieu Library of University of Melbourne, Melbourne*, presents a number of design strategies to create inspirational spaces i.e. maintaining openness and creative incorporation of built-in display spaces     307

15.1. Higher education learning space evaluation concept model 1 (from Rose-Munro & Majeed, 2017)     319

FIGURES AND TABLES

| 15.2. | Higher education learning space evaluation model concept 1a (from Rose-Munro & Majeed, 2017) | 320 |
| 16.1. | The three over-arching modes of learning theory (Bolton, 2005) | 328 |
| 16.2. | Adaptive teaching framework (Bolton, 2005) | 328 |

## TABLES

| 1.1. | Implementation outcomes variables (from Peters, 2013) | 15 |
| 1.2. | Mapping the objective research question and method (adapted from Peters, 2013) | 15 |
| 1.3. | Summary of the university-industry-government relationship (adapted from Etzkowitz, 2000) | 18 |
| 2.1. | Faculty interest in active learning models | 39 |
| 5.1. | Summary of findings | 99 |
| 7.1 | Factor analysis results for WIHIC | 138 |
| 7.2. | Means, standard deviations and gender differences (ANOVA result and effect size) for WIHIC scales | 141 |
| 7.3. | Simple correlation and multiple regression analyses of associations between learning environment scales and student enjoyment and achievement | 142 |
| 8.1. | The industrial model versus the inquiry model in education (derived from Leland & Kasten, 2002) | 152 |
| 8.2. | Design characteristics of learning spaces | 161 |
| 8.3. | Design characteristics of four main learning space types (adapted from Beckers, 2016a) | 161 |
| 8.4. | Respondents characteristics (N=697) (Beckers, 2016b) | 163 |
| 8.5. | t-values to identify significant differences between learning space preferences per task (Beckers, 2016b) | 166 |
| 9.1. | Different scenarios of the HBDS model | 198 |
| 10.1. | A categorisation of three main dimensions of student learning activities | 208 |
| 12.1. | Students' learning: Negotiating space, time and circumstances and institutional space development strategy (adapted from Boys, Melhuish, & Wilson, 2014, p. 17) | 249 |
| 13.1. | Campus members' location and sociological grouping preference | 274 |
| 13.2. | Campus members' location and observed activity | 275 |
| 14.1. | Key qualities of academic library spaces linked to their corresponding measures or quality indicators | 291 |
| 14.2. | List of academic libraries visited in Australia | 292 |
| 14.3. | Criteria of qualities in academic library spaces and their corresponding quality indicators | 308 |
| 15.1. | Success evaluation criteria, 1 indicates not achieved, 5 indicates successfully achieved | 323 |

# NOTES ON CONTRIBUTORS

**Neda Abbasi** is a Lecturer in Built Environment in the School of Engineering and Technology at Central Queensland University (CQU), Sydney campus. She comes from an architecture background holding a Master of Architectural Engineering from the Faculty of Fine Arts, University of Tehran, Iran, and has worked as a Research Fellow and Project Manager for five years, in the School of Architecture and Built Environment, Deakin University. Her research interest focuses on architecture, design and construction pedagogy and spaces and places of learning and teaching i.e. planning, design and post occupancy evaluation of educational environments. Following a Master thesis and project titled "The Youth House" which explored adolescents' psychological needs and preferences for different natural and built environments, she conducted her PhD research in the University of Melbourne titled "Pathways to Better Personal and Social Life through Learning Spaces" which examined contributions of school design to adolescent identity formation. She was involved in the development of a Tool for Evaluation of Academic Library Spaces (TEALS) in Deakin University (2011–2012) and has been conducting evaluation of academic library spaces since 2011 i.e. evaluation of Deakin University library at Burwood Campus (2011), University of Queensland libraries at St Lucia Campus (2012–2013) and University of Canberra library (2015). She has worked as the project manager and/or researcher on a number of projects funded by Australian Government Office for Learning and Teaching (OLT) i.e. Teaching and Assessing Team Learning in Architecture and Design-related Contexts (2011–2014), Global Canopy (2014–2016), and Building Resilience in Construction Graduates (2015–2016). In CQU, currently she is leading a project on Best Practice in Online Delivery of Architecture and Building Design Studios (2017–present).

**Ronald Beckers** is a senior lecturer in facility management at the HAN University of Applied Sciences in Nijmegen, the Netherlands. He holds a PhD in building planning and development from the University of Twente. His research focuses on the added value of corporate real estate and facilities on core processes of organisations, by aligning the working and learning environments with organisational and societal developments. Before he joined the HAN University of Applied Sciences, he was a consultant in the field of facility management and corporate real estate management. He can be contacted at Ronald.beckers@han.nl

**Flavia Curvelo Magdaniel** is a research fellow at the University of Delft specialising in corporate real estate. She is a co-author of Campuses, Cities and Innovation (2017). Beginning as a graphic designer she was later educated as an architect and was inspired by the cities and cultures she has experienced around the world. Flavia was born and grew up in La Guajira, a Caribbean region in Colombia. She moved to Bogotá to study Architecture within an outstanding Faculty of Arts, where she developed a passion for illustration. After working for four years as a designer she moved to the Netherlands in 2008 to pursue a masters education in Real Estate & Housing. In 2010, she obtained the degree of MSc at TU Delft. She is a research fellow in the University of Delft research centre on https://managingtheuniversitycampus.nl/campus-research-team/. Before and while working in her PhD research, Flavia performed graphic design works for the department of MBE, including the design of the dissertation "Managing the university campus", posters, research reports and marketing brochures for education and research.

**Mollie Dollinger** is a PhD candidate at The University of Melbourne's Centre for the Study of Higher Education. She is a higher education researcher studying student co-creation and the higher education student experience. Mollie has earned a Bachelor of Arts from The University of Arizona and Master's of Science from Indiana University. She has previously worked at Sichuan International Studies University in Chongqing, China.

**Robert A. Ellis** is a Professor and Dean (Learning and Teaching) across six faculties at Griffith University, Australia. Previously, he was the inaugural Director of eLearning at the University of Sydney and Associate Professor in the Institute for Teaching and Learning. He is a coordinating editor for Higher Education and co-series editor of Understanding Teaching and Learning Practice, both with Springer. He has been an Australian Research Council researcher since 2005, investigating quality in learning and teaching, the student experience of technology-enhanced learning and learning environments. His research program comprises over 80 journal, book and conference publications, aimed at making a meaningful social and disciplinary contribution to education and its participants through translational research outcomes.

**Kenn Fisher** practices both as a research academic and as an education/health planner as he seeks to link the development of research with practice through the concept of translational design. This is modelled on the evidence based design of health environments which itself derives from clinical medical research practice. As an Associate Professor in Learning Environments in the Faculty of Architecture, Building and Planning at The University of Melbourne Kenn has been involved for the past seven years in AU$5million worth of research projects for the Australian Research Council Linkage/Discovery and the Australian Government's Office of Learning and Teaching in the planning, design and use of new generation learning environments. He has published widely in peer reviewed journals and books, and has supervised and examined numerous doctoral candidates. As an Educational & Health Planning Consultant (0.5) he operates as a strategic facility planner involved in masterplanning, learning environment and workplace academy

NOTES ON CONTRIBUTORS

planning and brief writing internationally, having worked in France, the UK, USA, Italy, Thailand, Laos, Cambodia, Hong Kong, China, Malaysia, Australia and New Zealand.

**Barry J. Fraser** is a John Curtin Distinguished Professor at Curtin University in Perth, Australia, Editor-in-Chief of Springer's *Learning Environments Research: An International Journal* and Co-editor of Brill Sense's book series *Advances in Learning Environments Research.* He is a Fellow of the International Academy of Education, American Educational Research Association, American Association for the Advancement of Science, Academy of Social Sciences in Australia, Australian College of Educators and Academy of Technological Sciences and Engineering.

**Jacov Haina** is an architect and teaches Architectural Design in the Faculty of Architecture and Town Planning at the Technion–Israel Institute of Technology. His master's thesis dealt with the design of the University of the Future. He is currently completing a second master's degree in Philosophy at the University of Haifa. His current research includes the history of university architecture in Israel.

**Rifca Hashimshony** is an architect and an associate professor in the Faculty of Architecture and Town Planning at the Technion–Israel Institute of Technology. For many years she was assistant dean and deputy dean in charge of undergraduate studies. She teaches various design studios, and was involved in an international project initiated by Professor Alexander Tzonis of TU Delft, dealing with the design of the University of the Future. Among her research interests are the future of higher education, scientific education for young children, and building conservation. (Biography at the time of the first publication of the chapter in 2006.)

**Leah Irving** has a PhD in Education, a Master's degree in Professional Education and Training, a Master's degree in Art (Visual Art) and a Bachelor's degree in Art. For the past ten years Leah has held positions at Curtin University associated with learning design and development utilising technologies that include virtual worlds, 3D game environments, Alternate Reality Games and Augmented Reality. Prior to this she held similar positions in the K-12 and TAFE sectors. Leah's current position as Creative Learning Developer is with Curtin University's Learning Futures team within Curtin Learning and Teaching where she manages the development of a bespoke Challenge-based learning platform and works across the university on creative learning solutions.

Leah has a particular interest in augmented and virtual reality as learning mediators and has combined this interest with the university's commitment to integrate Indigenous Australian culture in learning and teaching. She has been successful in a number of eScholar research grants at Curtin University. One of these examined the efficacy for location-based augmented reality to embed cultural stories of the Wadjuk Noongar peoples in the urbanised landscape with the purpose of raising awareness

xix

NOTES ON CONTRIBUTORS

of Indigenous Australian culture in a university setting. Her current project builds on this prior research to explore the cultural significance of the Curtin University Bentley campus for the Wadjuk Noongar peoples through augmented reality, a 3D simulation of the Bentley campus and digitised cultural artefacts turning the entire Curtin campus into a learning landscape.

**Alejandra Torres-Landa Lopez** is an architect with a Master's Degree as a Teacher in Higher Education and a PhD in Anthropic Environment Science. The latter is where architecture is analyzed from the point of view of Anthropological Architecture of Nold Egenter). Dr Lopez has been working at the Autonomous University of Agauacalientes in Mexico since 1995 as a teacher and a researcher and throughout these years she has seen the impact buildings and information technology (IT) have in human activities. So, after her PhD studies (2014) Dr Lopez chose to focus on how educational infrastructure and IT are analyzed to identify the influence they have in teaching and learning in architecture. She also studies how space itself responds to new educational paradigms. In focusing on learning environments Dr Lopez teaches both bachelor and graduate students, in face to face programs as well as blended learning and online. She has also been teaching faculty members how to become online teachers, showing them how to work in the virtual space of an educational platform (Moodle) but mainly helping them change from a traditional teaching paradigm to a new one.

**Marian Mahat** is the lead Research Fellow of the Innovative Learning Environments and Teacher Change (ILETC) project at The University of Melbourne. As the Research Manager, she oversees all research activities and the dissemination of project findings including the management of Research Fellows and graduate researchers. Marian has over twenty years of professional and academic experience, spanning several Australian universities, the Australian Federal and local governments, as well as the private sector. Highly proficient in both quantitative and qualitative research methods, she has worked on collaborative projects, written numerous publications and presented in conferences in education. Her research focus is in student learning and outcomes in different learning and teaching contexts.

**Saadia Majeed** completed her Doctoral studies in the Department of Management at Monash University. She currently works as a Research Analyst in Learning Space Innovation in the Office of the DVC & VP (Education). She holds a double Master's degree in Environmental Sciences and Disaster Management. Her past research primarily concentrated on disaster risk management, policy and planning. She also worked developing an integrated governance approach to disaster risk management which is especially applicable in Bangladesh but also has the potential for wider application in other disaster-prone regions.

**Jacqueline Pizzuti-Ashby** is a researcher and educator who is intrigued by the transactional relationship between people and place. she studied this dynamic over

xx

12 years resulting in an award-winning dissertation "Designing for the future: A post-occupancy evaluation of the Peter Jones Learning Centre". Jaqueline is an international speaker on campus ecology and environmental design and facilitates workshops and presentations on designing spaces for creativity and innovation. She believes in the creative life and better understanding the connections we have to each other and our surrounding milieu. She also believes in giving a damn and high-fives that makes her palm tingle – and that a hearty laugh is priceless. Jacqueline is currently a project manager in the Faculty of Medicine at the University of British Columbia, assisting the Department of Family Practice in examining and redesigning its current clinical education placement model. Responsible for developing and administrating an environmental scan tool that assesses the current clinical education placement model in Family Practice and in the other UBC Health Professional programs; conducting a literature review; completing the thematic analysis and data synthesis; and developing distributed clinical education placement models to pilot in a proposed phase 2 of the project.

**Leanne Rose-Munro** is an educator, researcher and passionate about innovative learning spaces that offer enhanced opportunity for participation. Her research skills are evaluating innovative learning environments and the design affordances that enable inclusion in learning opportunities. After working in Education for 18 years, and becoming a member of the Melbourne University LEARN team, she started Learning Space Consultancy. Leanne's research interests are underpinned by Success Case Methodology (Brinkerhoff 2005) which accounts for performance management systems and the role that learning plays in it to achieve results. This has lead to theory building regarding policy and governance and the impact on the individual. In 2012, Leanne was a major contributor towards the Government Draft Standards Committee for the Department of Education and Early Childhood Development in Victoria that formulated hearing accessibility standards for learning spaces. In 2016 Leanne was appointed as Manager Learning Spaces at Monash University. In this role she evaluated higher education learning environments and identified design affordances that positively impact learning and teaching. Through leading design development initiatives and strategic thinking Leanne supported a diverse range of internal and external stakeholders involved in major learning space developments. Leading collaborations with a very talented interdisciplinary team has enabled the delivery of innovative future focussed on-campus buildings that are world leaders. In 2018 Leanne was appointed Program Director, STEMM Hub and Life Science Precinct, Major Projects Chancellery, The University of Melbourne. Using evidence-based inputs gained in prototyping and post-occupancy evaluations Leanne now provides design advice to stakeholders and senior decision-makers in University Major Projects. This work involves designing and developing project management strategy, enabling high performing teams, developing risk mitigation strategy with a focus on enabling transformational change.

NOTES ON CONTRIBUTORS

**Mahmoud Reza Saghafi** is an Associate Professor in the Faculty of Architecture & Urbanism at the Art University of Isfahan. He has 20 years' experience in international teaching, research and management experience as an academic member resulting in innovative teaching approaches, research led educational design and maximising student learning. Since acquiring his doctorate, he has had ten publications focusing on blended design studio education. Mahmoud also has 23 years of industry practice in architectural design which ran parallel to his academic career. His thesis was published as a book entitled *A Holistic Blended Design Studio Model: Exploring and Expanding Learning Opportunities* (LAP Lambert Academic Publishing, 2013).

**Panayiotis Skordi** is a Professor in the Department of Information Systems and Decision Sciences, Mihaylo College of Business and Economics, California State University, Fullerton, USA. He teaches statistics for which he has won outstanding teacher awards. He is a Fellow of the Institute of Actuaries.

**Ji Yu** has recently received her doctoral degree from the University of Cambridge. She holds an MA in education from Beijing Normal University and a BA in engineering from Tongji University in China. Her PhD thesis focuses on the relationships between learning space and student learning in higher education. The project adopted an evidence-based approach using mixed methods. She is particularly interested in incorporating contemporary student learning theories to explore the educative value of emerging new generation learning environments. She was a research assistant at Beijing Academy of Educational Sciences and project management assistant for UNICEF Child-Friendly School Project in China.

# PART 1

## EMERGING TRENDS IN HIGHER EDUCATION AND THEIR IMPACT ON THE PHYSICAL CAMPUS

KENN FISHER

# INTRODUCTION TO PART 1

The five chapters in Part 1 intersect in their evaluations and predictions of the university campus. They range from how evidence could be used to predict the future university, especially given the impact of technology; through using expert elicitation as a form of evidential prediction; an analysis of university campus structure and its relationship to the community and city; how specialist technology universities are innovating in response to government, industry and educational pressures to innovate; to, finally, how the university campus may need to evolve as it maintains a role as the 'third teacher'.

Chapter 1 explores the idea of translational research – more commonly experienced in medical research practice – and how this can be leveraged into evidence based transactional design as seen largely through the lens of health planners. It argues that translational research could be seen as translational design and could be adapted to educational planning and design practice.

This approach is applied in Chapter 2 wherein a mini meta-analysis of university future books and journals articles was shortlisted to 19 scholarly studies predicting the future. This was triangulated through an expert elicitation and a Delphi study to suggest seven future structural forms of university campuses. Chapter 3 picks up many of the drivers noted separately in Chapters 1 and 2 and suggests a single campus framework model which could be adaptive to future forces of change. This is perhaps less evidence-based but is very compelling nevertheless. Chapter 4 focusses on the Technology University as a sector and undertakes a comparative study of some 30 plus universities to identify how they have each responded to a triple helix consisting of university community/industry/government forces for change and innovation.

Finally, Chapter 5 seeks to unpack the barriers to change in how the university can continue to be an effective 'third teacher' in coming decades.

The five-chapter package is a very comprehensive overview of the context of university futures. Note that information technology futures – such as virtual and mixed reality, gamification, artificial intelligence and machine learning – are not tackled in detail as this sector is moving so fast this book would be redundant not long after printing. The book focuses on how the built campus can align the physical face to face experience with the virtual by being an adaptive space and place that can accommodate many virtual alternative futures.

© KONINKLIJKE BRILL NV, LEIDEN, 2019 | DOI: 10.1163/9789004391598_001

KENN FISHER

# 1. THE TRANSLATIONAL DESIGN OF UNIVERSITIES

*From Campus to Classroom*

### ABSTRACT

Transforming learning environment design thinking from primarily the 'look' or form must be accompanied by a renewed focus on functionality. The rapid emergence of broadband wireless means we can access information online anytime anywhere – in a virtual community or place – as the massive online open courseware (MOOC) and massive online campus courseware (MOCC) phenomenon have attested to. Should we now re-engineer our physical learning environments to ensure they are optimal for this form of knowledge construction? Many innovations have been developed to support this virtual/physical hybrid model but do they work? I argue that these innovations – or research projects – must be evaluated and the evidence of their efficacy gained used to translate innovate learning environments into working operational models in a scaled-up system- and campus-wide format. Translational design can be used to evaluate learning and knowledge environments to assist in improving learning outcomes.

### TRANSLATIONAL DESIGN

Translational design (Norman, 2009) derives from translational research which predominates in medical and health research practice. Such approaches have been adopted by health planners to develop an evidence-based approach to the design of medical and health facilities (HERD, 2018). Norman argues that translational research – when related to the designed environment – can be called translational engineering or translational design.

The design of university campuses and campus buildings over recent decades and indeed, over many centuries, is not particularly evidence-based. Whilst precedents and in some cases post occupancy evaluations (Cleveland & Fisher, 2014) are used by planners and designers, there is a scarce body of knowledge which provides a genealogy of peer reviewed scholarly evidence-based higher education physical environment design.

This book attempts to source evidence-based studies on campus planning and design primarily through the auspices of doctoral dissertation research. Other potential sources include several scholarly peer reviewed journals such as the International Journal of

© KONINKLIJKE BRILL NV, LEIDEN, 2019 | DOI:10.1163/9789004391598_002

K. FISHER

Learning Environments and, to a lesser degree, Environment and Planning D: Society and Space. Another less scholarly source includes the Society for College and University Planning. One of the issues about the difficulty of aggregating the knowledge base regarding campus planning and design is the cross-disciplinary nature of the sector.

What can be said about university campuses is that they are 'complex adaptive systems', or assemblages.[1]

> First, the university is "of human action, and not of human design". It is characterized by evolution, self-organization, and emergence. A historical analysis is necessary to understand its design. Second, the university has a unity, or "wholeness", to it. It cannot be split up or merged at will. A holistic analysis – as opposed to a reductionist analysis – is required to understand its design. (Lohmann, 2006)

The idea of campus to classroom suggests, too, that there is a hierarchy to these complex adaptive systems. The following sections in this Chapter begin at a campus 'town and gown' level and gradually move towards a classroom focus. The concept of a contemporary university is under massive pressure due to digital advances. The same can be said for the classroom for now, everywhere can be the classroom. Two questions arise here: 'what is the likely future role of a university campus?', and 'what is the likely future role of classroom?' Both of these roles operate within the context of three modalities – instructor led (formal or 'mode one'), student led (informal or 'mode two'), and social (third spaces, or 'mode 3') (Fisher, 2005; Gibbons et al., 2002). The ratio between these modalities is changing rapidly from the instructor led mode in a classroom to a multimodal model which has less instructor based face-to-face interaction, more peer-to-peer interaction, and evermore social interaction both on and off campuses with a blurring of the three modal boundaries.

Third spaces – where students can collaborate or work individualy in a variety of places of their choosing – are becoming fundamental to supporting the student experience in a digital and increasingly online world. International students in particular prefer to form their sense of community within the safety of a campus. This is resulting in a much greater development of informal, social and third spaces on campus. In some campuses the ratio of formal to informal is reaching 50:50 (Deed & Alterator, 2017; Beckers, 2016).

Such a transformation needs to be unpacked to understand what the impact of these digital and virtual drivers are to the traditional physical campus.

THE DIGITAL CAMPUS

Perhaps the most significant impact on campus design and planning has been the recent emergence of wireless broadband and its accompanying mobile digital devices (Huang et al., 2012). This means that academics and students can work virtually anywhere and anytime. However, the social construction of knowledge tends to draw teachers and learners together as they collectively learn from each other. This can only occur to a small degree in the virtual space and the natural desire of humans to form social gatherings is compelling. But what sorts of spaces should campuses offer in this digital context?

The affordances brought about by digital tools allows students to access online courses, connect to tele-teaching and collaborate virtually with colleagues in multiple locations. However, these developments are in their early stages and as such do not have an evidence base with which to evaluate their performance. Current findings suggest that the massive online open courses have high attrition rates and it is thought that this may be part due to the lack of personal contact in a face-to-face learning environment (Bower et al., 2014).

We are now seeing universities developing branch and satellite campuses to provide locations for teachers and students to combine a virtual with a face to face experience (Fisher, 2017). Another factor is that the allocation of formal, informal and social space is changing with students voting with their feet not to attend lectures. The most agile universities are converting libraries and some lecture theatres to informal space and blended active learning spaces. Active learning spaces are seeing gradual developments in evaluation of how these spaces work (Baepler et al., 2014). The scaling up of this type of space is quite slow, largely due to the incremental adoption of online technologies by academic teaching staff (de la Harpe et al., 2014).

In the process of designing new academic buildings, there is a significant issue in designing innovative technology enhanced learning environments and having current academic staff take up these opportunities. Given this reticence, the conversion of the existing 19th and 20th century university estates and assets – which are designed around a predominantly teacher-centred passive pedagogy – to a more student centred active form of learning is very slow to evolve. However, the need to upgrade these increasingly out of date facilities is providing many opportunities to experiment with new learning space topologies. There is also a significant growth in student learning commons and campus social hubs, with a focus on enhancing the student experience (Glass et al., 2012). But this raises the vexed question in terms of evidence-based planning and design: 'does the campus design support the educational function required?'

CAMPUS PLANNING AND DESIGN – DOES FORM FOLLOW FUNCTION?

With all this building activity, there still remains scarce evidence on the effectiveness of these sometimes-innovative forward-looking developments. This dilemma links to the notion of knowledge management with the transfer of knowledge embodied in the idea of project team developed tacit knowledge which has to be converted to published or documented explicit knowledge – such as post occupancy evaluations – to be scaled up and made available (Nonaka, 1991).

Both of these forms of knowledge tend to be held in the private sector by consulting firms such as architects, campus planners, engineers and other consultants, who tend

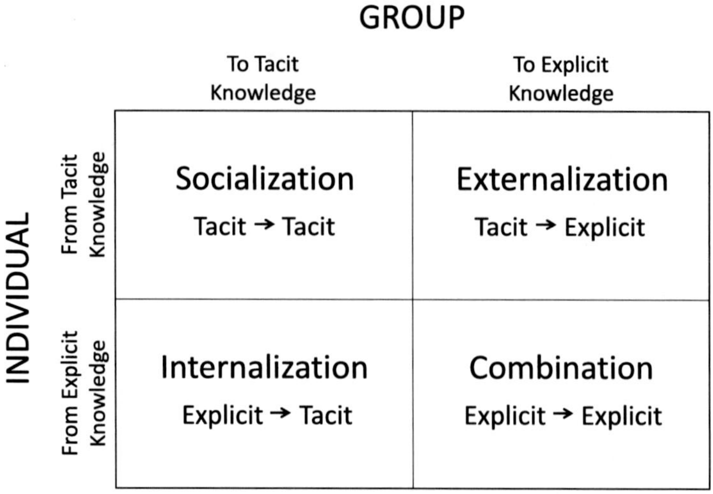

K. FISHER

## GROUP

|  | To Tacit Knowledge | To Explicit Knowledge |
|---|---|---|
| **From Tacit Knowledge** | **Socialization**<br>Tacit → Tacit | **Externalization**<br>Tacit → Explicit |
| **From Explicit Knowledge** | **Internalization**<br>Explicit → Tacit | **Combination**<br>Explicit → Explicit |

INDIVIDUAL

*Figure 1.1. Tacit: Explicit knowledge interchange (Nonaka, 1991)*

to retain this intellectual property. This knowledge becomes a form of competitive advantage in a private sector which is largely framed around a contested design and construction tendering environment.

Whilst these capital works programmes are invariably managed by in-house client-oriented project managers, and perhaps framed through the services of a university planning architect, the knowledge base is still not particularly available in most organisations. Where it is available, for example on the Internet (e.g. SCUP, 2018), the material is inevitably around a single recent masterplan example and some project overviews, with some universities having also developed design guidelines (for example, UTS, 2018). These guidelines are inevitably related to having consistent technical and regulatory standards across all projects so that all consultants working on building projects are working to the same university requirements.

So, to carry out an evidence-based approach, designers usually refer to architectural journals, which rarely focus on function; they rather prefer form as can be seen with a simple review of these journal venues. This lack has led to the development of the role of the educational and health planner, where the focus is primarily on function. This approach is usually in association with architects to create a form to house the function. That said, the use of educational planners in university projects is also scarce. In schools the role has been certified for those who wish to take this path, through the Association for Learning Environments (A4LE, 2018).

For this approach to develop, educational clients need to support the evidence-based educational planner approach, which some indeed do with in-house staff, but these organisations are the more progressive in that they predominantly have quite advanced learning environments development programs and practices linked with

8

# THE TRANSLATIONAL DESIGN OF UNIVERSITIES

academic professional development. Inevitably the development of new generation learning environments requires significant change management with a transition process running in parallel with the academic staff.[2]

In attempting to understand 'form-follows-function', planners and designers are faced with a very broad range of functions to house. Indeed, campuses range from the aforementioned single-storey vertical campus in a city, to extremely large complexes which resemble cities in themselves. At the extreme end of the spectrum sits the University of Mexico with 100,000 students and their own internal bus system. And, there are many options in between where the boundaries between the city and the campus are porous, permeable and blurred. Thus, planners and designers can be designing almost any element that may be built or inhabited in a normal city.

## TOWN AND GOWN

Another increasing complexity is the encroachment, in many cases, of university campuses intersecting with the city public – and private – realm. This may take a number of forms such as: independent faculties off the main campus; research institutes established either as independent entities; or as a research precinct such as bio medical hubs; research parks; technology parks; and elements of a digital or knowledge city (IASP, 2018).

University and city interaction can be two ways. Rather than just the university encroaching on the city domain, there is increasing interaction through what is known variously as 'commercialisation of intellectual property', 'community engagement', 'knowledge transfer' or 'joint venture partnerships'. This may be bringing community partners on to campus, or the university engaging with industry within industry facilities, or joining up with the community in various ventures such as a shared library.

The emerging concept of work-integrated-learning – to ensure that university graduates are 'job ready' – is increasing the level of industry engagement. Coupled with this physical engagement is the increasing use of teleteaching (as noted earlier), videoconferencing and other digital collaborative tools as cross disciplinary knowledge is developed in teams especially in relation to applied research and more particularly in medical teaching and practice (Scott-Kruse, 2016). In regard to basic research often these collaborations can be international as in many cases this form of research is highly specialised and partners tend to be located in other university institutions around the globe.

Thus, the university campus is becoming more permeable and porous and, indeed universities are exploring alternatives to the campus as 'mothership'. We are finding that there are various models of emerging campus topologies (Hashimshony & Haina, 2019). Research intensive universities have tended to traditionally be single campus based but, as globalisation grows at an alarmingly relentless pace, some of the elite universities are forming branch campus joint ventures with similar elite universities in other countries (QS, 2018). We are thus seeing campuses

9

supporting dual and more university brands where the synergy of those universities is collaborative rather than competitive. For example, the University of Cambridge in China, Harvard University likewise in China, and the University of New York with its distributed campuses around the globe.

One model which is taking off at a rapid pace is the idea of a vertical campus where universities such as Western Sydney University – which already has five major campuses – is developing vertical campuses located within major urban centres in the Greater Sydney Basin. Three or four new vertical campuses have just been opened around Western Sydney based on multiple-story purpose-built, but leased, towers which are fitted out to the university's requirements. These are leased on ten-year lease terms, usually with the right of a second ten years, which gives the university an option to retire from these locations should the digital campus become more popular and economically viable. The university can retract to its 'mother ship' campuses or could develop new vertical campuses in alternative locations.

The attraction of vertical satellite campuses is that the campus is effectively 'taken to the student' rather than students having to commute to distant major campuses. Thus, the Western Sydney University can offer a more accessible program to students of all types whether they be working in these major town centres, be part-time, mature age with or without families or, indeed, international students who are looking for a safe and secure educational experience co-located with all of the amenities that a city centre can offer, without being isolated on a traditional campus with its extant student colleges. Vertical campuses are yet to be fully researched in terms of how effective they are, although of course they are common place in such places as Hong Kong and Singapore, for example. Campus research has been focussed mainly on a horizontal scale to date (Green & Penn, 1997; Hashimshony & Haina, 2019).

Town and gown will continue to be a significant factor as university mission statements continue to address the benefits that a university can provide to its local constituency. Further to this, governments are increasingly demanding that universities become more relevant to society in terms of applied skills knowledge and research. This is not to say that pure or basic research will be neglected, it is simply to say that the balance will continue to shift. Universities operate within a triple helix model wherein teaching, research and community engagement all interact (Davis et al., 2009). Thus, the campus and the city both act as places of teaching/learning, research and community engagement and are increasingly intertwined as government funding for research continues to seek more commercially applied research outcomes for this financial support. Furthermore, learning environments in a digital world can be operating at any time and any place and often the city is a better bet for students after hours than a campus.

## LEARNING ENVIRONMENTS

Formal (mode 1) learning environments on a university campus are the most prone to significant change due to the aforementioned developments in online learning driven by wireless broadband and mobile communications devices. Whilst massive online open courseware (MOOC) and massive online campus courseware (MOCC) are in their early stages of development, increasingly they are becoming part of a hybrid teaching and learning model. These models – more commonly known as blended active learning environments – largely adopt the 'flipped classroom' approach in that students can learn online without a face to face instructor experience off-campus and bring that knowledge to a face-to-face instructor led experience on campus where the learnt material can be socially constructed as deep learning (Bower, 2014).

There is evolving evidence as to the effectiveness of these technology-assisted active learning models emerging in the scholarly literature (Baepler et al., 2014). It is perhaps this area – together with the rapid re-purposing of libraries – which lends itself to significant scholarly research thus forming a more coherent, if yet distributed, emerging evidence base. Such studies as Scale-Up, Active Learning Environments and the Learning Spaces Academy all attest to the experiments and pilot studies which are being evaluated.[3] These studies are all adding to the evidence-base although they are quite difficult to source across distributed and numerous academic journals due to the multi-disciplinary nature of these environments. Their construction, management and use involves discipline specialists, educational designers, academics, researchers, educational technology technicians, information technology technicians, architects, interior designers, furniture manufacturers, engineering services technicians, builders with many sub-contractors and so on. There is also the uneven nature of teaching practice across universities. Some of these developments can be tracked via professional associations, although these are not necessarily scholarly academic research-oriented venues for publications.[4]

## LIBRARIES

University libraries have been the most affected by advances in digital scholarship. With the online availability of an extraordinary range of resources, hard copy books have been less in demand. These are being moved from centrally accessible libraries on campus into off-site bookstores. The space made available from the removal of these books has been turned over to access by students as learning commons, or digital commons.

These library commons are effectively mode two or informal learning spaces. Increasingly they are adjacent to the aforementioned third spaces, or mode three environments which relate more to social interaction. An additional development of this approach is the development of precinct learning commons and third spaces or precinct learning hubs (Fisher, 2013a). These spaces have a multiple use, but the primary purpose is to create or foster cross disciplinary interaction between schools, faculties and research institutes.

There is ongoing debate regarding the role of the traditionally named library, but the evolution of libraries traces back three millennia and they have undergone continual change due to external drivers even then consisting of technological advances (Fisher, 2013b). This most recent transition is yet another example of technological forces impacting on the role of the library, requiring a recalibration of the functions it carries out. They now increasingly provide spaces used for individual and collaborative learning, social interaction, interdisciplinary interaction and information literacy support. This latter function is increasing as the rate of development of knowledge grows requiring specialised information navigating skills within specific disciplines. There is a valuable set of comparative statistics for library spatial analysis available about most Australian university libraries though, such as the Confederation of Australian University Libraries (CAUL, 2018).[5]

Anecdotally, it appears that library budgets are neither reducing and nor are their floor spaces diminishing. However, how those funds are spent, and what is contained in those floor spaces and where they are located is continually being adjusted. Above all libraries are amongst the most adaptive of all of the elements of a university campus. The library also forms a significant component of a university campuses social capital, especially for first year students (Budgen et al., 2014; Arup, 2017). A major part of library functions is to support international and non-local students informal and social activities and experience. Inevitably the international students are paying significant fees and are attached to the campus primarily for study and cultural interaction. The campus and the library provide both a safe, comfortable and affordable food space to enhance their student experience. To some degree these sorts of spaces are emerging in student housing satellite campuses surrounding the 'mother ship' campus.

## STUDENT HOUSING

The role of student housing, whether it be domiciled, shared housing, independently operated student residences, or campus-based student colleges, is becoming of increasing importance as students and parents alike seek to obtain an optimum student experience for the years at university. If one looks at the student demographic in universities globally, once again we clearly have a very complex adaptive system.

Student demographics vary widely from country to country, although there are generic similarities in various categories. Certainly, common to the United States, the United Kingdom, Canada, New Zealand and Australia, are a significant number of international students attending English-speaking courses either full-time for a complete undergraduate degree, for a semester exchange or for postgraduate studies. Domestically universities have national students who may travel across the country to another state or province, local students who may wish to live closer to their university after having left the parental home and also local commuter students (Jones, Lang, & LaSalle, 2016).

These non-home-based students require various forms of student accommodation and, in the cited cases, there is significant activity in third-party developed student housing, most often in high-rise apartment style projects. Many of these have arrangements with specific universities regarding 'pastoral' care together with a responsibility to enhance the student experience all of which is supported by their operations. Service agreements are developed to ensure that there is adequate support for a quality student off-campus lifestyle.

Yet there is little research on this, and what is available is either kept within competitive university housing developers and operators, or within individual university student housing departments. Some research material is available from the global corporate real estate firms such as Jones, Lang LaSalle and CBRE. It is possible to find a few scholarly publications on this subject, although it is not a sector that seems to have lent itself to academic research. These corporate real estate giants are also now penetrating the research laboratory domain as applied research links the commercial and industrial sector with the intellectual property developed by university research departments and institutes.

## RESEARCH, RESEARCH PARKS AND RESEARCH PRECINCTS

Historically research has evolved in a predominantly disciplinary specialist model represented on campus almost as silos in distinctive precincts. Whilst there is clearly a need for deep research within a highly specialised subject area, increasingly research is becoming inter- and cross-disciplinary. This is represented by global issues requiring multidisciplinary teams to solve such as climate to solve such thematic questions as climate change, resources, water security, food production, marine, biomedical and a range of other topics.

In the past decade technological advances have also seen the need for more appropriate facilities research practices. Also, the ageing estate following significant expansion across the globe in the 1970s is now well and truly reaching the end of its life cycle. This has provided the opportunity for research facilities to be reconfigured for a 21st-century digital operating model. There is also pressure from government funding authorities for universities to shorten the time taken to commercialise new intellectual property. Such pressure has encouraged greater interaction partnerships and collaboration between industry and academe. This has resulted in the emergence of research parks, bio-hubs and research precincts.

Research on the evidence base for the development of new research facilities resides predominantly in conference proceedings which inevitably are highly specialised in keeping with the nature of research specialisation. Perhaps an overarching oversight is available for campus planners and designers through developments tracked by associations of research parks and similarly knowledge cities (Brown, 2009; the Association of University Research Parks[6]; and the European Biotechnology Network[7]). There is a distinct connection between biomedical research sciences and the evidence-based research methodologies used in the health sciences by health planners. There is a significant evidence base in this specialised area which offers a potential lead to the sorts of methodologies which may be appropriate for other academic sectors.

## METHODOLOGIES AND SOURCES OF EVIDENCE

In terms of addressing sources of evidence, the key tool for pursuing these sources is linked closely with methodological models. These are extensive and, in some cases, quite complex and can be protracted taking weeks, months and years to develop. Some of these approaches are addressed in the other chapters in this book. A core consideration is either qualitative, or quantitative or a mixed methods approach to research. To a large degree qualitative and quantitative models are contested in that the quantitative can often be considered to be not significantly deep in its findings.

The qualitative on the other hand can delve much deeper through the notion of ethnography. One criticism of the latter is that in being deeper it is of necessity narrower and is therefore difficult to scale the findings to become a generalised form of evidence. Other critics argue that quantitative research can be seen to be too broad and often carried out through surveys and questionnaires, with little attempt to delve deeper into the findings from this methodology. Perhaps what is missing is a mixed methods approach where the outliers in the quantitative results can be followed up with focus groups, interviews or other qualitative approaches can be applied. To some extent this acts as a triangulation method where the results from alternative approaches can be compared and contrasted to arrive at a thoroughly

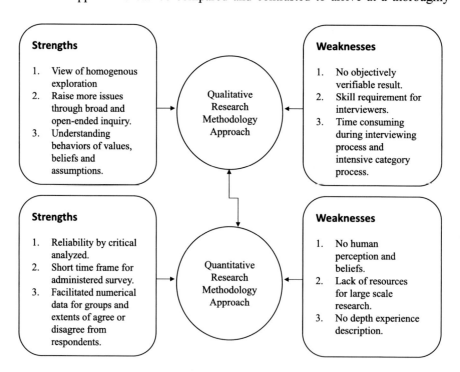

*Figure 1.2. Strengths and weaknesses of qualitative vs quantitative (Looi, 2014)*

THE TRANSLATIONAL DESIGN OF UNIVERSITIES

analysed evidence-based outcome. Various approaches are outlined in Zeisel et al. (2012) and Ulrich and Zimmer (2008).

Methods in educational planning are nowhere near as developed are those methods which are used in health facility planning evidence-based practice

*Table 1.1. Implementation outcomes variables (from Peters, 2013)*

| Implementation Outcome | Working definition | Related terms |
|---|---|---|
| Coverage | Benefit to target respondents | Reach, access, service spread |
| Sustainability | Extent to which intervention is scaled | Maintenance, durability, incorporation |
| Acceptability | Perception of stakeholders | Factors related to acceptability |
| Adoption | Intention | Uptake |
| Appropriateness | Fit or relevance | Perceived fit |
| Feasibility | Context | Practicality |
| Fidelity | Degree to which it retained original intent | Integrity, quality of delivery |
| Implementation Cost | Incremental cost of strategy | Marginal cost, total cost |

*Table 1.2. Mapping the objective research question and method (adapted from Peters, 2013)*

| Objective | Description | Question | Methods & data |
|---|---|---|---|
| Explore | Explore idea or phenomenon to make a hypothesis or generalisation | What are possible factors or agents for implementation strategy | *Qualitative methods*: grounded theory, ethnography, phenomenology, case studies, narrative approaches, informant interviews, focus groups, historical reviews. *Quantitative methods*: network analysis; cross sectional surveys. *Mixed methods*: combining the above. |
| Describe | Identify & describe phenomenon & correlates or causes | What is the context; main factors in this context | *Quantitative methods*: network analysis; cross sectional surveys. *Qualitative methods*: ethnography, phenomenology, case studies, narrative approaches, informant interviews, focus groups, historical reviews. Mixed methods: both of the above with convergence of data & analyses. |

*(cont.)*

K. FISHER

*Table 1.2. Mapping the objective research question and method (adapted from Peters, 2013) (cont.)*

| Objective | Description | Question | Methods & data |
|---|---|---|---|
| Influence | Test whether intervention produces expected outcome | | |
| With adequacy | Sufficient confidence that intervention and outcomes are occurring | Is coverage of a health intervention changing among beneficiaries of study? | Before-after time services in intervention recipients only; participatory action research |
| With plausibility | Greater confidence that outcome is due to intervention | Is outcome plausibly due to the intervention rather than other causes | *Concurrent, non-randomised cluster trials*: before and after cross-sectional studies; quality improvement studies. |
| With Probability | High calculated probability that outcome is due to intervention | Is outcome due to intervention? | *Partially controlled trials*: interventions in some areas and not others; effectiveness-implementation hybrids. |
| Explain | Develop/expand a theory to explain relation between concepts, reasons for events occurrence and how they occurred | How and why does intervention lead to behavioural effects | *Mixed methods*: both qualitative and quantitative inquiry with convergence of data and analyses: *Quantitative*: repeated measures of context; actors; depth and breadth of implementation across subunits; network identification; designs for confirmatory inferences; effectiveness-implementation hybrids. *Qualitative methods*: case studies; phenomenological and ethnographic with key interviews; focus groups; historical reviews. *Participatory action research.* |
| Predict | Use prior knowledge or theories to forecast future events | What is likely course of future implementation? | Quantitative: agent-based modelling; simulation and forecasting modelling; data extrapolation and sensitivity analysis (trend analysis, econometric modelling). Qualitative: scenario-building exercises; Delphi techniques from opinion leaders. |

THE TRANSLATIONAL DESIGN OF UNIVERSITIES

(McCullough, 2010; Centre for Health Design,[8] 2018 and HER Journal[9]). One of the purposes of this book is to seek to develop a more robust and scholarly evidence-based research practice based on much larger randomised control trials so that in education we can have a much greater level of confidence to replicate those projects and approaches which are found to clearly work.

Randomised controlled trials are not used in educational facility planning projects although some are beginning to emerge in the context of new generation learning environments. Yet there are very few studies which consider more than a handful of projects under evaluation. Ideally educational planners should use these health planning approaches to have improved scholarly evidence-based robust replicable evaluation studies.

An outline of the health planning approach is illustrated in the Tables 1.1 and 1.2.

## FUTURES RESEARCH

Part of the evidence base is to attempt to predict the future notwithstanding the difficulty of basing this on past evidence. However, there are various methodologies to achieve this with perhaps the most effective approach being based on the Delphi model (Helmer, 1967). This is closely related to 'expert elicitation' which is addressed in detail in the next chapter of this book.

Expert elicitation brings together 'experts' in a field who can collaborate on trends and make considered judgements on how the future might look. These concepts can be seen in Futures Journals and also in various reports such as one completed in 2012 for American Research Universities.

A consortium of leading research universities has cooperatively identified the core challenge and barriers that many institutions now face limiting the success of their research efforts. While the level of concern naturally varies, the study consistently revealed a number of core issues, that can be categorized into six categories; (1) Hyper-competition and Complexity, (2) Compliance and Indirect Cost Recovery, (3) Research Quality and Impact, (4) Planning and Decision Support, (5) Value of the Research University, and (6) Fragility of Research Administration and Leadership. (Elsevier, 2010)

Another higher education focussed series of studies undertaken through expert elicitation include the NMC Horizon Report (2017) studies.

## CONCLUSIONS: UNIVERSITY 2.0

Summing up, translational design is about seeking evidence to support planning, design and policy decisions in campus developments and in educational facilities design. With an uncertain and increasingly disruptive future, the external forces acting upon the university are exacerbating what is already a complex adaptive system. Historically the concept of the university has managed to survive a wide

17

Table 1.3. Summary of the university-industry-government relationship (adapted from Etzkowitz, 2000)

| University | | Industry | | Government | |
|---|---|---|---|---|---|
| Subjects | Keywords | Subjects | Keywords | Subjects | Keywords |
| Academic Culture | Academic Autonomy | Industry Culture | Industry Goal | Public Policy | Govt goal: strengthen economy |

**University**

Academic Culture — Academic Autonomy
- Quality
- Freedom to publish
- Revision of academic norms

*Academic function*: teaching, research; extension
*Inputs*: Government funds & industry sponsorship
*Outputs*:
Knowledge production, time to research, commercialisation of IP
- Types of commercialisation
- Problems with commercialisation
- Results of the academic-industry technology transfer
- Niches of market
- Exploitation of knowledge-based academic expertise
- Internal policy of patents
- Stability of the execution of research
- Legal instruments for cooperation
- Teacher evaluation cooperation

**Industry**

Industry Culture — Industry Goal

*Industry function*: national development
*Inputs*: knowledge
*Outputs*: new products; generation of dynamism; larger and faster technological innovation
- Niches of market
- Magnification of knowledge based
- Internal policy of patents
- Sponsorship
- Fiscal incentives for cooperation
- Employee evaluation cooperation

**Government**

Public Policy — Govt goal: strengthen economy
- Profit
- Royalties
- Revisions of industry norms
- Recognised academic development as academic (extension) and industry function
- Give support to research directed to market
- Give support to technological innovation integrated to academic research
- Give support to university and industry identify niches of market
- Economic development
- Government policy of patents
- Give support to sponsored research
- Give legal instruments and fiscal incentives to encourage cooperation
- Evaluation of university and industry results

(cont.)

| University | | Industry | | Government | |
|---|---|---|---|---|---|
| *Subjects* | *Keywords* | *Subjects* | *Keywords* | *Subjects* | *Keywords* |
| *Intermediate Offices* | • Function: connect teaching, research & extension resources, admin & internal marketing & comms. & external marketing; administering interaction process<br>• Organisational structure | *Agents* | • Function: connect in-home P&C with university P & D resources; administration internal comms to evaluate possibilities of interaction and industry possibilities; administration of the interaction process<br>• Organisational structure | *Politicians* | • Function: Stimulate interaction university & industry |
| *Relationship evaluation* | • Typology | *Relationship evaluation* | • Typology | *Relationship evaluation* | • Typology |
| *New University* | • 21st C university<br>• Entrepreneurial university<br>• New university mission: economic development<br>• New organisational structure: cross- & new disciplines; self-generating culture; more social space | *New Industry* | • 21st C Industry<br>• Industry based science<br>• New industry mission<br>• New organisational structure: cooperation projects, entrepreneurial centres of high technology in the vicinity of universities | *New Government* | • 21st C Government<br>• The new university and industry need a new government admin where scientific and technological infrastructure are integrated to the productive structure |

range of external disruptions for over a millennium, and the adaptations have not been cathartic but have been rather more incremental. However, it must be said the virtual campus could become a threat if – and only if – the face-to-face social construction of knowledge can be sustained to the same degree virtually. This remains true for the concept of clustering and precincts (Solvell, 2003), as like minds tend to gather to share ideas and create new knowledge in cross-disciplinary partnerships.

The 21st C external environment is such that any impact or:

> … transition is not to a pure market since no country is giving up subsidies entirely and some are creating new ones. Rather the transition is toward a mixed system of market forces and government incentives. East/West, North/ South: the interaction of government, industry and academia is shifting from previous modes of separation or control into a 'triple helix' of overlapping, yet relatively autonomous, spheres. (Etzkowiz, 2000, p. 330)

The triple helix refers to the academic – industrial – government forces acting on the university (not to be confused with the University of Melbourne's triple helix – see Davis, 2009). The external forces are summarised nicely in Table 1.3.

As evidence of this incremental change, over time universities have incrementally adapted to outside forces, exemplified by Harvard University:

> Harvard's great strength, which can be the strength of every university, is a pattern of innovation that is continuous and focused on the university's unique mission – without undue concern for either tradition or what other institutions are doing. Harvard steadily advances, heedless of any "ladder" or the crowd of would-be competitors. Harvard pragmatically climbs its own mountain. On a higher education landscape that needs institutions of many types, that is the one Harvard trait that all should emulate. (Christensen, 2012, p. 53)

Universities, as complex adaptive assemblages, function at a macro urban/ campus level, through to the micro, or classroom level, with third spaces (Soja, 1999) increasingly being exploited in between. This is supported for the 21st C university, with the far-sighted note in Table 1.3 by Etzkowitz (2000) who forecasts a need for 'social spaces increased'.

It is not surprising, then, that translational design – or evidence-based design – will become increasingly necessary for practising campus planners and designers as society embraces university 2.0 (Kulaklia & Mahoney, 2014) to continue their journey of alignment with web 2.0 and pedagogy 2.0 in yet another form of triple helix.

### NOTES

[1] https://casmodeling.springeropen.com

[2] These professional development programs require evidence in order to convince academic staff to move from a teacher centred pedagogy to a technology enhanced active learner centred model.

³ https://www.pkallsc.org/about/collaborating-partners/
⁴ See https://ascilite.org; www.educause.org
⁵ http://www.caul.edu.au/caul-programs/caul-statistics
⁶ http://www.aurp.net/what-is-a-research-park
⁷ http://european-biotechnology.net/services/linklist/cluster-bioregions-technology-parks.html
⁸ https://www.healthdesign.org/knowledge-repository
⁹ http://journals.sagepub.com/toc/her/current

## REFERENCES

ARUP. (2015). *Future libraries: Workplace summary and emerging insights.* London: ARUP.

Baepler, P., Walker, J., & Driessen, M. (2014). It's not about seat time: Blending, flipping, and efficiency in active learning classrooms. *Computers and Education, 78,* 227–236.

Bower, M., Delgarno, B., Kennedy, G., Lee, M., & Kenney, J. (2014). *Blended synchronous learning: A handbook for educators.* Canberra: Australian Government Office of Learning & Teaching.

Brown, A. S. (2009, November). Building a place for innovation. *Mechanical Engineering.*

Budgen, F., Main, S., Callcott, D., & Hamlett, B. (2014). The first year at university: Giving social capital a sporting chance. *The Australian Journal of Teacher Education, 39*(7). Retrieved from http://dx.doi.org/10.14221/ajte.2014v39n7.7

Christensen, C., & Eyring, J. (2012). *The innovative university: Changing the DNA of higher education.* San Francisco, CA: Jossey-Bass.

Cleveland, B., & Fisher, K. (2014). The evaluation of physical learning environments: A critical review of the literature. *Learning Environments Research, 17*(1), 1–28.

Davis, G., Obrien, L., & McLean, P. (2009). *Growing in esteem: Positioning the university of Melbourne in the global knowledge economy.* Retrieved from https://www.educause.edu/research-and-publications/books/tower-a…esteem-positioning-university-melbourne-global-knowledge-economy

Deed, D., & Alterator, S. (2017). Informal learning spaces and their impact on learning in higher education: Framing new narratives of participation. *Journal of Learning Spaces, 6*(3), 54–58.

de la Harpe, B., Thembi, B., McPherson, M., Fisher, K., & Imms, W. (2014). *Not a waste of space: Professional development for staff teaching in new generation learning spaces.* Canberra: Australian Government Office of Learning and Teaching.

Educause Australia Conference. (2007, April 29–May 2). *Advancing knowledge: Pushing boundaries.* Paper presented at the Educause Australia Conference, Melbourne.

Etzkowitz, H., Webster, A., Gebhardt, C., & Terra, B. (2000). The future of the university and the university of the future: Evolution of ivory tower to entrepreneurial paradigm. *Research Policy, 29*(2), 313–330.

Fisher, K. (2005). *Research into measuring the effectiveness of learning environments.* Paris: OECD.

Fisher, K. (2013a, July). *Transforming design thinking through the translational design of learning and knowledge environments.* HERDSA Conference, Auckland, New Zealand.

Fisher, K. (2013b). *The new learning environment: The campus as thirdspace.* Paper presented at the Conference of Australian University Directors of Information Technology, C.A.U.D.I.T., Melbourne.

Fisher, K. (2017). *Aligning the strategic campus plan with the institutional mission in 2030: University campuses as complex adaptive assemblages.* In Society for college and university planning, SCUP, Minnesota.

Gibbons, M., Limoges, C., Nowotny, H., Schwartzman, S., Seot, P., & Trow, M. (2002). *The new production of knowledge: The dynamics of science and research in contemporary societies.* London: Sage Publications.

Glass, C. (2012). Educational experiences associated with international students' learning, development, and positive perceptions of campus climate. *Journal of Studies in International Education, 16*(3), 228–251.

Green, M., & Penn, A. (1997). *Socio-spatial analysis of four university campuses: The implications of spatial configuration on creation and transmission of knowledge.* Proceedings Complex Buildings, First International Symposium, London.

K. FISHER

Hashimshony, R., & Haina, J. (2019). Designing the university of the future. In K. Fisher (Ed.), *The translational design of university learning environments*. Rotterdam, The Netherlands: Sense Publishers.

Helmer, O. (1967). *Analysis of the future: The DELPHI method*. Santa Monica, CA: Rand Corporation.

HERD. (2018). Retrieved May 19, 2018, from https://www.healthdesign.org/topics

Huang, R., Zhan, J., Hu, Y., & Yang, Y. (2012). *Smart campus: The developing trends of digital campus*. Beijing: Faculty of Education, Beijing Normal University.

IASP. (2018). Retrieved May 19, 2018, from https://www.iasp.ws/About-us/IASP-in-a-few-words

JLL. (2016). *Student housing: University partnerships in the UK*. London: Jones Lang LaSalle.

Joseph, A. (2008). A review of the research literature on evidence-based healthcare design (Part I). *Health Environments Research & Design, 1*(3), 61–125.

Kulaklia, A., & Mahoney, S. (2014). *Knowledge creation and sharing with web 2.0 tools for teaching and learning roles in so-called university 2.0*. Paper presented at the 10th International Strategic Management Conference, Procedia – Social and Behavioural Sciences, London.

Lohmann, S. (2006). *The public research university as a complex adaptive system* (Unpublished paper). University of California, Los Angeles, CA.

Looi, T. (2014). The strengths and weaknesses of research methodology: Comparison and complimentary between qualitative and quantitative approaches. *IOSR Journal of Humanities and Social Science (IOSR-JHSS), 19*(4), 99–104.

McCullough, C. (2010). *Evidence-based design for healthcare facilities*. Indianapolis, IN: Sigma Theta Tau International.

Nonaka, I. (1991). The knowledge-creating company. *Harvard Business Review, 69*(6), 96–104.

Norman, D. (2009). The research practice gap. *Interactions, 17*(4), 9–12.

Peters, D., Adam, T., Olakunle, A., Agyepong, A., & Tran, N. (2013). Implementation research and how to do it. *British Medical Journal, 347*, 6753. doi:10.1136/bmj.f6753QS

Scott-Kruse, C., Karem, P., & Shifflett, K. (2016). Evaluating barriers to adopting telemedicine worldwide: A systematic review. *Journal of Telemedicine and Telecare, 24*(1), 4–12.

SCUP. (2018). Retrieved from https://www.scup.org/page/index

Soja, E. (1999). *Thirdspace: Expanding the geographical imagination*. Cambridge, MA: Blackwell Publishers.

Solvell, O., Lindqvist, G., & Ketels, C. (2003). *The cluster initiative greenbook*. Stockholm: Bromma Tryck AB.

The Association for Learning Environments (A4LE). (2018). Retrieved May 19, 2018, from https://a4le.imiscloud.com/A4LE/Knowledge_Center/A4LE/Knowledge_Center/Advanced_Academy/Advanced_Academy_for_Learning_Spaces.aspx?hkey=fd47687c-900b-4423-b171-b5c9e5bf20c5

Top Universities. (2018). Retrieved May 19, 2018, from https://www.topuniversities.com/student-info/choosing-university/university-branch-campuses

Ulrich, R., Zimring, C., Zhu, X., DuBose, J., Seo, H., Choi, Y., Quan, X., & Anjali, J. (2008). Review of the research literature on evidence-based healthcare design (Part I). *Health Environments Research & Design, 1*(3), 61–125.

UTS Design Guidelines. (2018). Retrieved from https://www.uts.edu.au/sites/default/files/Design_Guidelines_160608.pdf

Zeisel, J., & Vischer, J. (2008). Process management: Bridging the gap between research and design. *Design & Health Scientific Review*, 57–61.

KENN FISHER

# 2. SCOPING THE FUTURE OF THE HIGHER EDUCATION CAMPUS

## ABSTRACT

Campus planners are required to design campuses to last for decades and even centuries, but the rapid fragmentation and availability of knowledge sources is necessitating a rethink of what it means to plan strategically. University vice chancellors and presidents the world over are now having to adopt an agile, adaptive and flexible strategic planning framework to deliver the university's mission, so how should campus planners and designers respond? This chapter reviews the scholarly literature and the expert views of practitioners in campus planning (both virtual and physical) to take a position on what campus planners might need to look out for over the next ten years as they strive to align the virtual and physical infrastructure with their respective university missions. The overall methodology used in this study is based around traditional doctoral research approaches, using a number of mixed method (qualitative and quantitative) research tools which include systematic literature reviews, Delphi study online surveys and selected interviews. The two-year study arrived at some conclusions as to what the university campus might look like in 2030.

## INTRODUCTION

Now the concept of learning environments – indeed all knowledge environments – clearly involves integrating the virtual and the physical but we do not yet know what these new generation learning and research environments will look like as they have begun to emerge only recently. Such significant tectonic shifts in the concept of the university campus as we have known it for centuries have been predicted (Chapman, 2006). This SCUP sponsored study reinforces Chapman's prescient arguments as it comes at a time when there are massive change drivers impacting on the physicality of the university campus concept brought about largely by the rapid rise of broadband mobile technologies.

The study reviews the scholarly literature and the expert views of practitioners in campus planning (both virtual and physical) to take a position on what campus planners might need to look out for over the next ten years as they strive to align the virtual and physical infrastructure with their respective university missions. In

© KONINKLIJKE BRILL NV, LEIDEN, 2019 | DOI: 10.1163/9789004391598_003

this context it could be said that there are two extremes or bookends to the scope of higher education provision at present.

The first is a relatively new model which is exemplified by Laureate University (founded in 2000), which has as its mission 'expanding access to quality higher education to make the world a better place' (Laureate, 2016). With over a million students and some 80 institutions in 25 countries aligning the strategic campus plan with the institutional mission offers many challenges. Conversely, at the other extreme, some of the oldest universities maintain a single institutional and campus model, such as the University of Cambridge (commemorating its 800th year), although there are signs of some joint ventures emerging with the likes of some institutions in China. Cambridge's mission is to 'contribute to society through the pursuit of education, learning, and research at the highest international levels of excellence' (Cambridge, 2016).

Clearly Laureate, as one of the largest universities on the planet, has a blended learning multi-campus model, whereas Cambridge favours a single campus face-to-face teaching and research model, but with global strategic partnerships. And, of course, there are all sorts of possibilities in between. So, there is no-one-size-fits-all solution to this emerging challenge of the future of the university campus. That said, the university concept has been challenged for decades, if not centuries, with new technologies being often cited as likely to make campus-place based learning obsolescent (Ernst & Young, 2014). Some authors categorise university typologies and identify trends which are impacting on each of those typologies.

The overall methodology used in this study is based around traditional doctoral research approaches, using a number of mixed method (qualitative and quantitative) research tools – namely systematic literature reviews, Delphi study online surveys and selected interviews – to arrive at some conclusions as to what the university campus might look like in 2026. That said, there is an argument for the constant updating of these concepts in line with Dovey's (2016) and Lohman's (2006) idea of complex adaptive assemblages.

Universities are complex. They need to be adaptive to constant change, especially in the digital age with its rapid rate of transformation. And they are assemblages in that they are a whole which itself consists of a wide range of elements, or assemblages. A 'complex adaptive assemblage' is a development of Deleuze and Guattari's (1987) notion of a 'complex adaptive system'. Dovey argues that the system itself is actually made up of many component parts, with many of these elements not working within a systematic framework but rather as separate assemblages which co-exist on a campus and which are impacted on by uncontrollable outside forces.

Using city planning and urban design concepts to approach the notion of campus planning through this lens is a means of developing connected lines 'from both sciences and humanities, not as a new ideology but as an integrated way of thinking about power, complexity, desire, place, adaptation, assemblage, emergence,

SCOPING THE FUTURE OF THE HIGHER EDUCATION CAMPUS

resilience and territory. The movement for territorialisation to deterritorialisation and reterritorialisation resonates with the adaptive cycle of resilience thinking with its foreloop of growth and conservation contrasted with the back loop of collapse and re-organisation' as illustrated in Figure 2.1.

These separate assemblages and their inter-relationships can be better understood in a campus context by using 'experts' in the fields of learning sciences, teacher professional development, educational technologies, learning environment/campus

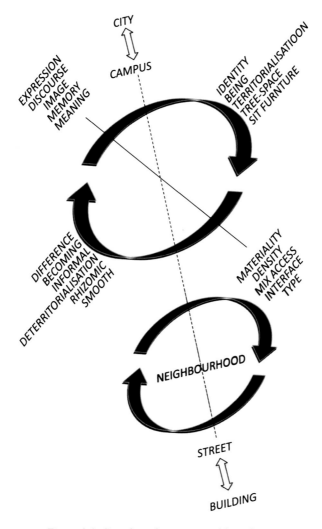

*Figure 2.1. Complex adaptive assemblage drivers
(adapted from Deleuze & Guattari, 1987, in Dovey, 2016, p. 269)*

25

K. FISHER

designers and others to form a cohesive idea of how the separate parts might form a whole. Lohmann (2006) notes that the university is:

> ... of human action, and not of human design. It is characterized by evolution, self-organization, and emergence ... [it] has a unity, or "wholeness", to it. It cannot be split up or merged at will. A holistic analysis – as opposed to a reductionist analysis – is required to understand its design ... unbundle the research university, and it will die. (p. 15)

External city urban planning and urban design drivers need to be complemented with internal drivers, as neatly suggested by Hashimshony and Haini (2019) in their proposition which illustrates how the digital and spatial might interact on campus. This project used both approaches to offer scenarios for campus typologies in 2030 in an evidence-based approach rather than simple statements of opinion.

## OVERVIEW

Scenarios are not meant to predict the future. They can be defined as "consistent and coherent descriptions of alternative hypothetical futures that reflect different perspectives on past, present and future developments which can serve as a basis for action" (OECD, 2006). They are tools for thinking about the future, which will be shaped partly through deliberate strategies and actions and partly by factors beyond the control of decision makers). With the OECD's note of caution in mind, this study sought to forecast possible future developments brought about by rapid online learning modalities (Coursera, 2015) and their impact on the campus-based face-to-face experience.

The evolution of the university campus has seen its 21st C presence become ever more multifaceted with a wide range of change drivers impacting on its ability to support its mission. Thus, this study used an evidence-based, Delphi lead, expert elicitation methodology (similar to the approach used in the annual NMC/Educause Horizon Report model (Johnston et al., 2014, 2015) to forecast how campuses might evolve over the next decade.

Several theoretical models – with some now well tested in practice – have been used to frame the research including the 'flipped classroom/campus' concept (Strayer, 2007) the 'sticky campus' (Lefebvre, 2014), expert elicitation (Meyer & Booker, 1991; Sullivan & Payne, 2011) and cognitive mapping (Jameson, 1996). This approach is also supported by Helmer's (1967) 'analysis of the future' modelling strategy encapsulated in the Delphi approach. Multiple issues are impacting on the future of the campus both as a whole and also as a series of interconnected learning and research environments. These issues are being considered in professional and academic forums such as at recent conferences (ARC, 2015). Indeed, the whole concept of flipped learning is in the early stages of a rigorous, scholarly evaluation (Freeman et al., 2014; Duke University, 2015).

26

Some of these issues were also canvassed in previous Chapman Prize winner reports. Boys et al. (2014) focussed on student perceptions of learning spaces, whilst Painter et al. (2013) focussed on the gaps in the research and also the need for some form of agreed taxonomy regarding the range of issues being considered in this research domain. Also, Johnson et al. (2015) examined peer engagement as a common resource on campus and explored the interaction patterns in institutions.

In continuing to build on that work, this SCUP study focused on the views of eminent researchers in both industry and academe to forecast how university campuses may change in the near future using the well-tested practice of expert elicitation (Sullivan & Payne, 2011).

## BACKGROUND

One approach advocated by Norman (2010) calls for a 'translational design' research model. This draws its influence from translational clinical medicine wherein research and practice are intertwined. In leveraging this concept to campus planning and design, translational design seeks a stronger focus on research in the design of learning environments in an age of transformation and uncertainty. This approach also links academe to industry, with each discipline informing the other through empirical research studies. Using this evidence-based planning and design (EBD) approach, first developed by health planners (HERD, 2015), the scholarly peer reviewed published literature can be evaluated.

An alternative way of unpacking the complexity of university strategic campus planning in a systematic manner is to frame the analysis within a student-learning trajectory – as advocated by Boys et al. (2014) – but filter this through the work of Kolb and Kolb's (2005) four learning elements. Kolb and Kolb suggest that four topologically nested sub-systems – the *micro; meso; exo; and macro* – inscribe the principle domains in which students learn.

The *micro* is represented by the student's immediate classroom, the *meso* is mediated by student residences, family and perhaps parallel online courses, the *exo* covers the policies and structures impacting on the student via campus culture and, finally, the *macro* is shaped by society's values and aspirations (such as valuing education over training, for example). The study also accesses research and knowledge transfer/community engagement in its analysis.

The first – macro – is shaped by society's values and aspirations and several institutional studies that draw on expert elicitation methods are worthy of note. Norton (2014) suggests that technology will have a significant impact on the campus experience. This campus-based face-to-face disruption has been acknowledged by Coursera (2015) and Laureate (Zogby & Zogby, 2014). Massive online open courseware (MOOC) has evolved at a rapid rate and now these courses recognise a need for an on-campus experience to support the online experience as completion rates in MOOC's have been significantly low at only 10% (The Economist, 2014).

There are clear implications here for campuses. For example, what support services should be provided on campuses, where are they best located and what would their built form look like? These needs are made explicit in the concept of affordances (Gibson, 1977), which develops a framework for infrastructure in support of teaching and learning modalities. Ensuring an effective on-campus experience for students is itself leading to innovation in course models, with partial online and partial face-to-face elements, which are 'branded' as blended active learning models – where the instructor time is reduced and replaced by an online component. It is also known as the 'flipped classroom'.

'Over half the 4,500 students at MIT take a MOOC as part of their course' (Economist, 2014). Thus, the concept of the 'sticky campus' is a key factor. The Universities increasingly provide a unique palette of knowledge sources and student experiences to ensure students will want to come and stay on 21st C campuses (Lefebvre, 2014). Various other equally – if not more – important issues are also in play, including Government framed research policy and funding, student fees and student debt, access and inclusion, overall funding of public vs private sources, and the internationalisation of both research and learning.

There is also a more recent questioning of how universities should be valued in the community; that is just by financial performance and graduation numbers, or rather a more balanced approach which couples these metrics with a more qualitatively valued assessment of the relative importance of the concept of the university to both the local community, the State and also to the production of new knowledge, including its transfer.

The second order – exo – includes policies and structures impacting on the student via campus culture. These impacts include internationalisation, research, community engagement, student services, academic professional development, educational technologies, human capital, the student experience and graduate attributes. In exploring how these themes impact on students, the annual Horizon Report (Johnston et al., 2016) outlines educational technology trends (that is the digital or the virtual) over short, medium and long-time frames.

One resulting physical impact as noted earlier is the 'flipped' classroom (Strayer, 2007). These environments require a re-mapping of the student experience in the context of graduate attributes. In terms of the built learning environment, student graduate attributes can be used as a means of calibrating how learning environments are designed and how well they actually work. Indeed, these are now being connected to so-called 'soft skills' such as entrepreneurship, startup strategies and cloud sourcing, all of which are skills not normally extant in a 'traditional' curriculum. The alignment with the institutional mission will also be through student graduate attributes at the institutional and also the faculty/discipline level.

The third element – meso – is mediated by student residences, family and also the abovementioned parallel online courses which in this case are called Massive Online Campus Courseware (MOCS). Kolb and Kolb (2005) suggest that the meso is mediated by student residences and family values. Linking this through the concept of the student experience may provide a fundamental way of understanding the influence of the meso. Suitably calibrated surveys and other qualitative research methodologies have been explored to provide evidence (Office of Learning and Teaching, 2016) that can be mapped onto a spatial campus framework.

This SCUP project argued for a stronger focus on the strategic imperative of universities through the cognitive mapping of the educational drivers now impacting on our teaching, learning and research programs. For example, additional recent findings from work by Laureate University (Zogby & Zogby, 2014) embraced the blended learning model to ensure their 850,000 student base is comfortable with a blended online and campus-based model. It should be noted that Laureate attracts students focused on education and training directed towards finding employment and that many of their institutes in 29 countries are vocationally oriented. At present, their predominant model is 40% campus face-to-face and 60% online but, tellingly, the university wishes to reverse that ratio through a blended study centre model.

The final element – micro – is represented by the student's immediate classroom. There is a slow transformation from the predominating passive, teacher-lead model of didactic lecture halls, towards a more active, learner centred, environment (Fisher & Newton, 2014). The arguments around funding ratios that have supported large lectures of 400–500 students in 1st year courses are now being eroded. More online analytics are being used to determine student learning outcomes, utilising all pedagogical models where lectures are found to be the least effective (Fisher & Ellis, 2017). Blended learning spaces are emerging where larger groups can still be taught and where the evidence shows that there are improved learning outcomes.

## RECENT DEVELOPMENTS

The use of analytics enables a more personalised constructivist approach to learning (Literatu, 2015). As noted earlier, students in the 'flipped' mode can remotely view online lectures through iTunes or YouTube at their leisure, but on campus they have a more active and engaged collaborative event with an instructor and their peers. Timetabling and space modelling have transformed the traditional 1-hour lecture and 2-hour tutorial to a 1-hour online e-Learning and a two-hour blended tutorial model.

Lecture theatres are being replaced by spaces such as active learning classrooms (ACL), technology enabled, active learning spaces (TEAL), immersive innovative learning environments (IILE's) and problem-based learning environments such as Conceive, Design, Implement and Operate (CDIO, 2016). This latter example is used largely in engineering and technology programmes (Keppell et al., 2012). These developments are supported by evidence-based evaluations which argue for a significant change of pedagogical practice and, accordingly, parallel changes in technology and the design of learning spaces to improve measured student learning outcomes.

The design response, in addition to the Innovative Learning Environments (ILE's) noted above, can include a campus wide network of distributed learning hubs and increased informal and social student learning thirdspaces (Fisher, 2005). These can be a distributed precinct, faculty, department or school discipline-based learning commons and are all designed to optimise the on-campus student experience as noted in Chapter 1.

Academic libraries are rapidly converting to centralised learning commons where books are making way for people, with some universities opting for automated book storage and retrieval to release book stack space for additional informal and social spaces for students. Libraries are effectively being re-engineering into cultural centres where campus social capital can expand (Johnston et al., 2014).

These issues are also covered in part by a research project Modelling of Complex Learning Environments (Ellis, Goodyer, Fisher, & Marmot, 2014). In its early phases this study synchronously mapped the digital/virtual behaviours of students over the physical to better understand how campus learning spaces will provide an improved student learning experience and engagement. It is a study that evaluates the recent past to predict what might emerge in the future.

The SCUP Chapman Award study took a very different approach in that it tapped into expert opinion as to what works, how and why, and which strategies were likely to dominate in the future to influence campus planning and design. Both studies complement each other, and both serve to inform a much larger examination of the 'wicked' problem that is: 'what will the campus of 2030 look like in aligning its affordances (Gibson, 1977) with the institutional mission'.

Hashimshony and Haina (2019) note that 'in identify(ing) transforming trends in society that are affecting the mission of universities, [they] analyse the impact of those trends on the institutional and spatial structure of universities, and then summarize the factors that planners should be paying attention to in the future design of their institutions'. This statement (which appears in one of the chapters in this book) – in a nutshell – suggests to this author the use of cognitive mapping (Jameson, 1996) as a means of understanding the impact of transformation and change in pedagogy on the design of future campuses. Unless we critically analyse and understand the dynamic forces acting on universities in the 21st C, we can never expect to design built infrastructure to effectively support learner needs in our rapidly evolving digital world.

Cognitive mapping is a perfect framework to more deeply understand learner needs and to map these over their potential impact on the physical learning environment. Jameson (1996) argues – in referencing Lynch's 'The Image of the City' (1960) – that 'to understand the city, you must first understand society'. From this logic comes the socio-pedagogical-spatial notion of 'flipping the campus'. That is, where students can work and learn anywhere. Instead of coming to campus to sit passively in lecture theatres students become active learners through collaborative workshops that are mediated and coached by academic 'guides' with the material acquired through various online managed digital portals.

Thus, the three prime campus spatial typologies – formal (teacher-centred), informal (learner centred) and social (collaborative) – are changing significantly in their mix, from the present 50:40:10 to perhaps 10:60:30. This is a highly complex area with the default position on many campuses being predominantly a process of incremental change. The industrial age classroom model of didactic teaching is still prevalent despite the inroads being made by online learning modalities. The evidence to date (Keppell et al., 2012; Fisher & Newton, 2014) points towards a more blended active-learning, digitally supported model. In summary this involves a mix of self-directed, collaborative, problem-based, immersive, active, integrated workplace and other forms of authentic learning in varying proportions, depending on the discipline, year level and subject complexity.

## METHODOLOGY

### Mixed Methods Research – Qualitative and Quantitative

This SCUP study used various tools to elicit views on the trends in campus planning over the years 2020–2030. The principal elements included:

- A scholarly systematic literature review of campus planning futures
- A review of a number of expert elicitation surveys undertaken by significant research bodies and institutes
- A Delphi Study and Proof of Concept of a SCUP members survey to elicit views of campus planners regarding campus futures
- This is coupled with a parallel study of Australian and UK University Directors of Estates and Chief Information Officers on their views of campus planning, both virtual and physical

The sources were triangulated for validation and cross-referencing to determine the most probable campus futures in the opinion of these 'experts'.

### Expert Elicitation

This approach is epitomised by the Delphi analysis approach. In 1967 Olaf Helmer noted:

> In my opinion the so-called soft sciences are on the verge of a revolution. The traditional methods of the social sciences are proving inadequate to the task of dealing effectively with the ever-growing complexity of forecasting the consequences of alternative policies and thus furnishing useful planning aid to high level decision makers in the public and private sectors. (Helmer, 1967, p. 3)

In so doing Helmer pointed out that new methods include operations research, mathematical modelling, simulation and also the notion of systematic utilisation of expert opinions. He also noted that use could be made of informed intuitive judgement which is based on the notion that 'projections into the future, on which public policy decisions must rely, are largely based on the personal expectations of individuals rather than on predictions from well-established theory' (p. 4). In this context he mentions the concept of expert opinion, which more recently has been framed as expert elicitation (Sullivan & Payne, 2011). The Delphi method involves a series of repeated exchanges between the researcher and the selected expert responses, gradually narrowing down the key themes which form the questions the answers of which are elicited from a wider group. This approach was taken in this study, with circa 40 'experts' responding to the iterations of the survey questions as they were continually refined.

Expert opinions were also sourced from various studies in the literature conducted by scholarly institutes including the NMR Horizon Report – Higher Education; NMR Report – HE Libraries; the Scottish Executive; Zogby Analytics; and various SCUP surveys such as SCUP Trends 2016 and this SCUP Perry Chapman 2015–2016 project.

For the quantitative questionnaire design the literature review assisted in framing the survey questions for the Delphi Phase of the project, arriving at the following key themes: University strategy; Student experience; Informal and social learning; Formal teaching and learning; Impact of technology; Staff experience; Research spaces; and Industry engagement. The following categories of university senior staff were selected as respondents: Directors and Planners of Estates; Directors of IT and CIO's; and Deputy Vice Chancellor/Deputy Presidents for Academic and separately for Research.

Approximately 60 targeted responses were received which indicated that these respondents had an interest in the topic and thus the data gained will be valid and reliable. One possible drawback of the questionnaire – the design of which highlights the extraordinary complexity of campus ecosystems – is that it would be difficult for one person to complete the questionnaire. Indeed, four or five Departments in a University might need to be consulted to complete the data required. The survey was managed through Survey Monkey and the data analysed using the tools available in that system.

*Qualitative Research*

This included an abbreviated systematic literature review, with three stages of review:

- *Conceptual* – The Rapid Structured Literature Review (RSLR) was used to formulate research aims, objectives and questions. From these a conceptual map of topic areas was created. Seminal articles were sourced from such venues as peer reviewed journals, professional journals, conference proceedings, market research, organisational literature, official statistics from Government and company sources and dissertations, theses and unpublished papers.

- *Operational* – The research design and methodology used data collection and quality assessment. Databases were searched using key words and strings. Tables were created of descriptive information and these were then reviewed to create thematic relationships and connections. A literature map was then extracted from the literature and then linked by theme, author, time series or a combination of these.
- *Sense making* – Discussions and interpretations picked up differences between authors' views in the RSLR. Key outcomes were then determined to inform key insights for practice. The overall findings from the RSLR were then compiled and further work identified for future study.

EXPERT ELICITATION SURVEY FINDINGS

*Expert Elicitation Survey Findings (from the Literature Review)*

This section summarises the combined findings from these surveys: NMR (2016) Horizon Mobile Devices, SCUP Trends (2016), Zogby and Zogby (2014) Survey of Students for Laureate 2020, the NMR (2016) HE Horizon Report, and the NMR (2014) Horizon Report HE Libraries. They are summarised here using the eight categories identified in the development of the questionnaire viz University strategy; Student experience; Informal and social learning; Formal teaching and learning; Impact of technology; Staff experience; Research spaces; Industry engagement. A source audit trail in a matrix is available for the following statements.

*University Strategy*

There is an ongoing debate as to whether the university as pubic good (Lambert, 2014) should focus on its local community or a global community. Funding often comes from local sources – government, industry and student fees. But revenue can also come from international sources. Note that the 'Brexit' is likely to see some UK universities establish offshore campuses in Europe to continue to secure research funding (Oates, 2016). Some of the higher order changes that the campus master plan will have to be adaptive to are advancing cultures of innovation; a re-thinking of how institutions work; competing models of education; keeping education relevant; embracing the need for radical change; rethinking the roles of educators; and defining and transitioning to new business models.

These drivers of change will also be impacted on by a proliferation of open educational resources; the need for greater innovation to stay competitive; and distributed learning options. So, whilst 74% of universities have campus masterplans connected to strategic plans (see survey hereunder), the latter is likely to be subject to some significant sources of disruption largely driven by technology developments and a related globalisation of education.

There is a growth in synthetic mergers of academic institutions – eg Laureate – with shared 'back of house' but many brands. So, whilst Laureate International

University is across 80 brands and is focussed on work related courses, other universities focus on their local community. In developing countries there can be more conservative responses than in the western world as well. There is rapid growth in China, Russia, and Malaysia which will challenge the US and England.

In the Western world there is a growing demographic change due to reducing middle classes which means there will be increasing lower social economic classes meaning greater development required. Some other issues include greater integration of planning at executive level, an entrenched infrastructure deficit in ICT and the potential for the open licensing of course material and online delivery models. There is an under-resourcing of campus infrastructure which could see an impact on the scaling of teaching innovations.

The Delphi survey – considered in more detail hereunder – noted that small numbers of universities are running summer semesters/trimesters (37%), and there is an expected growth (10%) in post graduate programmes, both national and international. It is predicted that there will be only a 10% growth for domestic undergrads, and little or no growth in international undergrads. Between 2010 & 2021 student enrolments aged 18 to 24 increased 10%; ages 25–34 increased 20%; and over 35 increases were 32%, which may indicate a changing of student needs on campus and online as these demographics develop over time.

### Student Experience

Key issues in this category begin with Millennials having different learning styles and expectations, as will generation Z students. There will be a demand for year-round learning, as 52% of students will expect classes to be delivered 24/7. There will be increasing value placed on the user experience and this will have a high priority. Students will expect their learning to be transient with constant upgrading of credentials. There will be a rise of more authentic assessment and a shift to deeper learning approaches accompanied by a focus on measuring learning, learning analytics and adaptive learning all supported by disability services.

The integration of international students will be paramount and student accommodation quality will need to be improved. There has been significant interest in student accommodation for local and international students by universities. There is a greater need for library study spaces accompanied by a need for improved BYOD (bring your own device) access and equity.

### Informal & Social Learning

There has been shown significant interest in growth of informal learning spaces and also the conversion of libraries to informal learning. Creating authentic learning opportunities and increased incidental learning are also cited. Some of the technology implications in informal learning include location intelligence, networked objects, BYOD, Cloud computing, the increase in issuing of Badges &

Microcredit for MOOC courses, the notion of the 'quantified self' and also the emergence of telepresence.

There will also be learning through augmented and virtual realities and the use of ePortfolios may mean more informal learning spaces for students to prepare these. Artificial intelligence is also likely to play a significant role. There will be increased use of blended learning designs, informal learning modalities and also an increase in personalised learning. More individual and group study spaces are needed.

*Formal Teaching & Learning*

Considerable interest in blended learning developments is evident. Also, there is a strong interest in laboratory-based facilities in active learning spaces. MOOCs are only being adopted at a slow rate, whilst BYOD is growing.

There is a strong interest in professional development for blended learning in part due to a search for increased relevance for formal teaching, learning and creative inquiry. This is seeing an increased development of the flipped classroom. There will be more crossover learning, and so called 'soft skills' are becoming more critical – communication skills, entrepreneurial concepts, startup concepts, self-directed learning, writing, critical thinking, and problem solving. Student disengagement (millennials and society) requires more experiential and active learning spaces.

There is an increase in the need to accredit professional programs and a focus on quality and rating tools. 50% of students now expect learning and assessment to be collaborative. This is all leading to a redesign of learning spaces to accommodate the aforementioned issues, but also to be sufficiently adaptive to support augmented and VR learning, makerspaces and the increased use of robotics in the workplace pushing back into academe to train students in these models. There is a move towards embedding libraries in the curriculum – with improved digital literacy – and alternative avenues of discovery leading to libraries possibly becoming closer to faculties.

*Impact of Technology*

There is likely to be an Increase in MOOC's offered to partner institutions eg through the Coursera network and in 2017 it was predicted that by 2020 MOOCs will have increased by 500%. It is expected that MOOC's will manage growth in student numbers without the need for more physical facilities although there is emerging evidence of the need for a face-to-face component in courses to ensure positive learning outcomes and to reduce attrition rates.

Kurzwell (2016) predicts a significant growth in AI by 2030, 3D printing will expand, wearables and VR will impact on learning and the Internet of Things will impact on teaching. Makerspaces will evolve for 21st C skills of making, doing, entrepreneurship, co-working and startup cultures. There will be increased online learning coupled with the emergence of machine learning.

There will be a need to support lower socio-economic cohorts in more flexible ways – more non-traditional students – in non-traditional institutions and in non-traditional educational models eg competency-based education. 50% of students will expect course material and technology/MOOCs to be ubiquitous. 33% expect most tuition to be online. There will be a need to manage radical change.

*Staff Experience*

There is continuing resistance to MOOC's, whilst 100% of students prefer blended learning. With the advent of machine learning it is possible that devices could replace faculty by 2030. Whilst university administrators are aiming for greater efficiencies through open plan workplaces, there is a move away in the industry from these open spaces to spaces which nurture staff, suggesting a rethinking of the workplace design and staff wellbeing. The increased integration of the library with academic programs may imply more distributed librarians and libraries.

*Research Spaces*

There is likely to be an increase in the separation of teaching and research as forecast by some. The gross floor areas (GFA) of research buildings are likely to grow by up to 10%. Research partnerships will include business and industry. Much research may move off campus to be closer to industry (Trachtenberg in Times HES, 2015). Whilst the study did not have the time or scope to delve deeply into research space futures, we nevertheless began to look at discipline specific spatial implications, but it became quickly clear that this is really another project – or projects – in itself, for a later day.

*Industry Engagement*

There is likely to be a much greater industry engagement with associated work integrated learning. Research partnerships will include business and industry and there will be more context-based learning. Industry linkages are likely to increase with the development of more research, science and technology parks and biohubs. Some research will move off campus in this context.

There will be a greater drive for public universities to seek further funding from these linkages. Also, there will be greater work integrated learning so that graduates are more 'job ready' in those institutions that are more focussed on professional training. Due to a shift to seeking job opportunities, students will study closer to home for qualifications there, and/or in their region. Teaching students for a robotic future will rapidly become the norm (30% of jobs will be automated in 65% of occupations). There will be a trend towards selecting courses in health care, computing, construction, and social services.

SCOPING THE FUTURE OF THE HIGHER EDUCATION CAMPUS

Student disengagement (millennials and society) requires more experiential and active learning modalities. 50%–70% of students expect there to be greater work integrated learning.

## SCUP DELPHI SURVEY RESULTS

*Expert Elicitation: SCUP Member Survey – Proof of Concept*

As noted elsewhere, the Delphi Approach requires the elicitation of some 30 respondents to test and further develop the survey. Most SCUP respondents were from the organisational and administration Departments of the University (68%). Teaching and research universities dominated (63%) followed by primarily teaching (21%). 90% of respondents were from the USA. 10% were in the CBD, 47% outside the CBD and 26% were regional/rural. 47% of the respondent's universities were of <10,000 students, whilst 21% were 50–75,000 students. Top ranking themes were – in top priority order – teaching, student experience, research and community engagement. 74% advised they connected their campus masterplan with their university mission. Of those 26% didn't, 5% thought it was not relevant, 5% were on the way, and 14% were 'other'.

Regarding cross disciplinarity, learning space strategy development and managing a digital learning environment, the chart indicates that circa 30% of respondents are working on all three. Another 25% have developed a digital strategy already but it is not yet university policy. 25% have cross disciplinarity as a policy whereas only 15% have a learning space strategy and a digital learning environment strategy in place. Cross disciplinarity is encouraged, according to the results, in four primary ways, with each of these scoring 4 to 5 in a Likert Scale of 0–5. These included interdisciplinary undergraduate courses (5), academic leadership, administrative and executive leadership and developing grant programs (all 4). Interestingly 38% of respondents said such concepts were not stated in their strategic documents (strategic plan, mission, values). 30% of respondents advised they would be developing new curriculum policies for the delivery of programmes, and 50% said that potentially they would for the use of an online learning platform.

In relation to periods of study, 79% of the respondent universities run a semester system, with only 5% a trimester system and 10% having a quarter or term model. 37% already have a summer extended timetable, with 21% 'experimenting' and 26% 'exploring' the option. 10% will not use it at all. Likert preferences for blended learning were 4.3; for online programmes 4.5; for after-hours programs 4.7; and for alternative languages 2.5.

A question was asked regarding growth in recruiting in the following categories: local post grad (PG) research, local PG coursework, local undergraduate (U/G), international PG research, international PG coursework and international U/G level. 30–50% of respondents expected up to a 10% growth in general student numbers over 10 years. International PG research was expected to rise to 30% saying they

37

would not be recruiting extra domestic PG research or coursework, whilst another 25% replied with a conflicting result saying they would not recruit extra local U/G or P/G.

In terms of students taking off-shore programs for a semester or two, 50% of respondents said that no PG students took these programs, whilst 30% said they did. At the undergraduate level 30% said that up to 10% of students took off shore programs, and another 20% of respondents said that 76–100% of students took these programs. The issues impacting on offshore uptake seemed to be evenly agreed that exchange rates, cultural, security and political issues were uppermost.

In relation to student accommodation, there was a consistent interest (30–40%) in the additional provision of accommodation for all student categories – on campus international, national/interstate and local within state students. This was repeated for supported off-campus categories as well. There was across the board interest at a lower level at around 20% for both categories. There were another 10% of respondents very interested in all categories except the off campus local/state students.

One question sought to elicit interest in the development of informal/social learning spaces including distributed learning commons. 42% saw a dramatic increase in provision. Conversion of library spaces to informal and social learning commons was seen as very important and highly likely at 32%. Another 10.5 % said it was being planning and a further 21% thought it potentially needed. Interest in collocating other services with the Library, such as student services, retail and IT were varied. 20% said they had already done so and will continue with this trend; 30% said potentially; and, interestingly, 25% said they would not. With regard to the centrality or distributed model of library – there were contrasting positions of about 70% having a strong focus on the central library but also 80% having a combination of central and distributed.

There was an all-round strong interest in developing blended learning pedagogies, spaces and programs on their campuses. When asked if respondents planned to evaluate new generation learning spaces, 10% said not likely and the remainder split evenly between already doing this and potentially they would look at it. A somewhat complicated question elicited answers related to work integrated learning (WIL), problem and project-based learning (PPBL), maker spaces (MS), clinical teaching models (CTM) and tele-teaching (TT) across faculty groupings. Broadly the *Highly Likely* results as follows.

The standout result of course is the interactive nature of teaching and learning in Medicine and Health Sciences, followed a fair way back by STEM, Engineering and Science. This is perhaps not surprising due to the laboratory nature of learning in these disciplines. But the standout once again is the Medical and Health interest in Tele-Teaching, due in part to telemedicine and the increase in robotic and micro surgery. One wonders why the other disciplines do not follow the lead, although it may be due to the lower cost and funding models of non-Medical programmes.

*Table 2.1. Faculty interest in active learning models*

|       | Biotech | Engineer | Human | STEM | Soc Sci | Medical |
|-------|---------|----------|-------|------|---------|---------|
| **WIL**  | 20% | 50% | 15% | 25% | 15% | 50% |
| **PPBL** | 50% | 45% | 20% | 50% | 20% | 50% |
| **MS**   | 20% | 25% | 15% | 20% | 10% | 25% |
| **CTM**  | 10% | 5%  | 5%  | 55  | 5%  | 50% |
| **TT**   | 10% | 10% | 5%  | 5%  | 5%  | 40% |

Another question elicited a trend towards an increase in blended learning but with supporting lecture-based programs, both rated at 3–4 out of the 6 Likert scale points. Bring your own devices had increased significantly, although the rate of reduction in university supplied desktop computers was falling very slowly. The growth of online presence, delivering online courses and in measuring the use of the online environment was essentially split evenly between a 'slow rate' and a 'steady rate'.

However, this did not translate to the adoption of MOOC's (despite MIT's uptake of 40%) with the majority of answers around parallel online, MOOC's and MOCC's rating 0–2 on the Likert scale. In this context when asked if there were funding issues prohibiting the uptake of these courses, 45% said no and 25% said yes, with the remainder not applicable. One peer reviewer in the Delphi study noted that in the USA there is some difficulty funding students to take online courses delivered out of the State in which they are undertaking their tuition.

There was a strong 'yes' to an increase in professional development for blended learning delivery, noting that they were already doing this, would expand and at a faster rate. Staff remuneration was likely to remain linked to both research and teaching, with some increase in the likelihood – although a slight drift away – focusing on research biased promotions. A second validating question noted the greater balance of *current* teaching and research positions vs both teaching only and research only. However, in 10 years-time it appeared that there might be a significant shift between teaching and research, with roughly 60% of respondents suggesting more teaching only positions, 20% suggesting more research only, and 20% suggesting that they would stay the same.

Regarding the % gross floor area of research buildings on campus, responses were evenly spread between 1–10%, 11–25% and 26–50%. Growth was estimated by 50% of respondents in 10 years to be 1–10%.

There appears to be a strong appetite for industry engagement. In terms of industry engagement through research and related parks, there seems to be little appetite from some universities which may well be teaching focussed. However there is certainly potential interest, and some currently being planned and already built or being built.

K. FISHER

## POSSIBLE HIGHER EDUCATOIN FUTURES TO 2030

### *University Typologies from the Literature*

Around six or seven models of university typologies were observed in the above literature review. These are consolidated hereunder and combined in various ways to develop a more overarching typology.

### *OECD (2006) Model*

These OECD scenarios correlate to some degree with other typologies hereunder. These are compared in the conclusions and a resulting model suggested. They include:

Scenario 1: Trend towards Open Networking
Scenario 2: Focus more on Serving Local Communities
Scenario 3: Responds to the New Public Responsibility
Scenario 4: Envisages Higher Education Inc.

| *Scenario 1* - **Open Networking** | *Scenario 3* - **New Public Responsibility** |
|---|---|
| • Highly internationalised network<br>• institutions collaborate in research - industry - student mobility.<br>• Greater range of options to students and researchers<br>• Premier institutions still network with each other<br>• Knowledge generated becomes available to all<br>• Open knowledge<br>• Student exchanges / study abroad<br>• MOOC's platforms | • Publicly funded but increasing public management - market forces /financial incentives<br>• Boundaries between public / private blur<br>• Postgraduate fees fully paid by the student<br>• Focus on quality of teaching / employability<br>• Increase differentiation - focus on strengths and local community<br>• Research less cross-border except for the<br>• Accountability, transparency, efficiency, effectiveness, responsiveness & vision<br>• Rising public debt has shifted cost to consumers<br>• More autonomy = greater entrepreneurship<br>• Research funding more competitive / project focus |
| *Scenario 2* - **Serving Local Communities** | *Scenario 4* - **'Higher Education Inc.'** |
| • Research continues to be internationally collaborative<br>• Teaching and research focussed on their local communities where funding derived<br>• Teaching focussed environment<br>• research largely left to Governments & more prestigious universities<br>• Backlash against globalisation<br>• Government research focussed on strategic security, natural sciences, life sciences & engineering<br>• Arts and humanities remaining a prime role for universities. | • HE institutions compete globally<br>• Research and teaching become disconnected - become separate 'core businesses'<br>• Vocational education increases its market share<br>• Many universities open branch campuses abroad and franchise educational programmes<br>• Emerging economies begin to specialise in their competitive advantages such as India in technology and agronomics in China<br>• Emerging economies also offer educational services to the developing world - trade liberalisation in education. |

*Figure 2.2. Four future university scenarios (OECD, 2006)*

40

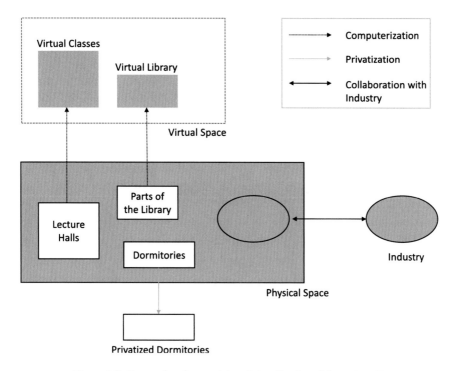

*Figure 2.3. Forces for change determining the size of the university
(from Hashimshony & Haina, 2014)*

*Hashimshony and Haina (2019) Model*

This model neatly suggests how the virtual and the physical might be inter-related. Since the time of writing of that article, these developments have begun to happen in significant ways in Australia, particularly the digitising of the library turning those spaces into learning commons, and the 'outsourcing' of student accommodation off campus. Increased links to industry are also emerging in some cases and consolidating and maturing in others. In particular work integrated learning is becoming more important as 'job ready' graduates are sought by employers.

*Crow and Dabars Model (2014)*

The genealogy of universities illustrated here by Crow and Dabars neatly suggests how the evolution of universities is now shaping the emergence of the New American University. Scaling up this concept across the university wide system will be problematical. Further densities of university campuses are also implicated depending on the siting of the university viz CBD, CBD edge, urban, rural.

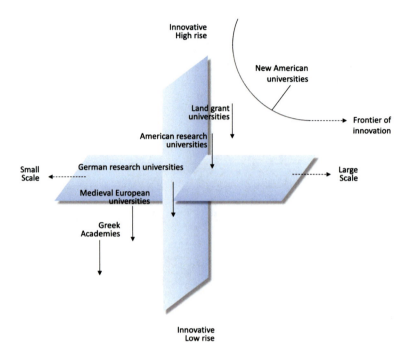

*Figure 2.4. The new American university and its origins (adapted from Crow & Dabars, 2014)*

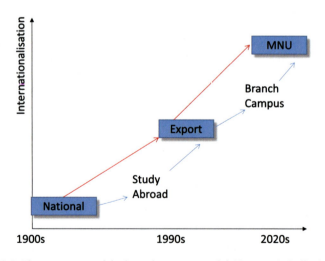

*Figure 2.5. The emergence of the branch campus model (Garrett & Gallagher, 2014)*

*Garrett and Gallagher Model (2014)*

This model sees universities evolving from nation serving institutions through an export of education model (via incoming international students to existing campuses) towards a branch campus model offshore. Laureate University is the most classic case of this Branch Campus model.

*Four Evolutionary Forms (Ernst & Young, 2012)*

This model seeks to establish four typologies, namely:

- Type 1: Current State – Status Quo
- Type 2: Streamlined Status Quo
- Type 3: Niche Dominators
- Type 4: Transformers

All currently exist, but have not been evaluated for performance per se.

| **INCREMENTAL CHANGE** | Type 1 – Current state<br>• Dominant model as broad-based teaching and research<br>• Supported by large asset base<br>• Large, predominantly in-house back office<br>*Examples*<br>• Expected slow pace of policy change<br>• Some focus on quality of teaching | Type 2 – 'Streamlined Status Quo'<br>• Continue as broad-based teaching and research<br>• Transform delivery of services<br>• Transform organisations<br>*Examples*<br>• Change in ratio of support staff to front line staff ie much lower support staff numbers |
|---|---|---|
| **STEP CHANGE** | Type 3 – 'Niche Dominators'<br>• Fundamentally reshape & refine services & operating 'markets'<br>• Concurrent shift in business model, organisation & operations<br>*Examples*<br>• Aalto University (focused disciplines)<br>• BPP University, UK (professional accredited quals with industry) | Type 4 – 'Transformers'<br>• Private providers & new entrants<br>• Carve out new positions in the traditional sector<br>• Create new markets which merge parts of higher education sector with other sectors<br>*Examples*<br>• Venture Garage, Aalto University<br>• Coursera |

*Figure 2.6. Four possible evolutionary scenarios for universities*
*(Ernst & Young, 2014)*

*Avalanche Universities Barber (2015)*

Barber suggested five typologies viz:

- The *elite university* where technology becomes a greater part of the learning process, benchmarking is against global peers, and partnerships with other universities, institutions and businesses are important (e.g. Yale's expansion into Singapore in association with the National University of Singapore).

K. FISHER

- The *mass university* that will mostly use online or blended approaches, perhaps partnering with other respected institutions and practitioners from business and other fields. Some will "shut their physical doors" (p. 57) to be entirely on line (similar to many newspapers).
- The *niche university*, each different from the rest, may comprise a beautiful campus in a small town, "a handful of global stars" on staff, very high fees, and/ or students drawn from the top echelon (examples include Oberlin and Williams in the USA, The New College of Humanities in the UK). As non-elite universities compete for students they will require offerings that are "sharper and clearer about what they offer and to whom" (p. 51).
- The *local university* may deliver to, and organize, local student experience with much of the content coming from large, elite universities (e.g. the local function of Indian Institutes of Technology set up to support its economy). As well, universities that teach subjects requiring face-to-face content and training (like medicine) will remain important.
- A fifth overarching typology – the *lifelong learning* mechanism – could lead to people who have developed expertise without ever attending a university but have drawn on a range of services and acquired relevant knowledge, being awarded qualifications bachelors and master's degrees similar to honorary doctorates for exceptional performance (e.g. Steve Jobs and Richard Branson).

*Amalgamation of Typologies (Fisher)*

If, for example, Transformers and Niche dominators are coupled with other key factors such as covered elsewhere in this report, a framework for testing could look like Figure 2.7. This takes account of the various change drivers established in the methodology development phase of the project, coupled with some of the typologies listed above. The author has either been on the research and teaching staff, has been an undergraduate or post-graduate student, or carried out masterplanning at the following six institutions which cover three of the Australian University models.[1] The three models include:

- The Group of Eight (research intensive plus teaching)
- The Australian Technology Network (teaching and research)
- The Innovative Research University Cluster (teaching and research)

A fourth informal grouping could be formed with the rural and regional universities. The six examples have been judged on the above criteria as an exercise in trialling the methodology outlined. This diagram illustrates the comparators of higher education learning vs professional training/teaching and research-intensive vs teaching intensive. It is this matrix which could be developed further on a global scale of university context and development. *These are the personal judgements of the author and are not meant to signify actual ratings of the individual universities.*

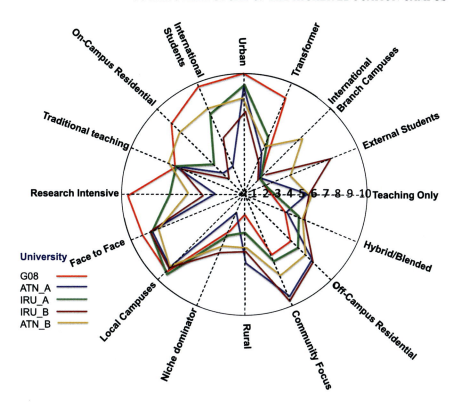

*Figure 2.7. Research intensive vs teaching; professional training vs higher education*

It is simply a possibly tool for establishing and comparing the future direction of universities of many typologies, with special interests which will specific to that institution and its mission.

## UNIVERSITY CAMPUSES AS COMPLEX ADAPTIVE ASSEMBLAGES – SUMMARY OF KEY ISSUES FOR CAMPUS PLANNING TO 2030

The following is a summary of key issues that are likely to impact on the development of university campuses over the next 10 years.

*Complex Adaptive Assemblages*

This study and the author's personal campus planning experience over some 50 or so campuses worldwide emphasise the complexity of university strategic campus planning in order to align with the university mission. The theoretical concept of 'complex adaptive assemblages' (Dovey, 2016 and Lohmann, 2006) suggests that this complexity must be combined with the ability of (many) universities to adapt,

K. FISHER

and that this adaptation has to integrate the needs and future aspirations of all its component parts ie the assemblage of parts.

Complex adaptive assemblages illustrate how such relationships dynamically respond to power, territoriality and de-territoriality. This interactivity relates to the term 'assemblage' which is translated from the French as akin to a 'layout', 'arrangement' or 'alignment'. It suggests at once a dynamic process and a diagrammatic spatiality' (Dovey, 2016, p. 283). Some of the elements (but not restricted to just these) which form that complex adaptive assemblage are addressed in summary form hereunder.

*Universities and Global Transformations*

There is likely to be an increased focus on the local community (for some universities), balancing the public good with the economically rationalist pressures on universities. There is likely to be a greater flow of international students from Asia – especially postgraduates – into the Western world, with Australia, the UK and the North America being the major recipients.

There will be further disruptions due to world affairs but also due to online learning evolution. Thus, universities will need to be both agile and resilient in accommodating these drivers of change. The student experience will be uppermost in the competition for enrolments. Whilst MOOCs will slowly develop in the next ten years as it is increasingly monetized, it is the advent of machine learning which will be a greater threat to the campus face-to face experience (although machine learning may take more than a decade to be proven).

There is an increasing belief that online learning will not develop the soft skills needed of graduates for professional futures, and an increased and focussed smaller group face-to-face experience will evolve. The student experience re quality, supported and affordable accommodation will still be a key part of the three to five years of a post high school student's formative university life prior to graduating into a professional life.

*Student Experience – Informal & Social Learning*

The social construction of knowledge with soft skills being a focus will be highly sought after. This will entail a growth in informal and social learning spaces, including maker and co-working spaces. This is exemplified by Nonaka's (1997) cycle of knowledge development and transfer. Note that Ba can be roughly translated from the Japanese for 'place'.

> The term *En* goes back to ancient Buddhism. It is still used, however, in Japanese everyday life. *En* corresponds to the belief that the world is filled with multitudinous unexpected meetings, or the feeling that we should appreciate those meetings and live together. It is the grace to accept the ongoing flood of encounters and events, no matter how unpredictable they would seem to be. *En* also means the "edge" or "margin." It implies an ambiguous

46

boundary that not only surrounds multiple kinds of living spaces but makes them interrelate and interpenetrate. The nature of those *En* boundaries and the resulting interpenetrative areas encourage humans to act and encounter each other. We call the group of architectural works in this exhibition "*En* architecture." *En* architects try to produce spatial worlds in which human beings can live positively. Each of their practices fosters the momentum to originate architecture in tandem with the countless interconnections that are occurring among people, things, and locality. This momentum is fostered by *En* as an invisible force operating external to human beings. (Introduction to the Japanese Pavilion, Venice Biennale 2016, Social Architecture)

## *Formal Learning*

There will be an increasingly rapid move to blended and authentic learning using learning analytics to support student learning. Possible machine learning will enhance this experience. There will be a transition from teacher centred learning to learner centred experiences through blended learning and the flipped classroom, coupled with entrepreneurial experiences linked to industry experiences through work integrated learning.

## *Impact of Technology and the Virtual/Physical Nexus*

Whilst this growth is slow there is likely to be an Increase in MOOC's offered to partner institutions and it is expected that MOOC's will manage growth in student numbers without need for more physical facilities. Makerspaces will evolve for 21st C skills of making, doing, entrepreneurship, co-working and startup cultures. There will be increased online learning coupled with the emergence of machine learning. There will be more non-traditional students in non-traditional institutions and in non-traditional educational models e.g. competency-based education. 50% of students will expect course material and technology/MOOCs to be ubiquitous. 33% already expect most tuition to be online.

## *Staff/Faculty*

Librarians will engage even more with curriculum to the extent that they may be 'embedded' within faculties to be closer to academic and curriculum development. Professional development for blended learning and flipped classroom experiences will become the norm.

## *Research Directions*

There is likely to be a 10% growth in research, with a focus on STEM, STEAM (includes Arts) and STEMM (includes Medicine). Research, science and technology

K. FISHER

parks are likely to grow as are bioscience hubs. There will be stronger links to industry with some research activities moving off campus in support of this development. Work Integrated Learning and internships will become the norm as will authentic learning, entrepreneurial and startup cultures.

*Integrated Strategic Planning*

SCUP has for many years advocated an integrated approach to strategic campus planning. However, all too often University planning is carried out in parallel silos without the individually developed strategies coming together, either during the planning process or at a point where they can be integrated to illustrate the links between key elements on a campus. If nothing else this study has served to illustrate the complexity of strategic campus planning and its connection to the university mission.

A final recommendation/outcome of this study is that there should be an integrated strategic campus planning committee in every university, with representatives from the key stakeholder groups.

This activity can be organised around the practice of the 'Campus Educational Overlay', which is a concept available from the author on request as the subject of another separate 40-page non-peer reviewed paper based on the author's experience with working, teaching, researching, studying and consulting at over 50 universities in Australia, New Zealand, Asia, the Middle East, the United Kingdom and the US.

## NOTE

[1]  In addition the author has worked across over 50 universities in New Zealand, Australia, Hong Kong, China, Malayasia; the Middle East; the United Kingdom and the United States.

## REFERENCES

ARC. (2015, April 22–24). *Academic resource conference in Oakland, California.* Retrieved from http://2015.wascarc.org/session/poster-sessions/flipped-campus-new-look-campus-experience-or-what-do-you-mean-i-have-go

Barber, M., Donnelly, K., & Rizvi, S. (2013). *The avalanche is coming: Higher education and the revolution ahead.* London: Institute for Public Policy Research.

Boys, J., Melhuish, C., & Wilson, A. (2014, May). *Developing research methods for analysing learning spaces that can inform institutional missions of learning and engagement.* Ann Arbor, MI: Planning for Higher Education (SCUP).

Cambridge. (2016). Retrieved August 28, 2016, from https://www.cam.ac.uk/about-the-university/how-the-university-and-colleges-work/the-universitys-mission-and-core-values

CDIO. (2015). Retrieved November 7, 2016, from http://www.cdio.org

Chapman, P. (2006). *American places: In search of the twenty-first century campus.* Westport, CT: Praeger Publishing.

Coursera. (2015). Retrieved from http://www.coursera.org

Coursera. (2015). *Undergraduate STEM course.* Retrieved August 1, 2015, from https://www.coursera.org/course/stemteaching

Crow, M., & Dabars, W. (2015). *Designing the new American university.* Baltimore, MD: Johns Hopkins University Press.

Deleuze, G., & Guattari, F. (1987). *A thousand plateaus*. London: Athlone Press.

Dovey, K. (2016). *Urban design thinking*. London: Bloomsbury Publishing.

Duke University. (2015). Retrieved from http://cit.duke.edu/blog/2015/02/flipping-classroom-fellowship-refining-flipped-class/

Economist. (2014, June 28). The future of the university: The digital degree. *The Economist*.

Ellis, R., Goodyer, P., Fisher, K., & Marmot, A. (2014). *Modelling the characteristics of complex learning spaces*. Canberra: Australian Research Council Discovery Grant Award.

Fisher, K. (2005). *The campus as thirdspace*. Camberwell: Australian Teaching and Learning Council.

Fisher, K. (2010). *A strategy for a distributed precint hub and spoke learning commons framework for the university of Adelaide* (Report to the Infrastructure Committee). Adelaide: University of Adelaide.

Fisher, K. (2013). *Transforming design thinking through the translational design of learning and knowledge environments*. Paper presented at the HERSDA (Higher Education Research and Development Society of Australia) Conference proceedings, Auckland, New Zealand.

Fisher, K., & Ellis, R. (2017). Translating translational research on space design from the health sector to higher education: Lessons learnt, and challenges revealed. In L. Carvalho, P. Goodyear, & M. de Laat (Eds.), *Place-based spaces for networked learning*. New York, NY: Routledge.

Fisher, K., & Newton, C. (2014). Transforming the twenty-first-century campus to enhance the net-generation student learning experience: Using evidence-based design to determine what works and why in virtual/physical teaching spaces. *Higher Education Research & Development Journal, 20*. Retrieved from http://dx.doi.org/10.1080/07294360.2014.890566

Freeman, S., Eddy, S., McDonough, M., Smith, M., Okoroafora, N., Hannah, J., & Wenderotha, M. (2014). Active learning increases student performance in science, engineering, and mathematics. *Psychological and Cognitive Sciences, 10*(1073), 28.

Garrett, G., & Gallagher, S. (2014). *From university exports to the multinational university: The internationalisation of higher education in Australia and the United States*. Retrieved June 5, 2015, from http://ussc.edu.ac/ussc/assets/media/docs/publications/1301_GarrettGallagher_HigherEd_Final.pdf

Gibson, J. J. (1977). The theory of affordances. In R. Shaw & J. Bransford (Eds.), *Perceiving, acting and knowing*. Hillsdale, NJ: Lawrence Erlbaum Associates.

Hashimshony, R., & Haina, J. (2006). Designing the university of the future. *Planning for Higher Education, 34*(2), 5–19.

HERD. (2015). Retrieved from http://her.sagepub.com

Jameson, F. (1996). Cognitive mapping. In M. Hardt & K. Weeks (Eds.), *Jameson reader* (pp. 277–288). Oxford: Blackwell.

Johnson, L., Adam, X., Becker, S., Estrada, V., & Freeman, A. (2015). *The NMC horizon report: 2015 higher education edition* (Horizon Report). Austin, TX: New Media Consortium (NMC).

Johnson, W., Nitecki, D., Khoo, M., Nathani, R., & Swaminathan, S. (2015). *Peer engagement as a common resource: Managing interaction patterns in institutions*. Ann Arbor, MI: SCUP.

Keppell, M., Souter, K., & Riggle, M. (Eds.). (2012). *Physical and virtual learning spaces in higher education: Concepts for the modern learning environment*. Hershey, PA: Information Science Reference.

Kolb, A. Y., & Kolb, D. A. (2005). Learning styles and learning spaces: Enhancing experiential learning in higher education. *Academy of Management Learning & Education, 4*(2), 193–212.

Kurzwell. (2016). Retrieved from http://www.kurzweilai.net/how-ai-may-affect-urban-life-in-2030

Lambert, M. (2014). *Privatization and the public good: Public universities in the balance*. Cambridge, MA: Harvard Education Press.

Laureate. (2016). Retrieved August 28, 2016, from http://www.laureate.net/AboutLaureate/Mission

Lefebvre, M. (2014). The library, the city, and infinite possibilities: Ryerson university's student learning centre project. *International Federation of Library Associations and Institutions, 40*(2), 110–115.

Literatu. (2015). Retrieved from http://www.literatu.com

Lohmann, S. (2006). *The public research university as a complex adaptive system*. Los Angeles, CA: University of California.

Lynch, K. (1960). *The image of the city*. Cambridge, MA: MIT Press.

Meyer, M., & Booker, J. (1991). *Eliciting and analyzing expert judgement: A practical guide*. Philadelphia, PA: SIAM.

K. FISHER

Norman, D. (2010). *The research – practice gap*. Retrieved from http://www.jnd.org/dn.mss/the_research-practic.html

Norton, A. (2104). *Mapping Australian higher education, 2014–2015*. Melbourne: Grattan Institute.

Oates, J. (2016). *British unis mull offshore EU campuses in post-brexit vote panic*. Retrieved from http://www.theregister.co.uk/2016/09/23/uk_profs_mull_euro_move/

OECD. (2007). *Centre for Educational Research and Innovation (CERI) – university futures*. Retrieved May 9, 2017, from www.oecd.org/edu/ceri/centreforeducationalresearchandinnovationceri-universityfutures.htm

Office of Learning and Teaching. (2016). Retrieved from http://www.olt.gov.au/resource-library?text=graduate+attributes

Painter, S., Fournier, J., Grape, C., Grummon, P., Morelli, J., Whitmer, S., & Cevetello, J. (2012). *Research on learning space design: Present state, future directions*. Ann Arbor, MI: SCUP.

Strayer, J. (2007). *The effects of the classroom flip on the learning environment: A comparison of learning activity in a traditional classroom and a flip classroom that used an intelligent tutoring system* (Unpublished doctoral dissertation). Ohio State University, Columbus, OH.

Sullivan, W., & Payne, K. (2011). The appropriate elicitation of expert opinion in economic models. *Pharmoeconomics, 29*(6), 455–459.

Temple, P. (Ed.). (2014). *The physical university: Contours of space and place in higher education*. Abingdon: Routledge.

Time Higher Education Supplement. (2015). *Future perfect: What will the university look like in 2030*.

Zogby, J., & Zogby, J. (2014). *2014 global survey of students*. Baltimaore, MD: Laureate University.

RIFCA HASHIMSHONY AND JACOV HAINA

# 3. DESIGNING THE UNIVERSITY OF THE FUTURE

## ABSTRACT

In discussions about the future of the university, little has been said about how these changes will affect its spatial layout, even though a university's physical characteristics must complement and strengthen its mission. This chapter addresses that issue and provides an overview of the physical layout of the future university that responds to 21stC drivers of change. It initially describes the development of the mission of the university in the western world and how that mission has determined the basic architectural prototypes of university design since the Middle Ages. Based on this review the authors re-examine these prototypes, identifying the main characteristics of contemporary society that are causing universities to re-evaluate their missions. They then analyse the impact of these changes on the institutional and spatial structure of the university. Four possible scenarios for the design of the future university are explored. The final section summarises the important factors that should be considered by higher education planners seeking to effectively direct the future design of their institutions.

## INTRODUCTION[1]

We are currently witnessing profound social, cultural, and technological changes that are transforming traditional institutions. The university (as defined by The Oxford Student's Dictionary of Current English as an "institution for advanced teaching, conferring degrees and engaging in academic research") is one of the institutions being transformed, as discussed in numerous recent articles (Delanty, 1998a, 1998b, 2001; Smith & Webster, 1997; Tzonis, 1999). The university remains the primary center of higher learning throughout the world, as well as the main repository of accumulated wisdom (Bell, 1973). It continues to be a powerful force even after half a millennium (Altbach, 1998). However, prevailing critiques raise doubts about the future of the university as an institution (Lyotard, 1984; Readings, 1996).

We disagree with these critiques. They do not consider the resiliency of these institutions and their ability to change to meet societal needs. Instead, we argue that universities will undergo major organisational and physical changes as they adapt their activities to meet present and future needs.

© SOCIETY FOR COLLEGE AND UNIVERSITY PLANNING, 2006 |
DOI: 10.1163/9789004391598_004

R. HASHIMSHONY & J. HAINA

In discussions about the future of the university, little has been said about how these changes will affect its spatial layout, even though a university's physical characteristics must complement and strengthen its mission. This article addresses that issue and provides an overview of the physical layout of the future university that responds to the above-mentioned changes. We first describe the development of the mission of the university in the western world and how that mission has determined the basic architectural prototypes of university design since the Middle Ages. Based on this review, we suggest that it is time to re-examine these prototypes. We identify the main characteristics of contemporary society that are causing universities to re-evaluate their missions and analyse their impact on the institutional and spatial structure of the university. We then discuss and evaluate four possible scenarios for the design of the future university. Finally, we summarise the important factors that should be considered by higher education planners seeking to effectively direct the future design of their institutions.

## THE GROWTH OF THE UNIVERSITY AS A SOCIAL INSTITUTION AND THE DEVELOPMENT OF ITS SPATIAL LAYOUT[2]

Although higher education existed in ancient times (e.g., Plato's Academy in Greece), its institutionalisation is attributed to the Middle Ages. The term "university" derives from the Latin *universitas*, meaning corporation or guild, since, in the medieval world, scholars were considered to be a guild of specialists.

Universities initially emerged as institutions in Paris and Bologna at the end of the 11th century. They evolved from the cathedral schools and continued the tradition of the preservation of knowledge that had previously been the responsibility of monasteries. These universities developed to meet the new needs of urban society for professional training, such as medicine and civil law, and had no permanent buildings. They operated from existing buildings, usually no larger than the size of a city block. Where necessary, universities were divided among several unconnected buildings located in different parts of the city.

As the number of students increased and more fields of study were added, it became necessary to build buildings to house university activities in one location. The creation of permanent structures marked the establishment of the university as an independent institution (Cobban, 1992).

The first important prototype for university design[3] was the single college[4] edifice, which later became the most common type of university building in England. The first college to be built was probably Merton College at Oxford, founded in 1264 (Figure 3.1A). Its distinct architectural structure – a square unit surrounding an internal court – reflected its social and educational character. It was designed to house nearly everything the students and their teachers needed: spaces to study, eat, sleep, and pray. According to Turner (1990), there were several reasons for the enclosed quadrangle in the design of the English college: the influence of the monastery

52

cloister, the assurance of protection from the outside, the ease of surveillance over students, and the optimal utilisation of small lots. This closed configuration reflects the severe character, the strict discipline, and the rigid daily routine of the college. Over time, as the number of students increased, additional colleges were founded, thus forming clusters (Figure 3.1B).

The university remained relatively unchanged from the Middle Ages until the late 18th and early 19th centuries, when religion gradually lost its dominant force and the European universities became institutions of modern learning and research. The Humboldt University of Berlin (founded by Wilhelm von Humboldt in 1809), in which modern standards of academic freedom were pioneered, is representative of these trends. The German model of the university as a complex of graduate schools performing advanced research and experimentation had a worldwide influence in defining the role of the university in society, but not in offering a new, innovative design.

The earliest American institutions of higher learning were Harvard University (founded in 1636), the College of William and Mary (1693), and Yale University (1701). The modern American university, arguably the most influential academic model today, derives from three basic ideas: the English collegiate model, the

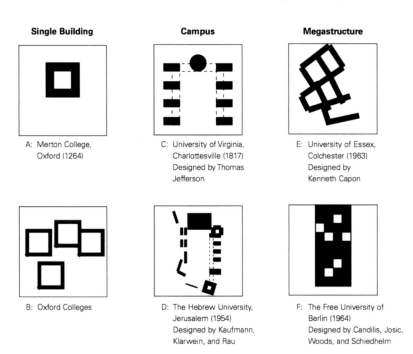

Figure 3.1. Main layout prototypes: Schematic presentation of examples

German research university of the 19th century, and the American concept of service to society (Altbach, 1998). The Morrill Act of 1862 refocused the mission of higher education by creating public-land-grant universities with a commitment to providing practical education for the new industrial society, thereby defining an important social role for American universities. The American universities represent the concept of an "academical village" – a term coined by Thomas Jefferson, the designer of the University of Virginia in Charlottesville in 1817 (Figure 3.1C), to describe universities as communities in themselves, where shared learning infused daily life, similar to the English colleges (Turner, 1990). But unlike the cloistered character of the European colleges, a more open and dispersed spatial model evolved in America. Jefferson's plan for the University of Virginia, for example, comprised pavilions, each with living quarters upstairs and classrooms downstairs. Each pavilion was identified with a specific subject and also served as the place of residence of the professor who taught that subject.

The Latin term *campus* (field) describes the distinctive physical character of American universities. It was first used to describe the college grounds, but gradually came to mean the entire property, including buildings, and later became the synonym for all university compounds.

Muthesius (2000) sees the use of the term *campus* as an attempt to distinguish the higher education institution from its surroundings and to define its isolated and independent character.

> According to Turner (1990, p. 4), campus sums up the distinctive physical qualities of the American college, but also its integrity as a self-contained community and its architectural expression of educational and social ideals.

The romantic idea of isolation from the city and civilisation came to its pure expression in the American college, located in nature and "removed from the corrupting forces of the city" (Turner, 1990, p. 12). In addition to the learning facilities, the American campus contains many other functions for students' comfort, including residence halls and sports facilities. This typology was later adopted by many designers for campuses throughout the world (e.g., Hebrew University in Jerusalem, designed by Kaufmann, Klarwein, and Rau [Figure 3.1D]).

At the beginning of the 20th century, universities blossomed throughout the world. Their organisational structures changed as additional fields of knowledge gave rise to the division of universities into different faculties and departments. However, in contrast to earlier periods when higher education remained largely a private enterprise in most countries, World War I strengthened the ties between the university and the state. The state increased its financial support; in return, academics provided research in support of the war effort. Universities no longer conducted research for their own sake, but tried to develop applied research for the benefit of society. The result was stronger collaboration with external factors, such as industries, and greater openness to the outside world.

Since World War II, there has been an increasing demand for higher education as a result of facilitated access to education through programs such as the 1944 GI Bill of Rights in the United States, the fact that the academic degree has become a means to upward mobility, and the need for more educated workers to support economic growth. As a result, new universities continue to be established all over the world, and existing universities have expanded to serve the growing number of students. In Britain alone, for example, at least six new universities were built during the 1960s.

The term "multiversity", first used by Kerr (1995), expresses the fact that university activities became increasingly complex from both the organisational and the spatial point of view. The physical dimensions of the campus became so large that the distances prohibited good communication among its different parts. The approach of duplicating architectural spaces no longer worked. The university required new and radically different designs to support the increasing complexity of its organisation. These new universities were designed as a single large concentrated building, called a "megastructure". The term "megastructure" usually means a vast structure, containing some of a city's functions, including dwellings, leisure, and commerce, that is able to adjust and grow according to specific needs, as described by Maki (cited in Banham, 1976, p. 217):

A large frame in which all the functions of a city or part of a city are housed. It has been made possible by present day technology.

A number of university designs were based on this spatial model, e.g., the University of Essex in 1963 (Figure 3.1E) and the Free University of Berlin in 1964 (Figure 3.1F).

The concept of the megastructure never fulfilled the designers' expectations. In many cases, its outsize, colossal dimensions caused the destruction of the existing urban fabric because it did not fit the scale of the existing buildings and the size of the city blocks. The megastructure also proved to be a failure in respect to flexibility, since it did not allow easy expansion or interchange of activities within the structure, as expected by the designers. This model was abandoned in the late 1960s.

## FACTORS THAT MAY DEFINE THE FUTURE UNIVERSITY

The highly varied and at times conflicting societal pressures placed on the university have generated discussion about the need to redefine the role of this institution to better serve the needs of contemporary society. Delanty (2001) argues that the university is still the only institution in society where one can find together the following four activities: research, education, professional training, and intellectual criticism. Indeed, universities have existed for so many years because of the special mix of these four roles in one institution. However, as a result of the changing demands placed on universities, the relative importance of each activity must be re-evaluated in the future. It is likely that the balance between research and teaching will change, while more tasks related to service to society may be added. Decisions made about balancing these activities will have a critical impact on the distribution of spaces within the university.

The following factors are particularly important in defining the nature of the future university: financial challenges, collaboration with industry, increasing student population and greater diversity, new patterns of teaching and learning, growth of interdisciplinary fields of knowledge, and openness to the community.

### Financial Challenges

As government support for universities has declined, these institutions have been forced to look for new funding sources. Commercialising knowledge, such as filing patents expected to generate revenues; designing and providing noncredit, cutting-edge educational programs for private and public sector employers; and cutting expenses by privatising some of the services offered to students and staff alike, such as residence halls, are some of the methods adopted by universities to cope with their financial difficulties. As a consequence of these changes, Jarvis (2000, p. 52) states that

> universities should now be more responsive to the demands of market, recognise the need to change their ways, be less independent and become more efficient.

### Collaboration with Industry

The character of industry is changing rapidly in the context of the competitive forces of an increasingly global economy. Particularly notable are the growing importance of information-based and high-technology industries and the central place of knowledge in today's economy (Bell, 1973; Castells, 1996; Toffler, 1981). The scientific knowledge that can be provided by universities is critical to the success of these industries and has encouraged the growth of collaboration between industry and university. However, while the commercialisation of knowledge helps universities solve some of their financial problems, it also reduces their past monopoly power over the creation of knowledge, since more research is performed today outside the walls of the university.

### Increasing Student Population and Greater Diversity

In recent years, the growing student population has become increasingly heterogeneous; universities are no longer reserved for the elite. Students come from much more diverse social classes, the proportion of female students has increased dramatically, and there is a growing demand from students who are older than the traditional college age and who are tied to a geographic location. This change reflects the democratisation of higher education, the importance of knowledge to our society, and the changing structure of the labour force, i.e., greater demand for educated workers (white-collar workers) and less demand for labourers (blue-collar workers). This rapid growth of a more diverse student population will further increase both the number and type of institutions of higher education and will affect, in turn, decisions about the missions and physical requirements of universities.

### New Patterns of Teaching and Learning

Major changes in technology that have occurred in recent years, particularly the improvements in computers and software and the rapid growth of Internet applications, have provided access to digital knowledge resources. This has greatly increased options for communication between individuals in different places at different times. These technological improvements have created the option of a virtual university in which virtual spaces replace the existing physical ones. Terms like "distance learning" and "electronic learning" represent the possibility of learning activities unrelated to time and place. However, these virtual universities generally do not offer students the kinds of informal interactions found in the traditional face-to-face campus learning experience that stimulate learning beyond the formal educational experience.

The task of universities to bring people together and allow for cross-fertilisation of minds is considered by some researchers as the main reason for their existence. Kumar (1997, p. 31) says in this respect, "I want to emphasise the informal side of university life, not as residual but a central feature of universities". Also, the "sense of community" and the "university spirit" created by physical spaces, an important part of the educational role of the university, do not exist at this time in the virtual university. Some combination of virtual and physical spaces might offer a solution.

### Growth of Interdisciplinary Fields of Knowledge

The classical university was based on a hierarchical structure of major disciplines that were then divided into sub-disciplines. This structure has been retained in the current university, as shown in Figure 3.2A. The faculties and departments, represented by the vertical elements, usually are located in a defined physical space. Interactions across disciplines, shown by horizontal elements, occur sporadically and often reflect only the interests of individual faculty working together in an interdisciplinary project.

In contrast, today's structure of knowledge is increasingly interdisciplinary in character, as shown in Figure 3.2B. In the future university, the horizontal elements

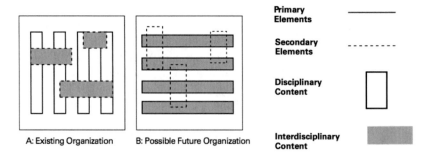

*Figure 3.2. Schematic description of changes in the organisational structure of the university*

containing the evolving interdisciplinary frameworks, which were secondary in the classical organisation (Figure 3.2A), may become primary elements. In time, these elements might also need defined physical spaces.

*Openness to the Community*

As a result of increasing standards of living and life expectancy, more people around the world have more leisure time. There is a large public seeking meaningful activities to fill its free time, and the university can be just the right framework for this population. The public opportunity to attend lectures, special courses, and evening activities may strengthen the image of the university as a central institution, responding to the needs of society. The implication is an increasing interaction between the university and the "outside world". As a result, the boundaries of the university campus will become more penetrable and its facilities will be used more efficiently for mixed activities.

## POSSIBLE EFFECTS OF INSTITUTIONAL CHANGES ON THE PHYSICAL STRUCTURE OF THE UNIVERSITY

The basic architectural prototypes of university design, as described previously, should be re-examined in view of the forces for change that are affecting the missions of higher education institutions. The design of a future university should be related to the expected changes in the activities of that institution.

Five variables typically are used to characterise the physical structure of existing universities and can be used to conceptualise the future university: size, spatial configuration, boundaries and accessibility, functional organisation, and location. An analysis of the impact of these variables gives us better insights into the possible spatial characteristics of the future university. These characteristics can serve as a point of reference for planners and policymakers and should also be examined with regard to considerations such as values, institutional goals, and pragmatic constraints.

## DESIGNING THE UNIVERSITY OF THE FUTURE

*Size (Small vs. Large)*

Size refers to the total built area, exclusive of open spaces between buildings. Figure 3.3 illustrates three forces for change that may affect the size of the future university. First, moving activities into the virtual space by use of distance learning and communication technologies may reduce or eliminate the need for large lecture halls, library study areas, and related spaces. Second, privatisation may cause some of the classic functions of the university, such as dormitories and sport facilities, to be located elsewhere, thus decreasing the area of the university. Finally, strengthening relations with industry may affect the size of the university in two opposing ways: new functions may be imported and located within the university compound, thereby increasing its size, while other functions may be exported and attached to existing industries, resulting in a decrease in the size of the university.

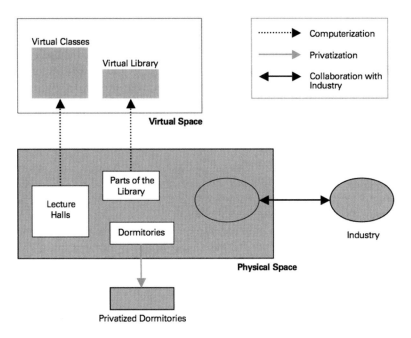

*Figure 3.3. Forces for change determining the size of the university*

*Spatial Configuration (Compact vs. Decentralised)*

The concept of the confined university, as in the campus and the megastructure, should be reconsidered since contradictory forces are in operation. On the one hand, the need for internal cohesion regarding new modes of knowledge production, the growing need for collaboration, and the importance of linking different fields of knowledge may encourage the continuation of centralisation. In contrast, as discussed previously, some current institutional trends indicate a tendency towards a higher degree of decentralisation due to privatisation and the option to study and work at home or elsewhere off campus. However, diffused spatial patterns may decrease possibilities for interpersonal interaction and harm the valuable sense of a university's community. The social quality of the university and the options it creates for diverse formal and informal interactions therefore also need to be considered.

*Boundaries and Accessibility (Open vs. Closed)*

The boundaries of the university are both physical and conceptual. They define the degree of accessibility to the university by determining the openness of the institution to different populations that are not part of the university community. The historical notion of the Ivory Tower embodies the isolated and closed character of many universities. This "closed-ness" is also typical of the previously-described spatial typologies. The growing need for collaboration with industry, the new openness to the community, and the changes in the organisational structure of the university may well result in the blurring of its physical boundaries. The integration of students and academic staff in the life of the community and the emerging social role of the university as a bridge to the public also become highly important.

*Functional Organisation (Zoning vs. Mixed Uses)*

Rigid functional organisation or spatial zoning was appropriate when departments were isolated and knowledge was divided into discrete disciplines. However, collaborative research and interdisciplinary knowledge can have a major influence on the spatial structure of the university. The need for an environment of mixed uses is enhanced by the existing possibility of studying and working from different places and by collaboration with industry. These changes can be implemented through the university's emerging interdisciplinary physical frameworks. Based on the new communication technologies, multifunctional buildings may also appear, mixing different knowledge operations (production, distribution, and preservation) with leisure activities and even residence. The mixed-uses strategy, with shorter physical distances between different functions, supports more flexible and spontaneous activities suited to current dynamic lifestyles.

A recent example of such a mixed-use building is the Stata Center at the Massachusetts Institute of Technology, designed by Frank O. Gehry (inaugurated May 2004). It houses three main tenants – the Computer Science and Artificial Intelligence Laboratory, the Laboratory for Information and Decision Systems, and the Department of Linguistics and Philosophy. In addition to the functional yet flexible work environment, it also contains lounges and gathering areas that are home to different research groups. A "town square" provides meeting and socialising opportunities; a sky-lit "student street", a public arcade for the MIT community, runs the entire length of the ground floor. There is also a cafe, a childcare center for 80 children, a fitness center, a faculty dining area, and many other related facilities.

*Location (Integrated vs. Isolated)*

Little can be said about the location of the future university relative to city environs. The concept of the university as a site of interconnectivity, epitomised by its increasing collaboration with industry and other knowledge institutions and by its growing openness to the community, can be considered conducive to a specific location inside a city or near industry or a community. Developments in communication technologies and transportation, on the other hand, minimise the importance of physical location.

It is probable that only some of the above-mentioned spatial tendencies will be realised. The alternative values for each of the five variables are represented in Figure 3.4. Different kinds of institutions can be formed, by applying different values to each variable, as will be demonstrated in the next section.

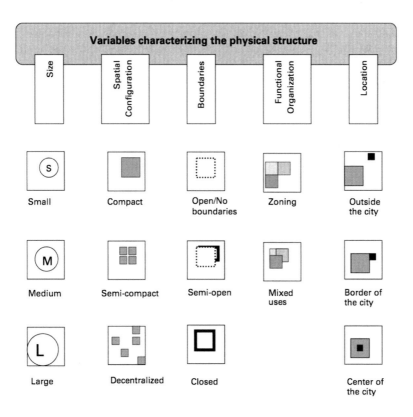

*Figure 3.4. Graphic presentation of alternative values for each spatial variable*

## THE DESIGN OF THE FUTURE UNIVERSITY: POSSIBLE SCENARIOS

The preceding discussion has shown that many factors will affect the decisions made by universities as they plan their future – whether they are existing institutions adapting to the forces of change or entirely new universities yet to be built. It is impossible to predict what the physical layout of the future university will be since there are myriad possible options.

There are three main uncertainties that we believe will be the major forces defining the future university:

- the volume of activities that will occur in the virtual space
- the degree to which the university will maintain its compact spatial configuration
- the degree to which the university will maintain its closed-ness

To illustrate some of these options, three basic scenarios[5] for future universities are discussed: the Mini-University, the New Campus, and the University-City. A fourth scenario is based on the combination of the first two scenarios. As shown in Figure 3.5, each scenario is generated by applying alternative values, possibly extreme ones, to the above three uncertainties to illustrate the different combinations and intensities of institutional changes. To make the scenarios more coherent and concrete, academic features such as fields of knowledge and/or the social nature of the university are also described. Figure 3.6 illustrates the characteristics of each scenario's physical structure in terms of the five spatial variables.

*Scenario 1: The Mini-University*

As shown in Figure 3.5A, this scenario is based on a large volume of activities being conducted in the virtual space, an organisation that is physically very compact, and institutional boundaries that are relatively closed.

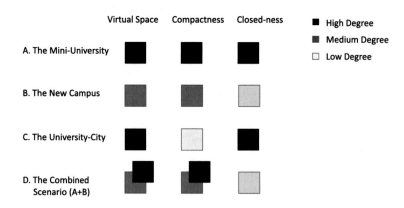

*Figure 3.5. Values applied to the three main uncertainties to generate the four scenarios*

This is the model of a compact urban university, containing only knowledge-related activities and based on intensive integration of activities in the virtual space. It is usually research-oriented, producing application-oriented and interdisciplinary knowledge. From the institutional point of view, this means high levels of privatisation and computerisation, but a low level of openness to the community. The Mini-University collaborates strongly with industry and other institutions such as hospitals. Although its core activity is research, it might also cater to exceptional undergraduate students who might later become researchers.

Functions such as leisure, culture, and housing are not included in this type of university; rather, these are privatised activities provided by the neighboring city. The university will be a single structure of indeterminate size, possibly even a skyscraper, consisting mainly of large computer laboratories, with little division into sub-territories. One could say that this Mini-University is an elaboration of the classic single building typology discussed previously.

This design will facilitate social interaction and face-to-face encounters in the computer laboratories and the spaces surrounding them. The physical space of this university serves as a collective bridge to the virtual space. It does not support the existence of disciplines requiring large physical spaces such as workshops or laboratories. The need for laboratory space will be satisfied by using either virtual laboratories or the laboratories at other institutions.

The characteristics of the Mini-University's physical structure are described below and are represented graphically in Figure 3.6A.

- Size: The size is small, due to the intensive integration of distance learning and communication technologies, and because additional functions such as cafeterias will be supplied by the surrounding neighborhood.
- Spatial configuration: The physical spaces are compact and concentrated in one unit, although other activities will be available via communication technologies.
- Boundaries and accessibility: The boundaries are semi-open and involve strong connections with other organisations, but little integration with the outside community since the university offers no benefits (e.g., cultural activities) to the community.
- Functional organisation: The variety of functions included in this type of university is limited, but the compact space is organised in a flexible manner since most of the activities are computer-based. It is possible to envision an elaboration of this type that would also include living quarters and other social and cultural elements, such as a skyscraper, returning to the concept of the traditional college.
- Location: The location is preferably in the city center, easily accessed by public transportation, and close to amenities such as food and leisure activities. The small size permits this university's integration into the city center from a financial point of view. However, the small size also permits its location on the borders of the city, if necessary, for example, to locate it in the vicinity of industry.

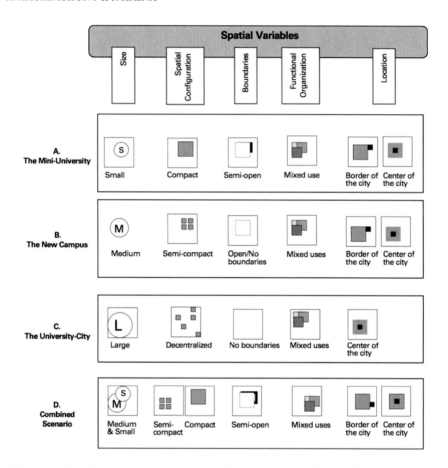

*Figure 3.6. Graphic presentation of the spatial characteristics of each of the four scenarios*

The Open University may serve as a partial example of a Mini-University. It started in England in the early 1960s as a genuinely multimedia concept, combining broadcast lectures with correspondence texts and visits to conventional universities. Thanks to the technological developments of the last decades, it developed into a distance learning university, although most of the courses include face-to-face components such as group tutorials, laboratory work, or field trips. In addition, periodic symposia are held at the Open University study centers dispersed throughout the country. These study centres also provide library services and learning aids and serve as a meeting place for students (with or without tutors). Unlike the Mini-University, the Open University is not research-oriented.

*Evaluation.* The Mini-University has low operational costs and is flexible regarding location. The internal configuration also allows for some degree of flexibility, but possibilities for growth are limited. It enables social encounters and interactions, but the traditional sense of community does not exist.

*Scenario 2: The New Campus*

This scenario is based on a medium volume of activities in the virtual space, a medium degree of compactness of the physical space, and open institutional boundaries (Figure 3.5B).

It is based on the campus typology, with separate buildings set in a green area, but in a more compact physical layout. This design thus maintains the classical character of the university, including spatial autonomy, while introducing necessary adaptations to present reality. From the institutional point of view, this means a low degree of privatisation, a medium degree of computerisation and collaboration with industry, and a very high degree of openness to the community.

The New Campus will act in two spaces – the virtual and the physical – simultaneously. The virtual space will mainly complement the physical one, thus allowing some of the physical spaces, like large lecture halls and libraries, to be replaced. This type of university will have some degree of collaboration with industry that can be based on the location of industries inside or close to the campus. An example is the establishment of the IBM Research Center inside the campus of the University of Haifa in Israel.

The campus will house a variety of functions, including residence halls, sports facilities, cultural centres, and museums. These will give a feeling of community to both the students and university personnel and will offer the possibility of cooperating with the neighboring community. The New Campus can provide various services to the community, including exhibitions, public lectures, and concerts.

The characteristics of the New Campus's physical structure are described below and are represented graphically in Figure 3.6B.

*Size.* The size is smaller than the traditional campus due to some increased use of computers, thereby allowing the replacement of physical spaces with virtual ones.

*Spatial configuration.* Most of the university functions continue to take place within the campus, while a few functions will be allocated outside its boundaries.

- Boundaries and accessibility: While the New Campus remains centralised, open boundaries will allow access to industry and the community.
- Functional organisation: While the general spatial configuration of the New Campus is similar to the typology of the classical campus, the classical division into faculties and departments will probably disappear over time, and the separate disciplinary units will be combined into interdisciplinary collaborative ones. Large lecture halls will probably be replaced by computer laboratories.

- Location: A variety of locations could be appropriate for this type of university, although locating it in urban surroundings might be more beneficial to the community.

The Technion–Israel Institute of Technology in Haifa is an example of a campus developing in this direction. Several multidisciplinary centres of excellence were established in recent years and ties with industry were strengthened. The faculty of medicine, its student dormitories, and the Rappaport Family Institute for Research in the Medical Sciences[6] are located next to a big hospital in downtown Haifa, far away from the main campus.

*Evaluation.* The New Campus supports the maintenance of the social character of the university and its identity. The space between the buildings plays an important role in creating opportunities for social encounters and formal activities, including interaction with the community. It also allows great flexibility in the allocation of new functions and growth. In addition, the open spaces can benefit those who prefer a more open and relaxed learning environment.

### *Scenario 3: The University-City*

In this scenario, a large volume of activities take place in the virtual space, the organisation is physically decentralised, and the institutional boundaries are open (Figure 3.5C).

The centrality of knowledge and its association with components of the urban system, such as schools, museums, industry, and leisure activities, blurs the limits between this type of university and the city. The university will be completely assimilated in the city and will become a unique entity. From the institutional point of view, this means a high degree of privatisation, a medium degree of computerisation, and a high degree of collaboration with industry and of openness to the community. A "City of Knowledge" can reflect a dramatic increase in learning and research. The university communities will cooperate with other knowledge communities in the city. The university will deal with many fields of knowledge and will act as a cultural and technological center for the whole region. Most of its functions will be knowledge-related, including high-technology industries, knowledge-related commerce, conferences, and museums, similar to the institution described by Tadmor:

> The scientific technological research university, therefore, in its unfolding "golden age", will not just be a large university campus, where students learn, engineers and managers train, and research is carried out, but rather it will become a major national-technology-science-complex; or rather a science-technology city with the university at its core, surrounded by a large array of buffer institutions, industrial parks, technological incubators, science related cultural activities, science oriented youth camps, and international meeting places. (2003, p. 22)

The characteristics of the University-City's physical structure are described below and are represented graphically in Figure 3.6C.

- Size: The size is large, due to the dramatic increase in learning and research activities.
- Spatial configuration: Different parts of the university will be located in different parts of the city.
- Boundaries and accessibility: There are no boundaries. The university and the city will be intermingled.
- Functional organisation: The organisation will be one of mixed uses.
- Location: The University-City will be located within the city limits.

*Evaluation.* The University-City opens new horizons for future developments and ideas with greater flexibility. The community of the university is the community of the city and thus is not a discrete community, but a variety of communities, each fulfilling, in some way, the classical tasks of the university. The parallel existence of different and diverse knowledge communities enables the collaboration and mutual fertilisation needed for producing knowledge.

It is the ultimate embodiment of the emerging knowledge society, emphasising both the democratisation of knowledge and its central role. It can provide varying spatial situations and balanced integration of green areas. Many parallel diverse systems will exist simultaneously, fulfilling the classical tasks of the traditional university.

*Additional Scenarios – Combining Basic Scenarios*

The Mini-University, the New Campus, and the University-City are three basic scenarios that can be combined to create new complex spatial organisations. For example, a combination of the New Campus and the Mini-University may result in a new type of university in which some parts will be similar to the Mini-University, and others similar to the New Campus. In this case, the Mini-University model will apply to only a few disciplines, such as medicine and computer science, both of which have strong links with external entities (like hospitals or industry). Hence, they may need to be situated outside the campus. In both cases, the platform of the campus remains important, both from the administrative and the practical point of view, by offering facilities such as laboratories that do not exist outside the campus.

These scenarios are created by applying more than one value to each uncertainty in the matrix that generates the scenarios (Figure 3.5D). Thus, for example, regarding the volume of activities in the virtual space, the figure illustrates that in the Mini-University, most of the activities happen in the virtual space, while in the New Campus, virtual spaces complement physical ones.

The combined scenario will thus be based on the following values: a combination of a large volume of activities with a medium volume of activities in the virtual space,

R. HASHIMSHONY & J. HAINA

a compact organisation with some degree of decentralisation, and open institutional boundaries. The characteristics of the Combined Scenario's physical structure are represented graphically in Figure 3.6D.

*Evaluation.* Because of the complex nature of this organisation, it provides various opportunities and offers the advantages of two spatial organisations incorporating new technologies and qualities in more than one way. It seems that this possibility represents a more realistic scenario for the future university, since it includes implementation of gradual changes in a flexible manner, rather than an extreme revolution.

### SUMMARY AND IMPLICATIONS FOR THE FUTURE

We have analysed the influence of social, cultural, economic, and technological changes over time on the structure of the university and have discussed the implications of these changes for the design of the future university. The design options were presented in three major scenarios that identify the key elements of the future university and can be used as guidelines for designers and policy makers.

However, when using these scenarios to conceptualise the university of the future, planners should pay particular attention to the following three key factors:

- *Using virtual space or physical space:* tradeoffs. It is most probable that future universities will be "bi-spatial" universities, with a combination of activities in both the virtual and the physical spaces. One of the key questions that designers of future universities must address is which physical spaces can and should be replaced by virtual spaces. It will be necessary to determine which qualities will make the physical spaces suitable for their new task as "bridging spaces" to support social interactions. Designers will have to design both physical and virtual spaces.

  Designers of the future universities must determine which physical spaces can and should be replaced by virtual spaces.

- *Relationship with industry.* Other issues arising from changes in the university institution relate to its cooperation and interrelations with industry. Designers will have to invent different strategies to provide spatial connections with industry. Will the university, or part of it, be located near industry? Will the industry be located next to, or inside, the university? Will some parts of the university become mobile and able to be located in different places at different times, according to specific needs?
- *Degree of integration with the community.* Increased openness to the community raises questions about the boundaries of the university and the desirable degree of integration with its surroundings. Some claim that a certain degree of spatial identity should be maintained together with the open boundaries. Planners and

DESIGNING THE UNIVERSITY OF THE FUTURE

designers will have to propose spatial schemes/layouts that combine these two conflicting qualities. Again, the notion of bridging spaces might be applied: in this case, bridging between the university and its immediate surroundings. These spaces may include functions linked both to the university and to the community, such as cultural centres, sport facilities, shops, and museums.

The universities of the future will take as many different forms as required to carry out their varied missions. Some of the decisions that will be made about their physical form will depend on future technological developments as yet unknown to us. Thus, we are only at the beginning of this discussion about the university of the future:

Massive and unstoppable changes are under way, but we are not passive subjects powerless to shape our fates. If we understand what is happening, and if we can conceive and explore alternative futures, we can find opportunities to intervene, sometimes to resist, to organise, to legislate, to plan, and to design. (Mitchell, 1995, p. 5)

## ACKNOWLEDGEMENTS

This research was supported by Technion VPR Fund.

This article is based on research towards a master's degree by Jacov Haina in the Faculty of Architecture and Town Planning, Technion–Israel Institute of Technology, Haifa, under the supervision of Rifca Hashimshony, Faculty of Architecture and Town Planning, Technion, and Alexander Tzonis, Faculty of Architecture, TU Delft, The Netherlands.

## NOTES

[1] This chapter originally appeared as Hashimshony, R., & Haina, J. (2006). Designing the university of the future. *Planning for Higher Education, 34*(2), 5–19. Reprinted here with kind permission from the Society for College and University Planning.

[2] Although universities have existed since the 12th century, there is, to date, no comprehensive and comparative overview of the historical development of university design, except for the research published by Turner (1990), which mainly surveys the architecture of universities in the United States since the beginning of colonial settlement. (In the introduction, Turner does include a brief description of the English college as the precursor of the American college.)

[3] This article focuses on spatial arrangement, rather than on architectural features such as shape, materials, or style.

[4] Although the term "college" was originally used to describe a type of institution and the physical layout in which it was housed, it is used today to describe any institution for higher education, usually offering only a first degree, in contrast with a "university", which offers research and graduate studies as well.

[5] Scenarios present alternatives and stimulate creative ways of thinking that can help decision makers evaluate possible futures by analyzing uncertainties related to known processes. Some attribute the development of scenario methodology to the Manhattan Project, and it has been used in various disciplines ever since (Carroll, 2000; Diaper, 2002; Hertzum, 2003; Wollenberg, Edmunds, & Buck, 2000). Because of the high degree of uncertainty, we have opted for the scenario methodology.

[6] The 2004 Nobel Prize Laureates in Chemistry, Avram Hershko and Aaron Ciechanover, came from this research centre.

## REFERENCES

Altbach, P. G. (1998). Forum comparative perspectives on higher education for the twenty-first century. *Higher Education Policy, 11*(4), 347–356.

Banham, R. (1976). *Megastructure: Urban futures of the recent past*. London: Thames & Hudson.

Bell, D. (1973). *The coming of post-industrial society: A venture in social forecasting*. New York, NY: Basic Books.

Carroll, J. M. (2000). *Making use: Scenario-based design of human-computer interactions*. Cambridge, MA: MIT Press.

Castells, M. (1996). *The rise of the network society*. Oxford: Blackwell.

Cobban, A. B. (1992). Universities: 1100–1500. In B. R. Clark & G. R. Neave (Eds.), *The encyclopedia of higher education* (pp. 1245–1251). Oxford: Pergamon.

Delanty, G. (1998a). Rethinking the university: The autonomy, contestation and reflexivity of knowledge. *Social Epistemology: A Journal of Knowledge, Culture and Policy, 12*(1), 103–113.

Delanty, G. (1998b). The idea of the university in the global era: From knowledge as an end to the end of knowledge? *Social Epistemology: A Journal of Knowledge, Culture and Policy, 12*(1), 3–25.

Delanty, G. (2001). *Challenging knowledge: The university in the knowledge society*. Buckingham: Open University Press.

Diaper, D. (2002). Scenarios and task analysis. *Interacting with Computers, 14*(4), 379–395.

Hertzum, M. (2003). Making use of scenarios: A field study of conceptual design. *International Journal of Human-Computer Studies, 58*(2), 215–239.

Jarvis, P. (2000). The changing university: Meeting a need and needing to change. *Higher Education Quarterly, 54*(1), 43–67.

Kerr, C. (1995). *The uses of the university* (4th ed.). Cambridge, MA: Harvard University Press.

Kumar, K. (1997). The need for place. In A. Smith & F. Webster (Eds.), *The postmodern university? Contested visions of higher education in society* (pp. 27–35). Buckingham: Open University Press.

Lyotard, J.-F. (1984). *The postmodern condition: A report on knowledge*. Manchester: Manchester University Press.

Mitchell, W. J. (1995). *City of bits: Space, place, and the infobahn*. Cambridge, MA: MIT Press.

Muthesius, S. (2000). *The postwar university: Utopianist campus and college*. New Haven, CT: Yale University Press.

Readings, B. (1996). *The university in ruins*. Cambridge, MA: Harvard University Press.

Smith, A., & Webster, F. (Eds.). (1997). *The postmodern university? Contested visions of higher education in society*. Buckingham: Open University Press.

Tadmor, Z. (2003). *The golden age of the scientific technological research university*. Retrieved from https://www.neaman.org.il/EN/Golden-Age-Scientific-Technological-Research-University

Toffler, A. (1981). *The third wave*. New York, NY: Bantam Books.

Turner, P. V. (1990). *Campus: An American planning tradition* (Rev. ed.). Cambridge, MA: MIT Press.

Tzonis, A. (1999). *Towards the university of the 21st century* (Unpublished paper).

Wollenberg, E., Edmunds, D., & Buck, L. (2000). Using scenarios to make decisions about the future: Anticipatory learning for the adaptive co-management of community forests. *Landscape and Urban Planning, 47*(1–2), 65–77.

FLAVIA CURVELO MAGDANIEL

# 4. THE RELATIONSHIP BETWEEN INNOVATION, CAMPUSES AND CITIES

*Lessons about Synergy from the Development
of the MIT in Cambridge*

### ABSTRACT

In the context of the knowledge-based economy (KBE), tech-campuses can be considered as strategic infrastructure resources to stimulate innovation. Tech-campuses comprise the land and buildings joined or separately developed by universities, Research and Development (R&D) companies and governments and used to accommodate technology-driven research activities (Curvelo Magdaniel, 2016). The science park is the most common type of tech-campuses, but the previous definition refers to a diversity of environments including the campuses of universities of technology and corporate R&D parks.

Since the late fifties, tech-driven research increasingly involves the interaction between universities, R&D companies and governments, which relationship is referred as the concept of the Triple Helix (Etzkowitz & Leydesdorff, 1995). This concept positions these three spheres as crucial in the knowledge society because the potential for innovation, entrepreneurship and economic development resides in their capacity to generate new institutions and social formats for knowledge creation, diffusion and application. Although some of these new formats take place in tech-campuses, it is difficult to demonstrate how the built environment can possibly stimulate innovation. My doctoral thesis explored the relationship between innovation and the built environment at the urban level. It looked at the campus as a physical and functional area that is part of the city. In this sense, the research approach fits very well the "town and gown" component of this book, but with a focus on technology campuses or "campuses that accommodate technology-driven research" as the main activity.

This definition includes campuses of universities of technology but also corporate campuses. Indeed, the main conclusions are derived from the in-depth case studies of the MIT campus (university campus) and the High-Tech Campus Eindhoven (corporate campus). Thus this chapter focuses on the relationship between innovation, campuses and cities using an evidence based approach from the case of MIT.

© KONINKLIJKE BRILL NV, LEIDEN, 2019 | DOI: 10.1163/9789004391598_005

F. CURVELO MAGDANIEL

## INTRODUCTION

Broadly, the relationship between innovation and the built environment has been studied mostly at the building level. There is a body of researchers linking built environment characteristics with knowledge sharing behaviour in knowledge-intensive organisations (Appel-Meulenbroek, 2014; Appel-Meulenbroek et al., 2017; Becker, 2007; Oseland et al., 2011; Toker & Gray, 2008; Waber et al., 2014). Although many studies have tried to measure (qualitatively and quantitatively) the impact of physical characteristics of workplaces on knowledge sharing behaviour based on similar theoretical assumptions, this has been difficult in practice and the evidence remains thin.

At the urban and regional level, studies consider that creating a healthy and attractive social climate is key in the development of human capital for innovation in cities and regions (Drucker & Goldstein, 2007; Fernández-Maldonado & Romein, 2008; Van Den Berg et al., 2005). For instance, the presence of universities and their activities is regarded as influential of regional milieu by attracting a concentration of highly educated people at a particular location (Drucker & Goldstein, 2007). Similarly, universities are seen as major players in urban regeneration because they can act both as promoters of business innovation and in terms of their civic and social outcomes (Fernández-Esquinas & Pinto, 2014).

Accordingly, a city's capacity to attract and retain human capital relates both to the quality of its knowledge base (e.g. universities and knowledge institutes, among others) and to other aspects defining quality of life (e.g. housing, safety, cultural amenities, diversity, etc.). Although the importance of the built environment supporting innovation processes is growing, there is little research relating how the built environment could enhance the Triple Helix relationship. Indeed, investing in the development and management of physical infrastructure that supports the creation, diffusion and application of knowledge can be seen as a way to strengthen these relationships (Van Winden et al., 2008).

A recent study, positioned the built environment as catalyst for innovation through the development of tech-campuses (Curvelo Magdaniel, 2016; Curvelo Magdaniel et al., 2018). Herein, the catalyst role of tech-campuses in innovation is demonstrated by real estate decisions and interventions facilitating five interdependent conditions required for innovation in particular contexts. First, location decisions and area development facilitate the long-term concentration of innovative organisations in cities and regions.

Second, interventions enabling the transformation of the built environment at area and building levels facilitate the climate for adaptation along changing technological trajectories over time. Third, large-scale real estate interventions facilitate the synergy among universities, industry and universities. Fourth, location decisions and interventions supporting image and accessibility define the innovation area by emphasising its distinct identity, scale and connectivity features. Fifth and last, real estate interventions enabling access to amenities increase the diversity/density

THE RELATIONSHIP BETWEEN INNOVATION, CAMPUSES AND CITIES

of people and social interaction regardless of the distinct geographical settings in which the concentration of innovative activities takes place. This article explains and describe the third proposition above, by asking: *what campus interventions have facilitated the synergy between the spheres in the Triple Helix and how?*

This chapter aims to outline concepts influencing the collaborative process of campus development and provide understanding on how the built environment can possibly stimulate innovation by strengthening university-industry-government relationships. The theoretical and empirical information used in this chapter are part of a PhD dissertation (Curvelo Magdaniel, 2016) grounded in the field of Corporate Real Estate Management.

CONCEPTS

*The Built Environment as Catalyst for Innovation*

Curvelo Magdaniel (2016) proposed six conditions (3 demand and 3 supply) required to stimulate innovation in organisations involved in the development of technology campuses – e.g. universities of technology, R&D companies and cities/regions. Each condition has a different function in the process of knowledge creation and its application, which is relevant for the competitive advantage of these organisations. These conditions are distinguished into demand-driven conditions and supply-driven conditions (see Figure 4.1).

Demand-driven conditions refer to those resulting from deliberated activities of local stakeholders within the three organisational spheres involved in campus development (universities of technology, R&D firms and local governments). Demand-driven conditions for innovation are (1) Long-term concentration of innovative organisations; (2) Climate for adaption along changing technological trajectories over time; (3) Synergy among organisational spheres (university-industry-government). These local conditions are likely to be similar across industrialised regions regardless the different contexts in which innovative organisations locate.

Supply-driven conditions refer to those shaped by physical and functional characteristics of the region in which the organisations above locate and conduct their activities. These conditions are shaped by the geographic settings of the hosting city/region and ultimately by the location characteristics of tech-based research organisations within such city/region. Supply-driven conditions for innovation are: (4) Identity of the innovation area; (5) Diversity of people and density of social interaction. These local conditions are likely to be unique in each context.

A last condition is distinguished as a facilitator for all these conditions and positioned in between demand- and supply-driven conditions: (6) the built environment as catalyst. In fact, built environments like tech-campuses are the result of both, deliberated organisational goals supporting primary process and the singular geographic settings in which organisations locate. Thus, the facilitating role of the built environment as catalyst for innovation is strongly dependent on the other five

73

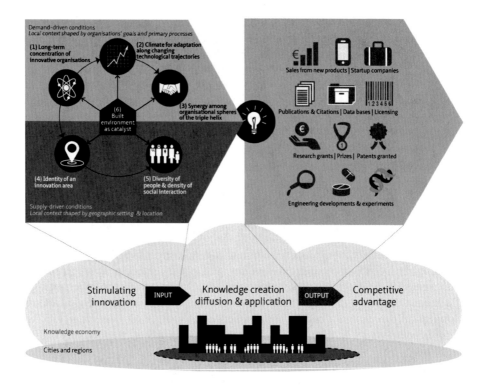

*Figure 4.1. Input conditions (left) in the conceptual model explaining the proposition of the built environment as catalyst for innovation. These interdependent conditions are required to create and apply knowledge (innovation as a process in the middle) conducting to different outputs (right) (from Curvelo Magdaniel, 2016, p. 326)*

conditions – i.e. the built environment can facilitate conditions for innovation if interventions are steered in a way that match specific organisational demands with the unique supply conditions of their local contexts. Although the conditions for innovation are interdependent, this chapter focus on illustrating one proposition that refers to the third condition of the model explained as follows.

*Synergy among Organisational Spheres of the Triple Helix*

To be able to create and apply knowledge, regions and cities need the long-term presence of innovative organisations (1st condition for innovation). Beyond that, an institutional climate for innovation is required (2nd condition), which results from the ability of the regions/cities to take advantage of and to exploit the technological developments of their local innovative organisations. Reaching this climate demands collaborative efforts among regional stakeholders in the three organisational spheres:

governments, industry and academia. Most of the efforts take the form of incentives targeted to reach their shared vision on competitive advantage driven by innovation.

The success in implementing such incentives rely largely in the synergy among the stakeholders in these three spheres to assume and play different and unconventional roles. For instance, universities, firms and governments can be leaders, entrepreneurs, funders and promoters when implementing the different incentives (e.g. investing in research, creating firms and jobs, strengthening local networks, funding real estate development and marketing the region as a place to work, live and study). This synergy among organisational spheres in the Triple Helix (3rd condition) functions as the activation energy required to carrying on the processes of knowledge creation and application in the entire system of the model.

In theory, this is referred to as the organising capacity of a region to develop one or more activities of the knowledge city (Van Den Berg et al., 2005). These activities include some of the aspects such as attracting and retaining knowledge workers and creating and applying knowledge as important processes of innovation. Accordingly, 'organising capacity is understood as the ability of those responsible for solving a problems to convene all concerned partners (public and private, internal and external), in order to jointly generate new ideas and formulate and implement a policy that responds to fundamental developments and creates conditions for sustainable economic growth' (Van Den Berg et al., 2005).

In an earlier research, Van Den Berg et al. (1997) defined organising capacity as the entire process including 'the identification of needs, the development of ideas and policies, the implementation of them and the monitoring of results'. Important to carry on this entire process are a vision, strategic networks, leadership, political and societal support and communication (Van Den Berg et al., 2005).

This definition can be applied to the Triple Helix concept as the concerned partners creating the conditions to stimulate innovation in an area. According to Etzkowitz (2008), 'role-taking' increases the interactions between each of these spheres, which identities are enhanced through new ways of relationships with other spheres. The proactive role of the stakeholders in the Triple Helix is an important aspect of this condition because their relationships determine the actions that will trigger interaction between innovators concentrated in an area. The quality of these relationships is crucial because each of these spheres has its own interests on innovation, which is in turn influenced by the different meanings each give to this concept (Kostoff, 2003).

For instance, when looking at output indicators of innovation, which are mainly measures of performance (e.g. patents, licensing, start-ups, prototypes, etc.), their significance varies according to the type of organisation and their own core processes and aspirations. For example, the sales flowing from new products are more relevant for R&D firms as the amount of Nobel Laureates is for universities, or the number of R&D spin-offs per square kilometre is for local governments. Understanding these differences and the orientation of the different organisations towards innovation is relevant to organise their capacities to stimulate innovation in ways that benefit them all.

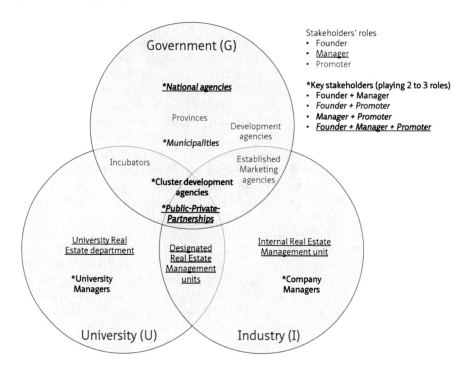

*Figure 4.2. Overview of the main stakeholders influencing the demand for developing tech-campuses framed into the Triple Helix model (Etzkowitz, 2008) (from Curvelo Magdaniel, 2016, p. 108)*

Correspondingly, the synergy created in a region through a concerted allocation of roles and activities strengthen the attractiveness of the innovation area for organisations, which are willing to locate and/or remain in a particular location. In practice, the flow of incentives is mainly evidenced at strategic level. For instance, many tech-campuses and cities worldwide have an intended knowledge-based and/ or science and technology policy or vision (Curvelo Magdaniel, 2017). Accordingly, the involvement of different stakeholders in the three spheres of the triple Helix is common in the development of tech-campuses.

Although, the interests of these stakeholders may differ, stimulating innovation and encouraging socio-economic development – among others – are common goals in the KBE. Similarly, empirical information from 39 tech-campuses worldwide suggests that various stakeholders take different and overlapping roles in campus development: founder, manager and promoter (Curvelo Magdaniel, 2016). For instance, promoters of tech-campuses are increasingly represented by hybrid (and sometimes non-traditional) structures involving public and private parties (Figure 4.2).

Similarly, Curvelo Magdaniel (2016) observed that the incentives to attract and retain research organisations are more explicitly addressed in specific contexts

THE RELATIONSHIP BETWEEN INNOVATION, CAMPUSES AND CITIES

where the development of the campuses is a top-down approach led by local and/ or national governments. This is the case of many campuses in Asia that have been declared special research and development zones that give advantages to companies on regulatory standard requirements. In other regions, the incentives are softer and targeted to increase the attractiveness of the areas for knowledge workers in terms of safety, social security and quality of living.

## METHODS

This chapter uses a single case study to illustrate the concept of synergy in campus development described in the previous section and its facilitating role to stimulate innovation in a particular context. The tech-campus studied in this chapter is home of the Massachusetts Institute of Technology (MIT), which is one of the most prestigious research universities of the world. Next to five schools with a community of more than 22,000 members, there are over 200 companies located in properties of the MIT. This tech-campus is located in the city of Cambridge within the Greater Boston area, where more than 60 campuses of universities and colleges locate.

This concentration of higher education institutions is well known for its scientific excellence in research and technological advancements, which has positively influenced the transformation of this region in one of the most prosperous of the world. This transformation is a process which has evolved along with interrelated developments in education, technology and economy in which universities such as the MIT have played a crucial role (Saxenian, 1985).

This case is particularly interesting to explain the research proposition that large-scale real estate interventions facilitate the synergy among universities, industry and government. In-depth study of this case has the likelihood of offering theoretical insight (Eisenhardt & Graebner, 2007) because of its exemplarity highlighting the general aspects described in the conceptual framework to explain the selected proposition.

First, this tech-campus emerged and developed to accommodate technology-based research as its main activity. Second, stimulating innovation is explicitly addressed as a goal of the organisations involved in the MIT campus development. Similarly, these organisations have had success in realising this goal measured by input and output indicators.[1] These criteria make this case a paradigmatic one. According to Flyvbjerg (2006), a paradigmatic case 'operates as a reference point and may functions as a focus for the founding of schools of thought'. Nonetheless, it is safe to acknowledge that successful innovation is hard to define because its measurement is becoming more complex in the knowledge based economy (KBE).

### Data Collection

The information analysed and presented in this chapter relies on data collected by means of twelve open and semi-structured interviews, observations in site, web search, attendance of seminars, review of documents and relevant readings. An overview of the data collection sources and evidence collected is illustrated in Figure 4.3. The data was collected during the period September 2014 – December 2015. The interviews, observations and attendance of seminars took place during a two-weeks field trip to the MIT campus and its surroundings in October 2014.

For the interviews, three experts were contacted via e-mail and two of them responded (i.e. the campus planner during the period 1960–2000 and the campus real estate manager since 2000). These interviews include about 10–15 open questions aimed to gain knowledge on the campus development process from each expert's experience. The interviews were often divided in two parts. The first part sought for

| DATA COLLECTION PLAN | | |
|---|---|---|
| | SOURCES | EVIDENCE COLLECTED |
| Type 1: Open and semi-structured interviews | Interviewees Role 1 - Experts subject of study | Targeted and insightful Facts, Opinions, leads of the case study topic – perceived causal explanations |
| | Interviewees Role 2 - Key-informants subject of study | Facts, context and leads to facts |
| | Interviewees Role 3 - Experts object of study | Insights, context |
| Type 2: Site observations | Event 1 - Seminar Understanding MIT at the School of Architecture and Planning (2 sessions, 3 speakers from MIT Corporation) | Insight into cultural features of the context, opinions and leads to the facts |
| | Event 2 - Seminar Changing Cities at the Media Lab (2 sessions, 3 speakers Lecturer at the Media Lab) | Insight into cultural features of the context, opinions and leads to the case study topic |
| | Event 3 - Opening of the University Industry Demonstration Partnership Fall Meeting | Insight into cultural features of the context |
| | Event 4- Site walks | Photography and other records of events on real time covering the context of the case |
| | Event 5 - Informal drinks at MIT Student Center with lecturer, students and planner, | Make inferences about the context – clues worthy for investigation |
| | Event 6 - Informal dinner at Kendall Square with Planners (former at MIT and current at Masdar City) | Insight into cultural features of the context, opinions and leads to the facts. |
| | Event 7 - Informal talk at the Venture Café in the CIC | |
| | Event 8 - Meeting with students at Media Lab, | |
| | Event 9 - Informal dinner with Post Doc researcher working at Stata Center. | |
| Type 3: Documentation | Doc type 1 - Maps and Photos of the campus collection at MIT Museum archives | Exact information containing references, details of the development of the campus covering a long span of time. |
| | Doc type 2 - Official briefing and administrative documents and reports | Exact information containing facts, names, references, and details of the subject of study. |
| | Doc type 3 – Literature of existing empirical research or formal studies of the same case | Broad-coverage information of the subject of study over time, with details of events and references of the subject of study |
| | Doc type 4 – News clippings and other articles appearing the mass media | Exact information containing facts, names, references, and details of the subject of study. |
| Type 4: Open access mapping applications | App 1 – Google Earth | Exact information containing details of the physical the development of the campus covering a long span of time – imagery over time. |
| | App 2 – Esri Maps | Specific information containing physical details of the subject of study - imagery. |
| | App 3 – Mapnificent and Google maps | Specific information containing physical details of the subject of study – accessibility & connectivity. |

*Figure 4.3. Data collection plan (from Curvelo Magdaniel, 2016, p. 463)*

the visions and decisions that have influenced the development of each campus in order to identify the strategies aimed to stimulate innovation. The second part asked about the implementation of such strategies and to which extent they considered the built environment helped attaining this goal.

Two other experts with particular knowledge about innovation dynamics in the Boston-Cambridge area were contacted and responded via e-mail (i.e. two senior researchers on technology-driven real estate). These interviews include about 10 open questions aimed to gain insight into particular contexts influencing each campus development. The interviews were often divided in two parts concerning innovation in the hosting region. The first part focuses on the perceived relationship between innovation and physical infrastructure. The second part focused on external developments influencing the development of the MIT campus.

Key informants were contacted incrementally either as suggested by experts or as indicated in reports while documenting the case. In total, 14 key informants were contacted via-email and 10 of them responded. This group of interviewees involved professionals in diverse fields including urban planners, real estate managers, facility managers, innovation policy officers, and lecturers on innovation and entrepreneurship. These interviews were tailored enquiries on particular campus development phases, strategies or decisions. They focused on campus development history in general.

*Data Analysis*

This study combined both deductive and inductive approaches for data analysis. The use of rich and extensive descriptions, tables, maps, and figures was central to the generation of insights. Besides, it helped to cope with the amount of qualitative data collected. The systematic use of notes, drawings and diagrams were organised through manual coding and categorisations in personal diaries and Excel sheets. An iterative analytical procedure is used to sharpen the constructs by displaying enough evidence for the case with examples, anecdotal reports and descriptions.

## RESULTS

*Urban Area Development (UAD) as a Large-Scale Real Estate Intervention*

Over two different periods of technological advancements, the MIT in collaboration with public and private sectors have been involved in the development of three major urban areas surrounding the academic property. These are Technology Square, Kendall Square and University Park @MIT (see Figure 4.4). The developments of these areas began during the Space age and the ICT industrial revolution and some of them spanned along the Digital and Information age up to today.

These areas have accommodated the changing activities resulted from the evolving knowledge base and industrial renewal across different technological paradigms that characterized Massachusetts' innovation climate (Curvelo Magdaniel, 2016). Although

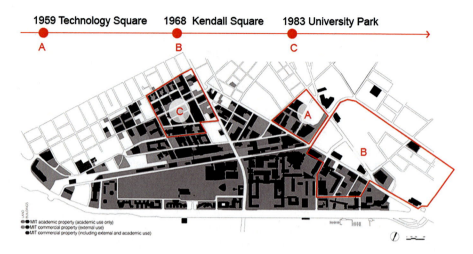

*Figure 4.4. Location of urban areas developed by the MIT in collaboration with public and private partners since 1959. Green: Urban area developments. Grey: The MIT's owned land. Black: The MIT's owned/leased buildings (Curvelo Magdaniel, 2016, p. 256)*

this chapter focuses on one condition for innovation, UAD is a particular intervention that has facilitated all interrelated conditions for innovation in the framework described before in Figure 4.1. Thus, the following paragraphs outline, with as many examples as possible, how the developments of these three areas increased the synergy between public and private parties by channelling the flow of incentives. Simultaneously, it shows how UAD changed the identity of Cambridge as an innovation area, attracted innovators to locate near to the MIT campus, increased the density of functions in the city, and ultimately, contributed to accelerate the innovation climate.

*Technology square.* In the late 1950s, the city of Cambridge pursued an urban renewal project in one of its industrial districts east of Cambridge. The area intended for development comprised residential land, known as the Roger's Block and industrial land, accommodating a major plant of the Lever Brothers Soap Factory established in Cambridge since 1898. Two important events accelerated the urban renewal project in the area. In 1957, the municipality demolished the Roger's Block and in 1959, the headquarters of the Lever Brothers moved to New York and soon afterwards the plant closed. This situation left a complex of 30 buildings of the manufacturing plant vacant and hundreds of people unemployed.

Thus, the demolition of the whole area was imminent since the city lost revenues coming from the employment and property taxes generated by this company. In 1959, the Mayor of the city contacted the MIT to develop the vacant site and the MIT saw an opportunity for investment. In 1960, the MIT and Cambridge began the plans to convert the 6-hectares plot into an offices and R&D complex. In 1962, the MIT partnered with the real estate firm Cabot, Cabot & Forbes (CC&F), to begin the construction of the project. This marked a precedent, since it was the first time an educational institution worked together with a private firm to create a business environment (Simha, 2001).

By 1967, the first four buildings of the complex were ready and Polaroid set up its headquarters in Technology Square as well as others such as IBM, government agencies and the MIT's research groups. At the beginning of the 1970s, the MIT sold its interest in Technology Square to CC&F but continued renting space for special research projects. During the 1980s Draper Laboratories – which became an independent research institute from the MIT in 1973 – begin the construction of a new building in Technology Square. In 2001, the MIT purchased the entire complex with the intention to maintain it as a tax-paying commercial property. This MIT's decision has benefited the city, which by 2014 was still receiving real estate tax revenues from this area and at the same time has reached its economic development goal of converting a former depressed industrial area into an R&D complex. Today, Technology Square is a mixed use built environment that accommodates several offices, biotechnology labs and street-level retail in 11,000 m² (Figure 4.5).

*Kendall Square.* During the space age in the 1960s, NASA funded research programs in Cambridge involving Harvard University and the MIT. The expected accommodation of NASA's research activities triggered the redevelopment plan for Kendall Square area in East Cambridge. According to Simha (2001), 'Technology Square's success inspired the NASA Electronics Research Centre to set up its headquarters in the adjacent Kendall Square in 1967'.

At the beginning of the 20th century, the land use of East Cambridge was dominated by industrial manufacturing plants. In the period 1964 – 1966, the Boston Redevelopment Authority (BRA) oversaw the economic benefits for the region from NASA's presence and presented an urban renewal proposal for Kendall Square to clear the old industrial use. The proposal was presented to the MIT because financing this urban renewal project would require the MIT's cooperation and commitment

*Figure 4.5. Technology Square in 2014*

to the city of Cambridge.[2] After the MIT agreed to provide credits for the city, Cambridge invited NASA to locate its centre here.

In 1968 the BRA, the Cambridge Redevelopment Authority (CRA) and NASA began the renovation works of the 12-hectares plot. The clearing of the old industrial uses took place between 1967 and 1975 and the sale of the redevelopment land took longer than expected because of the economic recession. Within that period and after changes in the federal administration in 1969, NASA announced the termination of its Cambridge's activities. The new building erected for NASA's research centre became vacant, but soon the CRA found a new occupant: the federal Department of Transportation (DOT) Research Center. In 1971, the DOT released 4.5 hectares of land that they considered a surplus. The CRA considered the option to sell the site to the MIT for academic purposes but the Institute was interested in maintaining its academic activities compact. Instead, they proposed to convert the site into a housing neighbourhood.

During the period 1974–1977 there was an active planning process for Kendall Square involving proposals and negotiations of different parties including the MIT. It began in 1974, when the MIT and East Cambridge Planning Team proposed a plan for a lively 24/7 neighbourhood of mixed use including housing. This plan was based on 1964's study commissioned to Kevin Lynch, professor at the School of Planning and Architecture at that time, who had been leading the project 'The Image of the City'.

In his report, Lynch outlined that Kendall Square was an undefined space bordering the campus with opportunities for a lively mixture of commercial, office, cultural, hotel and housing developments. The plan was rejected because the city had in mind a more commercial and industrial development for this area. In 1975, the CRA proceeded with the plan with changes allowing housing but not as a required function. Finally, in 1977 the Zoning plan was approved in line with the comprehensive Zoning Ordinance Review of Cambridge. For the first time, mixed development zones for a variety of different land uses on a common site were proposed.

In 1979, Boston's Properties was selected as developer for the project, whose design proposal was highly criticized by the MIT. The main oppositions were against the group of massive buildings proposed along Main Street and the lack of public space, which increased the built density around the campus. During the early 1980s, the proposal began development as well as increasing traffic congestion issues. The planning of the new Kendall MBTA[3] Red Line began in 1983 while a new hotel was being developed in the site where the new subway station was to be located. In 1986, the MIT participated in the design of the Kendall/MIT subway station, which construction in the 1990s would improve the connectivity of Cambridge in the region. As Boston's Properties continued the mixed industrial and commercial development up today, the results have been criticized for being monolithic and lacking sufficient services.

In 1999, the Cambridge Innovation Centre (CIC) was established in Kendall Square, which became one of the earliest co-working spaces for start-up companies in the U.S. The CIC began offering affordable and flexible real estate for young entrepreneurs in the area. CIC's founder began renting space-floor from the MIT's owned building located in One Broadway. Soon, CIC's business model became successful accommodating a growing number of start-ups, other medium and large firms that established at CIC. In 2014, the CIC rents from the MIT half of the space available in the same building (~28,000 sqm) providing office space for over 500 companies, of which nearly 450 are start-ups.

In addition, CIC offers venue for social meetings and organises networking events for their tenants and the Kendall square community. The success of this model has inspired the launch of LabCentral in 2013, a 2,600~ sqm facility which is the first shared laboratory space for start-up companies in life-sciences biotech industries in Cambridge.

During the 2000s, several R&D companies, research institutions and venture capital (VC) have located in Kendall Square. Most of them conduct businesses or research in the biotech and pharma sectors, but also in IT and Data and more recently in energy fields. Examples of those are the Broad Institute in 2001, Genzyme in 2003, VMWare in 2004 (the first company from Silicon Valley to establish in Kendall Square), followed by Google in 2005 and Microsoft New England R&D centre (NERD) in 2007. These and other companies as well as the local businesses located in the area are part of the Kendall Square Association (KSA), founded in 2009 to help drive the direction of the area. They are actively strengthening the network of companies and institutions in the area, by organising events, informing Kendall Square residents about developments in the area and building the identity of the innovation area.

In 2011 the city of Cambridge released a planning study for Kendall square which study area includes a 10-hectares parcel of the MIT academic property. The same year the Institute formally filed a rezoning petition for this area. The MIT community raises its awareness about the need for a long term planning that considers the preservation of academic land resources and social inclusion that can be hindered with the commercial development emerging in Kendall Square area. Recently, a design committee for MIT's Kendall Square Initiative was established to supervise and guide the design principles of the area.

This committee, formed by faculty from the MIT School of Architecture and Planning and the MIT community, is a form of participatory planning and design to ensure high quality of the built environment and alignment with the current planning and design principles of the MIT campus. The first outcome of this initiative is the MIT Gateway to Kendall Square Zoning petition, which was approved by the Cambridge City Council in 2013. According to the MIT News office, 'the new zoning preserves existing academic development potential and enables the creation of new housing, retail, lab and commercial space, as well as more engaging open space and way-finding'. The MIT's vision of mixed-use neighbourhood for Kendall Square persists from the 1970s up to today.

In 2014, the Kendall Square continues under development and it is facing a spatial and functional transformation. It has become denser resembling the image

*Figure 4.6. Kendall Square in 2014*

of a financial and business district rather than a university environment. The strong presence of large corporations such as Google, Microsoft and Novartis are dominant in the landscape (Figure 4.6). Although there has been improvement efforts, the public space is still poor in some areas and the existing shops and restaurants as well as the new residential development are getting expensive for the students' and Cambridge's communities. These and other concerns are raised regarding the development of Kendall Square, which are issues related to urban area development as a catalyst for stimulating innovation.

*University Park @MIT.* University Park @MIT is a mixed use development of commercial, private laboratory, incubator and residential functions, located North East of Massachusetts Avenue in the parcels once-occupied by the Simplex Wire & Cable Co. This company was a manufacturer of wire and cable for telephones established in Cambridge since 1888. In 1969, this company was sold to a company in New York that decided it was not viable to continue operating in Cambridge and moved the operations to Maine – another state in New England. The property was placed in the market and after the success experienced with Technology Square, the MIT saw the potential of transforming the industrial district into a housing and commercial development. This time the Institute did not consider allocating any academic use or the MIT's related research projects in the area. Between 1970–1971 the MIT acquired the property of 74,500 m².

In the years that followed, the MIT conducted a study aiming to identify the site's needs, considering the interests of the Cambridge's community on housing development. This led to a complex process of negotiations with the city and the community before the plan was completed. In 1983, the MIT selected Forest City Enterprises (FCE) as developers for the site. In 1985, the City Council appointed a Planning Committee involving representatives of the MIT, FCE and the Cambridge's

*Figure 4.7. University Park @MIT in 2014*

community. In 1987, these parties completed a Masterplan, which was approved by the City Council in 1989. This masterplan was changed because of rezoning in the Cambridgeport Industrial District in 1992, including more areas for parks and student housing in the development. The same year the development of the area began.

University Park @MIT is an example of real estate development in which the MIT established a long-term relationship with the community, because of the social component of housing development. The construction works took longer than a decade in completing the plan. Today, University Park is a mixed use neighbourhood, including 37,000 m$^2$ of residential use, 150,000 m$^2$ of commerce, a large Biotech innovation Center and high quality of public space and green areas (Figure 4.7).

## DISCUSSION AND RECOMMENDATIONS

*Large-Scale Real Estate Interventions Facilitate the Synergy in the Triple Helix*

Two types of large-scale real estate interventions have facilitated the synergy among stakeholders in the Triple-Helix. The re-development and renewal of areas in the MIT campus have been long-term processes that demanded strategic alignment, agreements and commitment between the different organisations involved. This enabled to strengthening the relationship and trust among local stakeholders who worked together and changed roles over decades, while foreseeing a mutual benefit. Developing these areas increased the chances for collaboration and building trust among these spheres while enabling the channeling of the flow of incentives towards targets that did retain and/or attract economic activities in Cambridge when it was needed.

The development of the three urban areas described above aimed mainly to support the strategic mission of the MIT in the long-term, which turned out to have unexpected impacts. For instance, these developments have helped to establish and maintain a collaborative relationship between the MIT and the city of Cambridge in fostering the economic development of the city. Over the years, the MIT has acquired land in Cambridge to secure its accommodation growth in the long term, while its presence in the city and the tax-exempt status of its academic land has been employed

F. CURVELO MAGDANIEL

by its hosting city in fostering development. In addition, UAD has facilitated the concentration of firms in Cambridge accelerating the process of technology transfer and the fulfilment of the MIT's mission of applying knowledge into practice.

This chapter has demonstrated how a concerted agenda created synergy among organisational spheres that were able to play non-traditional roles in accomplishing their goal of stimulating innovation to remain competitive. In this case, the MIT assumed a non-traditional role as both a planner and a real estate developer and became increasingly proactive in the creation of clustering of R&D firms, which has increased the job opportunities and income from taxes for the city of Cambridge.

These empirical findings validate existing theoretical concepts outlining this required synergy and role-taking ability, such as the organising capacity of cities in the knowledge economy (Van Den Berg et al., 2005) and the triple helix relationships in regions (Etzkowitz, 2008; Etzkowitz & Leydesdorff, 1995). Although the role of industry has been more passive in the MIT campus development, they have played an essential part in fulfilling the shared planning and development goals of the universities and the municipality.

Overall, UAD at MIT showed the involvement of various stakeholders in campus development. These stakeholders have different perspectives on urban area development as a catalyst for innovation because they perceive innovation in different ways according to their ambitions and perspectives on the built environment. Therefore, some issues arise when the incompatibility of their ambitions generate a lack of balance in campus interventions. These situations can reduce the function of the built environment as a catalyst for innovation and they could hinder the processes leading to innovation in the area in the long term. These issues, which are not exclusive to a single intervention but strongly linked to UAD, will be discussed below.

*Commercial Development vs. Academic Accommodation*

Since the late 1990s, there has been a change in focus in land acquisition policies at the MIT. The allocation of campus' land resources and area development efforts to commercial uses has been raising a conflict between specific stakeholders, whose perspectives on the built environment as a catalyst for innovation are incompatible.

Decision makers and controllers of the MIT campus' properties perceive the commercial development of urban areas around Kendall Square as an opportunity to generate income that will sustain the Institute's mission while keeping an entrepreneurial environment around campus. For instance, during the development of the MIT's Kendall Square initiative, the Institute abandoned its commitment to reserve the land south of Main Street for academic purposes. As a result, the 10-hectares parcel of the MIT academic property will be converted into a mixed-use development including new housing, retail, lab and commercial space. Similarly, academic land reserves have been leased to private firms for long terms, closing off the MIT's academic expansion in North Campus.

86

This initiative led by leaders of the Institute and controllers of the MIT's properties have been supported by the City of Cambridge, because there is an alignment in their ambitions. With this type of development, the city will benefit because of the revenues coming from property taxes, while succeeding in their ambition to create an attractive 'place to live, work and do business' as part of their economic development strategy. This alignment in ambitions has strengthened the relationship between the MIT and the City of Cambridge for decades.

The coordination of their strategies has been based on a collaborative model of mutual respect and understanding. Nevertheless, the strategic nature of such a relationship is increasingly built on financial ties, in which the lack of long-term planning can result in uncontrolled development that can be followed by political action. Between 2011 and 2012, members of the MIT community organised a committee to be formally involved in the planning of Kendall Square. The involvement of the community in this project is an initial MIT's political stand to ensure the long-term (social and financial) sustainability of this area in line with the future growth and expansion of the Institute as well as the preferences of its main users (i.e. academic staff and students).

Academic leaders and influential members of the MIT community have perceived the commercial development as a threat for the Institute's future in accommodating academic growth and fulfilling its academic mission. Accordingly, this group of stakeholders argues that ensuring the institute's growth of academic space is as important as generating income to sustain its mission. Indeed, they perceived the emphasis on commercial development as a paradoxical strategy, which is focusing on short-term financial returns at the expense of long-term welfare of the MIT. The implications of this strategy for the MIT's financial operations can be roughly drawn in possible scenarios.

If the MIT schools would need space that has been allocated for commercial use, they would have to pay for it at the high market price. In the end, if schools have financial trouble in accommodating growing education or research programs, they will have to get the financial support of the Institute. This can result in formal buying decisions in getting back those properties to academic use, which will de-capitalise the Institute's endowment. In addition, such decisions will raise political disagreements with the city that will suffer in the moment the MIT decides to take such land off the city's tax roll.

If that is not the case, the schools will have to lease more properties from other commercial parties at high costs. The Institute must subsidise the cost of the rent, or the schools will have to raise capital outside the MIT to buy buildings or rent space at the cost of their research programs. In the last scenario, the MIT schools and departments will be threatened by their academic competitors because the sponsors of research programs are unlikely to spend their budgets on space rather than on actual research.

Overall, there is a need for a healthy debate between these stakeholders to bring balance and to avoid uncontrolled development, which in the end can be a threat to innovation because the MIT's mission of educating and advancing research can

F. CURVELO MAGDANIEL

be compromised without both, ensuring academic space and generating income to support the Institute's core business. The poor communication between these stakeholders and the cultural differences in their practices are not facilitating the required space for debate.

Decision makers and controllers are aware of the risks on the long term, but keep their position on investing the MIT's capital according to the real estate opportunities while 'learning by doing' on the process. The MIT community have manifested their opinions and reactions to this strategy through formal communication channels (e.g. the MIT Faculty Newsletter) in order to raise these concerns among students, faculty, staff, alumni, parents and more. Nevertheless, the periodic changes in administrations – both, in the MIT and the City of Cambridge – are major obstacles to have a continuous and healthy debate in overcoming this issue.

*Attracting Firms vs. Retaining Talent*

The allocation of area development efforts to commercial uses is having an impact on campus life, in which the fostering of a mixed working, academic and social environment is raising major concerns among specific stakeholders. Similarly, their perspectives on the built environment as a catalyst for innovation are different. Particularly, those concerned with UAD in relation to two other interventions facilitating other conditions for innovation in the model: the development of physical connectors and shared facilities.

The City of Cambridge, as well as real estate developers and investors, see the mixed-use development around the MIT campus as an opportunity to boost the entrepreneurial environment in Cambridge. The undeniable success stories of Technology Square and University Park @MIT facilitating the establishment of companies, is been replicated in Kendall Square since 1968. However, its development over such a long period has taken a different scale and character shaped by distinct socio-economic events in context. Indeed, the municipalities are acting upon the booming of the biotech and pharma cluster out of the advancements in biomedical research with urban development strategies aimed to sustain the presence of firms and research institutions in close proximity to the talent in academic institutions. For instance, the development of mixed-used districts and transit-oriented development are example of these urban strategies present in Kendall Square.

Nevertheless, the fostering of that mixed environment for 'working, living and doing business' is overlooking 'studying' as part of that existing environment and more important, as an essential activity in the city. Students and young people represent a considerable share of Cambridge's population and in Kendall Square. Nowadays the high concentration of firms and the intensification of commercial developments in Kendall Square are creating other problems. The area is becoming crowded and expensive. First, the dense concentration of users in the area generates traffic congestion with an environmental impact, which is a target for improvement in the transit-oriented strategies. Second, the high rental prices of housing, office

88

and retail space are increasing the costs of living in the area, which can become unaffordable for the young community of entrepreneurs and students.

These issues are related and strengthened by the different perspectives on the built environment between real estate developers and users. For instance, the lifestyles and commuter preferences of young knowledge workers are urban oriented. They see physical proximity and connectivity as strengths to boost their productivity. Some of them are willing to pay higher prices for urban real estate instead of moving to suburban areas. This situation is optimal for commercial real estate developers, who see physical proximity as an opportunity to boost their profitability.

However, commercial real estate development needs to be controlled, especially around universities because many young people (e.g. students) cannot afford it. In this regard, there is a need for more involvement from the municipality and representatives of the communities, to create a balanced mixed-use development which considers the income difference among individuals who are an essential part of their promoted 'entrepreneurial ecosystem'. For instance, investments in affordable housing, public transportation and public space are crucial to enable a healthy environment for all the involved communities in Kendall Square area.

Another issue derived from the efforts to strengthen the proximity between firms in the area and the talent in the MIT campus is the promotion of an ideal collaborating environment that obscures the reality about the complex processes leading to innovation (e.g. technology transfer). The historical incompatibility of ambitions between industry and academy regarding innovation is not easy to solve through mixed-area developments or shared facilities initiatives. For instance, examples of shared facilities at the MIT campus facilitating a diversity of people and density of social interaction as the fifth condition for innovation (Curvelo Magdaniel, 2016; Curvelo Magdaniel et al., 2018), involve people either in academy, or in industry but not the mix of the two. That is because the innovation targets and research processes of these two spheres are contrasting.

MIT focuses on advancing knowledge from fundamental research and transferring technology through licensing mechanisms, while firms in the private sector focus on generating revenues from research and development. Thus, the separation between university and industry is a policy established at MIT, after learning from experiences sharing research laboratories (Nelsen, 2005). Indeed, the mentality differences between academy and industry protecting their intellectual property failed in their efforts to build a proper and healthy relationship. For instance, MIT's Technology Transfer Office (TTO) focuses on establishing a relationship with industry as a founding partner while keeping the MIT's research focus on fundamental sciences.

Similarly, fostering entrepreneurship is not a kind of magic resulting from placing industry next to academic talent. There is a long path between having an idea and developing it into a new product, which takes time, incentives and support. Many MIT graduate students in the fields of science and engineering struggle to develop research topics that they can simultaneously base their dissertation and take their inventions to market. Thus, some of them have to push their academic work aside knowing that their ideas are more likely to succeed if they are fostered by themselves rather than licensed to a company.

The MIT has helped them by attracting investors, finding venture capital and keeping people interested on MIT's ideas. In this context, the new real estate developments aimed to accommodate young emerging entrepreneurs next to venture capital firms comes opportunistically to support and strengthen this flow of incentives. Nevertheless, these are also commercial activities driven by incentives for income. Therefore, it is important to understand that the process of producing scientifically based commercial ideas emerges and it is nurtured in a different context.

Overall, these remarks are important to understand that the proximity between university and industry, in this case, has evolved naturally and it is not to be forced. Therefore, the strategies encouraging their proximity – such as mixed-use development – have to be planned and implemented carefully, considering they are different spheres that collaborate while keeping their own status and ambitions.

*Balance in Meaning of Innovation*

The previous discussion has helped to identify a dual perception of innovation among stakeholders involved in campus development. On the one hand, stakeholders who focus on campus as an accommodation solution tend to perceive innovation as a process driven by the exchange of ideas. They seek to facilitate people's activities and processes through the built environment. Therefore, the concentration of R&D firms around MIT campus is seen as an opportunity to encourage a creative environment leading to the discovery and the application of knowledge in attaining their goals.

On the other hand, stakeholders who focus on campus as an asset resource tend to perceive innovation as a market driven by the exchange of capital. They seek to maximize investments through the built environment and to increase real estate value. Therefore, the concentration of R&D firms around MIT campus is seen as an opportunity to encourage commercial area development in attaining their goals. Although, their actions are driven by this second perception, they also promote the first one.

The two issues described above are results of these two conflicting perceptions among stakeholders. For instance, focusing on commercial developments over academic accommodation and attracting firms over retaining talent, are examples in which the perception of innovation as a market driven by exchange of capital is increasingly dominant in campus development. However, this unbalance can also inhibit the role of the built environment as a catalyst for innovation in MIT campus. Therefore, there are important points of attention to consider in the future development of the MIT campus.

First, having a shared vision of innovation is not enough for the MIT and the city of Cambridge. It takes stakeholder's consensus in delineating goals and, most importantly, stakeholder's commitment in using their resources – e.g. the

THE RELATIONSHIP BETWEEN INNOVATION, CAMPUSES AND CITIES

built environment – to attain the desired vision for the future. For campus and city managers, the main challenge is ensuring the continuity of goals and their implementation because of the short-term condition of their appointments. Thus, acting upon the changing demand should be seen as a task that takes place in a long-term perspective.

Second, the physical integration of MIT campus in the city can be used as an advantage to strengthen the collaboration between public and private partners and to negotiate when dealing with the challenges of potential shortcoming of academic space, poor public space, traffic issues and affordability of students' housing. For campus and city planners, the main challenge is reaching the balance among the different ambitions of stakeholders involved in the development of MIT campus. Thus, opening spaces for debate leading to participatory planning is recommended. In this sense, we may revise the conceptual model, in which the synergy facilitated by the built environment is a Quadruple Helix (Leydesdorff, 2012), including the society and communities of individuals in the development of tech-campuses.

## ACKNOWLEDGEMENTS

The author thanks the interviewees who participated in this case study. Specially, those experts whose knowledge and experience in campus planning made these case descriptions rich and valuable.

## NOTES

[1]   Although the MIT campus is known as a successful case in terms of outputs in its own context, the complete list of input and output indicators that supports this selection can be found in the appendices of the PhD dissertation in which this chapter is based.
[2]   According to Simha (2001), the city of Cambridge received from the Federal Government over US$5 million in credits, used by the city to write off its share of the Kendall Square Urban Renewal Project. These credits were based on the MIT's land purchases for educational use.
[3]   Massachusetts Bay Transportation Authority (MBTA) is the public operator of most bus, subway, commuter rail and ferry routes in the Greater Boston, Massachusetts's area.

## REFERENCES

Appel-Meulenbroek, H. R. (2014). *How to measure added value of CRE and building design: Knowledge sharing in research buildings* (PhD doctoral thesis). Technische Universiteit Eindhoven, Eindhoven.

Appel-Meulenbroek, H. R., De Vries, B., & Weggeman, M. (2017). Knowledge sharing behavior: The role of spatial design in buildings. *Environment and Behavior, 49*(8), 874–903.

Becker, F. (2007). Organizational ecology and knowledge networks. *California Management Review, 49*(2), 42–61.

Curvelo Magdaniel, F. T. J. (2016). *Technology campuses and cities: A study on the relation between innovation and the built environment at the urban area level* (PhD doctoral thesis). Delft University of Technology, Delft.

Curvelo Magdaniel, F. T. J. (2017). *Campuses, cities and innovation. 39 international cases accommodating tech-based research.* Delft: TU Delft, Faculty of Architecture, Department of Management in the Built Environment.

F. CURVELO MAGDANIEL

Curvelo Magdaniel, F. T. J., De Jonge, H., & Den Heijer, A. C. (2018). Campus development as catalyst for innovation. *Journal of Corporate Real Estate, 20*(2), 84–102.

Drucker, J., & Goldstein, H. (2007). Assessing the regional economic development impacts of universities: A review of current approaches. *International Regional Science Review, 30*(1), 20–46.

Eisenhardt, K. M., & Graebner, M. E. (2007). Theory building from cases: Opportunities and challenges. *Academy of Management Journal, 50*(1), 25–32.

Etzkowitz, H. (2008). *The Triple Helix: University-industry-government innovation in action.* New York, NY: Routledge.

Etzkowitz, H., & Leydesdorff, L. (1995). The Triple Helix: University-industry-government relations: A laboratory for knowledge-based economic development. *EASST Review, 14*, 14–19.

Fernández-Esquinas, M., & Pinto, H. (2014). The role of universities in urban regeneration: Reframing the analytical approach. *European Planning Studies, 22*(7), 1462–1483.

Fernández-Maldonado, A. M., & Romein, A. (2008). A knowledge-based urban paradox: The case of Delft. In T. Yigitcanlar, K. Velibeyoglu, & S. Baum (Eds.), *Knowledge-based urban development: Planning and applications in the information era* (pp. 221–238). Hershey, PA: Information Science Reference.

Flyvbjerg, B. (2006). Five misunderstandings about case-study research. *Qualitative Inquiry, 12*(2), 219–245.

Kostoff, R. N. (2003). Stimulating innovation. In L. Shavininia (Ed.), *The international handbook of innovation.* Oxford: Elsevier Science.

Leydesdorff, L. (2012). The Triple Helix, Quadruple Helix, …, and an n-tuple of helices: Explanatory models for analyzing the knowledge-based economy? *Journal of the Knowledge Economy, 3*(1), 25–35. doi:10.1007/s13132-011-0049-4

Nelsen, L. L. (2005). The role of research institutions in the formation of the biotech cluster in Massachusetts: The MIT experience. *Journal of Commercial Biotechnology, 11*(4), 330–336.

Oseland, N., Marmot, A., Swaffer, F., & Ceneda, S. (2011). Environments for successful interaction. *Facilities, 29*(1–2), 50–62.

Saxenian, A. (1985). Silicon valley and route 128: Regional prototypes or historic exceptions. *Urban Affairs Annual Reviews, 28*, 81–105.

Simha, O. R. (2001). *MIT campus planning: An annotated chronology.* Cambridge, MA: Massachusetts Institute of Technology.

Toker, U., & Gray, D. O. (2008). Innovation spaces: Workspace planning and innovation in US university research centers. *Research Policy, 37*(2), 309–329.

Van Den Berg, L., Braun, E., & Van Der Meer, J. (1997). *Metropolitan organising capacity: Experiences with organising major projects in European cities.* Aldershot: Ashgate Publishing.

Van Den Berg, L., Pol, P., Van Winden, W., & Woets, P. (2005). *European cities in the knowledge economy: The cases of Amsterdam, Dortmund, Eindhoven, Helsinki, Manchester, Munich, Munster, Rotterdam and Zaragoza.* Aldershot: Ashgate Publishing.

Van Winden, W., Carvalho, L., Yigitcanlar, T., Velibeyoglu, K., & Baum, S. (2008). Urban competitiveness in the knowledge economy: Evolution paths of the Portuguese metropolises. *Knowledge-Based Urban Development–Planning and Applications in the Information Era, 203–220.*

Waber, B., Magnolfi, J., & Lindsay, G. (2014, October). Workspaces that move people. *Harvard Business Review.*

ALEJANDRA TORRES-LANDA LOPEZ

# 5. "THE THIRD TEACHER" OF THE XXI CENTURY

*Educational Infrastructure, Its Problems and Challenges*

### ABSTRACT

Learning is a personal and an internal process influenced by different external factors. In the formal educational system learning is affected mainly by professors (first teacher), classmates (second teacher) and educational infrastructure (third teacher). The last element creates environments in which teaching and learning processes take place. The impact educational infrastructure has in academic achievements has been registered by many researchers (Strange & Banning, 2001; Shneider, 2002; Fisher, 2005; Lippman, 2010; and Torres Landa López, 2013).

Nevertheless, it seems that Mexican Higher Educational Institutes (HEI) are being built the same way as in the past, therefore they don't respond either to new educational paradigms, or the inclusion of emerging technology.

This chapter refers to some problems "the third teacher" (i.e. the educational infrastructure) faces. Firstly, most schools and universities have been built to respond to specific needs of training, principally manual skills reacting to the Industrial Revolution (Robinson, 2011), but the postmodern society of XXI century requires different approaches (Lyotard, 1999). Secondly, new information technology (IT) has changed the way people communicate and relate to each other. These include changes that affect directly the teaching and learning process and thus the educational infrastructure (Oblinger, 2005).

Thirdly, designing Higher Educational infrastructure must be addressed differently than designing educational infrastructure for early schooling stages, as the students that enter universities are young adults and have different characteristics than children. Therefore, instead of grounding the design in pedagogy it must be an andragogy approach to tackling the problem.

### INTRODUCTION

People learn all the time, anywhere, anytime; it's a personal and an internal process in which new knowledge is constructed by reorganizing mental diagrams, based on previous knowledge and experiences (Díaz Barriga Arceo & Hernández Rojas, 1999), influenced by different external factors. In the Formal Educational System (FES) learning is affected mainly by professors which are considered to be the *first teacher* as he or she is responsible to design strategies to help students achieve a

© KONINKLIJKE BRILL NV, LEIDEN, 2019 | DOI: 10.1163/9789004391598_006

learning goal. The Formal Education System (FES) is a systematic and deliberate process where strategies are deliberately designed to meet certain learning objectives and society has given this role mainly to schools (Mesanza López, 1999).

But, many times students mention that they learnt more from their classmates and their peers, and they reason that is why they are the *second teachers*. This happens in most cases because the generational gap between teachers and students creates a barrier that can't let communication flow freely. Furthermore, there is a *third teacher* in the FES, referring to the learning environment, as already the Reggio Emilia approach (Lippman, 2010) has pointed out, that space is a key source of educational provocation and insight, space that is conceived within an educational infrastructure.

The impact educational infrastructure has on academic achievements has been registered by many researchers, such as Strange and Banning (2001) who analyzed educational spaces and how the physical infrastructure affects learning outcomes. They quote Winston Churchill, who said: "We shape our buildings; thereafter they shape us" and they specify the different distances to be taken into consideration when designing a proposed space. This might include the difference between an intimate, personal, social or public scale, otherwise known as proxemics.

Shneider (2002), in analysing the relationship that learning achievement has to educational infrastructure, addresses the negative impact that a "sick building" could have in the educational process. When educational infrastructure has bad qualities on acoustics, lights, temperature, among others it can be considered as having a "sick building syndrome". Fisher (2005) highlights how the evaluation of learning environments has focused on technical issues, but there has to be a qualitative and quantitative measurements in order to have the whole picture. Fisher presents some layout proposals responding to different learning activities. Lippman (2010) brings up again the concept of educational infrastructure as the third master that had already been proposed half a century ago. Torres Landa López (2013) has undertaken a research study of the Mexican Higher Educational infrastructure that concludes with urging a change in how classrooms are conceived and how workshops, laboratories and libraries, as learning spaces, must be reimagined. They should be seen as places where ideas and thoughts can be shared within infrastructure that can work as a social catalyzer where people can interact between each other and with the space itself (Augé, 1996).

Nevertheless, it seems the findings and conclusions of these and other studies haven't been taken into consideration in the design-and-build process of educational infrastructure, because many of them are still being built the same way as in the past. Thus, they don't respond either to new educational paradigms, or the inclusion of emerging technology.

SOME PROBLEMS THE THIRD TEACHER FACES IN THE 21ST C CENTURY

Although learning is a multifactorial process, designers, architects and people in charge of educational infrastructure can help create better learning environments to enhance learning achievement. It's often said that the proper identification of a problem is

50% of the solution, therefore, three big problems of "the third teacher" (educational infrastructure) have been acknowledged. Three main problems were some of the conclusions of the author's PhD research including: *an anthropic conflict at the Mexican Higher Education Institutes; problems and challenges educational infrastructure faces for teaching, and learning History of Architecture* (Torres Landa López, 2013).

*Much Existing Educational Infrastructure is Built within Old Paradigms*

Many schools have been built to respond to specific needs of training, principally manual skills reacting to the Industrial Revolution (Robinson, 2011), but the postmodern society of the 21st C requires different approaches (Lyotard, 1991) as illustrated in Figure 5.1.

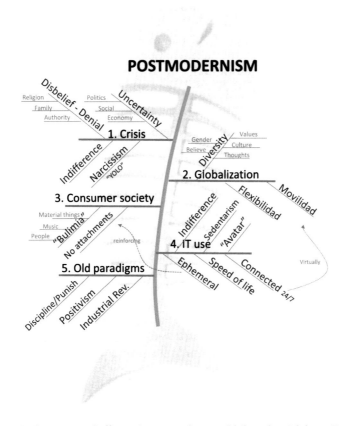

*Figure 5.1. The cause and effects of a postmodern world (based on Ishikawa Diagram)*

In the 20th C, society was considered to exist in a Modernist World where the 'subject' was mistrusted, since any subject had to be perceived from 'objective' observation and through human senses, otherwise it would be doubted. The subjectivity had no scientific value because it couldn't be validated objectively so it was denied.

In contrast, the object was overvalued and considered trustworthy; objectivity had credit and positivistic studies were based on quantitative data and were analyzed from an objective point of view, giving a sense of security. The boom of information technology (IT), predominantly with the computers in 1960s, came to reinforce these ideas, as it was thought that everything could be understood even within a binary relation of a 0–1.

At the same time, the evolution of IT changed the way people communicate and how people relate between each other, changes that directly affect the teaching and learning process (Oblinger, 2006). Therefore, educational infrastructure should be built differently, but do we see fundamental changes?

Postmodernist ideas evolved to oppose modern beliefs. Postmodernity prints different characteristics in society which can be identified from an analysis of causes and effects as seen in Figure 5.1.

To understand 21st C society's characteristics a cause and effect diagram was developed showing that students and teachers in the Higher Education sector are shaped by a number of factors such as:

- Political, economic and social crisis is a common way of life all around the world since the beginning of the 21st C. This has caused a level of uncertainty in people, since everyone can have their own references and anything that is said is "okay". This uncertainty drives people to deny religious beliefs, family and authority in general. Therefore, it is not surprising that young people have the motto "YOLO" referring to "you only live once". The reflection of the narcissism of this generation sees many people only caring for themselves without considering the past, the present and, clearly, not the future.
- On the other hand, globalization has allowed a "reduction" in the size of the world, generating a great diversity of gender, creed, thoughts, culture and values, provoking a great flexibility in all areas of human life. Postmodernism is an era in which there is a record of greater mobility (physical and/or virtual) and with it an exaggerated and exhausting speed of the way of life as it is perceived and lived.
- Society of the last decades of the 20th C, and at the beginning of 21st C, is considered as a consumer society. This can be compared to the idea that the world has "bulimia", because people buy compulsively and then throw everything away, the same way if they are objects, music and even people. With it, in their relationships, there is less attachment or compromise to many forces in these times.
- These characteristics are further reinforced by new technologies, especially because of information and communication technologies (ICT) that have increased the detachment from 'things'. Truth is no longer important as a person can be anybody else in the virtual environments, anyone can create an "avatar" with different

features of real life. The speed at which technology changes, including computer systems' formats, encourages the ephemeral way that millennials are living.

- All the above contributes to the crises mentioned in previous paragraphs and the changes needed can't be completed because of the strong old structures society has from the past, where people are educated under a positivist approach. For instance, the solutions given to serve the Industrial Revolution were very successful; for example, for the educational system there were International political programs to build educational infrastructure to reach most of population at the beginning of the 20th C; it worked so well that it is a paradigm difficult to break (Robinson, 2010).

The changes of society are evident, and people should work out innovative ways to respond to new needs.

*The Characteristics of Students in Higher Education*

One of the changes that must be made is the way Higher Educational (HE) infrastructure is designed. First, the approach for designing HE infrastructure should be addressed differently than the one taken when designing educational infrastructure for school stages, as the students that enter universities are young adults and have different characteristics than children. Therefore, instead of grounding the design in pedagogy it should be an andragogic approach to tackle the problem.

As andragogy is the science of adult education that focuses on the student, just like the constructivist model that many higher educational instituted based their curricula on. Andragogy takes advantage of adults' characteristics, therefore, learning strategies are designed to promote their autonomy, their previous experiences and knowledge. This is all used to build new content where the student's interest on the subject is the motivation needed to achieve learning objectives and, in many cases, students at this age are working in paid employment, so applying what they are learning allows significant and deeper learning.

At the same time students of HE have the ability to organize their time which allows the promotion of an adult-oriented educational process which includes flexibility. Such characteristics that can be increased through the use of ICT (Rodríguez Rojas, 2003).

*Active Learning Spaces*

Recent studies (Torres Landa López, 2016) have shown that new educational paradigms are pointing to major changes in the teaching and learning process, alterations exposed in:

- New Syllabus, as they become more flexible and their main objective drives from teaching to learning, so the student becomes the center of the educational process, and learning's goals aims to a high level of thinking, where students develop their skills to analyze, synthesize, problem solving, team work, among others (Abdullah et al., 2011).

- Nowadays, learning is perceived as a nonlinear process, replacing the thought of a linear one; according to Raffaele Simone (quoted by Carmona Ochoa, 2015) this preconception of a linear way of thinking (sequential intelligence) was originated with the ability of writing and reading as it gave human being an alphabetic vision, as it allows the acquisition of information from a linear series of visual symbols.
- It's also seen a change in schools, where learning by repetition stopped being the most frequent activity in classrooms, migrating to an active learning approach, where students are more participative and collaborative.
- And furthermore, boundaries between disciplines are vanishing, one example is biomimicry (Benyus, 1997) where the knowledge of Biology crosses the borders of design, architecture and engineering disciplines.
- From what was said earlier, it's clear the urge to see learning from an holistic point of view, where interaction, communication and social compromise are leading trends (Brown & Long, 2006).

Consequently, if the activities in the teaching and learning process are changing, educational infrastructure that conceives the space where the interaction of teachers and students take place, it's also mutated or should be transformed. Some trends that stamp the beginning of a new course for the design and construction of learning spaces is revealed in the following ways:

- Planning and design guidelines are altered, as the interpretation of the problem starts by aiming to build for learning instead of for teaching.
- Educational infrastructure provides spaces that endorses interaction between students, teachers, administrative staff, family and society; these spaces should be considered good neighbors (O'Donnell Wicklund Pigozzi and Peterson, VS Furniture, & Bruce Mau Design, 2010).
- Information technology (IT) blends into the physical infrastructure allowing ubiquitous learning.
- Every corner is designed to favor learning, formal and informally (Brown & Long, 2006).
- The flexibility of the syllabus mentioned before obligates spaces to be less specialized (Abdullah et al., 2011). There should be a variety of spaces, e.g. galleries, studios, labs; every corner is designed to enhance learning, therefore there has to be a good access to technology (Fisher, 2005).
- IT becomes a transformer, as it helps to change the sequential intelligence approach of learning, as mentioned before, to a non-alphabetic vision, as people receive simultaneous signals from television, videogames and Internet, information where order in not important (Carmona Ochoa, 2015).
- The building itself is a teaching tool (Crane, 2008), this dimension of physical infrastructure has been a constant in Mexican schools, as it can be seen in many O'Gorman' schools (Arias Montes, 2005).

## "THE THIRD TEACHER" OF THE XXI CENTURY

- Changes in furniture has become a priority, as active learning demands flexibility on different settings and arrangements.

The doctoral research done in Mexico (Torres Landa López, 2013) reviewed and analysed all the authors quoted above and helped to get different points of view of the problem; it gave the opportunity to identify similar research so, on the one hand it followed some of the methodology the authors used and on the other hand, it helped to figure new questions, such as the importance that libraries have been gaining in the educational process.

### Libraries as Learning Spaces

As pointed above, the morphology of the physical space and the IT of the educational infrastructure have an impact on the learning outcomes, but they are not the only dimension, as the high level way of thinking process like, the

*Table 5.1. Summary of findings*

| Dimension | Elements | How | Why |
|---|---|---|---|
| Physical | Inadequate:<br>• Space morphology<br>• Noise control<br>• Temperature control<br>• Sunlight diffusion<br>• Air quality<br>• Equipment<br>• Flexibility of classrooms<br>• Furniture design<br>• Handicapped access | • Creates uncomfortable and unpleasant environments<br>• Makes it difficult to implement different learning activities<br>• Generates boundaries to access education | • It hinders the actors of the educational process (teacher and students) to be receptive and able to build new knowledge<br>• It doesn't respond to different learning styles of students<br>• Inhibit inclusion |
| Technological | IT absence, obsolescence, insufficiency or bad use:<br>• Computers<br>• Electronic boards<br>• Mobile devises<br>• Software<br>• Internet<br>• LMS (e.g. Moodle) | • Inhibits innovation<br>• Closes communication channels<br>• Limits andragogy characteristics of adult students<br>• Hinders old educational paradigm changes | • Students spend more time in automata's chores<br>• Traditional communication is the only way to interact<br>• New research can't be reached and use to enhance learning |
| Documental | Deficiency or insufficiency of:<br>• Traditional libraries<br>• Virtual libraries<br>• Reading spaces | • Hinders the development of generic competences such as: search and identify data; analysis and synthesis information | • Not been in contact with the latest findings, it's harder to build new knowledge. |

99

ability to search and find the right information, the capacity to decodify symbols, categorize, classify, find patterns, analyze and synthetize (Vargas Beal, 2011), what illustrates the importance of the references, what it should and was taken as the third dimension (Fig 5.1).

The results of the research done in Mexico (Torres Landa López, 2013) demonstrated that all HEI studied have traditional (physical) libraries, and many of them have virtual libraries. The access to the information is not as easy as it should be, especially in virtual environments. This could be because many people are not familiar with new technology or because the metaphors used to design these environments are done more from the informatic point of view. And, although many students admit it's quite easy to access the traditional libraries, they don't use them often, sometimes because it's not close to the classrooms where they are, other times because their academic schedule is so tight that they prefer to google the information, even if they know it might not be the best data they could get.

Mexican HEI have to encourage the habit of reading, but the infrastructure has to change in order to see a change of behavior in students, because when the students were asked where do they read, they say they do it in libraries, in their classrooms, in the gardens, even in hallways, but are these spaces prepared for these activities? Some of the pictures taken in the HEI visited show the opposite, as students have to sit on the floor or under the strong sunbeam to have a place to review some lines.

For many years, libraries have been considered only as book containers and warehouses, but in the last decades they have been transformed from places where books were very jealousy kept, to more open and public spaces, where anyone can take, read and enjoy a book (Eco, 1981), allowing the creation of more dynamic and inclusive spaces so people can use their bibliographic collections.

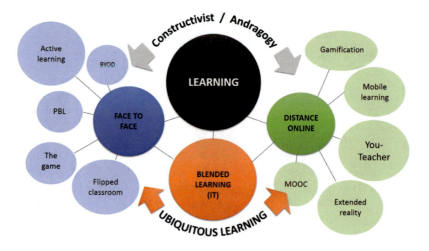

*Figure 5.2. Educational trends*

General outcomes from the research (Torres Landa López, 2016), can point out from the Mexican Higher Education Institutes that were studied some elements of their infrastructure that influence learning outcomes, asserting how and why it happens.

## CONCLUSION

Educational infrastructure of Higher Education Institutes must be a social catalyzer and must be seen more than a set of classrooms, laboratories and buildings. This infrastructure needs to be considered as a learning environment where ideas, thoughts and people meet, where individuals relate between each other and where persons interact with the space itself. Infrastructure should be designed by a transdisciplinary team, considering that it's for adult people, and so designed with an andragogy approach and an understanding of educational trends (Figure 5.2).

## REFERENCES

Abdullah, N. A. G., Beh, S. C., Tahir, M. M., Ani, A. I. C., & Tawil, N. M. (2011). Architecture design studio culture and learning spaces: A holistic approach to the design and planning of learning facilities. *Procedia – Social and Behavioral Sciences, 15*, 27–32. Retrieved from http://doi.org/10.1016/J.SBSPRO.2011.03.044

Arias Montes, J. V. (2005). *Juan O' Gorman: Arquitectura Escolar 1932*. México: UAM-A, UNAM, UASLP.

Augé, M. (1996). *Los no lugares*. España: Gedisa.

Benyus, J. (1997). Echoing nature. Why biomimicry now? In J. Benyus (Ed.), *Biomimicry: Innovation inspired by nature*. New York, NY: Harper Collins.

Brown, M., & Long, P. D. (2006). Trends in learning space design. In D. G. Oblinger (Ed.), *Learning spaces* (pp. 9.1–9.11). Washington, DC: EDUCAUSE. Retrieved from https://www.educause.edu/research-and-publications/books/learning-spaces/chapter-9-trends-learning-space-design

Carmona Ochoa, G. (2015). *Ciudades imaginarias y sociedades virtuales*. México: Universidad de Guadalajara, Universidad Autónoma de Coahuila.

Crane, S. (2008). New paradigms for educational facilities. In S. Crane (Ed.), *7o Congreso Internacional INIFED*. México: INIFED.

Díaz Barriga Arceo, F., & Hernández Rojas, G. (1999). *Estrategias docentes para un aprendizaje significativo. Una interpretación constructivista*. México: McGraw Hill.

Eco, U. (1981). *De Biblioteca*. In Conferencia ofrecida en la Biblioteca Comunale de Milán, Italia. Retrieved from http://dialnet.unirioja.es/servlet/fichero_articulo?codigo=283515

Fisher, K. (2005). *Research into identifying effective learning environment: Evaluating quality in educational facilities*. Retrieved from http://www.oecd.org/dataoecd/26/7/37905387.pdf

Lippman, P. C. (2010). *Can the physical environment have an impact on the learning environment?* Retrieved from http://www.oecd.org/dataoecd/50/60/46413458.pdf

Lyotard, J.-F. (1999). *La Condición postmoderna* (Vol. 19). Grandes obras del pensamiento contemporáneo.

Mesanza López, J. (1999). *Diccionario de las Ciencias de la Educación*. México: SANTILLANA.

Oblinger, D. (2006). *Learning spaces*. Washington, DC: EDUCAUSE. Retrieved from https://www.educause.edu/research-and-publications/books/learning-spaces

O'Donnell Wicklund Pigozzi and Peterson, A. I., VS Furniture, & Bruce Mau Design. (2010). *The third teacher: 79 ways you can use design to transform teaching & learning*. New York, NY: Abrams.

Robinson, K. (2010). *Changing educational paradigms*. Retrieved from https://www.youtube.com/watch?v=zDZFcDGpL4U

A. TORRES-LANDA LOPEZ

Rodríguez Rojas, P. (2003). La andragogía y el constructivismo en la sociedad del conocimiento. *Laurus, 9*(15), 80–89.

Shneider, M. (2002). *Do schools facilities affect academic outcomes? National clearinghouse for educational facilities.* Retrieved from http://www.ncef.org/pubs/outcomes.pdf

Strange, C. C., & Banning, J. H. (2001). *Educating by design: Creating campus learning environments that work.* San Francisco, CA: Jossey-Bass.

Torres Landa López, A. (2013). *Un conflicto antrópico en las Instituciones de Educación Superior Mexicanas. Problemas y retos de la infraestructura educativa en la enseñanza y aprendizaje de la Historia de la Arquitectura.* Aguascalientes: Universidad Autónoma de Aguascalientes.

Torres Landa López, A. (2016). *"El Tercer Maestro" para el siglo XXI. Infraestructura educativa para el aprendizaje ubicuo.* Aguascalientes: Universidad Autónoma de Aguascalientes. Retrieved from http://www.uaa.mx/direcciones/dgdv/editorial/docs/el_tercer_maestro.pdf

Vargas Beal, X. (2011). *Infraestructura Educativa Documental y su relación con la docencia de la Historia de la Arquitectura.* Aguascalientes: Universidad Autónoma de Aguascalientes.

# PART 2

# THE SOCIO-CULTURAL IMPLICATIONS IN ALIGNING VIRTUAL AND PHYSICAL LEARNING SPACES

KENN FISHER

# INTRODUCTION TO PART 2

Part 2 explores the socio/pedagogical and cultural aspects of the university campus and the six chapters seek to apply evidence-based approaches to six campus planning and design elements. Having stated that this book does not address in detail the rapid digital transformations providing pressure for the campuses to adapt to, Chapter 6 does look at how academics – rather than buildings – need to adapt. It examines the virtual world of learning and how a place-based experience can be achieved in an online world. Chapter 7 continues the focus on academic teachers in looking at 'classroom culture' and how the inhabitants of learning environments – including students – might adapt to blended, mixed online-face to face pedagogies.

Chapter 8 responds to the growing use of online pedagogies in face to face learning environments. Anecdotally the need for informal learning spaces has seen a shift towards a ratio of 50:50 teacher:student centred spaces (or formal:informal). This chapter compiles the evidence for this shift in significant detail through evidence-based methodologies. Chapter 9 develops the theme of blended learning using the architectural teaching studio as a case study. Evidence is built through mixed methods research to conclude that blended learning improves student learning outcomes. Chapter 10 seeks to determine a model which links students perceptions of learning and their cognitive, affective and regulatory learning styles to a variety of learning spaces. Once again a mixed method approach is used to develop an evidence-based model.

Chapter 11 then ties the previous chapters together linking the teacher virtual, student informal, combined blended and the student learning spatial experience to arrive at an evidence-based model.

© KONINKLIJKE BRILL NV, LEIDEN, 2019 | DOI: 10.1163/9789004391598_007

LEAH IRVING

# 6. VIRTUAL WORLDS IN HIGHER EDUCATION

*Embodied Experiences of Academics*

ABSTRACT

Significant changes in higher education are challenging ways of being for academics. The rapid development of technologies combined with influences of globalization on higher education is creating an increasingly different environment for university learning and teaching. Massive increases in student numbers from around the globe now accessing higher education has required universities to adapt their learning spaces on and off campus in order to meet growing expectations. Increasingly, online technologies are utilized in creating new learning environments to cope with these changing dynamics. Virtual worlds are part of a wide range of technology-mediated learning spaces currently used by universities that are challenging established pedagogies, practices and ways of being an academic. This chapter explores how academics experience virtual worlds as pedagogical places. Using the virtual world Second Life™ as a lens, it examines the changing nature of embodiment, pedagogy and place for academics and the significance these changes have for academic identity and practices. A hermeneutic phenomenological approach following van Manen (1990) is used for this inquiry and is framed by post-phenomenological philosophies of human-technology relations after Ihde (1990, 1998, 2002, 2011) and Verbeek (2005, 2008). Theories of extended embodiment established by Merleau-Ponty (1962) and Heidegger (1962) underpin understandings of experiences mediated through the avatar.

One-on-one interviews were conducted with academics having direct experience using Second Life for learning and teaching. Data were analysed through hermeneutic phenomenology and discourse analysis approaches. This interpretive research method uses data extracts to include the reader in the process. The results from this research indicate virtual worlds are places where academics dwell pedagogically. Virtual worlds can be creative, playful, agential and collegial places for academics where they engage with student avatars in a pedagogically caring way. The virtual world place is a figured world that influences ways of being and ways of feeling and has strong implications for academics' professional identity and how they see themselves as academics in these spaces. The results from this research have implications for the professional development of academics as we move further into the 21st century and virtual learning spaces become the norm – if they are not already so.

© KONINKLIJKE BRILL NV, LEIDEN, 2019 | DOI: 10.1163/9789004391598_008

L. IRVING

## INTRODUCTION

More and more, online technologies are utilized in creating learning environments to accommodate large numbers of students who are, in most cases, geographically dispersed and require flexibility around their work and/or family lives. Virtual worlds are part of a wide range of technology-mediated learning spaces currently used by universities to meet these complex needs that are also presenting challenges for established pedagogies, practices and ways of being an academic.

This chapter draws upon research from my PhD thesis that explored how academics' experienced virtual worlds as pedagogical places. The focus of this chapter offers a perspective on the embodied nature of being an academic in the increasingly technologized world of universities today. It uses the virtual world Second Life™ as a lens to examine the changing nature of embodiment for academics and the significance this has for academic identity and practices. A hermeneutic phenomenological approach following van Manen (1990) is used for this inquiry and is framed by post-phenomenological philosophies of human-technology relations after Ihde (1990, 1998, 2002, 2011) and Verbeek (2005, 2008). Theories of extended embodiment established by Merleau-Ponty (1962) and Heidegger (1962) underpin understandings of experiences mediated through the avatar.

Virtual worlds are an integral part of a wider range of new and emerging technologies often referred to as Information and Communication Technologies (ICT) that form part of a technology continuum reaching back over at least three decades. While these technologies were initially viewed more as tools for learning (Kennedy, Dalgarno, & Gray et al., 2007; Kennedy, Judd, Churchward, & Gray, 2008) this viewpoint has shifted to encompass possibilities for rich learning environments that support situated learning experiences where the boundaries between informal and formal spaces are blurred and virtual spaces are layered with physical spaces (Keppell & Riddle, 2012).There is however, very little research or understanding of academic's learning and teaching experiences in these spaces (Westberry, McNaughton, Billor, & Gaeta, 2013) or the challenges these spaces may present for embodied teaching practices and professional academic identities.

## THEORIES AND PERSPECTIVES OF EMBODIMENT

This section briefly outlines the theories and perspectives which guide this study's understanding of how technology-mediated spaces such as virtual worlds can be, and are, experienced in ways that are meaning making and/or meaningful (Thomas & Brown, 2009), just as (although in different ways) non-digital places can be. In order to understand how academics perceive digital artefacts such as avatars, buildings, landscapes and interactive objects that are the materiality of the virtual world this inquiry is framed within the concepts of technology-mediated experience and technological intentionality after Ihde (1979, 1990, 1998, 2002,

108

2011) and Verbeek, (2005, 2008). Technological artefacts, according to Ihde, can be experienced not in the same ways as we experience physical artefacts, but nonetheless they are experienced in some way and this experience can be interpreted. Through Ihde's (1979, 1990, 2010) concept that technology has the capacity to transform perception and his framework of human–technology relations, this research seeks to establish ways in which to understand and discuss how academics experience 'being' an academic in technology-mediated teaching and learning places and spaces.

*Embodiment*

The primary interest in embodiment for this current study is the idea of extended body originating from Merleau-Ponty (1962) and Heidegger (1962) that have been taken up by others such as Ihde (1990, 1998, 2002) and Verbeek (2005) to incorporate relations with technology. It is Merleau-Ponty's (1962) theory of embodiment and perception that this research bases the understanding of how experiences of virtual worlds are possible through the embodied avatar.

Merleau-Ponty (1962) introduced a phenomenology of embodiment that considered the lived body as a way of experiencing the world. For Merleau-Ponty the body cannot be viewed purely and as an object that is a collection of organs, fluid, muscle, bone, skin and so forth. Rather it is a schema that is an all-perceiving union of mind and body and is the bodily intentionality of being in the world.

Embodiment for Merleau-Ponty therefore is a holistic sensing of the world not specific senses operating independently but in unison everything combines to interpret the life-world. It is a pre-reflective state of knowing where the body is in space and is much as a perceiving body as it is a body to be perceived by others. Furthermore, Merleau-Ponty insists that the body is the reference point from which all else in the world is perceived and experienced.

For Merleau-Ponty, artefacts and technologies become part of the body schema. To articulate this concept, he uses the example of the blind man's cane becoming a seamless extension of the person's body in their experiencing of the world, it is not the cane so much that is experienced, but rather the footpath or objects encountered through the cane. Another of Merleau-Ponty's examples is that of a feather in a woman's hat. He describes the woman's ability to negotiate doorways and so forth without damaging the feather in her hat because she has a tacit knowledge of where the feather is. The feather according to Merleau-Ponty, has become part of the woman's body schema and is embodied by the woman. In this current study this concept refers to the avatar becoming part of the academic's body schema. Interestingly, neurological and behavioral studies are finding the plasticity of the human brain enables the body schema to extend through objects and artifacts reconfiguring the space around it (see for example Steptoe, Steed, & Slater, 2014).

L. IRVING

*Embodied Tools*

In a similar vein Heidegger (1962) describes tools in terms of ready-to-hand and present-at-hand. A very simplistic explanation of this theory is a tool/artifact/technology ready-to-hand is when a technology with a specific purpose is used unconsciously by the user and thus becomes an extension of the user's body. Heidegger's well-known example is a carpenter using a hammer; the hammer has a particular intentional use (e.g. to hammer nails) and becomes an extension of the carpenter's arm. The carpenter may experience the metallic hardness of the nail and/or the texture of the wood but is not so much conscious of the hammer. The hammer becomes present-at-hand when it breaks or is not in use, it is there "objectively present" (Verbeek, 2001).

Brey (2000) notes however that a technology such as a hammer is also for acting on the world not just perceiving the world via the technology. Therefore, artefacts both extend the body and experience of the environment is perceived and acted upon through them (Brey, 2000). The point of explaining these examples is to suggest the extension of the academics body is experienced through the avatar's motility in the virtual world. Moreover, the theories of Merleau-Ponty, Heidegger, Ihde and Verbeek's extended body and human-technology relations assist in answering the research question of how virtual world places are experienced in a pedagogical way for academics. The avatar, I propose, mediates experiences of teaching and learning in the virtual world for academic.

*Human-Technology Relations for Interpreting Environmental Experiences*

Ihde builds on Heidegger's (1962) philosophy of technology and being to suggest that there are new ways of experiencing that are parallel to corporeal experiencing. Ihde's (2002) perspective of embodiment follows Merleau-Ponty and is discussed in terms of knowing where your body is in space, being able to "know" the extremities of your body as you move about the world and negotiate spaces that includes knowing you can fit through spaces without measuring yourself against them. Moreover, Ihde's (1990, 2002) theory of human-technology relations includes technologies integrated with the bodily experiencing of the world and hermeneutic in that technologies can be interpretive devices for experiencing the world. Technologies can be embodied by their users and they can mediate embodiment and play a mediation role between humans and their environment. Ihde's phenomenological approach to technology provides a framework for analysing the phenomenon of technology-mediated experience.

*Avatars and Embodiment*

In virtual worlds the user or virtual world participant is represented in-world by an avatar which they chose from existing templates or customize their own. The avatar becomes an extension of the user to experience and be experienced (by other avatars).

It also enables the user to interpret certain things in the virtual world environment. Non-verbal cues and signals of body language in concrete world are biologically and cultural determined (Wainwright, 2010; White & Gardner, 2013) and are interpreted by others as part of communication exchange. Avatars in current virtual worlds do not have the capacity to enact the subtleties of body language but there are many possible avatar actions that signify certain things as part of communicating with others and more complex nuances are on the near horizon (see for example Mancini, Ermilov, Castellano, Liarokapis, Varni, & Peters, 2014; Goldberg, Christensen, Flash, Giese, & Malach, 2015).

The currently available actions in conjunction with the spoken or typed word add levels of complexity to interaction and communication in a virtual world and must be interpreted by other users who in turn respond through their avatar. This is not a hermeneutic human-technology relation in the true Ihde (1990, 2002) sense but it does entail hermeneutic analysis of the other avatar in relation to ones' own avatar in order to understand what is being communicated. Moreover, the physicality of the virtual world, the graphical 3D environment needs interpreting in order for the avatar to interact with it. For example, a learning space in a virtual world may have interactive objects that facilitate learning and these need to be interpreted as 'things' to be interacted with in a certain way. The avatar is then directed to interact with them. Pearce (Pearce & Artemesia, 2006a, p. 1) refers to it as ""spatial literacy" – the ability to read and interpret meaning and narrative embedded in virtual space in a particular way". The user is continually interpreting the environment and the interaction by the avatar in ways that co-shape the user's experience of the [virtual] world.

Ihde (2002) suggests a phenomenological understanding of our sense of being a body in the world is motile, perceptual and emotive and has two perspectives. The sense of being a body in the world is what Ihde calls body 1 or the here-body and suggests another socially and culturally constructed perspective which he calls body 2 or over-there body. Body 2 refers to how our body is transcribed or inscribed through and with our social and cultural context. In a similar vein to Merleau-Ponty (1962) the here-body or myself-as-body is not to be delimited by the skin surface or the outline of the body. Ihde insists the here-body has a kind of sensing which goes beyond its perimeter that still belongs to the intentional body or is still part of the intentional body and extends beyond the skin. An example Ihde uses to illustrate this is of a martial arts person being able to sense or anticipate blows from behind and can execute blows or "… aim one's activity beyond any simple now-point" (2002, p. 6).

Body 2 is over-there body and is the body that observes itself. Ihde describes this phenomenon through the example of asking his students to describe in a phenomenological way, the experience of skydiving. A percentage of the class described in the here-body and gave a relatively full sensorial account that included the feel of the wind in their face and ground rushing towards them gives a sick feeling in the stomach. The rest of the class gave an over-there body account as if spoken in the third person. Ihde describes this as similar to when someone describes an out of body experience; they describe the experience in the "I" context but as

L. IRVING

an observer. This is much the same as the way a person is represented in-world by an avatar. The default viewpoint a person participating in a virtual world is from behind their avatar and is the predominant viewpoint used for general use. This is demonstrated further a little later in this chapter through transcript extracts.

*Avatar Identity as Discourse Identity*

The concept of avatars as expressions of identity has generated considerable interest (see for example Yee, Ducheneaut, Yao, & Nelson, 2011) particularly around large-scale online virtual worlds and gameworlds. The perspective on identity this research takes is that identity is developed and experienced within specific contexts or as Gee (2000, 2001) describes as being a 'kind of person' in a given context. For Gee, everyone has multiple identities that they enact or act through in a specific context.

The relevance of different kinds of identities for this study is that the identity generated by the avatar reflects upon the user (person behind the avatar) or is shaped by the user. While Gee (2000) suggests identity is a useful "analytical lens" to understand education it is also a useful perspective in looking at how avatars extend the identity of the virtual world user, in this case the academic.

Gee offers four categories in which to view identity – nature N-identity, institution I-identity, discourse D-identity and affinity A-identity, however he insists these are not necessarily separate from each other. Gee often uses D-identity with a capital D as in Discourse and it the form used in this chapter. While Discourse identity is most relevant for this research, institution identity would also be relevant for academics because the university bestows or authorizes a certain kind of identity.

*Institution Identity*

Institution identity (I-identity) is an identity authored by an institution and is an identity performed through the discourses associate with that institution (Gee, 2000). For example, the identity of a medical doctor and the power of that identity, are authorized through the discourses associated with the medical institution. This not only refers to a hospital, although the hospital is a central author, but the entire institution of medicine. For academics the institution is a university and a particular position in a university held by the academic influences how others perceive them and indeed equally important, how they perceive themselves. A professor is authored an identity via the institution that has certain rights, privileges, expectations, and so forth.

*Discourse Identity*

Discourse identity with a capital D, is distinguish from discourse that is interaction through language. It is an "identity-kit" and is connected to "being" in the world or ways of being in the world. Gee clarifies this as being in the world and being a kind of person in the world. While Discourse identity incorporates interaction through speaking and writing it has a more complex meaning that encompasses a range of associations, understandings, practices, knowledge, interactions, conventions and so forth. People have multiple identities and multiple life-worlds coinciding with those identities. In a virtual world the academic is an academic avatar in a space and therefore may encounter new or different ways of being an academic through their avatar in a different space. Indeed, technologies are enabling new identities and multiple identities that change the way we think about the world and ourselves (Turkle, 1995).

## EMBODIED PLACE AND IDENTITY

This section addresses the research question that asks, "How do academics experience embodiment in a virtual world". In this study embodiment was experienced by academics through the avatar in a virtual world in two main ways. It was experienced through the shaping of academic identity projected by avatar and through experiencing being or dwelling in the virtual world. In the following sections, quotes from transcripts are indented and presented as extracts in order to highlight the participants' voices so as to ground the findings in the data and also to allow the reader to join in the process of interpreting and making meaning. The names used are fictional in order to preserve the privacy of participants and to personalize rather than represent the participant as a code.

What is evident is an intrinsic connection between corporeal academic and their avatar supporting similar claims of human/avatar connection by others (Blascovich & Bailenson, 2011; Yee & Bailenson, 2007). However, whereas Yee and colleagues take a psycho-behavioral perspective in understanding this connection the findings of this study are framed by post-phenomenological concepts of technology mediation (Ihde, 2002; Verbeek, 2005) where experiences of reality (e.g. the virtual world, relationship with students, teaching) is mediated by the avatar through an embodied extension the academic.

From a phenomenological perspective, all places are embodied because a place does not exist without being existent for someone or somebody (as per Merleau-Ponty, 1962). Within environmental psychology a dimension of a person's identity is experienced through the individual's cognition of the physical world they live in (Lengen & Kistemann, 2012). Place and the production of place is closely linked to identity, which includes identity of place and identity of the person in relation to the place. In some cases, particularly in environmental psychology, this is referred to as place-identity that is a concept initially defined by Proshansky (1976). Place-identity is the intersection of who we are and where we are in the world or rather who is often strongly connect with where we are (Dixon & Durrheim, 2000). Proshansky defines place-identity as "… those dimensions of self that define the individual's personal identity in relation to the physical environment by means of a complex pattern of conscious and unconscious ideas, feelings, values, goals, preferences, skills, and behavioural tendencies relevant to a specific environment" (1978, p. 147). Korpela

L. IRVING

(1989) a recognized as a leader in this field of research insists emotional attachment to place is central to the concept of place-identity.

*Virtual World Places Echoing Concrete Places*

It is often questioned why the environments of 3D virtual worlds resemble the physical world when the options are really only limited by the imagination of the designer. But as Relph (2007) points out "… imagined places have to bear resemblances to real places if they are to be comprehensible" (p. 3). However some find it perplexing when the very learning environments universities are endeavouring to transcend such as classrooms and lecturer theatres are recreated using a 21st century technology such as virtual worlds.

Norman's (2013) well-known work on interface design prioritises a key design principle for the function of something to be easily understood. People search for cues and signs embedded in the design in order to interpret their meaning and purpose. Therefore, classrooms and lecture theatres, pathways and walls are all cues that draw upon what is known to guide activity and interaction until such time suggest Seamon (2014b) and Relph (2007) that a sign system for virtuality is commonly understood. Furthermore, Horan (2000a) suggests digital places need thoughtful design if they are to become meaningful places that and should respect "… functional and symbolic associations" (p. 15).

Twinning and Peachey (2009) point out, that in virtual worlds, rooms and buildings and so forth are not necessary for shelter from the elements; they have no function in this sense. Therefore, the materiality of virtual worlds, the buildings, artefacts, objects and so forth, are signifiers for something. They are used in ways such as to set a scene or invoke a feeling but, because virtual artefacts can also be interactive, they are actionable and agentive. In the transcript extract below, the sign systems of simulated digital artefacts are plumbed so as to establish the backdrop of a figured world that has an expected code of behaviour. The materiality of the virtual space in this case is used, therefore, as a device to support expected behaviour and an expected way of being for students:

> I've got a PowerPoint projector that I can use on slides. I've got a podium in the centre and they've got seats to sit on and I tend to use that, not for long periods of time, but just to set the tone that they're university students here. That we are pursuing an academic objective and that their role is to learn, rather than just to play. But saying that, one of the things I found out is you start off with that and then you teleport down …. (Arthur)

When new practices are built, we often draw on old or established practices (Gee, 2011). Artefacts are drawn from the concept of 'lecture theatre'. The podium references institutional academic power and authority. The lecturer at the podium is the focus of the student mass, the expert divulging knowledge. In virtual worlds, almost anything is possible: people fly, teleport to other lands or places and morph

114

into different forms, but in most cases things in SL replicate or simulate real-world scenes and practices. The idea of authentic experiences of virtual world place as embodied is an interesting dilemma because the avatar only exists in its motile sense within the virtual world and the academic only exists in the concrete world. However, while virtual environments such as Second Life may be deficit in sensorial experience there may be other ways of experiencing place that are equally powerful but in different ways.

For example, the transcript extract above is but one section of the transcript as a whole and, while it strongly orientates towards an identity of control and authority, the whole transcript from this research participant (Arthur) comes across more as an academic who is highly innovative and creative pedagogically. Arthur did not conduct his virtual class in one place but took students to many places throughout SL and was extremely innovative in his pedagogical approach; therefore, he used known cues, for example, the simulated lecture theatre, so as to establish identities for himself and his students in order for appropriate behaviours to be adopted.

*Embodied Professional Identity*

Professional identity is discussed through the lens of embodiment as the cultural and discursive dimensions of being an academic. Ihde's (1990) two main human-technology relations of embodiment and hermeneutic frame the analysis in conjunction with Merleau-Ponty's (1962) perception of embodiment and van Manen's (1990) phenomenological existential dimensions of lived time, embodiment, spatiality and relationship in the academics' experiences. In particular, Gee's (2011) discourse analysis is used as an analytical tool to interpret participant descriptions of professional identity that helped in suspending my own presumptions and biases to focus deeply on what the text was saying.

The professional academic attitude of academics in this study was expressed from two perspectives; through the embodied avatar and the corporeal academic, the real person at the computer interacting with the virtual world. Other researchers have found that the look of the avatar including the body shape and colour and the clothing, has significant consequences for how others see the avatar and make that connection with the corporeal person (see Yee & Bailenson, 2007; Pena et al., 2009; Merola & Pena, 2010; Martey & Consalvo, 2011). For the majority of participants in this current study, presenting a professional academic persona (both appearance and behaviour) was crucial. This was achieved through creating an avatar that looked like them to some extent but most importantly looked and acted like their perceptions of what is meant to be an academic.

The nature of this study is phenomenological, which aims at understanding how a phenomenon is experienced as it is lived. The phenomenal body is the perspective from which the world is experienced as bodily being-in-the-world (Merleau-Ponty, 1962). Therefore, for this research study embodiment is a central focus for understanding how virtual world phenomena are experienced by academics.

Historically, the body has been central in the teaching and learning experience until the recent technological developments enabled distance education on a massive scale through online learning.

Although much of higher education courses are either wholly or partially online these days, the body is seen for many as a central element of the teaching and learning process (see for example, van Manen, 1990; Bresler, 2004; Nguyen & Larson, 2015; Latta & Buck, 2006; Perry & Medina, 2011). Latta and Buck (2006) for example insist that "… embodied teaching and learning is about building relationships between self, others, and subject matter; living in-between these entities" (p. 317).

While new haptic and tangible technologies mean the body is increasingly becoming an interface (Facer, 2011) and advances in virtual reality allow a more tactile, sensorial experience such as those demonstrated through dental education simulations (see Kolesnikov, Zefran, Steinberge, & Bashook, 2009; Bakker, Lagerweij, Wesselink, & Vervoorn, 2010) this is in the future. Moving to a more sensorial embodied experience will be incremental and part of these incremental steps is avatar embodiment in virtual worlds, which allow academics to insert their body back into pedagogical relations in online learning environments. Understanding experiences associated with being an academic avatar will be of benefit in preparing future academics for teaching in these kinds of environments.

*Avatar Embodiment and Academic Identity*

In recent versions, Second Life membership comes with a library of avatars to choose from that can be modified for personalisation. Previously there was a need for technological skills associated with building and scripting to create a professional looking avatar that went beyond using the basic avatar created via the customisation toolset. Professional in this context refers to being a competent and experienced user of Second Life – not a newbie. Academics did not want to appear a newbie and also wanted to present a professional look consistent with being an academic in order to be seen in-world as an academic and a confident user of Second Life. Just as it is important for academics to be confident in the lecture theatre or classroom it is important for their confidence as an academic being in-world to be technically competent with the virtual world interface and avatar and for the physical look of the avatar to signify professionalism.

Therefore, to be professional is to be a competent user of the virtual world technology (Second Life) and for the avatar to have a certain look that reflects the academic corporeal look to some extent in a professional signification. While the corporeal academic is always enmeshed or melded with their avatar in what Gee (2014, p. 94) calls the "projective identity", In post-phenomenology it is not so much about identity but more with being-in-the-world in a way that is mediated by technology through a certain kind of human-technology relation. Analysis reflect my interpretation of data using Gee's (2000, 2004, 2008, 2011, 2014) Discourse analysis to my fully understand the dimensions professional identity and hermeneutic phenomenology and post-phenomenology to understand the sense of being in a virtual world in an experiential, interpretive and technology-mediated way.

The findings of this research indicate there are (at least) three essential elements for professional identity embodied by the avatar; avatar appearances, co-construction with other avatars and the connection or relationship academics have with their avatar. Moreover, the materiality of the avatar signals a reconfiguration of professional identity for academics. The avatar augments their professional identity in the concrete world to some extent but is also a separate academic identity specific to the avatar. Academic avatar identity is governed by the structures of the virtual world, which is a figured world that has different modalities of signification and offers opportunities for different kinds of professional identity and agency.

*Extended Body and Proprioception*

Proprioception is a term often used in medical and physical rehabilitation contexts. In this sense which refers to the sensory information that gives the ability to know of one's position and movement. Body position is perceived both at the conscious and unconscious levels. The information of conscious proprioception is utilized to facilitate complex motor activity, while unconscious proprioception is important to coordinate basic posturing during sitting, standing and simple movement activities (Johnson & Soucacos, 2010).

The sense of extended embodiment was experienced by academics through the avatar, which contributed to their experience of identity and heightened their sense of being there, of co-presence with others and to be socially present. As stated previously, conceptualising extended embodiment is framed by Merleau-Ponty's (1962) perception of body extended schema and Ihde's (2002) embodied human-technology relation, which underpin this study. According to Ihde the technology must become more or less transparent retracting from the persons consciousness; they do not see or feel the technology and so forth.

In many cases it is possible for the technology of the virtual world to recede in consciousness to the extent where that the virtual world in some cases is experienced as a sense of Flow as described by Csikszentmihalyi (1991). Flow was experience more strongly when participants were building and developing in the virtual world, which is discussed later under the heading of Place. However, flow was also experienced through the avatar engaging in activity with artefacts and with other avatars and demonstrates the depth of engagement that is possible. Flow has several features according to Csikszentmahlyi defined as heightened concentration where someone is fully immersed in a process or activity and through which the goals and actions of that activity are challenging and but achievable and involves creativity.

The state of Flow is dependent upon the sense of embodiment the academic has with the avatar, which is in turn dependent upon experiencing proprioception. Proprioception brings in the human technology relations theory underpinning the understanding of embodiment in a virtual world. Proprioception is sensing the perimeters of the body in space and its position and movement through space. The avatar becomes the embodied periphery, the external perimeter of body schema for the corporeal academic and mediates the experiences of teaching, dwelling pedagogically and the pedagogical relationship with their students.

*Avatar Appearance*

Currently it is difficult to obtain a close facial resemblance to a Second Life avatar although some highly skilled digital artists achieve impressive results. A reasonable body resemblance however is relatively easily achieved even for beginner users. It was important for academics in this study to have their avatars to bear some physical resemblance to them. This was not so the students would recognize them because many students did not ever meet the academic in the concrete world. Therefore, it was of personal importance to the academic for their avatar to look like them and had a bearing on building a connection between academic and their avatar. There is a significant distinction between the academic seeing his or herself as the avatar and seeing his or herself represented by the avatar.

This is an important element of teaching in a learning space that is unfamiliar and new. Teaching in a virtual world was a substantial shift for all participants of this research study regardless of their technical ability because the medium is an emerging area. Confidence is critical to the success of teaching in any capacity especially where technologies are involved (see for example Kimball, Stables, Wheeler, Wosniak, & Kelly, 1991; Courneya, 2011) and for academics to connect with their avatar was also connected with their teaching confidence.

Consistent among participants was the need for an academic's avatar to project the appropriate professional identity. It was important for academics' avatars to look a certain way even though each had a different concept of what that look was and what the look meant. To look professional was the aim but professional to a large extent was a subjective interpretation albeit drawing upon shared social and cultural cues. It took considerable time for most academics to be satisfied with their avatar's appearance. Finding a professional look was not an easy task for many and generally a conservative look with business attire being the favoured clothing style. While it was not important for an avatar to look exactly like the academic participant it should look similar to them.

> For starters I always want to look professional, that's always my aim in real life or in Second Life, so as soon as she looked professional, a bit similarish [sic] to me. Some people say she looks like me. I mean she doesn't, she's a lot younger. (Lucy)

Virtual world research indicates the look of the avatar including the body shape and colour and the clothing, has significant consequences for how others see the avatar and how the corporeal person sees them (see Yee & Bailenson, 2007; Pena et al., 2009; Merola & Pena, 2010; Martey & Consalvo, 2011). This current study's findings demonstrates that research participants were acutely aware of how their students saw them and their attire influenced how they saw themselves as professionals.

One participant had difficulty finding his 'academic identity' in his avatar and the experience teaching was uncomfortable and insecure for him. The performative limitations of the avatar restricted this academic's ability to project his natural way of teaching, which was very kinetic. As Irwin (2011) notes, the ability of the avatar is not consistent with the ability of the person operating it. Therefore, although the avatar is an extension of the corporeal academic's embodiment it does not encompass all abilities of the academic. This can present a problem if an academic is an experienced virtual world user and confident in the identity of his avatar in contexts other than being an academic such as social or gaming. This can lead to avatar identity being inadequate and consequently teaching experiences in a virtual world are frustrating and unsuccessful.

There is a significant distinction between the academic seeing themselves as the avatar and seeing themselves represented by the avatar. I have interpreted this as an important element of teaching in a learning space that is unfamiliar and new. Teaching in a virtual world was a substantial shift for all the participants of this research study regardless of their technical ability, because the medium is an emerging area. Confidence is critical to the success of teaching in any capacity, especially where technologies are involved (see, for example, Cunningham & Kimball, 2011; Courneya, 2011), and for academics to connect with their avatar was also connected with their teaching confidence.

*Transient Identities*

While most participants in this research had just the one avatar which they used for professional and social contexts in some instances, participants adopted different avatar identities for given contexts within SL. An extract from Michael's transcript demonstrates the transient nature or fluidity of identity that is a conscious construction of specific cues signifying different kinds of being:

> Identity is really at the centre of shaping your avatar because when you go into role play … you're shifting away from the identity of authority into the identity of diversity. (Michael)

In a teaching context, Michael tends to view the avatar as a practical tool for achieving something, while according to Michael it is a tool for participating in an activity, a cue to be read by students, and is not a state of being. The following extract occurs after discussing a role-playing scenario on diversity and, while Michael once again utilises purposefully constructed identities, he slips into a sense of being there through extended embodiment:

> If you've ever done this before, gone around in Second Life as a person not of your demographic, things happen that you weren't expecting to have happen to

you and I use the wheelchair on purpose, because I offended a lot of people by running around in a wheelchair in Second Life because they were angry at me whether I was really in one or not so – is my identity handicapped?

And:

You don't necessarily have to convey yourself all of the time, especially when you get into role play. (Michael)

The use of language by Michael is consistent with the ways in which other participants talk as if they are doing something in SL rather than the avatar doing something. There is an extended embodiment through the avatar and the experience of motility by "running around in a wheelchair". For example, the first part of the first sentence is directed to me, the researcher, asking if I have done something similar to the participant: "gone around in Second Life". Michael does not pose the question in terms of my avatar, but to me.

Firstly, there is an assumption that my avatar and I are one, just as Michael and his avatar are one. Secondly, "gone around" is a very casual term meaning both to physically move around a space but also to assume a persona or identity with an intention. Michael's use of it encompasses all of these definitions; therefore, he is signifying a geographical navigation of a space in an assumed persona with intent. The intent was to challenge others' perception of a given persona and identity – a person of diversity. It is not the regular persona or identity of his avatar, the one that represents Michael, but a new persona and identity embodied by his avatar.

Moreover, this passage creates a sense of avatar agency and intentionality, which contrasts with phenomenological or philosophical intentionality and simply means having a reason and purpose. The line indicating Michael "offended a lot of people" by "running around in a wheelchair" suggests others in SL place value and trust in avatars as being authentic identities and agents. Michael concludes with "You don't necessarily have to convey yourself all the time", indicating there is a genuine sense of self at times other than in this case, specific learning scenarios that require different personas for role-play. The ability for Michael to quickly switch the identity of his avatar to incorporate a new body shape, colour and so forth is for authenticity in the pedagogic activity, but this also indicates there is a 'true self' for the avatar. The avatar's 'true self' is the avatar identity that Michel and the other participants perceive as their real avatar identity.

### Co-Constructed Identity

Identity is largely a co-construction with others or is shaped by how others perceive us (Blommaert, 2005). We are aware of our body as others see it and experience it (Merleau-Ponty, 1969), which shapes our understanding of ourselves. Other virtual world users see the avatar as the extended embodiment of the academic, which shapes how the academic see himself or herself. The avatar as Pearce (2006, p. 1) notes, has "… the dimensions of both seeing oneself and being seen by others". In this study academic identity was co-constructed through the behaviour of student avatars. When student avatars were behaving in an out of control way that disrupted the class they were shaping the academics identity as someone who is not in control and possibly unprofessional and the academic saw him or herself as thus.

Therefore, the co-construction of identity is through how the academic perceives the student sees them (their avatar) as played out through the student's behaviour. Similarly, students who are engaged in learning and are not disruptive co-shape the academics identity as professional. In the following extract Marco, who is an experienced 3D gamer as well as a teaching academic, experiences a loss of control of his class and in the face of a guest speaker is embarrassed:

> One thing I found in both classes which really surprised me was something that I would definitely take into account before teaching again in Second Life, was giving students a chance to basically blow off steam as avatars, because in both classes, it was in a class session for the first time that the groups had really – while we'd encouraged them to make their avatars on their own, the first time they really experienced the space was in class session and I found [with] the law students it was like having middle schoolers on a field trip. They were just running amuck. We had a guest speaker and I was like 'Oh my gosh, this looks terrible'. (Marco)

Marco taught this class face to face as well as in SL and, while it is unclear if he experienced trouble with face-to-face classroom behaviour, his shock and consternation at their behaviour in SL indicates this was not his usual experience with this class. In this instance there appears to be an inability for students to move beyond their concept of a virtual-world space as an informal, fun place where they can display behaviour consistent with how they act in informal virtual spaces they may inhabit in the social lives. In doing so they are co-constructing Marco's professional identity to by unprofessional, at least in Marco's eyes.

This study's concept avatar identity development is consistent for the most part with Warburton's (2008) mapping of the development of avatar identity; technical competence, threshold of care, schism, managed instability and multiple avatars. Some of which are useful in discussing the identity disruption academics may experience. According to Warburton there are a number of critical points for what he describes as developing a relationship with your avatar. Technical competency is one of the first critical elements need to start to connect with the avatar and 'threshold of care' is a process of building social and cultural capital in building friendships and connections and so forth and actually coming to care about your avatar. What could have been an issue for the academic in this study who experienced frustration through the restricted ability of their avatar is a combination of Warburton's next two elements; schism and managed instability. Schism refers to the tension between multiple roles (or identities) the avatar engages in and 'managed instability'

L. IRVING

is the "… flux between playful and professional modes of in-world existence" (Warburton, 2008, para 6).

A conclusion can be drawn from this section of discussion of academic identity that there is a need for academics to be aware of the intricate nature of academic avatar identity and that if academics have an existing avatar there may be conflicts with that identity and the one they are trying to portray as an academic. According to Warburton (2008) others have found solutions in having multiple avatars, which addresses the issue of managing multiple identities but in turn can bring other issues into the mix and academics need to be aware of this.

This current study contributes to an emerging interest of the avatar/player relationship within the area of games study. Extended embodiment as phenomenal body and proprioception is gaining increasing interest as an area of research within the philosophy of games. Martin (2012) for example discusses the game avatar as a phenomenal extended body after Merleau-Ponty's (1945, 1962) theory but also in terms of a prosthetic, which is not a direction I take with this research. Peachy and Childs (2011) approach avatars from the prosthetic perspective also however, this does account for the deep connection and sense of identity participants in this current study had with their avatar. The perspective I take, which is a perspective shared by Norgard (2011), is that the avatar is taken into the player's body schema not as a prosthetic extension.

Others have researched avatar embodiment but in different contexts and perspectives from this research study. Puvirajah and Calandra (2015) for example, use a case study approach to examine the embodied experience of a teacher as part of a teacher preparation program. The student teacher enacts being a teacher through role-play scenario in a virtual world. Puvirajah and Calndra approach the extended body as embodied cognition and associate it more in terms of with a Cartesian mind body/split where the mind is project into the 3D space and into the avatar. This perspective where the avatar is a projection of an identity is pursed by others particularly within the context of video games (see Hutchinson, 2007; Filiciak, 2003) or cyborg-like extensions (Cleland, 2010) and prosthetics 9. These examples differ from this current research study's perspective that argues the avatar is embodied by the corporeal person and is part of the academic's body schema.

*Embodied Skills*

Experiencing embodiment through the avatar allowed academics to interact with artefacts in the virtual world and experience pedagogic activity. Most of the literature on extended embodiment is in a corporeal concrete world sense however; theoretically these concepts apply to the avatar in the virtual world being the extended embodiment of the corporeal academic. Brey (2000) offers an observation on Merleau-Ponty's (1962) embodied relations and artefacts that are useful in understanding the ways in which the avatar as the extended body engages with the virtual world.

VIRTUAL WORLDS IN HIGHER EDUCATION

Brey notes that artefacts can mediate two kinds of motor skills that are taken into the body schema as "… a medium through which motor skills are expressed" (Brey, 2000, p. 9); as navigational and interactive. Merleau-Ponty's concept of the body schema described in terms of the way in which a feather on a woman's hat is taken into the body schema; the woman navigates her environment without damaging the feather in her hat through sensing the feather as part of her body schema, as described earlier, is a navigational motor skill according to Brey.

The ability for the avatar to manoeuvre about the virtual world 3D landscape and architecture involves proprioception – and is akin to the feather in the woman's hat in that knowing the spatial relations of the avatar as if it were one's own body. Interactive skills are used generally with handheld tools and Brey uses examples such as hammer and remote control and so forth. While interactive and navigational motor skills are in corporeal contexts.

The findings from the current study suggest the avatar is an embodied artefact in that it allows the corporeal person to navigate the virtual world and interact with virtual world artefacts to experience that world in a certain way – mediated through the avatar. Embodying an avatar incorporates both navigation and interactive motor skills in order for the avatar to operate in an unencumbered way through the dextrous use of input devices – keyboard and mouse for example. The input devices control the spatial and sensorial motor skills that are experienced by the corporeal academic via the avatar.

Virtual worlds are not experienced in the full sensorial modality possible in our physical world however Egoyan (2007) suggests the virtual world is experienced as performance rather than sensation. The virtual embodiment through an avatar is experienced through proprioception – the ability to sense the position and location and orientation and movement of the body and its parts. This perspective is of interest for a number of researchers of human interaction design exploring the nexus of body and technology interactions. Larssen and colleagues (Larrsen, Robertson, & Edwards, 2007) for example introduce a feel dimension to interaction design that incorporates knowledge of one's body orientation in space and its relation to things in space with the body as reference point.

This perspective is gaining popularity among embodied game designers where game interaction is a bodily experience. The introduction of Nintendo Wii® has brought embodied game interaction to the general public on a large scale through console-based interfaces where physical bodily gestures interact with game elements. The rise of mobile games, particularly those using geographic information systems (GIS) bring another level to embodied games creating hybrid spaces that combine virtual and physical spaces (Farman, 2013; Richardson, 2011; Irving & Hoffman, 2014) engaging bodily movement through spaces while interacting with virtual artefacts.

Others have researched avatar embodiment but in a different contexts and perspectives from this research study. Puvirajah and Calandra (2015) use a case study approach to examine the embodied experience of a teacher as part of a teacher

L. IRVING

preparation program. This is in a role-play scenario where a student teacher enacts being a teacher. This perspective where the avatar is a projection of an identity is pursed by others particularly within the context of video games (see Hutchinson, 2007; Fliciak, 2003). Some researchers pursue the idea of cyborg-like extensions (Cleland 2010; Becker, 2000), the effect of avatar appearance in computer-mediated interviews (Behrend et al., 2012) and avatar behaviour (Yee, 2007). Each of these areas has overlaps with the direction I have pursued but my findings are quite distinctive in having a specific phenomenological approach with a pedagogical focus.

*Dwelling as an Extended Intentional being through One's Avatar*

Dwelling is a key theme of phenomenological study. To dwell is to be fully immersed, to dwell in a place and to dwell in a specific state; to dwell in the state of pedagogy, to dwell in the state of creativity, to dwell in the state of caring. I use the concept to dwell in a place in the phenomenological sense of a state of being as in Bachelard's (1964) human space rather than dimensional space. Dwelling in a virtual place, as an avatar is an experience of extended embodiment, which I argue can be understood as a combination consistent with Ihde's (2002) embodied human-technology and Merleau-Ponty's (1962).

Briefly alterity human–technology relation is embodied in that the technology is taken into the corporeal body, not as a concrete technological artefact but as a digital artefact that is taken in at an emotional level. Ihde (1990) asserts that it is not possible (at the moment) to have a fully sensorial embodied experience in virtual environments however I argue that just as Ihde states that when certain technologies mediated experience one aspect phenomenon is heightened at the same time as diminishing other aspects the limitations of a virtual world work in a similar way. Dwelling is integral to experiencing the extended body and to dwell in a virtual place *that is demonstrated through transcript extracts below*, is seemingly not possible without the connection of with the avatar as extended body.

*Live Experience: Time, Place Relations and Embodiment*

The existential dimensions of phenomenological lived experience are being an academic in a virtual world through an avatar, as well as being a corporeal academic. The avatar here is an extension of what Ihde (2002) calls the here-body (the all-sensing corporeal body) and the over-there-body (disembodied). In the following statement, Lucy is describing a typical class in SL that is held at 7.30 in the evening, Australian Eastern Standard Time. Most of Lucy's students are in the Asia–Pacific region, but many are also from Europe. None are from the Americas, because the time difference makes synchronous interaction difficult:

For most of them, they've probably had their meal, they've put their young kids to bed if that's what they've got. Actually that's another thing that I've

124

noticed is the conversations, they go 'Oh, my child's sitting on my lap'. You can't do that even in a real workshop, or 'Hold on, my child's just awake, I'll just go and settle them'. You couldn't do that, you wouldn't even know they were unsettled, but you can do that in those circumstances. (Lucy)

The lived time for the academic and students is different. Lived time and space are two phenomenological existentials (van Manen, 1990). The lived time of the academic involves an hour of time set aside in the evening that for her would normally be the time for domesticity; preparing and eating a meal with her family, relaxing and winding down from the day's academic activity, reading or watching television. However, in order to have a class time to suit off-campus students, this normally domestic time is instead an hour of professional academic activity. The students' lived time overlaps domesticity and mothering, with lived time for being a student and the activity of academic lived time. Lucy acknowledges this in pointing out the uniqueness of this overlap for students. This overlap of lived time and lived space, and indeed the other existentials of lived relationship and lived corporeality (embodiment), is experienced by the academic in the following extract from Arthur's transcript:

I do find that there is a group of students who are more willing to come up and ask me questions in Second Life than they are willing to line up at the end of class and come up and ask me questions in real life, so it's a nice opportunity for them to log in and they can ask me questions. I do usually have most of my slides that I teach during the day loaded in Second Life, so I can quickly pull those out and we can look at a slide and I can explain a particular topic or something like that ... while I'm sitting on the couch watching TV, or whatever, and can help students answer questions and help them with particular things that they're doing. (Arthur)

The lived time and space for Arthur is overlapping professional and domestic time and place. The lived space is both a comfortable couch in front of the TV and also "there" which refers to the material space of SL that is inhabited by his avatar. The lived relation is in this case between academic and student and is one of caring. The lived embodiment or corporeality is experienced through the motile, emotive and perceptual body (the here-body) (Ihde, 2002) and the extended here-body that is the avatar.

These two entities are not entirely separate and, just as Gee (2011, 2014a, 2014b) states that there is a melding of identity between the corporeal body and the avatar, so too do the here-body and the extended here-body overlap. An interesting dimension of this finding is the double mediation through which this relationship is experienced; this is not to be confused with a similar term used in family law courts as a means of dispute resolution. I use the term 'double mediation' to make sense of the relationship between academic and student, which is mediated by each avatar via the corporeal academic and the corporeal student.

The findings of this study demonstrates that academics are able to incorporate a thoughtful, caring pedagogy in a virtual world learning space and that being an academic is a central and essential role without being teacher-centred. Unlike online learning that is dominated by asynchronous learning management systems where connecting pedagogically with students is difficult, the virtual world provides a synchronous learning space which academics co-habit with students, moreover in a collegial way. The double mediation, a term I use to describe the academic mediated by the avatar interacting with the student mediated by their avatar, creates closeness through distance. The distance is being together twice removed. Therefore, while much of the literature examining virtual worlds for teaching and learning is focused on learning design and pedagogical approaches (see Salmon, 2009; Stoerger, 2012; Whitton 2012; Boulos et al., 2007) this is generally from the student perspective or learning affordances and academics do not feature strongly. This is not to advocate for teacher-centred pedagogy but to caution that we do not lose sight of the significant role academic play in the pedagogical process, which can be supported by virtual worlds.

This study reveals an intrinsic connection between the corporeal academic and their avatar, supporting similar claims of human/avatar connections (Blascovich & Bailenson, 2011; Yee & Bailenson, 2007). However, whereas Yee and colleagues take a psycho-behavioural perspective in understanding this connection, the current study is framed by post-phenomenological concepts of technology mediation (Ihde, 2002; Verbeek, 2005) where *experiences* of reality (e.g. the virtual world, relationships with students, teaching) are mediated by the avatar through an embodied extension of the academic. Embodiment was experienced by academics through their avatars in a virtual world in two main ways. It was experienced through the shaping of academic identity projected by the avatar and through experiencing *being* or dwelling in the virtual world.

There are (at least) three essential elements for professional identity embodied by the avatar: avatar appearance, co-construction with other avatars and the connection or relationship academics have with their avatar. Moreover, the materiality of the avatar signals a reconfiguration of professional identity for academics. The avatar augments their professional identity in the concrete world to some extent, but is also a separate academic identity specific to the avatar. Academic avatar identity is governed by the structures of the virtual world, which is a figured world that has different modalities of signification and offers opportunities for different kinds of professional identity and agency.

## REFERENCES

Bachelard, G. (1994). *The poetics of space* (M. Jolas, Trans.). Boston, MA: Beacon Press.

Bakker, D., Lagerweij, M., Wesselink, P., & Vervoorn, M. (2010). Transfer of manual dexterity skills acquired in the simodont, a dental haptic trainer with a virtual environment, to reality: A pilot study. *Bio-Algorithms and Med-Systems, 6*(11), 21–24.

Blascovich, J., & Bailenson, J. N. (2011). *Infinite reality: The hidden blueprint of our virtual lives.* New York, NY: Harper Collins.

## VIRTUAL WORLDS IN HIGHER EDUCATION

Blommaert, J. (2005). *Discourse: A critical introduction*. Cambridge: Cambridge University Press.

Bresler, L. (2004). *Knowing bodies, moving minds: Towards embodied teaching and learning*. Dordrecht: Kluwer Academic Publishers.

Brey, P. (2000). Technology and embodiment in Ihde and Merleau-Ponty. In C. Mitcham (Ed.), *Metaphyscis, epistemology, and technology: Research in philosophy and technology* (Vol. 19). London: Elsevier/JAI Press.

Cleland, K. (2010). Prosthetic bodies and virtual cyborgs. *Second Nature, 3*, 72–99. Retrieved from http://www.kathycleland.com/wp-content/uploads/Cleland_Prosthetic_Bodies.pdf

Courneya, C. A. (2011). On teaching confidence and creativity. *Medical Education, 45*(11), 1070–1071. doi:10.1111/j.1365-2923.2011.04130.x

Csikszentmihalyi, M. (1991). *Flow: The psychology of optimal experience*. New York, NY: Harper Collins.

Cunningham, C. A., & Harrison, K. (2011). The affordances of second life for education. In G. Vincenti & J. Braman (Eds.), *Teaching through multi-user virtual environments: Applying dynamic elements to the modern classroom* (pp. 94–119). Hershey, PA: IGI Global.

Dixon, J., & Durrheim, K. (2000). Displacing place-identity: A discursive approach to locating self and other. *British Journal of Social Psychology, 39*(1), 27–44.

Ducheneaut, N., We, M.-H., Yee, N., & Wadley, G. (2009). *Body and mind: A study of avatar personalization in three virtual worlds*. Paper presented at the Proceedings of the SIGCHI Conference on Human Factors in Computing Systems, Boston, MA.

Egoyan, M. (2007). *Virtual embodiment*. Retrieved from http://embodiedresearch.blogspot.com.au/2007/12/virtual-embodiment.html

Facer, K. (2011). *Learning futures: Education, technology and social change*. New York, NY: Routledge.

Farman, J. (2013). *The mobile story: Narrative practices with locative technologies*. Hoboken, NJ: Taylor & Francis.

Filiciak, M. (2003). Hyperidentities: Postmodern identity patterns in massively multiplayer online role-playing games. In M. J. Wolf & B. Perron (Eds.), *The video game theory reader*. New York, NY: Routledge.

Gee, J. P. (2000). Identity as an analytic lens for research in education. *Review of Research in Education, 25*, 99–125.

Gee, J. P. (2003). *What do video games have to teach us about learning and literacy?* New York, NY: Palgrave Macmillan.

Gee, J. P. (2004). *Situated language and learning: A critique of traditional schooling*. New York, NY: Routledge.

Gee, J. P. (2005a). Semiotic social spaces and affinity spaces: From the age of mythology to today's schools. In D. Barton & K. Tusting (Eds.), *Beyond communities of practice: language, power, and social context* (pp. 214–232). New York, NY: Cambridge University Press.

Gee, J. P. (2007). *What video games have to teach us about learning and literacy*. New York, NY: Palgrave Macmillan.

Gee, J. P. (2008). *Social linguistics and literacies: ideology in discourses* (3rd ed.). Abingdon: Routledge.

Gee, J. P. (2011). *An introduction to discourse analysis: Theory and method* (3rd ed.). New York, NY: Routledge.

Gee, J. P. (2014a). *Unified discourse analysis: Language, reality, virtual worlds and video games*. Retrieved from http://CURTIN.eblib.com.au/patron/FullRecord.aspx?p=1715785

Gee, J. P. (2014b). *How to do discourse analysis: A toolkit* (2nd ed.). Hoboken, NJ: Taylor & Francis.

Goldberg, H., Christensen, A., Flash, T., Giese, M. A., & Malach, R. (2015). Brain activity correlates with emotional perception induced by dynamic avatars. *NeuroImage, 122*, 306–317.

Heidegger, M. (1962). *Being and time* (J. Macquarie & E. Robinson, Trans.). Oxford: Blackwell.

Horan, T. A. (2000a). *Digital places: Building our city of bits*. Washington, DC: ULI-the Urban Land Institute.

Ihde, D. (1990). *Technology and the life world: From garden to earth*. Bloomington, IN: Indiana University Press.

Ihde, D. (1998). *Expanding hermeneutics: Visualism in science*. Evanston, IL: Northwestern University Press.

Ihde, D. (2002). *Bodies in technology* (Vol. 5). Minneapolis, MN: University of Minnesota Press.

L. IRVING

Ihde, D. (2009). *Postphenomenology and technoscience: The Pekin university lectures.* New York, NY: SUNY Press.

Ihde, D. (2011a). Stretching the in-between: Embodiment and beyond. *Foundations of Science, 16*(2–3), 109–118. doi:10.1007/s10699-010-9187-6

Ihde, D. (Producer). (2011b). *Embodiment and multi-stability* [video]. Retrieved from https://vimeo.com/49101825

Ihde, D., & Selinger, E. (2003). *Chasing technoscience: Matrix for materiality.* Bloomington, IN: Indiana University Press.

Irving, L., & Hoffman, J. (2014). *Nyungar place stories pilot: Using augmented reality for indigenous cultural sustainability.* Paper presented at the Ascilite, Dunedin.

Johnson, E. O., & Soucacos, P. N. (2010). Proprioception. In J. H. Stone & M. Blouin (Eds.), *International encyclopedia of rehabilitation.* Retrieved from http://cirrie.buffalo.edu/encyclopedia/en/article/337/

Kennedy, G. E., Dalgarno, B., Gray, K., Judd, T. S., Waycott, J., Bennett, S., Maton, K., Krause, K.-L., Bishop, A., Chang, R., & Churchward, A. (2007). *The net generation are not big users of web 2.0 technologies: Preliminary findings.* Paper presented at the ICT, Providing choices for learners and learning, Ascilite, Singapore.

Kennedy, G. E., Judd, T. S., Churchward, A., & Gray, K. (2008). First year students' experiences with technology: Are they really ditical natives? *Australasian Journal of Educational Technology, 24*(1), 108–122.

Keppell, M., & Riddle, M. (2012). Distributed learning spaces: Physical, blended and virtual learning spaces in higher education. In M. Keppell, K. Souter, & M. Riddle (Eds.), *Physical and virtual learning spaces in higher education: Concepts for the modern learning environment* (pp. 1–20). Hershey, PA: IGI Global.

Kolesnikov, M., Zefran, M., Steinberg, A. D., & Bashook, P. G. (2009). *PerioSim: Haptic virtual reality simulator for sensorimotor skill acquisition in dentistry.* Paper presented at the IEEE International Conference on Robotics and Automation (ICRA 2009), Kobe, Japan.

Korpela, K. M. (1989). Place-identity as a product of environment self-regulation. *Journal of Environmental Psychology, 9*, 241–256.

Larssen, A. T., Roberston, T., & Edwards, J. (2007). *The feel dimension of technology interaction: Exploring tangibles through movement and touch.* Paper presented at the Proceedings of Tangible and Embedded Interaction, Baton Rouge, LA.

Latta, M. M., & Buck, G. (2008). Enfleshing embodiment: "Falling into trust" with the body's role in teaching and learning. *Educational Philosophy and Theory, 40*(2), 315–329. doi:10.1111/j.1469-5812.2007.00333.x

Lengen, C., & Kistemann, T. (2012). Sense of place and place identity: Review of neuroscientific evidence. *Health & Place, 18*(5), 1162–1171. Retrieved from http://dx.doi.org/10.1016/j.healthplace.2012.01.012

Mancini, M., Ermilov, A., Castellano, G., Liarokapis, F., Varni, G., & Peters, C. (2014). Effects of gender mapping on the perception of emotion from upper body movement in virtual characters. In R. Shumaker & S. Lackey (Eds.), *Virtual, augmented and mixed reality: Designing and developing virtual and augmented environments* (Vol. 8525, pp. 263–273). Cham: Springer International Publishing.

Martey, R. M., & Consalvo, M. (2011). Performing the looking-glass self: Avatar appearance and group identity in second life. *Popular Communication: The International Journal of Media and Culture, 9*(3), 165–180.

Martin, P. (2012). *A phenomenological account of the playing body in avatar based action games.* Paper presented at the 6th International Conference on the Philosophy of Computer Games, Madrid. Retrieved from http://youtube.com/watch?v=qb5jeF-UcX0

Merleau-Ponty, M. (1962). *Phenomenology of perception.* London: Routledge & K. Paul. [original 1945]

Merola, N., & Peña, J. (2010). The effects of avatar appearance in virtual worlds. *Journal for Virtual Worlds Research, 2*(5). doi:10.4101/jvwr.v2i5.843

Nguyen, D., & Larson, J. (2015). Don't forget about the body: Exploring the curricular possibilities of embodied pedagogy. *Innovative Higher Education, 40*(4), 331–344. doi:10.1007/s10755-015-9319-6

Norgard, R. T. (2011, April 6–9). *The joy of doing: The corporeal connection in player-avatar identity.* Proceedings of the Philosophy of Computer Games Conference, Athens, Greece. Retrieved from https://gameconference2011.files.wordpress.com/2010/10/thejoy1.pdf

128

VIRTUAL WORLDS IN HIGHER EDUCATION

Norman, D. A. (2013). *The design of everyday things: Revised and expanded edition.* New York, NY: Basic Books.

Peachey, A., & Childs, M. (2011). *Reinventing ourselves: Contemporary concepts of identity in virtual worlds.* Dordrecht: Springer.

Pearce, C. (2006a). *Communities of play: The social construction of identity in persistent online game worlds.* Retrieved from http://homes.lmc.gatech.edu/~cpearce3/PearcePubs/PearceSP-Final.pdf

Perry, M., & Medina, C. (2011). Embodiment and performance in pedagogy research: Investigating the possibility of the body in curriculum experience. *Journal of Curriculum Theorizing, 27*(3), 62–75.

Proshansky, H., Ittelson, W., & Rivlin, L. (Eds.). (1976). *Environmental psychology: People and their physical settings* (2nd ed.). Oxford: Holt.

Puvirajah, A., & Calandra, B. (2015). Embodied experiences in virtual worlds role-play as a conduit for novice teacher identity exploration: A case study. *Identity, 15*(1), 23–47. doi:10.1080/15283488.201 4.989441

Relph, E. C. (2007). Spirit of place and sense of place in virtual realities. *Techne: Research in Philosophy and Technology, 10*(3), 17–25.

Richardson, I. (2011). The hybrid ontology of mobile gaming. *Convergence: The International Journal of Research into New Media Technologies, 17*(4), 419–430.

Seamon, D. (2014b). Physical and virtual environments: Meaning of place and space. In B. A. Boyt Schell, G. Gillen, M. E. Scaffa, & E. S. Cohn (Eds.), *Willard and Spackman's occupational therapy 12th edition* (pp. 202–215). Baltimore, MD: Lippincot Williams and Wilkins.

Steptoe, W., Steed, A., & Slater, M. (2013). Human tails: Ownership and control of extended humanoid avatars. *IEEE Transactions on Visualization and Computer Graphics, 19*(4), 583–590.

Stoerger, S. (2012). Breaking away: How virtual worlds impact pedagogical practices. In Y. Harrison Hao & Y. Steve Chi-Yin (Eds.), *Handbook of research on practices and outcomes in virtual worlds and environments* (pp. 431–450). Hershey, PA: IGI Global.

Thomas, D., & Brown, J. S. (2009). Why virtual worlds can matter. *International Journal of Learning and Media, 1*(1), 37–49. doi:10.1162/ijlm.2009.0008

Turkle, S. (1995). *Life on the screen: Identity in the age of the internet.* New York, NY: Simon & Schuster.

Twining, P., & Peachey, A. (2009). Open virtual worlds as pedagogical research tools: Learning from the schome park programme. In A. Tatnall & A. Jones (Eds.), *Education and technology for a better world.* New York, NY: Springer.

Van Manen, M. (1990). *Researching lived experience: Human science for an action sensitive pedagogy/ Max Van Manen.* Albany, NY: State University of New York Press.

van Manen, M. (2014). *Phenomenology of practice: Meaning-giving methods in phenomenological research and writing.* Walnut Creek, CA: Left Coast Press.

Verbeek, P.-P. (2001). Don Ihde: The technological lifeworld. In H. Achterhuis (Ed.), *American philosophy of technology: The empirical turn* (pp. 119–146). Bloomington, IN: Indiana University Press.

Verbeek, P.-P. (2005). *What things do: Philosophical reflections on technology, agency, and design/ Peter-Paul Verbeek* (R. P. Crease, Trans.). University Park, PA: Pennsylvania State University Press.

Verbeek, P.-P. (2008). Cyborg intentionality: Rethinking the phenomenology of human–technology relations. *Phenomenology and the Cognitive Sciences, 7*(3), 387–395. doi:10.1007/s11097-008-9099-x

Wainwright, G. (2010). *Understand body language.* London: Hodder Education.

White, J., & Gardner, J. (2013). *The classroom x-factor: The power of body language and non-verbal communication in teaching.* New York, NY: Routledge.

Warburton, S. (2008). *Loving your avatar: Identity, immersion and empathy.* Retrieved from http://warburton.typepad.com/liquidlearning/2008/01/loving-your-ava.html

Warburton, S. (2009). Second life in higher education: Assessing the potential for and the barriers to deploying virtual worlds in learning and teaching. *British Journal of Educational Technology, 40*(3), 414–426. doi:10.1111/j.1467-8535.2009.00952.x

Westberry, N., McNaughton, S., Billot, J., & Gaeta, H. (2013). *Lost in space: Physically, virtually, and pedagogically.* Paper presented at the Research and Development in Higher Education, The Place of Learning and Teaching, Auckland, New Zealand.

Whitton, N., & Moseley, A. (2012). *Using games to enhance learning and references 360 teaching: A beginner's guide*. New York, NY: Routledge.

Yee, N., & Bailenson, J. N. (2007). The proteus effect: The effect of transfored self-represtnation on behaviour. *Human Communication Research, 33*(3), 271–290.

Yee, N., Bailenson, J. N., & Ducheneaut, N. (2009). The proteus effect. *Communication Research, 36*(2), 285–312. doi:10.1177/0093650208330254

Yee, N., Ellis, J., & Ducheneaut, N. (2008). The tyranny of embodiment. *Artifact, 2*(2), 88–93. doi:10.1080/17493460903020398

PANAYIOTIS SKORDI AND BARRY J. FRASER

# 7. THE ASSESSMENT OF THE PSYCHOSOCIAL LEARNING ENVIRONMENT OF UNIVERSITY STATISTICS CLASSROOMS

## ABSTRACT

This chapter draws on the field of learning environments and focusses on some of the pedagogical, social and psychological aspects of classroom environments associated with the design of university settings. Although most past learning environment research has focused on school settings, this chapter applies these research traditions to the teaching and learning of university-level statistics. With a sample of 375 students studying business statistics at a university in California, we developed and validated a questionnaire to assess student perceptions of psychosocial aspects of their classroom environments (e.g. teacher support, involvement, task orientation and equity) and investigated some determinants of classroom environment (sex, age, ethnicity) and some effects of classroom environment on student outcomes (achievement, enjoyment, statistics anxiety).

## LITERATURE REVIEW

By the time students graduate from university, they have spent nearly 20,000 hours in educational institutions (Fraser, 2001). Although historically evaluation in education has been based on achievement outcomes, evaluating the educational environment provides the opportunity to identify and correct weaknesses so that maximum benefit can be achieved by both teachers and students.

Classroom environment research built on the pioneering independent foundations laid by Moos and Walberg that was carried out over 40 years ago and which, in turn, was influenced by the theoretical contributions of Lewin (1936), Murray (1938) and Pace and Stern (1958). Moos' research led to the development of the Classroom Environment Scale CES (Moos & Trickett, 1974), whereas Walberg developed the Learning Environment Inventory LEI (Walberg & Anderson, 1968). Because this ground-breaking work recognised that students' perceptions are important social and psychological factors in classrooms, the classroom environment was evaluated through the eyes of the students (Fraser, 1986, 2012).

An enduring scheme for classifying human environments into three dimensions was developed by Moos (1974). *Relationship Dimensions* identify the nature and intensity of personal relationships within the environment and assess the extent to which people

© KONINKLIJKE BRILL NV, LEIDEN, 2019 | DOI: 10.1163/9789004391598_009

are involved in the environment. *Personal Development Dimensions* assess the basic directions along which personal growth and self-enhancement tend to occur. *System Maintenance and System Change* involve the extent to which the environment is orderly, clear in expectations, maintains control and is responsive to change.

Even though some learning environment research was carried out at the institutional level in higher education (Halpin & Croft, 1963; Pace & Stern, 1958; Stern, 1970), relatively little research had been undertaken at the classroom level in higher education. One possible explanation is that very few suitable instruments exist to assist with the research. This gave rise to the development of the College and University Classroom Environment Inventory (CUCEI) for use in small classes of up to 30 students (Fraser & Treagust, 1986; Fraser, Treagust & Dennis, 1986). However, no specific instruments have been developed to assess learning environments for university business statistics, which are predominantly taught using a combination of computer laboratories and lectures.

*Instruments for Assessing Classroom Environment*

Because Walberg's LEI and Moos' CES were intended for teacher-centred classrooms, the Individualised Classroom Environment Questionnaire (ICEQ) was developed for assessing those dimensions that distinguish individualised from conventional classrooms (Fraser, 1982, 1990). The final published version of the ICEQ contains 50 items (10 items in each of 5 scales called Personalisation, Participation, Independence, Investigation and Differentiation). The five possible frequency responses are Almost Never, Seldom, Sometimes, Often and Very Often.

The Science Laboratory Environment Inventory (SLEI) was created to assess the uniqueness of science laboratory classes at the senior-high school or higher-education levels (Fraser & McRobbie, 1995). It contains 35 items (7 items in each of its five scales of Student Cohesiveness, Open-Endedness, Integration, Rule Clarity and Material Environment). The SLEI was field tested and validated using a sample of over 5,447 students in 269 classes in six different countries, namely, the USA, Canada, England, Israel, Australia and Nigeria, and then cross-validated with a sample of 1,594 students in 92 classes in Australia by Fraser and McRobbie (1995).

Also the SLEI was cross-validated in Singapore with 497 tenth grade students from three independent schools (Quek, Wong, & Fraser, 2005) and a sample of 1,592 tenth grade students (Wong & Fraser, 1995), in Korea using a sample of 439 high school students (Fraser & Lee, 2009) and in the USA with 761 high-school biology students in Florida (Lightburn & Fraser, 2007).

The Constructivist Learning Environment Survey (CLES) assists teachers and researchers to assess the degree to which a classroom's environment is consistent with the constructivist view and to assist teachers to reflect on their epistemological assumptions and reshape their teaching practice (Taylor, Fraser, & Fisher, 1997). It contains 35 items (7 items in each of its 5 scales) with the five possible frequency responses of Almost Never, Seldom, Sometimes, Often and Almost Always.

The scales are called Personal Relevance, Uncertainty, Critical Voice, Shared Control and Student Negotiation. The CLES has been cross-validated by Nix, Fraser, and Ledbetter (2005) with 1079 students in 59 science classes in North Texas, by Aldridge, Fraser, Taylor, and Chen (2000) with 1081 students in 50 classes in Australia and 1879 students in 50 classes in Taiwan, and by Aldridge, Fraser and Sebela (2004) with 1864 grade 4–6 mathematics learners in 43 classes in South Africa.

Because the What Is Happening In this Class? (WIHIC) was used in our study, it is described in more detail here. The extensiveness of research using the WIHIC is reflected in reviews by Khine et al. (in press) and Fraser (2012). Khine and colleagues tabulated 24 studies in which the WIHIC had been used in Australia, China, Greece, Indonesia, Israel, Jordan, Qatar, Singapore, Turkey, Uganda, the United Arab Emirates and the USA. Fraser (2012) tabulated 21 studies in which the WIHIC had been used in Australia, Taiwan, UK, Canada, Indonesia, Singapore, India, South Africa, Korea, the United Arab Emirates and the USA (California, New York and Florida).

Many researchers have incorporated into their research only those WIHIC scales which are most salient for their particular study. For example, based on the WIHIC, Aldridge, Laugksch, Seopa and Fraser (2006) developed and validated the Outcomes-Based Learning Environment Questionnaire (OBLEQ) in the South African Sepedi language, which includes four scales from the WIHIC. The OBLEQ was used to monitor the implementation of outcomes-based classroom instruction in South Africa. Giallousi, Gialamas, Spyrellis, and Pavlatou (2010) developed and validated the How Chemistry Class is Working (HCCW) questionnaire using two WIHIC scales. When the HCCW was administered in Greece and Cyprus in the Greek language, more positive classroom environment perceptions were found among Cypriot students than Greek students.

The Technology-Rich Outcomes-Focused Learning Environment Inventory (TROFLEI) incorporates a wide range of dimensions which were important when using ICT program delivery in a new post-secondary school. Specifically, the TROFLEI incorporates all of the WIHIC's seven scales in addition to the three further important scales of Differentiation, Computer Usage and Young Adult Ethos. The TROFLEI has both actual and preferred forms, is responded to on a five–point frequency scale (Almost Never, Seldom, Sometimes, Often and Almost Always) and was validated with a sample of 2,317 students from grade 11 and 12 classes from Western Australia and Tasmania (Aldridge & Fraser, 2008).

The Constructivist-Oriented Learning Environment Survey (COLES) (Aldridge, Fraser, Bell, & Dorman, 2012) provides teachers with feedback from students regarding their perceptions of teachers' teaching practices in order to allow teachers to make changes to improve the learning environment. The COLES includes six scales from the WIHIC (leaving out only the Investigation scale), Differentiation from the ICEQ, Young Adult Ethos from the TROFLEI, and Personal Relevance from the CLES.

P. SKORDI AND B. J. FRASER

The most distinctive feature of COLES is the inclusion of two new scales related to assessment: Formative Assessment (extent to which students feel that their assessment tasks make a positive contribution to their learning); and Assessment Criteria (extent to which assessment criteria are explicit and known so that the basis for judgements is transparent). The validity and reliability for the COLES were established using a sample of 2043 grade 11 and 12 students from 147 classes in Western Australia (Aldridge et al., 2012).

*Past Research on Learning Environments*

The applications of learning environment assessments in past educational research and educational psychology are reviewed by Fraser (2012, 2014) and Burden and Fraser (1993). Selected applications are described below.

*Associations between student outcomes and environment.* Fraser (1994) tabulated 40 past studies showing that associations between student outcome measures and learning environment perceptions have been replicated for a variety of cognitive and affective outcomes, classroom environment instruments and samples ranging across countries and grade levels. Using the aforementioned SLEI, associations between classroom environment and cognitive and affective outcomes were found for high-school chemistry classes in Australia using the SLEI (Fraser & McRobbie, 1995; McRobbie & Fraser, 1993), senior-high school biology students in Australia (Fisher, Henderson, & Fraser, 1997) and chemistry students in Singapore (Wong & Fraser, 1996).

Teh and Fraser (1995) conducted a study in Singapore using high-school geography students in computer-assisted instruction classrooms and found associations between classroom environment, achievement and attitudes. Associations were found between student outcomes and perceived patterns of teacher–student interaction using the Questionnaire on Teacher Interaction (QTI) for Australian high-school biology students (Fisher, Henderson, & Fraser 1995) and primary-school mathematic students in Singapore (Goh & Fraser, 2000). Fraser and Butts (1982) reported links between the classroom environment and science students' attitudes.

*Evaluation of educational innovations.* Classroom environment instruments can be used to evaluate educational innovations. For example, students reported that, after the introduction of a computerised database, their classes became more inquiry oriented (Maor & Fraser, 1996). Classroom environment measures were used in Singapore for evaluating computer-assisted learning innovations (Teh & Fraser, 1995) and computer application courses for adults (Khoo & Fraser, 2008). In the USA, Spinner and Fraser (2005) evaluated an innovative mathematics program in terms of learning environment criteria.

An evaluation of a teacher professional development program in Texas involved 445 students in 25 classes using an innovative form of the CLES which had a

134

side-by-side response format so that students could provide their perceptions of THIS classroom and OTHER classroom. Students of teachers who had experienced the professional development (THIS classroom) perceived higher levels of Personal Relevance and Uncertainty relative to the comparison classes (OTHER classroom) (Nix, Fraser, & Ledbetter, 2005).

Lightburn and Fraser (2007) involved 761 high-school students in south-eastern USA in using the SLEI in an evaluation of the effectiveness of using anthropometric activities. They found that, relative to a comparison group, the anthropometry group had significantly higher scores on some SLEI and attitude scales. An innovative science course for prospective elementary school teachers in Southern California was evaluated by Martin-Dunlop and Fraser (2008). When learning environment scales selected from the WIHIC and SLEI were administered to 525 female student teachers taking this innovative course, very large differences (of over 1.5 standard deviations) were found between students' perceptions of the innovative course and their previous courses.

Afari et al. (2013) involved 352 students taking college-level mathematics classes in the United Arab Emirates in investigating whether the use of games in their mathematics classes was effective for improving their perceptions of the learning environment and their attitudes towards mathematics. Students exposed to in-class mathematics games perceived more teacher support, involvement, personal relevance, enjoyment of mathematics lessons and academic efficacy.

*Improving learning environments.* An important application of learning environment ideas is teachers' and instructors' use of classroom environment questionnaires in action research aimed at improving their classrooms based on a fundamental five-step procedure suggested by Fraser (1981): (1) assessing actual and preferred learning environment using a questionnaire; (2) providing feedback to teachers based on students' responses to the questionnaire; (3) reflection and discussion based on feedback from the questionnaire in order to identify which aspects of the learning environment might be chosen for change and to consider teaching strategies that might be used; (4) implementing an intervention over a period of time in an attempt to change the learning environment; and (5) re-administration of the questionnaire to students at the end of the intervention period to determine whether students perceive their learning environment differently from before.

Practitioners' applications of this technique were facilitated by the availability of preferred forms (Byrne, Hattie, & Fraser, 1986; Yarrow, Millwater, & Fraser, 1997) and short forms (Fraser & Fisher, 1983) of learning environment questionnaires. Reported case studies using this approach were reviewed recently by Fraser and Aldridge (2017).

The English version of the CLES was administered by mathematics teachers in South Africa to 1864 grade 4–9 students (Aldridge, Fraser, & Sebela, 2004). During the intervention stage of this study some teachers were able to increase the constructivist orientation of their classrooms, reinforcing the value of using the CLES to provide feedback to guide change. Aldridge et al. (2012) used the 11-scale COLES to investigate the feasibility of teachers using feedback from their students'

P. SKORDI AND B. J. FRASER

actual and preferred learning environment perceptions in action researched intended to improve their classrooms. They found that the feedback was useful and led to the implementation of classroom changes that resulted in improvements in their classroom learning environments.

*Gender differences in learning environment perceptions.* A gender achievement gap has existed and fluctuated over the years (Kafer, 2007), but males have usually scored higher than females on standardized mathematics tests (Amelink, 2009; College Board, 2010). Because of the absence of any noteworthy research into gender differences in achievement in statistics, mathematics achievement was used as a proxy because mathematics self-concept and statistics achievement are related (Benson, 1989).

Stereotype threat (Steele & Aronson, 1995), in which the stereotype acts as a self-fulfilling prophecy, has been suggested as a contributing factor in female students achieving less well than male students in mathematics courses (Inzlicht & Ben-Zeev, 2000; Keller & Dauenheimer, 2003; Quinn & Spencer, 2001; Schmader, Johns, & Barquissau, 2004; Spencer, Steele, & Quinn, 1999).

Ogbuehi and Fraser (2007) conducted a study of 661 middle-school students from four inner-city schools in California using modified versions of the CLES, the WIHIC and some attitude scales. They found gender differences for student Negotiation and Task Orientation from the CLES and that female students perceived the classroom environment more positively than did the male students. For achievement and students' attitudes to mathematics, no statistically significant differences were found. Taylor and Fraser (2013) found that females perceived a more positive classroom environment and were less anxious about learning, but had greater anxiety regarding evaluation.

## OUR STUDY OF UNIVERSITY STATISTICS CLASSROOM ENVIRONMENTS

### Methods

*Sample.* A learning environment questionnaire was administered in Southern California to 12 university classes whose sizes ranged from 30 to 210 students. A sample of 375 students from the total group of 638 registered students completed every questionnaire item and provided both enjoyment and achievement scores. Some students chose not to take part, but the majority of non-participants were not in class on the day when the survey was administered. The sample consisted of 52% females and 48% males and the ethnic breakdown was 28.0% White, 35.5% Asian and 22.7% Hispanic, with the remaining students being of other ethnicities. Most students (81%) were taking the class for the first time, with only 19% repeating the class.

All students were enrolled in a business statistics course for non-business majors in one of two universities in Southern California (one PhD-awarding and one not). The PhD-awarding university held courses over a 10-week quarter in a lecture theatre

136

which was not a laboratory, and which involved three 50-minute meetings per week. The non-PhD-awarding university had 15-week semesters and two 75-minute class meetings a week. Data were also collected at this university from the summer classes, which ran over 5 weeks with 130-minute class sessions on 4 days of the week. All classes were held in laboratories in which students had access to computers.

*What Is Happening In this Class? (WIHIC) questionnaire.* According to Dorman (2003), the WIHIC questionnaire is the most-frequently used classroom environment instrument around the world and has achieved almost bandwagon status. The WIHIC has 56 items, with 8 items in each of 7 scales and five possible frequency responses are Almost Never, Seldom, Sometimes, Often and Almost Always indicates how often a practice is undertaken (Aldridge, Fraser, & Huang, 1999).

The WIHIC's seven scales are:

- *Student Cohesiveness* – Extent to which students know, help, and are supportive of one another
- *Teacher Support* – Extent to which the teacher helps, befriends, trusts and shows interest in students
- *Involvement* – Extent to which students have attentive interest, participate in discussions, perform additional work, and enjoy the class
- *Investigation* – Emphasis on the skills and processes of inquiry and their use in problem solving and investigation
- *Task Orientation* – Extent to which it is important to complete activities planned and to stay on the subject matter
- *Cooperation* – Extent to which students cooperate with one another on learning tasks
- *Equity* – Extent to which the teacher treats student equitability.

We considered that the WIHIC's scales were relevant to university statistics classrooms, which comprised the setting for our study. We selected the WIHIC because of its proven validity and reliability in many studies around the world (Fraser, 2014; Khine et al., in press). All of the WIHIC's 56 items are listed in full in the Appendix.

## Results

*Factorial validity and internal consistency reliability of WIHIC.* To check the structure of the WIHIC, we used the responses of our sample of 375 statistics students in conducting a principal axis factor analysis with oblimin rotation[1] and Kaiser normalization.[2] The two criteria used for the retention of any item were that it must have a factor loading of at least 0.35 with its own scale and less than 0.35 with all other scales.

The factor analysis results for the 56-item 7-scale WIHIC for our sample are shown in Table 7.1. Only factor loadings of 0.35 and above are shown in the table.

137

## P. SKORDI AND B. J. FRASER

*Table 7.1 Factor Analysis Results for WIHIC*

| Item No | Factor Loadings | | | | | | |
|---|---|---|---|---|---|---|---|
| | Student Cohesiveness | Teacher Support | Involvement | Investigation | Task Orientation | Cooperation | Equity |
| Stu Coh 1 | 0.56 | | | | | | |
| Stu Coh 2 | 0.69 | | | | | | |
| Stu Coh 3 | 0.43 | | | | | | |
| Stu Coh 4 | 0.75 | | | | | | |
| Stu Coh 5 | 0.38 | | | | | | |
| Stu Coh 6 | 0.35 | | | | | | |
| Stu Coh 7 | 0.53 | | | | | | |
| Stu Coh 8 | 0.40 | | | | | | |
| Tea Sup 1 | | 0.65 | | | | | |
| Tea Sup 2 | | 0.78 | | | | | |
| Tea Sup 3 | | 0.66 | | | | | |
| Tea Sup 4 | | 0.62 | | | | | |
| Tea Sup 5 | | 0.74 | | | | | |
| Tea Sup 6 | | 0.75 | | | | | |
| Tea Sup 7 | | 0.62 | | | | | |
| Tea Sup 8 | | 0.48 | | | | | |
| Invol 1 | | | 0.71 | | | | |
| Invol 2 | | | 0.81 | | | | |
| Invol 3 | | | 0.65 | | | | |
| Invol 4 | | | 0.73 | | | | |
| Invol 5 | | | 0.68 | | | | |
| Invol 6 | | | 0.57 | | | | |
| Invol 7 | | | 0.48 | | | | |
| Invol 8 | | | 0.55 | | | | |
| Inves 1 | | | | 0.69 | | | |
| Inves 2 | | | | 0.62 | | | |
| Inves 3 | | | | 0.84 | | | |
| Inves 4 | | | | 0.64 | | | |
| Inves 5 | | | | 0.79 | | | |
| Inves 6 | | | | 0.80 | | | |
| Inves 7 | | | | 0.82 | | | |
| Inves 8 | | | | 0.72 | | | |

*(cont.)*

ASSESSMENT OF THE PSYCHOSOCIAL LEARNING ENVIRONMENT

*Table 7.1 Factor Analysis Results for WIHIC (cont.)*

| Item No | Factor Loadings | | | | | | |
|---|---|---|---|---|---|---|---|
| | Student Cohesiveness | Teacher Support | Involvement | Investigation | Task Orientation | Cooperation | Equity |
| Tas Orn 1 | | | | | 0.64 | | |
| Tas Orn 2 | | | | | 0.62 | | |
| Tas Orn 3 | | | | | 0.65 | | |
| Tas Orn 4 | | | | | 0.59 | | |
| Tas Orn 5 | | | | | 0.76 | | |
| Tas Orn 6 | | | | | 0.59 | | |
| Tas Orn 7 | | | | | 0.68 | | |
| Tas Orn 8 | | | | | 0.64 | | |
| Coop 1 | | | | | | 0.71 | |
| Coop 2 | | | | | | 0.78 | |
| Coop 3 | | | | | | 0.76 | |
| Coop 4 | | | | | | 0.71 | |
| Coop 5 | | | | | | 0.77 | |
| Coop 6 | | | | | | 0.84 | |
| Coop 7 | | | | | | 0.81 | |
| Coop 8 | | | | | | 0.79 | |
| Equ 1 | | | | | | | 0.65 |
| Equ 2 | | | | | | | 0.72 |
| Equ 3 | | | | | | | 0.60 |
| Equ 4 | | | | | | | 0.84 |
| Equ 5 | | | | | | | 0.83 |
| Equ 6 | | | | | | | 0.84 |
| Equ 7 | | | | | | | 0.75 |
| Equ 8 | | | | | | | 0.81 |
| % Variance | 3.19 | 6.15 | 5.04 | 7.98 | 3.63 | 28.71 | 9.54 |
| Eigenvalue | 1.79 | 3.44 | 2.82 | 4.47 | 2.03 | 16.07 | 5.34 |
| Alpha Reliability | | 0.87 | 0.91 | 0.91 | 0.92 | 0.87 | 0.95 |

$N= 375$

*Factor loadings less than 0.35 have been omitted from the table.*
*Principal axis factoring with varimax oblimin and Kaiser normalization.*

P. SKORDI AND B. J. FRASER

At the bottom of Table 7.1, the eigenvalue[3] and percentage variance for each scale are shown. Factor analysis of the 56-item WIHIC replicated the clear factor structure found in previous research (Aldridge et al., 1999; Pickett & Fraser, 2009; Zandvliet & Fraser, 2004, 2005). All 56 items were retained because each item had a factor loading of at least 0.35 with its own scale and less than 0.35 with the other six WIHIC scales.

The bottom of Table 7.1 shows that the proportion of variance accounted for ranged from 3.19% to 28.71% for different WIHIC scales. Together, the seven scales of the WIHIC accounted for a total of 64.24% of the variation. Scale eigenvalues ranged between 1.79 and 16.07, therefore satisfying the cut-off criterion of 1.0 for meaningfulness (Kaiser, 1974).

Internal consistency reliability refers to how closely items within a scale inter-correlate and therefore measure a common construct. In our study, we used Cronbach's alpha coefficient as a measure of internal consistency as reported in Table 7.1. Alpha coefficients[4] for different WIHIC scales ranged from 0.87 to 0.95. Overall, Table 7.1 supports the strong *a priori* factor structure and internal consistency reliability of all WIHIC scales for our sample of university statistics students in California.

*Gender differences in learning environment perceptions.* Because the WIHIC exhibited satisfactory validity when used with our sample, we used our WIHIC data as a source of dependent variables for investigating student gender as a determinant of classroom learning environment. In order to reduce the Type I error rate associated with performing any univariate tests for individual WIHIC scales, MANOVA[5] was performed for the seven WIHIC scales as a set prior to conducting or interpreting any univariate ANOVA analyses. Because Wilks' lambda[6] criterion revealed statistically-significant gender differences for the set of seven dependent variables as a whole, gender differences were interpreted separately for each WIHIC scale.

An effect size was also calculated for each scale as a measure of the magnitude of the difference between genders using Cohen's (1988) $d$,[7] which is defined as the difference between two means divided by the pooled standard deviation. Cohen hesitantly categorized effect sizes as small ($d = 0.2$), medium ($d = 0.5$) and large ($d = 0.8$) and stated that "there is a certain risk inherent in offering conventional operational definitions for those terms for use in power analysis in as diverse a field of inquiry as behavioural science" (p. 44). The effect size is a useful measure of the practical significance of a difference.

Table 7.2 reveals three general patterns. First, gender differences were statistically significant ($p<0.05$) for the two WIHIC scales of Student Cohesiveness and Task Orientation. Second, the magnitude of significant gender differences was medium for Task Orientation (0.45 standard deviations) but fairly small for Student Cohesiveness (0.25 standard deviation) according to Cohen's (1988) criteria. Third, whereas males' scores were slightly higher than females' scores for Investigation, females' scores were higher than males' scores for all other WIHIC scales.

140

ASSESSMENT OF THE PSYCHOSOCIAL LEARNING ENVIRONMENT

*Table 7.2. Means, standard deviations and gender differences
(ANOVA result and effect size) for WIHIC scales*

| Scale | Item Mean | | Item SD | | Difference | |
|---|---|---|---|---|---|---|
| | Male | Female | Male | Female | F | Effect Size |
| Student Cohesiveness | 3.42 | 3.62 | 0.79 | 0.78 | 5.90* | 0.25 |
| Teacher Support | 3.58 | 3.61 | 0.84 | 0.97 | 0.29 | 0.03 |
| Involvement | 2.56 | 2.68 | 0.90 | 0.94 | 1.32 | 0.13 |
| Investigation | 3.03 | 2.90 | 0.88 | 0.92 | 1.44 | -0.14 |
| Task Orientation | 4.22 | 4.47 | 0.61 | 0.53 | 17.98** | 0.45 |
| Cooperation | 3.02 | 3.28 | 1.13 | 1.13 | 2.22 | 0.23 |
| Equity | 4.31 | 4.43 | 0.71 | 0.76 | 1.51 | 0.16 |

*$p<0.05$, **$p<0.01$
Males ($n = 181$); Females ($n = 194$)

*Associations between classroom learning environment and student enjoyment and achievement.* Associations between classroom learning environment dimensions and two types of student outcomes (enjoyment of statistics classes and statistics achievement) were investigated using simple correlation and multiple regression analyses.

Enjoyment was assessed with a scale based on the Test of Science Related Attitudes (Fraser, 1981) and achievement was based on weighted and standardised scores achieved in four in-class multiple-choice tests. The learning environment scales were used as the independent variables and enjoyment and achievement were the dependent variables.

For the Enjoyment of Statistics scale, Table 7.3 shows that all the scales of the WIHIC – with the exception of Investigation – correlated positively and statistically significantly with Enjoyment. Students enjoyed the class more when they had direction and the class was well planned (Task Orientation), when they felt that the teacher helps them (Teacher Support), when there was more cooperative learning (Cooperation), when the class was interesting and students were allowed to participate (Involvement), when there was a friendly atmosphere (Student Cohesiveness), and when students were treated equally by the teacher (Equity).

The multiple correlation between WIHIC scales and the Enjoyment of Statistics scale was statistically significant. The regression weights in Table 7.3 indicate that Task Orientation was the only independent determinant of Enjoyment. Perhaps students' enjoyment of statistics classes for non-statistics majors at the university level is influenced by the way in which a teacher controls and conducts the class.

For achievement, Table 7.3 reveals a statistically-significant simple correlation for Student Cohesiveness, Involvement, Investigation, Cooperation and Equity. As well, the multiple correlation between achievement and the set of seven WIHIC scales was statistically significant. Inspection of regression coefficients shows that

141

P. SKORDI AND B. J. FRASER

*Table 7.3. Simple correlation and multiple regression analyses of associations between learning environment scales and student enjoyment and achievement*

| Scale | Enjoyment of Statistics | | Statistics Achievement | |
|---|---|---|---|---|
| | r | β | r | β |
| Student Cohesiveness | 0.15** | 0.09 | 0.14** | 0.19** |
| Teacher Support | 0.16** | 0.12 | 0.03 | 0.10 |
| Involvement | 0.13* | 0.01 | 0.15** | 0.15* |
| Investigation | 0.07 | 0.01 | 0.11* | 0.06 |
| Task Orientation | 0.17** | 0.12* | 0.09 | 0.05 |
| Cooperation | 0.12* | 0.01 | 0.13* | 0.23** |
| Equity | 0.11* | 0.02 | 0.11* | 0.09 |
| Multiple Correlation R | | 0.22** | | 0.26** |

$*p<0.05, **p<0.01$
$N=375$

Student Cohesiveness, Involvement and Cooperation were statistically-significant independent predictors of achievement when the other classroom environment scales were mutually controlled.

It is noteworthy that all bivariate and multivariate associations between classroom environment and the two student outcomes of enjoyment and achievement were positive, suggesting the importance of a positive learning environment for promoting student outcomes. This replicates considerable past research in many countries reviewed by Fraser (2014, 2012). However, it is noteworthy that generally the magnitudes of the relationships between classroom environment and student outcomes in Table 7.3 are relatively small compared with magnitudes reported in past research (Fraser, 2012). A possible explanation for this pattern is that other factors (e.g. students' prior educational experiences, the instructor, the peer group) could be more influential than the learning environment in influencing those student outcomes in university statistics classrooms.

## CHAPTER SUMMARY AND CONCLUSION

Although the design and redesign of spaces for learning and teaching often are intended to change or create specific types of pedagogical and psychosocial learning environments, it is uncommon to monitor the evolution of these learning environments. For example, when Prain (in press) monitored the perceptions of 2500 students over three years in four new schools, the innovative design of which aimed to promote personalised learning, students' perceptions of personalised learning did not improve.

In this chapter, we have attempted to show how ideas, methods and constructs from the field of learning environments might be applied to monitoring the success of educational spaces in promoting changes in important pedagogical and psychosocial dimensions. To do this, we have provided a brief literature review on the conceptualisation, assessment and application of learning environments, as well as reporting a study of the learning environments of university statistics classrooms.

In order to answer our study's first research question, statistical analyses were undertaken to establish if our questionnaire assessing learning environment (WIHIC) was valid and reliable for our sample of university statistics students. Factorial validity was clearly established for the WIHIC and the internal consistency reliability for all scales was supported using alpha coefficients.

MANOVA was used to answer our second research question concerning gender differences in classroom environment perceptions. Females' scores were significantly higher than males' scores for Student Cohesiveness and Task Orientation. Effect sizes for significant gender differences ranged between approximately a quarter and a half of a standard deviation (i.e. in the small to medium range).

To answer our third research question concerning outcome–environment associations, simple correlation and multiple regression analyses were conducted to reveal that student enjoyment and achievement each were significantly related to some of the WIHIC's learning environment scales. In particular, Task Orientation was a significant independent predictor of enjoyment of statistics and Student Cohesiveness, Involvement and Cooperation were significant independent predictors of statistics achievement.

## APPENDIX A

*Listing of Items in the What Is Happening In this Class? (WIHIC)*[8]

### Student Cohesiveness

1. I make friends among students in this class.
2. I know other students in this class.
3. I am friendly to members of this class.
4. Members of the class are my friends.
5. I work well with other class members.
6. I help other class members who are having trouble with their work.
7. Students in this class like me.
8. In this class, I get help from other students.

### Teacher Support

1. The teacher takes a personal interest in me.
2. The teacher goes out of his/her way to help me.
3. The teacher considers my feelings.

P. SKORDI AND B. J. FRASER

4. The teacher helps me when I have trouble with the work.
5. The teacher talks with me.
6. The teacher is interested in my problems.
7. The teacher moves about the class to talk with me.
8. The teacher's questions help me to understand.

*Involvement*

1. I discuss ideas in this class.
2. I give my opinions during class discussions.
3. The teacher asks me questions.
4. My ideas and suggestions are used classroom discussions.
5. I ask the teacher questions.
6. I explain my ideas to other students.
7. Students discuss with me how to go about solving problems.
8. I am asked to explain how I solve problems.

*Investigation*

1. I carry out investigations to test my ideas.
2. I am asked to think about evidence for my statements.
3. I carry out investigations to answer questions coming from discussions.
4. I explain the meaning of statements, diagrams, and graphs.
5. I carry out investigations to answer questions that puzzle me.
6. I carry out investigations to answer teacher's questions.
7. I find out answers to questions by doing investigations.
8. I solve problems by using information obtained from my own investigations.

*Task Orientation*

1. Getting a certain amount of work done is important to me.
2. I do as much as I set out to do.
3. I know the goals of this class.
4. I am ready to start class on time.
5. I know what I am trying to accomplish in this class.
6. I pay attention during this class.
7. I try to understand the work in this class.
8. I know how much work I have to do.

*Cooperation*

1. I cooperate with other students when doing assignment work.
2. I share my books and resources with other students when doing assignments.

144

3. When I work in groups in this class, there is teamwork.
4. I work with other students on projects in this class.
5. I learn from other students in this class.
6. I work with other students in this class.
7. I cooperate with other students on class activities.
8. Students work with me to achieve class goals.

*Equity*

1. The teacher gives as much attention to my questions as to the other students' questions.
2. I get the same amount of help from the teacher as do other students.
3. I have the same amount of say in this class as other students do.
4. I am treated the same as other students in this class.
5. I receive the same encouragement from the teacher as other students do.
6. I get the same opportunity to contribute to class discussions as other students.
7. My work receives as much praise as other students' work.
8. I get the same opportunity to answer questions as other students.

## NOTES

[1] Oblimin rotation https://stats.stackexchange.com/questions/113003/the-difference-between-varimax-and-oblimin-rotations-in-factor-analysis
[2] into Kaiser normalization www.psych.unl.edu/psycrs/statpage/pc_rot.pdf
[3] Eigenvalue https://www.researchgate.net/post/What_is_the_physical_significance_of_eigenvalues_and_eigenvectors2
[4] Alpha coefficients https://stats.idre.ucla.edu/spss/faq/what-does-cronbachs-alpha-mean/
[5] MANOVA http://online.sfsu.edu/efc/classes/biol710/manova/MANOVAnewest.pdf
[6] Wilks' lambda http://www.blackwellpublishing.com/specialarticles/jcn_9_381.pdf
[7] Cohen's '*d*' http://rpsychologist.com/d3/cohend/
[8] The WIHIC was developed by Fraser, Fisher, and McRobbie (1996) and Aldridge, Fraser, and Huang (1999). The frequency response alternatives of Almost Never, Seldom, Sometimes, Often and Almost Always are scored, respectively, 1, 2, 3, 4 and 5.

## REFERENCES

Afari, E., Aldridge, J. M., Fraser, B. J., & Khine, M. S. (2013). Students' perceptions of the learning environment and attitudes in game-based mathematics classrooms. *Learning Environments Research, 16*, 131–150.

Aldridge, J. M., & Fraser, B. J. (2008). *Outcomes-focused learning environments: Determinants and effects* (Advances in learning environments research series). Rotterdam, The Netherlands: Sense Publishers.

Aldridge, J. M., Fraser, B. J., Bell, L., & Dorman, J. P. (2012). Using a new learning environment questionnaire for reflection in teacher action research. *Journal of Science Teacher Education, 23*, 259–290.

Aldridge, J. M., Fraser, B. J., & Huang, I. T.-C. (1999). Investigating classroom environments in Taiwan and Australia with multiple research methods. *Journal of Educational Research, 93*, 48–62.

Aldridge, J. M., Fraser, B. J., & Sebela, M. P. (2004). Using teacher action research to promote constructivist learning environments in South Africa. *South African Journal of Education, 24*, 245–253.

Aldridge, J. M., Fraser, B. J., Taylor, P. C., & Chen, C.-C. (2000). Constructivist learning environments in a cross-national study in Taiwan and Australia. *International Journal of Science Education, 22*, 37–55.

Aldridge, J. M., Laugksch, R. C., Seopa, M. A., & Fraser, B. J. (2006). Development and validation of an instrument to monitor the implementation of outcomes-based learning environments in science classrooms in South Africa. *International Journal of Science Education, 28*, 45–70.

Amelink, C. (2009). Literature overview: Gender differences in science achievement. *SWE-AWE CASEE overviews* (3/2/14 ed.).

Burden, R. L., & Fraser, B. J. (1993). Use of classroom environment assessments in school psychology: A British perspective. *Psychology in the Schools, 30*(3), 232–240.

Byrne, D. B., Hattie, J. A., & Fraser, B. J. (1986). Student perceptions of preferred classroom learning environment. *The Journal of Educational Research, 80*(1), 10–18.

Cohen, J. (1988). *Statistical power analysis for the behavioral sciences* (2nd ed.). Hillsdale, NJ: Lawrence Earlbaum Associates.

College Board. (2010). *SAT percentile rank of males females and total group, 2007.* Retrieved from http://www.collegeboard.com/prod_downloads/highered/ra/sat/SAT_percentile_ranks_males_females_total_group_critical_reading.pdf

Dorman, J. P. (2003). Cross-national validation of the What Is Happening In this Class? (WIHIC) questionnaire using confirmatory factor analysis. *Learning Environments Research, 6*, 231–245.

Fisher, D. L., Henderson, D. G., & Fraser, B. J. (1995). Interpersonal behaviour in senior high school biology classes. *Research in Science Education, 25*, 125–133.

Fisher, D. L., Henderson, D. G., & Fraser, B. J. (1997). Laboratory environments and student outcomes in senior high school biology. *American Biology Teacher, 59*, 214–219.

Fraser, B. J. (1981). Using environmental assessments to make better classrooms. *Journal of Curriculum Studies, 13*(2), 131–144.

Fraser, B. J. (1982). Individualized classroom environment questionnaire. *American Journal of Education, 3*(2), 72–73.

Fraser, B. J. (1986). *Classroom environment.* London: Croom Helm.

Fraser, B. J. (1990). *Individualised classroom environment questionnaire.* Melbourne: Australian Council for Educational Research.

Fraser, B. J. (1994). Research on classroom and school climate. In D. L. Gabel (Ed.), *Handbook of research on science teaching and learning* (pp. 493–541). New York, NY: Macmillan.

Fraser, B. J. (2001). Twenty thousand hours. *Learning Environments Research, 4*, 1–5.

Fraser, B. J. (2012). Classroom learning environments: Retrospect, context and prospect. In B. J. Fraser, K. G. Tobin, & C. J. McRobbie (Eds.), *Second international handbook of science education* (pp. 1191–1232). New York, NY: Springer.

Fraser, B. J. (2014). Classroom learning environments: Historical and contemporary perspectives. In N. G. Lederman & S. K. Abell (Eds.), *Handbook of research on science education* (Vol. 2, pp. 104–119). New York, NY: Routledge.

Fraser, B. J., & Aldridge, J. M. (2017). Improving classrooms through assessment of learning environments. In J. P. Bakken (Ed.), *Classrooms: Assessment practices for teachers and student improvement strategies* (Vol. 1, pp. 91–107). New York, NY: Nova.

Fraser, B. J., & Butts, W. L. (1982). Relationship between perceived levels of classroom individualization and science-related attitudes. *Journal of Research in Science Teaching, 19*(2), 143–154.

Fraser, B. J., & Fisher, D. L. (1983). Development and validation of short forms of some instruments measuring student perceptions of actual and preferred classroom learning environment. *Science Education, 67*(1), 115–131.

Fraser, B. J., Fisher, D. L., & McRobbie, C. J. (1996, April). *Development, validation, and use of personal and class forms of a new classroom environment instrument.* Paper presented at the annual meeting of the American Educational Research Association, New York, NY.

Fraser, B. J., & Lee, S. S. U. (2009). Science laboratory classroom environments in Korean high schools. *Learning Environments Research, 12*(1), 67–84.

## ASSESSMENT OF THE PSYCHOSOCIAL LEARNING ENVIRONMENT

Fraser, B. J., & McRobbie, C. J. (1995). Science laboratory classroom environments at schools and universities: A cross-national study. *Educational Research and Evaluation, 1*, 289–317.

Fraser, B. J., & Treagust, D. F. (1986). Validity and use of an instrument for assessing classroom psychosocial environment in higher education. *Higher Education, 15*, 37–57.

Fraser, B. J., Treagust, D. F., & Dennis, N. C. (1986). Development of an instrument for assessing classroom psychosocial environment at universities and colleges. *Studies in Higher Education, 11*, 43–54.

Giallousi, M., Gialamas, V., Spyrellis, N., & Pavlatou, E. A. (2010). Development, validation, and use of a Greek-language questionnaire for assessing learning environments in grade 10 chemistry classes. *International Journal of Science and Mathematics Education, 8*, 761–782.

Goh, S. C., & Fraser, B. J. (2000). Teacher interpersonal behaviour and elementary students' outcomes. *Journal of Research in Childhood Education, 14*(2), 216–231.

Halpin, A. W., & Croft, D. B. (1963). *Organizational climate of schools.* Chicago, IL: Midwest Administration Center, University of Chicago.

Inzlicht, M., & Ben-Zeev, T. (2000). A threatening intellectual environment: Why females are susceptible to experiencing problem-solving deficits in the presence of males. *Psychological Science, 11*, 365–371.

Kafer, K. (2007). *Taking the boy crisis in education seriously: How school choice can boost achievement among boys and girls.* Paper presented at the Independent Women's Forum, Washington, DC.

Kaiser, H. (1974). An index of factorial simplicity. *Psychometrika, 39*, 31–36.

Keller, J., & Dauenheimer, D. (2003). Stereotype threat in the classroom: Dejection mediates the disrupting threat effect on women's math performance. *Personality and Social Psychology Bulletin, 29*, 371–381.

Khine, M. S., Fraser, B. J., Afari, E., Oo, Z., & Kyaw, T. T. (in press). Student perceptions of the learning environment in tertiary science classrooms in Myanmar. *Learning Environments Research, 21*(1), 135–152. doi:10.1007s10984-017-9250-0

Khoo, H. S., & Fraser, B. J. (2008). Using classroom psychosocial environment in the evaluation of adult computer application courses in Singapore. *Technology, Pedagogy and Education, 17*, 67–81.

Lewin, K. (1936). *Principles of topological psychology.* New York, NY: McGraw.

Lightburn, M. E., & Fraser, B. J. (2007). Classroom environment and student outcomes among students using anthropometry activities in high-school science. *Research in Science & Technological Education, 25*, 153–166.

Maor, D., & Fraser, B. J. (1996). Use of classroom environment perceptions in evaluating inquiry-based computer-assisted learning. *International Journal of Science Education, 18*, 401–421.

Martin-Dunlop, C., & Fraser, B. J. (2008). Learning environment and attitudes associated with an innovative science course designed for prospective elementary teachers. *International Journal of Science and Mathematics Education, 6*, 163–190.

McRobbie, C. J., & Fraser, B. J. (1993). Associations between student outcomes and psychosocial science environment. *The Journal of Educational Research, 87*, 78–85.

Moos, R. H. (1974). *The social climate scales: An overview.* Palo Alto, CA: Consulting Psychologists Press.

Moos, R. H., & Trickett, E. J. (1974). *Classroom environment scale manual.* Palo Alto, CA: Consulting Psychologists Press.

Murray, H. A. (1938). *Explorations in personality.* New York, NY: Oxford University Press.

Nix, R. K., Fraser, B. J., & Ledbetter, C. E. (2005). Evaluating an integrated science learning environment using the Constructivist Learning Environment Survey (CLES). *Learning Environments Research, 8*, 109–133.

Ogbuehi, P. I., & Fraser, B. J. (2007). Learning environment, attitudes and conceptual development associated with innovative strategies in middle-school mathematics. *Learning Environments Research, 10*, 101–114.

Pace, R. C., & Stern, G. G. (1958). An approach to the measurement of psychological characteristics of college environments. *Journal of Educational Psychology, 49*, 269–277.

Pickett, L. H., & Fraser, B. J. (2009). Evaluation of a mentoring program for beginning teachers in terms of the learning environment and student outcomes in participants' school classrooms. In A. Selkirk &

M. Tichenor (Eds.), *Teacher education: Policy, practice and research* (pp. 1–15). New York, NY: Nova Science Publishers.

Prain, V. (in press). Using quantitative methods to evaluate students' post-occupancy perceptions of personalised learning in an innovative learning environment. In S. Alterator & C. Deed (Eds.), *School space and its occupation: The conceptualisation and evaluation of innovative learning environments.* Rotterdam, The Netherlands: Sense Publishers.

Quek, L. C., Wong, A. F. L., & Fraser, B. J. (2005). Student perceptions of chemistry laboratory learning environments, student–teacher interactions and attitudes in secondary school gifted education classes in Singapore. *Research in Science Education, 35,* 299–321.

Quinn, D. M., & Spencer, S. J. (2001). The interference of stereotype threat with women's generation of mathematical problem-solving strategies. *Journal of Social Issues, 57,* 55–71.

Schmader, T., Johns, M., & Barquissau, M. (2004). The costs of accepting gender differences: The role of stereotype endorsement in women's experience in the math domain. *Gender Roles, 50,* 835–850.

Spencer, S. J., Steele, C. M., & Quinn, D. M. (1999). Stereotype threat and women's math performance. *Journal of Experimental Social Psychology, 35,* 4–28.

Stern, G. G. (1970). *People in context: Measuring person–environment congruence in education and industry.* New York, NY: Wiley.

Taylor, B. A., & Fraser, B. J. (2013). Relationships between learning environment and mathematics anxiety. *Learning Environments Research, 16,* 1–17.

Taylor, P. C., Fraser, B. J., & Fisher, D. L. (1997). Monitoring constructivist classroom learning environments. *International Journal of Educational Research, 27,* 293–302.

Teh, G. P. L., & Fraser, B. J. (1995). Development and validation of an instrument for assessing the psychosocial environment of computer-assisted learning classrooms. *Journal of Educational Computing Research, 12*(2), 177–193.

Walberg, H. J., & Anderson, G. J. (1968). Classroom climate and individual learning. *Journal of Educational Psychology, 59,* 414–419.

Wong, A. F. L., & Fraser, B. J. (1996). Environment-attitude associations in the chemistry laboratory classroom. *Research in Science and Technological Education, 14,* 91–102.

Yarrow, A., Millwater, J., & Fraser, B. J. (1997). Improving university and primary school classroom environments through preservice teachers' action research. *International Journal of Practical Experiences in Professional Education, 1,* 68–93.

Zandvliet, D. B., & Fraser, B. J. (2004). Learning environments in information and communications technology classrooms. *Technology, Pedagogy and Education, 13,* 97–123.

Zandvliet, D. B., & Fraser, B. J. (2005). Physical and psychosocial environments associated with networked classrooms. *Learning Environments Research, 8,* 1–17.

RONALD BECKERS

# 8. LEARNING SPACE DESIGN
# IN HIGHER EDUCATION

## ABSTRACT

The significant changes in higher education learning and teaching over the past decades, such as increased information and communication technology, and evolving learning theories have resulted in the dilemma whether higher education institutions can facilitate tomorrow's learning and teaching in today's or even yesterday's school buildings.

The purpose of this chapter is to illustrate the spatial implications of 'new ways of learning' in higher education. It therefore first describes the developments in higher education learning and teaching. Next, it presents a framework that elucidates the alignment of the physical study environment with learning theories and educational processes in higher education. Furthermore, the chapter covers the design and space characteristics of contemporary learning spaces. The chapter also addresses which learning spaces higher education students prefer for their study activities and it illuminates the students' design preferences for the physical learning environment based on a quantitative study that involved 697 Dutch business management students.

The chapter concludes with some learning space planning guidelines and practical implications. We show that 'new ways of learning' cause a shift in learning settings in school buildings with a growing attention to facilitating autonomy, interaction and knowledge exploration anytime and anywhere. Increasingly every square meter of the built environment has the potential to support the learning activities of a student, from home to the classroom and all kinds of other settings in between, such as a coffee house, café, restaurant, bar, museum, library and public spaces, such as streets, parks or public transport. Nevertheless, the findings of the qualitative study show that students prefer quiet learning spaces for study activities. Students favour quiet, closed learning space at the university, such as project rooms for collaborative activities or quiet areas to study individually. Regarding their learning space, students' value functional attributes of the physical learning environment as most important.

The content of this chapter contributes to a better understanding of the alignment of learning space to the evolving needs that come from new ways of learning supported by advanced information and communication technology. The presented framework and the findings presented in the chapter can be used by higher education institutions to support learning space planning and strategic decision-making about the physical learning environment.

© KONINKLIJKE BRILL NV, LEIDEN, 2019 | DOI: 10.1163/9789004391598_010

R. BECKERS

## INTRODUCTION[1]

This chapter addresses the alignment of learning space design with higher education learning and teaching. Higher education has gone through substantial changes in the past decades (Beckers, 2016a; Marais, 2011; Collis & Van der Wende, 2002). Today's schools and universities should prepare young people for tomorrow's knowledge economy by teaching them 21st century skills (Voogt & Pareja Roblin, 2012; Ananiadou & Claro, 2009). This demands a new scope on learning and teaching processes, which build upon traditional behaviourist, cognitivist, and social constructivist learning and teaching approaches (Marais, 2011; Foster, 2008). These new ways of learning can be characterised as a shift from a supply-driven approach of learning to more customised and demand oriented ways of learning (Van Aalst & Kok, 2004). This requires self-directed students who take responsibility for their own learning process, and learn how to build and use networks, cooperate with others, and make use of information and communication technology (ICT) as a tool to find resources that can help them to achieve their learning goals. In so-called flipped classroom concepts (Abeysekera & Dawson, 2015), students use the Internet for watching web lectures at home or in other places and come to universities to meet for social reasons, for working together on assignments, and for face-to-face contact with their tutors.

The changing context of higher education leads to reconsidering the physical study environment and to exploring how new learning spaces can be used to support an effective pedagogical transition (Adams Becker et al., 2017; Marmot, 2012). There is much research available about new learning and teaching approaches in higher education and the link with the physical learning environment shows increased attention in literature. Nevertheless, the subject can still be experienced as an under-researched topic (Boddington & Boys, 2011; Temple, 2008).

Therefore, this chapter aims to contribute to a better understanding of how to align higher education school buildings and learning spaces with the developments in learning and teaching. It first describes the developments in higher education learning and teaching. Next, it will elucidate the alignment of the physical study environment with learning theories and educational processes in higher education. Furthermore, the chapter covers the design of learning spaces and space characteristics. Finally, the chapter concludes with some learning space guide lines and practical implications.

## DEVELOPMENTS IN HIGHER EDUCATION LEARNING AND TEACHING

### New Ways of Learning

In the past century, educational approaches were dominated by traditional psychological theories such as behaviourism, cognitivism, and constructivism (Merriam, Caffarella & Baumgartner, 2007). In behaviourism, learning is basically linked to objective, observable changes in behaviour (Zimbaro, Johnson, & McCann, 2009; Ashworth, Brennan, Egan, Hamilton, & Sáenz, 2004). This assumption

LEARNING SPACE DESIGN IN HIGHER EDUCATION

is well-known by the stimulus-response experiments of Pavlov in the 1920s and Skinner's use of reinforcement to strengthen behaviour by operant conditioning in the 1950s (Zimbaro et al., 2009). In education, the behaviourist approach aimed at the reproduction of learned knowledge to show that learning had occurred. Techniques of rewards and punishments were used to stimulate learning behaviour. The behaviourist learning theory has long been, and still is, widely used in higher education classrooms. Shreeve (2008, p. 24) mentions lecture based learning as a method of teaching [that] promotes superficial learning and utilises assessment methods that reward student reproduction of facts.

Due to the results of increased research about knowledge processing in the brain, the behaviourist paradigm shifted to a cognitivist philosophy after World War II. Cognitivists such as Piaget, Vygotsky and Bruner stated that learning is a mental process, which is not necessarily observable in changed behaviour (Zimbardo et al., 2009; Illeris, 2007). Cognitivists focus on learning as a process of meta-cognition in which concepts such as perception, memory, problem solving, creativity, and thinking are important (Ashworth et al., 2004). The ideas about cognitivism further evolved into the constructivist theory. This theory is derived from the idea that learners construct knowledge based on their experiences (Foster, 2008; Volman, 2006; Van Aalst & Kok, 2004; Shuell, 1988). Learners link new information to existing knowledge so every person constructs its own unique interpretation of reality. Constructivist theorists extended the traditional focus on individual learning to address the collaborative and the social dimensions of learning (Ashworth et al., 2004). This social constructivist approach supposes that learning results from social interaction and that knowledge and understanding are constructed when individuals engage socially and communicate with each other, through shared problems and tasks (Foster, 2008). An example of social constructivism in current higher education is problem based learning (PBL) (Shreeve, 2008; Kayzel, 2004), in which

[students work] in small learning groups, discuss and explore individual knowledge and research findings to arrive at a group solution or course of action. (Shreeve, 2008, p. 24)

These and other social constructivist approaches require a different role of the teacher. According to Martin, Katz, Morris, and Kilgallon (2007, p. 13),

the role of the teacher needs to change from the sage on the stage to the guide on the side.

Leland and Kasten (2002) showed similar trends by comparing a traditional industrial model with a new inquiry model. The industrial model was devised after the factories at the end of the 19th century and the inquiry model resulted from developments in learning and teaching (Table 8.1).

Just like PBL and other modern didactic approaches, the inquiry model of Table 8.1 shows the basic aspects of 'new learning' or 'new ways of learning'. New learning refers to new kinds of learning processes and new instructional methods,

151

R. BECKERS

*Table 8.1. The industrial model versus the inquiry model in education
(derived from Leland & Kasten, 2002)*

| Characteristics | Industrial Model | Inquiry Model |
| --- | --- | --- |
| Learning model | Behaviourism | Social constructivism |
| Purpose of education | Conformity, obedience Prepare learner for factory job | Critical thinking, creativity Prepare learner for information/ technology |
| Structure | Classes graded by age Homogenous groups | Multi-age classes Heterogeneous groups |
| Curriculum | Fact based, traditional skills | Problem solving, 21st century skills |
| Instruction | Text-based, transmission | Multiple sources, transaction |
| Assessment | Uniform, standardised | Authentic, diverse |
| Role of the student | Passive, receive knowledge | Active, construct knowledge |
| Role of the Teacher | Foreman, clerk | Co-learner, facilitator |

which occur because society requires new learning outcomes (Simons, Van der Linden, & Duffy, 2000). New learning is a response to the perception that the traditional transfer model of knowledge in education is not satisfactory (Volman, 2006). This causes a shift in education from a supply-driven approach to a more demand-driven policy (Ashworth et al., 2004; Van Aalst & Kok, 2004). According to new learning approaches, students have to be active and self-regulative in their learning process. New ways of learning are linked to real issues and occur in real learning contexts (Adams Becker et al., 2017). This comes to the fore in the concepts of authentic learning (Volman, 2006) and context-rich learning (Simons et al., 2000), which resulted into the development of communities of learning and practice (McLaughlin & Mills, 2008; Smith & Bath, 2006).

*Technology in Education*

An additional driver for change is the availability of information and communication technology (ICT) in society and in education, enabling new ways of learning and teaching (Davies, Mullan, & Feldman, 2017; Sursock, 2015; Collis & Van der Wende, 2002). The traditional learning theories such as behaviourism, cognitivism, and social constructivism existed without computer technology in education (Van der Zanden, 2009). The development of ICT in the classroom led to a new learning theory called connectivism (Marais, 2011; Siemens, 2005). Connectivism is an answer to the debate about changing learning theories due to alternative ways of information storage, processing, and recall through devices and through networked connections. Connectivism, like social constructivism, builds on interaction too, but goes further than the interaction between persons (Siemens, 2005). According to Siemens (2005), constructivists would likely see the network solely as a social medium for interaction, while a connectivist additionally sees the network itself (referring to all available information sources) as an extension of the human mind. So, not only learning from others, but also learning in, as well as from social, digital or virtual networks. In connectivism, know-how and know-what are supplemented with know-where, which refers to the understanding of where to find knowledge that is needed (Siemens, 2005). As such, connectivism fulfils the need for teaching current students 21st century skills where learners move beyond content consumption and into stages of critical thinking, collaboration, and content creation (Downes, 2007). Also, connectivism is aware of globalisation in education as presented by Miller, Shapiro and Hilding-Hamann (2008) and Oxford University (2015). Connectivism shows opportunities in learning, which were impossible without ICT. This makes connectivism a learning theory for the digital age (Siemens, 2005).

A connectivist way of thinking matches the current generation students in higher education. These modern students differ in their use of technology in daily life. Literature indicates this generation as the net generation (Oblinger & Oblinger, 2005) or digital natives (Prensky, 2001). They can always be online and can have access to the whole world for both social ends and educational needs. By bringing their devices into the classroom, this generation of students is a trigger for change in education (Veen & Vrakking, 2006). The increase of ICT in education makes it easier for students to have access to a huge source of data. The lecturer no longer has the exclusive rights on knowledge supply (Van Aalst & Kok, 2004). He or she has become one of the many sources in the students' network, which can be consulted for educational goals.

*Aligning Learning Spaces with Learning and Teaching in Higher Education*

The developments in education have influenced the relationship between students and teachers, the relationship among students, and the way these relationships are supported by learning spaces (Beckers & Van der Voordt, 2013; Long & Holeton, 2009; McLaughlin & Mills, 2008; Jamieson et al., 2000). Originally, Oblinger (2005, p. 15) defined learning spaces in higher education as

> regularly scheduled physical locations designed for face-to-face meetings of instructors and students.

Due to the new trends in learning and teaching, other studies used the term learning spaces in a broader context as the facilities where learning takes place (JISC, 2006; Marmot, 2006). According to Brown (2005, p. 124).

> [l]earning spaces encompass the full range of places in which learning occurs [...].

Naming learning spaces in this way might be confusing for educational experts. There is an enormous number of scientific studies about the concept of 'learning'.

To state it bluntly, many researchers define learning more or less similar to Simons and Ruijters (2004, p. 212), who argue that

> Learning refers to implicit or explicit mental and/or overt activities and processes leading to changes in knowledge, skills or attitudes […].

This suggests that learning is generally in one's head and occurs permanently during the day and independently from the physical setting. In this chapter about learning spaces, learning refers to the context of education, school or university, and the term 'learning spaces' and 'study spaces' are used interchangeably.

The relationship between learning and teaching and the environment in which learning and teaching takes place has been widely studied (Higgins, Hall, Wall, Woolner, & McCaughey, 2005). Higgins et al. (2005) studied more than 200 academic references, which show that particularly basic variables of the physical environment such as air quality, temperature, noise, and several design features influence educational processes and student performance. However, according to Fisher (2005a, 2001), the real impact of school buildings on learning and teaching is mainly theoretical rather than empirically proven. In practice, there are many intervening variables that obscure the relationship between learning spaces and learning activities of students (Gislason, 2010). It is likely that a good teacher in a bad building will lead to better results than a poor teacher in a very well utilised building. Nevertheless, the past decades even more studies have addressed alignment of learning space characteristics and learning and teaching approaches in higher education.

Alignment can be described as bringing into harmony things that differ or could differ. Regarding to buildings, there are three stages that are relevant for aligning the physical environment with organisations (Szigeti & Davis, 2005). First, organisations should formulate why they require a built facility and next what their requirements are, in terms of the expected results of the core processes. Finally, the organisation need to formulate which spatial settings can meet the requirements. Duffy, Craig, and Gillen (2011) built on the same idea with their 'purpose-process-place' framework. Purpose, process and place refer to the spatial arrangements and adjacencies ('place'), which have to be deployed in such a way that working practices ('processes') can contribute to enhance the goals ('purpose') of the organisation (Figure 8.1).

The 'purpose-process-place' perspective can be used to develop a learning space framework to identify spatial implications of new ways of learning in higher education (Beckers et al., 2015).

*Figure 8.1. The purpose-process-place framework (visualised after Duffy et al., 2011, in Beckers, Van der Voordt and Dewulf, 2015, p. 3)*

## PURPOSE, PROCESS AND PLACE IN HIGHER EDUCATION

*Purpose of Education*

A traditional perception of the purpose of a school was formulated by the American educational reformer Dewey at the start of the 20th century. Dewey's vision on the purpose of schools was to transfer knowledge and prepare young people to participate in America's democratic society (Rodgers, 2002). The developments in education showed that in the 20th century, the ideas about knowledge transfer in education were mainly based on traditional learning theories such as behaviourism, cognitive theory and constructivism (Merriam, Caffarella, & Baumgartner, 2007). In the 21st century these three theories were supplemented with connectivism as a learning theory that builds upon ICT possibilities (Marais, 2011; Kop & Hill, 2008; Siemens, 2005). The foregoing led to a shift in the purpose of teaching and learning from 'school' as a place of instruction in the 19th century, to a place to produce learning in the late 20th century (Barr & Tagg, 1995) and to a place to construct knowledge in the 21th century (Siemens, 2008). Nowadays schools aim to be an institution where learning for students is a co-production with their peers and their teachers, instead of simply consuming knowledge and instructions in a classroom. Therefore, all four of the above-mentioned learning theories have their own merits and should be applied in curricula. Ashworth et al. (2004, p. 10) emphasise that

> [...] it would be more advantageous for educators of the future to take a more eclectic approach where learning theory is concerned, as more than one theory could accommodate the needs of the self-directed, experimental and lifelong learners of the future.

The development of the four learning theories can be characterised by two shifts in ways of learning. First, the development from behaviourism to cognitivism implies an increase of self-regulation in learning (Chen, 2002; Zimmerman, 1989).

> Self-regulated learning emphasises autonomy and control by the individual who monitors, directs, and regulates actions towards goals of information acquisition, expanding expertise, and self-improvement. (Paris & Paris, 2001, p. 89)

Second, in contrast to behaviourism and cognitivism, social constructivism and connectivism emphasise social interaction (Van der Zanden, 2010; Siemens, 2005). Where social constructivism is, to some extent, associated with self-regulation (Paris & Paris, 2001), connectivism is strongly related to self-regulated learning (Türker & Zingel, 2008) and the learner's autonomy (Kop & Hill, 2008). The four learning theories can be placed in a two-by-two matrix with 'self-regulation in learning' on the horizontal axis and 'social interaction in learning' on the vertical axis (Figure 8.2).

155

*Figure 8.2. Purpose of education (derived from Beckers et al., 2015)*

*Education Processes*

The four described learning theories are reflected in different educational processes with a variable power distribution between student and teacher. Trigwell, Prosser, and Waterhouse (1999) formulated three processes founded on two extremities of the student-teacher spectrum: a teacher-focussed strategy, a student-focussed strategy, and a teacher-student interaction strategy in between. Illeris (2007) mentions three similar interactions between students and teachers and calls these 'teaching directions' from a teacher perspective, teaching directions from a student's perspective and a teaching direction in which both teachers and students are involved.

The traditional teacher-centred way of teaching is based on behaviourism (Freiberg & Lamb, 2009). The behaviourist learning theory has had a substantial influence on education, for example, leading to programmed instructional approaches (Jones & Brader-Araje, 2002). Behaviourism in schools placed the responsibility for learning directly on the shoulders of the teachers (Jones & Brader-Araje, 2002) and was based on fixed rewards for positive student behaviour (Freiberg & Lamb, 2009). Shreeve (2008) described this didactic form as lecture-based learning, where learning is derived from the instructor imparting what is known about a subject and, thus, hopefully resulting in knowledge transfer. According to Ashworth et al. (2004, p. 7),

> Cognitivism meant a shift away from teacher-centred methods of course delivery and more freedom for students to choose the type of learning that suits them best.

Such students have to be self-regulated learners.

They personally initiate and direct their own efforts to acquire knowledge and skills rather than relying on teachers, parents, or other agents of instruction. (Zimmerman, 1989, p. 329)

The impact of social constructivist theories in education can be seen in the focus on working in small groups (Jones & Brader-Araje, 2002). The emphasis is on having students working together, while sharing ideas and challenging each other's perspectives.

Crucial to social constructivism is the idea that knowledge and understanding are constructed when individuals engage socially and communicate with each other, through shared problems and tasks. Most social constructivist models, therefore, stress the need for collaboration among learners. (Foster, 2008, p. 93)

Social constructivist literature mentions different didactic forms, like problem-based learning, collaborative learning, and cooperative learning (Foster, 2008). A characteristic of all educational processes that fit the social constructivist theory is the shift in the teacher's role from

the sage on the stage to the guide on the side. (Martin, Katz, Morris, & Kilgallon, 2007, p. 13)

New learning processes in connectivism are based on network learning (McLaughlin & Mills, 2008). In network learning, everyone is a node in a collaborative learning process. According to Siemens (2008), the difference between connectivism and the previously mentioned social constructivism is that constructivists suppose that knowledge transfer occurs by socialisation, and connectivists are connecting nodes involving both people and other sources. Hence, while a constructivist would likely see the network solely as a social medium for interaction, a connectivist additionally sees the network as an extension of the mind (Siemens, 2005). Wang (2008) described the learner-interface interaction as an important component of a technology-based interactive learning environment. This has led to virtual education, which can be characterised as a form of asynchronous tuition (Shabha, 2004).

Learners might move away from classroom groups and a tutor to online networks and important nodes on these networks, and the role of the teacher will further decrease. (Kop & Hill, 2008, p. 9)

The impact of the four learning theories on educational processes can also be mapped in a matrix with the same axes as in Figure 8.2. The designations of the four process quadrants in the matrix of Figure 8.3 are derived from Wang (2008) and Moore (1989). The conventional behaviourist educational instruction model was described by Moore (1989) as a relationship between the instructor and the learner. He characterised the self-regulated (cognitive) learner in relation to the content and the social constructivist learner in relation to other learners. In connection to ICT developments in education, Wang (2008) added the relation between the learner and the interface.

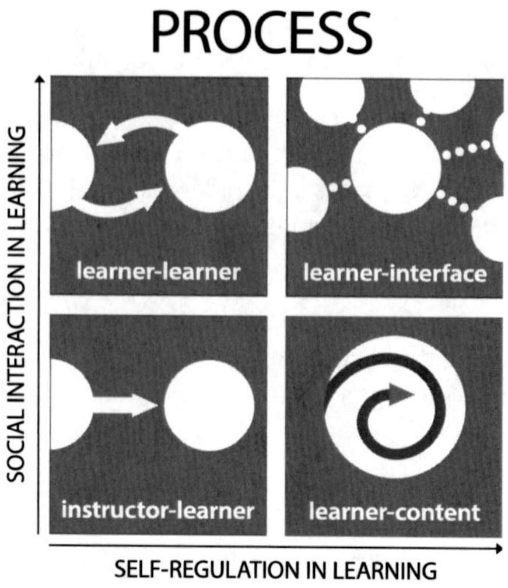

# PROCESS

*Figure 8.3. Education processes (derived from Beckers et al., 2015)*

The four processes are not mutually exclusive. They are all valuable and complementary, and a curriculum is usually composed from a palette of different teaching and learning processes (Kolb, 1984).

## Place; Learning Settings

Traditional school environments still focus on accommodating the transmission of knowledge rather than on learning objectives and learning outcomes, which can be achieved in different ways (Punie, 2007).

> The design of classrooms optimises instructor transmission. In the traditional classroom floor plan, students receive content packaged and presented with a 'one-size-fits-all' approach, regardless of the learners' unique needs or styles. (Brown & Long, 2006, p. 93)

The increase of self-regulated learning in education implies a shift in the role of the physical learning environment.

> In order to self-regulate, learners must be able to control their attention. Often this process entails clearing the mind of distracting thoughts, as well as seeking suitable environments that are conductive to learning (e.g., quiet areas without substantial noise). (Winne, 1995 as cited in Zumbrunn, Tradlock, & Roberts, 2011, p. 11)

Influenced by social constructivist theories in education, formal teaching spaces for large groups, like traditional classrooms, are becoming less common than smaller, less formal settings where students can learn from one another as well as from their

## LEARNING SPACE DESIGN IN HIGHER EDUCATION

appointed teachers (Marmot, 2006). This leads to the need for project rooms and small group settings, which support project-based learning and other forms of active learning (Fisher, 2005a).

For new ways of learning, students need more informal areas where they can meet face-to-face and have contact with their virtual network sources (Foster, 2008). Others mention informal or social learning spaces as a development in university buildings (Harrop & Turpin, 2013; Matthews, Andrews, & Adams, 2011). According to Matthews et al. (2011), informal social learning spaces refer to student learning outside of designated class time. Earlier, Oldenburg (2001) defined the social learning space as a physical and/or virtual area that is not predominantly identified with either social or work/study perspectives, but transcends both (Oldenburg, 1991 as cited in Wiliamson & Nodder, 2002). New university buildings have progressively shown such environments, for instance, Techno Cafés, which include high-quality services and technology to facilitate individual and group work (Foster, 2008).

Figure 8.4 adds the physical learning environment to the former quadrants that referred to 'purpose' and 'process'. Here the quadrants build on relevant learning space classifications in literature (e.g., Beard & Wilson, 2007; Marmot, 2006; Fisher, 2005b, 2003). Fisher (2003) presented a 'learning environments matrix', showing a clear overview of learning settings with different levels of self-regulated spaces and/ or collaborative spaces. He distinguished four edges of the learning space spectrum: the classroom setting, project space, personal study space, and the Internet café. The four edges correspond with Fisher's typology of four learning settings from 2005. Analogous to Fisher's work, four categories of learning spaces were defined in the right hand box of Figure 8.4, using the same axes as in the other two matrices. In the figure each of the education processes and the underlying need for interaction or self-regulation has a specific physical learning setting to match:

1. A setting for large groups (e.g. classroom or lecture hall);
2. An individual learning setting for concentration;
3. A setting for small group work (e.g. project room);
4. Informal open space settings, often with catering services.

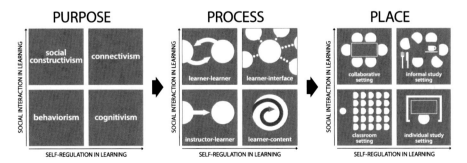

*Figure 8.4. Framework for aligning learning space with educational purpose and process (Beckers, 2016a, p. 40)*

The next step is to determine how the four learning space settings of Figure 8.4 can be further characterised.

## LEARNING SPACE CHARACTERISTICS

Literature shows that poorly designed buildings can restrain students to come to the university (Kuntz, Petrovic, & Ginocchio, 2012), whereas well-designed buildings or campuses may help to attract students (Price, Matzdorf, Smith, & Agahi, 2003). Many studies address the characteristics of the physical learning environment that might influence learning and teaching (Yang, Becerik-Gerber, & Mino, 2013; Harrop & Turpin, 2013; Walden, 2009; Woolner, Hall, Higgins, McCaughey, & Wall, 2007; Jamieson, 2003; Schneider, 2002; Fisher, 2001; Earthman, 1998), in particular comfort and aesthetics. These characteristics are linked to lighting, air quality, temperature, acoustics, furniture, and colour. Yang et al. (2013) showed that students' perception of attributes, such as air quality and temperature, are highly influenced by the design of classrooms. Students also perceive furniture to be important. Particularly for informal learning spaces, Harrop and Turpin (2013) found that students frequently described lighting and natural light as important. Temperature was only mentioned by a few students. Somerville and Collins (2008) endorsed the importance of comfortable, reconfigurable furniture in a functional, inspiring space. Jamieson's (2003) aesthetic aspects concerned interior design elements, such as colour schemes, quality and type of floor coverings, and decorative features. Other studies emphasised the importance of natural elements in learning environments for students' attachment to their learning environment, such as nature murals in indoor settings (Felsten, 2009), natural views (Benfield, Rainbolt, Bell, & Donovan, 2015), and plants (Bakker & Van der Voordt, 2010). Another aspect of the physical learning environment is the layout (Jamieson, 2003), which encompasses the arrangements of settings and the space between these settings. Layout also refers to how the physical environment facilitates students to move through and between study areas and to work within an area, either individually or with others. Studies by Yang et al. (2013), Sommerville and Collins (2008), and Fisher (2001) noticed the relevance of the spatial layout in relation to students' learning. Sommerville and Collins (2008) found that students prefer open, unconfined learning environments. According to Yang et al. (2013), students' appraisal heavily relies on spatial attributes, especially visibility, ICT facilities, and other facilities that are provided. Concerning ICT facilities, access to these resources is important to the majority of learners (Sandberg Hanssen & Solvoll, 2015; Harrop & Turpin, 2013) and usually refers to PCs, printers, large screens, access to the Internet, and software.

According to Jamieson (2003), four key characteristics of the physical learning environment should be taken into account related to supporting learning and teaching: comfort of the environment, aesthetic impact of the environment, layout of the environment, and fit-out (provided services). Building on the literature, these four characteristics of the physical environment can be operationalised as in Table 8.2.

LEARNING SPACE DESIGN IN HIGHER EDUCATION

*Table 8.2. Design characteristics of learning spaces*

| Layout | Comfort | Aesthetics | Fit-out/services |
|---|---|---|---|
| Central location of learning settings; Transparency/openness; Retreat; Diversity of learning settings; Convenience to meet. | Natural lighting; Temperature; Furniture; Size of working surface. | Colour; Floor finishing; General finishing & decoration; Plants. | Desktop computers; Printing facilities; WiFi; Food and beverages. |

*Table 8.3. Design characteristics of four main learning space types (adapted from Beckers, 2016a)*

*I. Classroom setting*

| Layout | Comfort | Aesthetics | Fit-out/services |
|---|---|---|---|
| Mostly closed rooms with 30 seats (50 m²) or more. Lecture halls up to 400 seats. Seats face the lecturer in a front position in the room. | Formal, functional and movable furniture (tables and chairs) or fixed chairs and tables in lecture halls. Size of working surface is about 0.5 m²/seat. Controlled temperature. Natural lighting is usually limited. | Finishing and decoration is functional and generic. | Bring your own device and use WiFi. Smartboard central in the room or decentral smaller presentation screens on the walls. |

*II. Collaborative setting for small groups*

| Layout | Comfort | Aesthetics | Fit-out/services |
|---|---|---|---|
| Open or closed settings, often scattered through the building. Closed project rooms (10 m²) for retreat. Open settings with movable tables and chairs in learning areas. Preferably not situated directly in or near circulation areas. | Setting with a large table and 4 to 8 seats. Working surface is about 0.5 m²/seat. Controlled temperature in closed project rooms; temperature difficult to control in open areas. Often lack of natural light. | Finishing and decoration in project rooms is functional and generic, in open areas more decorated and colourful. | Bring your own device and use WiFi. Presentation screen on the wall in project rooms. Near coffee corner. |

*(cont.)*

R. BECKERS

*Table 8.3. Design characteristics of four main learning space types*
*(adapted from Beckers, 2016a) (cont.)*

| III. Individual study setting | | | |
|---|---|---|---|
| *Layout* | *Comfort* | *Aesthetics* | *Fit-out/services* |
| Closed settings in personal cockpits (5 m²) or open settings in learning landscapes. Preferably not situated directly in or near circulation areas. | Functional furniture, comparable with office workspace (desk and chair). Often lack of natural light. Controlled temperature in personal cockpits; temperature difficult to control in open learning landscapes. | Finishing and decoration in personal cockpits is functional and generic, in open areas more decorated and colourful. | Bring your own device and use WiFi in combination with fixed desktop computers and printing facilities. |

| IV. Informal study setting | | | |
|---|---|---|---|
| *Layout* | *Comfort* | *Aesthetics* | *Fit-out/services* |
| Open and transparent. Combined with other functions, such as the entrance hall, corridors, atria. | Combination of formal and informal furniture. Limited attention for the size of working surface. Temperature is difficult to control, because of the layout and the size of these areas. Usually limited natural lighting. | Situated in colourful and decorated building areas. | Bring your own device and use WiFi. Supported by a coffee corner or a catering area. |

Combining the four learning settings of the learning space framework with the attributes of Table 8.2, enables to discern the learning settings by their design characteristics, as shown in Table 8.3.

## STUDENTS' LEARNING SPACE PREFERENCES

In order to develop appropriate physical learning environments that are aligned with the requirements of higher education students, the student experiences should be a key aspect of research into learning spaces. According to Jessop et al. (2012), the students' voice is too often missing in research into this topic. Therefore, this paragraph pays attention to the interaction between learning activities in higher education and the physical environment from a student perspective.

162

LEARNING SPACE DESIGN IN HIGHER EDUCATION

The results are based on a study that was conducted at the HAN University of Applied Sciences in The Netherlands (Beckers, Van der Voordt, & Dewulf, 2016). The sample was selected from 985 business management students in Nijmegen. The questionnaire was filled in by 697 students (71% response rate). The age, study year, gender, and living situation of the respondents are presented in Table 8.4. An impression of the learning settings in the Nijmegen building is shown in Figure 8.5.

In the questionnaire, the students indicated the importance of the seventeen items related to comfort of the environment, aesthetical aspects of the environment, the layout, and the fit-out of the environment (Figure 8.6). Figure 8.6 presents the seventeen items that indicate the importance of the physical study environment for students from most important to less important. The figure shows that students value functionality as more relevant for their physical study environment than for instance aesthetical aspects. The main item for students is the availability of WiFi in the environment. IT elements, like the presence of desktop computers and printing facilities in the study environment are important as well, but other aspects, such as natural light, temperature, comfort of the furniture, and enough working space are more important in the eye of the students. The same goes for the possibility to eat

*Table 8.4. Respondents characteristics (N=697) (Beckers, 2016b)*

| Variable | Number | Percentage | Variable | Number | Percentage |
|---|---|---|---|---|---|
| Gender | | | Living Situation | | |
| Male | 336 | 48,2% | With parents | 452 | 65,0% |
| Female | 361 | 51,8% | Student house | 181 | 26,0% |
| | | | Other | 64 | 9,0% |
| Age | | | Study year | 316 | 45,4% |
| 17 years | 59 | 8,5% | first year | 267 | 38,4% |
| 18 years | 100 | 14,4% | second year | 112 | 16,1% |
| 19 years | 148 | 21,3% | third year | 1 | 0,1% |
| 20 years | 155 | 22,3% | fourth year | 1 | 0,1% |
| 21 years | 110 | 15,8% | missing | | |
| 22 years | 63 | 9,0% | | | |
| 23 years | 31 | 4,5% | | | |
| > 23 years | 29 | 4,0% | | | |
| missing | 2 | 0,3% | | | |

An open area with student workstations

An open area with lounge seats in the corridors

Closed project rooms for students

An informal study space near the café

*Figure 8.5. Impression of learning settings in the Nijmegen building (Beckers, 2016b)*

163

and drink in the physical study environment. Layout aspects, such as a variety in spaces for retreat and meeting space, or the location of study spaces in the building, are less important to students. Aesthetical aspects of the physical environment, like colour or the finishing and decoration in the building, are perceived as not important in relation with study activities.

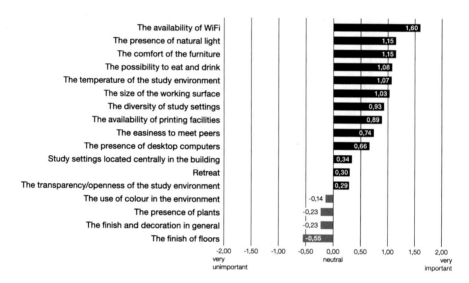

*Figure 8.6. Mean values regarding the importance of characteristics of the physical study environment in higher education buildings (N=697) (Beckers, 2016b)*

## LEARNING SPACE IN A BROADER PERSPECTIVE

Mostly, the spatial settings of Table 8.3 and Figure 8.4 are related to educational buildings. However, particularly the ICT developments of the past ten years have shed a different light on learning and teaching space. Nowadays, in this virtual world students can have access to study resources from anywhere, which means learning or study space is not limited to university buildings. Analogous to 'the city is the office' (Harrison, 2002), every square meter of the built environment has the potential to support the learning activities of a student, from home to the classroom and all kinds of other settings in between, such as a coffee house, café, restaurant, bar, museum, library and public spaces, such as streets, parks or public transport (Radcliffe, Wilson, Powell, & Tibbetts, 2008; Oldenburg, 2001). This perspective on higher education learning spaces is shown in the framework of Figure 8.7.

Knowing that students could choose for any place to conduct their study activities, the study at the HAN University of Applied Sciences aimed to determine the study place preferences of the students as well. Therefore, the questionnaire included questions to address which learning spaces students prefer for individual study

LEARNING SPACE DESIGN IN HIGHER EDUCATION

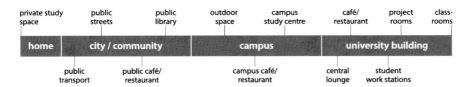

*Figure 8.7. Higher education learning space framework
(adapted from Beckers et al., 2015)*

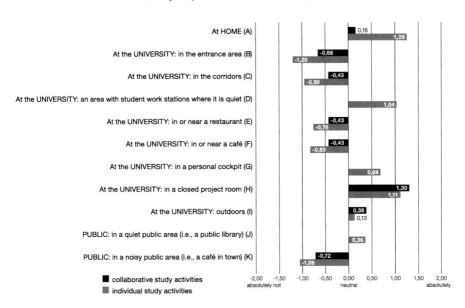

*Figure 8.8. Mean values regarding the learning space preferences
(N=697) (adapted from Beckers, 2016b)*

activities that require concentration, and for collaborative study activities in small groups with peers that require communication. The collaborative study activities concerned working on group assignments and did not refer to social activities, such as hanging out, having lunch, or just drinking coffee. Students were asked to indicate their preference – based on a five-point Likert scale, for several learning settings from the learning space framework, for both study activities, i.e. at home, at the university/campus, or in public spaces. The learning spaces at the university fit with the settings from Figure 8.4, namely: individual settings, settings for small groups, and informal settings. Classrooms were excluded from the study, because classrooms are mostly scheduled and used for instructions, so students usually cannot choose these settings for individual or collaborative activities. The results, as presented in Figure 8.8, show that students prefer to do individual study activities that require concentration, at home. For these activities students do not favour open, noisy

165

R. BECKERS

Table 8.5. t-values to identify significant differences between learning space preferences per task (Beckers, 2016b)

| Learning space | Mean difference | t-value | df | Sig. (2-tailed) | d | 95% CI LL | UL |
|---|---|---|---|---|---|---|---|
| Home | | | | | | | |
| A | 1.09 | 21.76 | 645 | 0.00 | 1.11 | 1.01 | 1.20 |
| University | | | | | | | |
| B | 0.54 | −15.92 | 688 | 0.00 | 0.63 | −0.61 | −0.48 |
| C | 0.52 | −14.38 | 685 | 0.00 | 0.58 | −0.59 | −0.45 |
| D | − | − | − | − | − | − | − |
| E | 0.33 | −8.67 | 690 | 0.00 | 0.35 | −0.41 | −0.26 |
| F | 0.40 | −10.64 | 690 | 0.00 | 0.41 | −0.47 | −0.32 |
| G | − | − | − | − | − | − | − |
| H | 0.19 | −5.68 | 689 | 0.00 | 0.24 | −0.25 | −0.12 |
| I | 0.25 | −7.01 | 689 | 0.00 | 0.22 | −0.33 | −0.18 |
| Public | | | | | | | |
| J | − | − | − | − | − | − | − |
| K | 0.34 | −8.82 | 685 | 0.00 | 0.35 | −0.41 | −0.26 |

settings, such as an atrium, corridors, the entrance area of the university building or an area with workstations for students, where talking is allowed. Catering areas, such as restaurants or grand cafés, are not popular either. When students work on individual study activities, they prefer to do these in closed, quiet learning spaces, such as individual cockpits or project rooms. An area with student workstations where it is quiet because talking is not allowed is sufficient as well. Other learning spaces than at home or at the university are not popular for individual study activities. Even when these spaces are explicitly meant for studying in silence, such as a library. Also, students do not prefer busy public spaces, like a café in town, for study activities.

For collaborative study activities with peers in small groups, students actually have one favourite place, namely closed project rooms. All other learning spaces are valued as rather neutral or even as not popular for working together on study activities. In the questionnaire, a specific question was formulated regarding the preference of working together face-to-face or through online networks, such as FaceTime, Skype or WhatsApp. 63% of the respondents preferred face-to-face contact to virtual contact. 11% preferred virtual contact more. The other 26% were neutral in their opinion.

The overall picture of Figure 8.8 shows a similarity between the preference of most learning spaces for individual activities and collaborative tasks. If a learning space is preferred or not preferred for individual activities, these spaces are preferred or not preferred for small group work as well. Nevertheless, an interesting question is whether there are significant differences between the two activities and to what extent specific learning space is more or less preferred for individual or collaborative activities. The t-values in Table 8.5 illustrate significant differences between the mean learning space preferences for individual and collaborative study activities.

Cohen's d in Table 8.5 shows a large significant difference between the preference to do individual or collaborative study activities at home, and also a medium difference for the preference to do study activities in busy areas at the university (e.g., entrance area, corridors, catering area, or a café). Small differences occur for the preference for quiet, closed learning space (project rooms) and outdoor spaces.

## IMPLICATIONS FOR PRACTICE

The design of the physical learning environment 'suffers' from its long-lasting history. In school buildings, the same problems occur as with the railway system. Both concepts go back more than 100 years, which may frustrate innovation. According to Jessop et al. (2012), dominant models of teaching, such as teacher-centred approaches may have shaped the configurations of rooms. Therefore, space may place boundaries over developments in higher education learning and teaching, like new or alternative pedagogies.

The insights of the research in this chapter could be used to support learning space planning in higher education buildings. Nevertheless, one of the main insights for practice is that the developments in education do not result in a revolutionary change of traditional learning settings, such as classrooms. The influence of developments in education on educational buildings will be closer to an evolution, rather than a revolution. Yet, the research gives many insights for learning space planning that may lead to a better alignment of learning spaces with learning and teaching in the future.

The first recommendation for higher education institutions is to aim for creating activity based study environments for students to support concentration, routine work, and communication. The purpose-process-place framework of Figure 8.4 in this chapter could be a valuable conceptual tool that can contribute to learning space planning. Besides classrooms, the framework presents settings that support individual

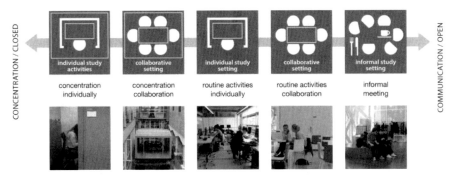

*Figure 8.9. Settings for an activity based learning environment (classrooms excluded) (Beckers, 2016, p. 163)*

study activities and settings that support communication. To sufficiently support the need of students for retreat, individual settings are preferably differentiated in closed settings for concentrated study and open space with workstations or laptop plug-ins for routine study activities and activities that do not specifically require concentration. The settings for communication are refined in three types. First, settings that support formal communication referring to collaboration. Second, settings for informal communication referring to meeting each other for routine activities. Third, settings that support activities that require concentration and retreat. This adds two closed settings that support study activities from concentration to communication (Figure 8.9).

In current practice, the imbalance between the settings of Figure 8.9 leads to misalignment. Besides traditional classrooms, higher education institutions mainly create informal meeting space in educational buildings, because the multi-functionality of these settings is highly overrated. To appropriately support study activities of students, higher education institutions could offer quieter (closed) learning spaces for retreat.

A second recommendation for higher education practice is to situate learning settings in relation to other spatial settings, such as instruction space, working space for teaching staff and circulation space, in an appropriate way. This supports the development towards communities of learning and practice (McLaughlin & Mills, 2008; Smith & Bath, 2006). Many higher education institutions focus on creating generic space for multi-use in terms of 'the campus as learning space'. Often, this is at the expense of students who want to identify themselves with a group and want to recognise that group in the building. The crux here is to find a balance between efficiency measures, such as generic space, and user preferences regarding dedicated areas for specific user groups. Specific spatial principles are:

- Create dedicated areas for learning communities that include three key elements: a teaching staff area, a student area, and areas for programmed instruction rooms (still mostly traditional classrooms) and for ad-hoc interaction between students and staff.
- Create mixed zones with informal meeting space for contact between students and staff, and among staff or students. Decentral informal learning spaces are areas where students can eat and drink while doing their work. Catering services, other than basic hot drinks, are not necessarily present in these areas. Extensive catering areas are centrally situated in the building.
- Student areas and the staff areas contain a balanced mix of settings that support concentration, routine activities, and communication.
- Distinguish physical learning environments that particularly support study activities or social activities in educational buildings.
- Learning spaces for students are separated from circulation areas, such as corridors or the entrance area. Yet, meeting spaces are close to circulation areas to stimulate chance encounters.

- Create generic instruction areas in between two learning communities, which both can use, besides their dedicated instruction rooms.
- Situate student areas next to the instruction rooms. Due to new concepts such as blended learning and flipped classroom, the information-transmission component of face-to-face lectures is moving out of class time (Abeysekera & Dawson, 2015). Traditional instructional education, with the teacher as sage on the stage, is decreasing in favour of students doing assignments in small groups during programmed instructions, where the teacher is the guide on the side. These cooperative learning activities, where students are working in small groups led by a teacher, demand other spaces than the traditional classroom. Therefore, spaces for small group work are preferably nearby to the classrooms, to support the increasing flexibility in education processes. So, create a learning environment that meets the increased variety in didactical approaches in higher education teaching supported by ICT.
- Create flexibility in the learning environment (e.g., adaptable furniture and equipment, movable walls and flexibility in building technology). Other possibilities are flexibility in use, by using generic furniture, so that students and staff could use each other's space in mixed zones.

Finally, additionally to the former principles, higher education institutions could increase opportunities for experimenting on a small scale with spatial concepts for the classroom of the future, such as new technology enabled active learning environments (Fisher & Newton, 2014; Park & Choi, 2014). These are hybrid instruction areas or intelligent classrooms that combine ICT developments in education with new didactical forms where students are not consumers of education, but active and self-regulative learners. Of course, new physical environments should match the learning and teaching approaches. But, according to Oblinger (2005), new learning spaces are themselves agents for change. By changing the environment, the users might be stimulated to think about adapting their activities to the environment.

## FINAL DISCUSSION AND CONCLUSION

The results of this study contribute two main insights to the current knowledge about the physical learning environment and learning spaces in higher education. First, the study shows that students, regardless of individual or collaborative study activities, prefer a quiet study environment with sufficient possibilities for retreat. This is similar to the results of Price et al. (2003), who found quiet spaces as one of the most relevant study facilities of universities. Harrop and Turpin (2013) also argued retreat to be a key attribute of the physical learning environment. But how is this related to the increase of informal learning spaces in higher education buildings? These spaces are noisy and crowded and are therefore not popular with students for doing their study activities. Nevertheless, several studies show the relevance of these spaces (Sandberg Hanssen & Solvoll, 2015; Higgins et al., 2005).

An explanation could be that informal spaces are deemed important but mostly for supporting other aspects of higher education learning such as serendipitous encounter and ambient sociality (Crook & Mitchell, 2012). So, a general conclusion that catering areas and informal learning spaces are not important is not convenient. These spaces are relevant to support social activities at the university, but are less preferred for study activities.

Second, students value the physical learning environment mainly based on effectiveness rather than experience. Students attach importance to functional aspects of the environment, such as sufficient natural light, a nice temperature, functional furniture, and sufficient resources. Environmental aspects that support collaboration, such as the convenience to meet peers are perceived important as well. Aesthetical aspects of the physical environment are less relevant for students to support study activities. These results confirm the findings of Jessop et al. (2012). They also found that students are mostly concerned about the functional aspects of learning spaces and that they are not overly concerned about aesthetics. Nevertheless, literature shows the relevance of the increasing experience factor in society (Pine & Gilmore, 1999) that shows up in higher education as well (Beckers & Van der Voordt, 2013). Schools must be fun and attractive. Higher education is not only about learning and teaching, but above all about the whole context and atmosphere in which learning and teaching take place. This results in catchy and trendy interiors and furniture in higher education buildings that increasingly look like shopping malls with atria containing restaurants and grand cafés. An attractive university building is an important instrument to attract and retain students and staff (CABE, 2005; Price et al., 2003).

Once again, differences between the findings of the aforementioned studies can be attributed to the scope of said studies. Building conditions do matter (Price et al., 2009). Well-designed learning environments are relevant for the image of the institution and to support end-user satisfaction. Furthermore, learning spaces in many modern university buildings fulfil minimum standards. Once these are attained, the impact of place characteristics on preferred learning spaces may be less significant (Higgins et al., 2005). Education buildings and facilities may be considered commodities or hygiene factors. They can motivate students to a certain extent, but students are most aware of the environment when it is not satisfactory.

Finally, the current study aimed to address preferences for the physical learning environment. Despite the sample of nearly 700 respondents, the study involved students of one Dutch UAS in a specific building in Nijmegen. Besides, these were all business students and the study focussed on two specific study activities. Further research that involves students from other disciplines, in more different buildings and in other countries would be a preferable next step, to look for differences or to endorse the findings of this Nijmegen study. Also, a study to student preferences for social study spaces that are designed for social activities, might be interesting as well.

To conclude, learning space preferences of higher education students mainly result from their goal support and evolving study activities. This is a significant finding, because the expectation is that future activities in higher education learning and teaching will be different from current activities. Traditional instructional approaches for larger groups will shift into more collaborative activities in small groups, in which students are self-directed learners. This shift in activities will have significant consequences for the requirements for higher education physical learning environments. Therefore, the findings of this research can be used by facility managers of higher education institutions in order to support contemporary learning with suitable, future-proof learning spaces.

## NOTE

[1] The content of this chapter is derived from the Ph.D. dissertation of R. Beckers (2016a).

## REFERENCES

Abeysekera, L., & Dawson, P. (2015). Motivation and cognitive load in the flipped classroom: Definition, rationale and a call for research. *Higher Education Research & Development, 34*(1), 1–14.

Adams Becker, S., Cummins, M., Davis, A., Freeman, A., Hall Giesinger, C., & Ananthanarayanan, V. (2017). *NMC horizon report: 2017 higher education edition.* Austin, TX: The New Media Consortium.

Ananiadou, K., & Claro, M. (2009). *21st century skills and competences for new millennium learners in OECD countries* (OECD education working papers No. 41). Paris: OECD.

Ashworth, F., Brennan, G., Egan, K., Hamilton, R., & Sáenz, O. (2004). Learning theories and higher education. *Level, 3*(2), 1–16.

Bakker, I., & Van der Voordt, T. (2010). The influence of plants on productivity: A critical assessment of research findings and test methods. *Facilities, 28*(9–10), 416–439.

Bar, R. B., & Tagg, J. (1995). From teaching to learning. *Change, 27*(6), 13–25.

Beard, C., & Wilson, J. P. (2006). *The experiential learning: A best practice handbook for educators and trainer* (2nd ed.). London: Kogan Page Limited.

Beckers, R. (2016a). *A learning space Odyssey* (PhD dissertation). University of Twente, Enschede.

Beckers, R. (2016b). Higher education learning space design: Form follows function? In S. Balslev Nielsen & P. A. Jensen (Eds.), *Research papers for EuroFM's 15th research symposium at EFMC2016, 8–9 June 2016 in Milan, Italy* (pp. 99–109). Lyngby: Polyteknisk Forlag.

Beckers, R., & Van der Voordt, T. (2013, May 22–24). *Facilitating new ways of learning in Dutch higher education* (pp. 25–35). International Journal of Facilities Management, EuroFM Journal, Conference papers 12th EuroFM Research Symposium, Czech Republic, Prague.

Beckers, R., Van der Voordt, T., & Dewulf, G. (2015). A conceptual framework to identify spatial implications of new ways of learning in higher education. *Facilities, 33*(1–2), 2–19.

Beckers, R., Van der Voordt, T., & Dewulf, G. (2016). Learning space preferences of higher education students. *Building and Environment, 104,* 243–252.

Benfield, J. A., Rainbolt, G. N., Bell, P. A., & Donovan, G. H. (2015). Classrooms with nature views evidence of differing student perceptions and behaviors. *Environment and Behavior, 47*(2), 140–157.

Boddington, A., & Boys, J. (2011). Reshaping learning – An introduction. In A. Boddington & J. Boys (Eds.), *Re-shaping learning: A critical reader* (pp. xi–xxii). Rotterdam, The Netherlands: Sense Publishers.

Brown, M. (2005). Learning spaces. In D. Oblinger & J. L. Oblinger (Eds.), *Educating the net generation* (pp. 12.1–12.22). Washington, DC: Educause.

Brown, M., & Long, P. (2006). Trends in learning space design. In D. G. Oblinger (Ed.), *Learning spaces* (pp. 9.1–9.11). Washington, DC: Educause.

CABE. (2005). *Design with distinction. The value of good building design in higher education.* London: Commission for Architecture and the Built Environment.

R. BECKERS

Chen, C. S. (2002). Self-regulated learning strategies and achievement in an introduction to information systems course. *Information Technology, Learning and Performance Journal, 20*(1), 11–25.

Collis, B., & Van der Wende, M. (2002). *Models of technology and change in higher education*. Enschede: CHEPS.

Crook, C., & Mitchell, G. (2012). Ambience in social learning: Student engagement with new designs for learning spaces. *Cambridge Journal of Education, 42*(2), 121–139.

Davies, S., Mullan, J., & Feldman, P. (2017). *Rebooting learning for the digital age: What next for technology-enhanced higher education?* (HEPI Report 93). Oxford: Higher Education Policy Institute.

Downes, S. (2007). *Learning networks in practice*. Ottawa: National Research Council Canada.

Duffy, F., Craig, D., & Gillen, N. (2011). Purpose, process, place: Design as a research tool. *Facilities, 29*(3–4), 97–113.

Earthman, G. I. (1998). *The impact of school building condition and student achievement, and behaviour* (pp. 2–26). Presented at the International Conference The Appraisal of Educational Investment European Investment Bank/Organization for Economic Coordination and Development, Luxembourg.

Felsten, G. (2009). Where to take a study break on the college campus: An attention restoration theory perspective. *Journal of Environmental Psychology, 29*, 160–167.

Fisher, K. (2001). *Building better outcomes: The impact of school infrastructure on student outcomes and behaviour: Schooling issues digest*. Canberra: Department of Education, Training and Youth Affairs.

Fisher, K. (2003). *Facility planning study for the Bank Negara Malaysia Corporate University*. Adelaide.

Fisher, K. (2005a). *Research into identifying effective learning environments* (pp. 159–167). Paper for OECD/PEB, Evaluating Quality in Educational Facilities, Lisbon.

Fisher, K. (2005b). *Linking pedagogy and space*. Footscray: Victoria University Australia, Department of Education and Training.

Fisher, K., & Newton, C. (2014). Transforming the twenty-first-century campus to enhance the net-generation student learning experience: Using evidence-based design to determine what works and why in virtual/physical teaching spaces. *Higher Education Research & Development, 33*(5), 903–920.

Foster, C. (2008). *Learning for understanding: Engaging and interactive knowledge visualization*. Durham, NC: Technology Enhanced Learning Research Group, Durham University.

Freiberg, H. J., & Lamb, S. M. (2009). Dimensions of person-centered classroom management. *Theory into Practice, 48*(2), 99–105.

Gislason, N. (2010). Architectural design and the learning environment: A framework for school design research. *Learning Environment Research, 13*, 127–145.

Harrison, A. (2002). Accommodating the new economy: The SANE space environment model. *Journal of Corporate Real Estate, 4*(3), 248–265.

Harrop, D., & Turpin, B. (2013). A study exploring learners' informal learning space behaviors, attitudes, and preferences. *New Review of Academic Librarianship, 19*(1), 58–77.

Higgins, S., Hall, E., Wall, K., Woolner, P., & McCaughey, C. (2005). *The impact of school environments: A literature review*. Newcastle: Design Council.

Illeris, K. (2007). *How we learn*. London & New York, NY: Routledge.

Jamieson, P. (2003). Designing more effective on-campus teaching and learning spaces: A role for academic developers. *International Journal for Academic Development, 8*(1–2), 119–133.

Jamieson, P., Fisher, K., Gilding, T., Taylor, P., & Trevitt, A. (2000). Place and space in the design of new learning environments. *Higher Education Research & Development, 19*(2), 221–236.

Jessop, T., Gubby, L., & Smith, A. (2012). Space frontiers for new pedagogies: A tale of constraints and possibilities. *Studies in Higher Education, 37*(8), 189–202.

JISC. (2006). *Designing spaces for effective learning. A guide to 21st century learning space design* (Joint Information Systems Committee). London: Higher Education Funding Council for England.

Jones, M. G., & Brader-Araje, L. (2002). The impact of constructivism on education: Language, discourse, and meaning. *American Communication Journal, 5*(3), 1–10. Retrieved May 1, 2013, from http://ac-journal.org/journal/vol5/iss3/special/jones.pdf

Kayzel, R. (2004). *De belofte van het nieuwe leren*. Retrieved April 18, 2011, from http://www.cop.hva.nl/artefact-1592-nl.html

172

LEARNING SPACE DESIGN IN HIGHER EDUCATION

Kolb, D. A. (1984). *Experiential learning: Experience as the source of learning and development.* Englewood Cliffs, NJ: Prentice-Hall.

Kop, R., & Hill, A. (2008). Connectivism: Learning theory of the future or vestige of the past? *International Review of Research in Open and Distance Learning, 9*(3), 1–13.

Kuntz, A. M., Petrovic, J. E., & Ginocchio, L. (2012). A changing sense of place: A case study of academic culture and the built environment. *Higher Education Policy, 25*(4), 433–451.

Leland, C. H., & Kasten W. C. (2002). Literacy education for the 21st century: It's time to close the factory. *Reading and Writing Quarterly, 18*(1), 5–15.

Long, P. D., & Holeton, R. (2009). Signposts of the revolution? What we talk about when we talk about learning spaces. *Educause Review, 44*(2), 36–48.

Marais, N. (2011). Connectivism as learning theory: The force behind changed teaching practice in higher education. *Education, Knowledge and Economy, 4*(3), 173–182.

Marmot, A. (2006). *Spaces for learning. A review of learning spaces in further and higher education.* Edinburgh: Alexi Marmot Associates and haa design by order of Scottish Funding Council. Retrieved April 15, 2013, from http://www.sfc.ac.uk/publications/spaces_for_learning_report.pdf

Marmot, A. (2012). *Matching post-16 estate investment to educational outcomes* (Alexi Marmot Associates by order of Scottish Funding Council). London: Alexi Marmot Associates.

Martin, P., Katz, T., Morris, R., & Kilgallon, S. (2007). A learning space for creativity: Early findings. In J. Barlow, G. Louw, & M. Price (Eds.), *Connections: Sharing the learning space. Articles from the learning and teaching conference 2007* (pp. 13–17). Brighton: University of Brighton Press.

Matthews, K. E., Andrews, V., & Adams, P. (2011). Social learning spaces and student engagement. *Higher Education Research & Development, 30*(2), 105–120.

McLaughlin, P., & Mills, A. (2008). Where shall the future student learn? Student expectations of university facilities for teaching and learning. In *Preparing for the graduate of 2015. Proceedings of the 17th annual teaching and learning forum.* Perth: Curtin University of Technology.

Merriam, S. B., Caffarella, R. S., & Baumgartner, L. M. (2007). *Learning in adulthood: A comprehensive guide.* San Francisco, CA: John Wiley & Sons.

Miller, R., Shapiro, H., & Hilding-Hamann, K. E. (2008). *School's over: Learning spaces in Europe in 2020: An imagining exercise on the future of learning* (JRC scientific and technical reports). Luxembourg: European Commission Joint Research Centre Institute for Prospective Technological Studies.

Moore, M. G. (1989). Editorial: Three types of interaction. *The American Journal of Distance Education, 3*(2), 1–6.

Oblinger, D. (2005). Leading the transition from classrooms to learning spaces. *Educause Quarterly, 28*(1), 14–18.

Oblinger, D., & Oblinger, J. L. (2005). *Educating the net generation.* Washington, DC: Educause.

Oldenburg, R. (1999). *The great good place* (2nd ed.). Philadelphia, PA: Da Capo Press.

Oldenburg, R. (2001). *Celebrating the third place: Inspiring stories about the 'great good places' at the heart of our communities.* New York, NY: Marlowe and Company.

Paris, S. G., & Paris, A. H. (2001). Classroom applications of research on self-regulated learning. *Educational Psychologist, 36*(2), 89–101.

Park, E. L., & Choi, B. K. (2014). Transformation of classroom spaces: Traditional versus active learning classroom in colleges. *Higher Education, 68*(5), 749–771.

Pine, J., & Gilmore, J. (1999). *The experience economy.* Boston, MA: Harvard Business School Press.

Prensky, M. (2001). *Teaching digital natives.* London: Sage Publications.

Price, I., Clark, E., Holland, M., Emerton, C., & Wolstenholme, C. (2009). *Condition matters: Pupil voices on the design and condition of secondary schools* (Project report). Reading: CfBT Education Trust.

Price, I., Matzdorf, F., Smith, L., & Agahi, H. (2003). The impact of facilities on student choice of university. *Facilities, 21*(10), 212–222.

Punie, Y. (2007). Learning spaces: An ICT-enabled model of future learning in the Knowledge-based society. *European Journal of Education, 42*(2), 187–199.

173

R. BECKERS

Radcliffe, D., Wilson, H., Powell, D., & Tibbetts, B. (2008). *Designing next generation places of learning: Collaboration at the pedagogy-space-technology nexus*. Brisbane: The University of Queensland.

Rodgers, C. (2002). Defining reflection: Another look at John Dewey and reflective thinking. *Teachers College Record, 104*(4), 842–866.

Sandberg Hanssen, T.-E., & Solvoll, G. (2015). The importance of university facilities for student satisfaction at a Norwegian University. *Facilities, 33*(13–14), 744–759.

Schneider, M. (2002). *Do school facilities affect academic outcomes?* Washington, DC: National Clearinghouse for Educational Facilities (NCEF).

Shabha, G. (2004). An assessment of the effectiveness of e-learning on university planning. *Facilities, 22*(3–4), 79–86.

Shreeve, M. W. (2008). Beyond the didactic classroom: Educational models to encourage active student involvement in learning. *Journal Chiropractic Education, 22*(1), 23–28.

Shuell, T. J. (1988). The role of the student in learning from instruction. *Contemporary Educational Psychology, 13*(3), 276–295.

Siemens, G. (2005). *Connectivism: A learning theory for the digital age*. Retrieved November 7, 2012, from http://Connectivism.ca

Siemens, G. (2008). *Learning and knowing in networks: Changing roles for educators and designers, ITFORUM 2008*. Retrieved November 7, 2012, from http://itforum.coe.uga.edu/Paper105/Siemens.pdf

Simons, P., & Ruijters, M. (2004). Learning professionals: Towards an integrated model. In H. P. A. Boshuizen, R. Bromme, & H. Gruber (Eds.), *Professional learning: Gaps and transitions on the way from novice to expert* (pp. 207–229). Dordrecht: Kluwer Academic Publishers.

Simons, P. R. J., Van der Linden, J., & Duffy, T. (2000). *New learning: Three ways to learn in a New Balance*. Dordrecht: Kluwer Academic Publishers.

Smith, C., & Bath, D. (2006). The role of the learning community in the development of discipline knowledge and generic graduate outcomes. *Higher Education, 51*(2), 259–286.

Somerville, M. M., & Collins, L. (2008). Collaborative design: A learner-centered library planning approach. *The Electronic Library, 26*(6), 803–820.

Sursock, A. (2015). *Trends 2015: Learning and teaching in European Universities*. Brussels: EUA Publications.

Szigeti, F., & Davis, G. (2005). *What is performance based building?* Canada: PeBBu Network.

Temple, P. (2008). Learning spaces in higher education: An under-researched topic. *London Review of Education, 6*(3), 229–241.

Trigwell, K., Prosser, M., & Waterhouse, F. (1999). Relations between teachers' approaches to teaching and students' approaches to learning. *Higher Education, 37*(1), 57–70.

Türker, M. A., & Zingel, S. (2008). Formative interfaces for scaffolding self-regulated learning in PLEs. *eLearning Papers 9*, 1–15. Retrieved April 29, 2013, from http://www.elearningeuropa.info/files/media/media15975.pdf

Van Aalst, H., & Kok, J. M. (2004). Het nieuwe leren. *JSW, 89*(4), 11–15.

Van der Zanden, A. H. W. (2010). *The facilitating university* (PhD dissertation). Eburon, Delft.

Veen, W., & Vrakking, B. (2006). *Homo Zappiens*. Londen: Continuum International Publishing Group.

Volman, M. (2006). Het 'nieuwe leren': Oplossing of nieuw probleem? *Pedagogiek, 26*(1), 14–25.

Voogt, J., & Pareja Roblin, N. (2012). A comparative analysis of international frameworks for 21st century competences: Implications for national curriculum policies. *Journal of Curriculum Studies, 44*(3), 299–321.

Walden, R. (Ed.). (2009). *Schools for the future*. Géttingen: Hogrefe & Huber Publishers.

Wang, Q. (2008). A generic model for guiding the integration of ICT into teaching and learning. *Innovations in Education and Teaching International, 45*(4), 411–419.

Williamson, A., & Nodder, C. (2002). Extending the learning space: Dialogue and reflection in the virtual coffee shop. *ACM SIGCAS Computers and Society, 32*(3), 1.

Woolner, P., Hall, E., Higgins, S., McCaughey, C., & Wall, K. (2007). A sound foundation? What we know about the impact of environments on learning and the implications for building schools for the future. *Oxford Review of Education, 33*(1), 47–70.

Zimbardo, P. G., Johnson, R. L., & McCann, V. (2009). *Psychologie, een inleiding*. Amsterdam: Pearson Education.

Zimmerman, B. J. (1989). A social cognitive view of self-regulated academic learning. *Journal of Educational Psychology, 81*(3), 329–339.

Zumbrunn, S., Tradlock, J., & Roberts, E. D. (2011). *Encouraging self-regulated learning in the classroom: A review of the literature*. Richmond, VA: Metropolitan Educational Research Consortium (MERC), Virginia Commonwealth University.

MAHMOUD REZA SAGHAFI

# 9. IMPLEMENTING GROUNDED THEORY IN RESEARCH ON BLENDED LEARNING ENVIRONMENTS

## ABSTRACT

Grounded theory as an inductive and exploratory research method has not any hypothesis. Therefore, data analysis process turn into a challenge that should be solved; how to organize and analyze the qualitative data? This paper presents the implementation of Grounded Theory as a research methodology in the field of design education. It illustrates how to analyze, organize, and transform data in an inductive approach till reach to a theory. By doing so, different unrelated data will be organized as a tree until form a holistic model. Each experience in grounded theory needs an innovative approach responding to unique challenges during the research process. The research aims to explore the limitations and benefits of a face-to-face design studio as well as a virtual design studio as experienced by architecture students and educators in order to find the optimal combination for a blended environment to maximize learning. While the studio environment has been promoted as an ideal educational setting for project-based disciplines, few qualitative studies have been undertaken in a comprehensive way. This study responds to this need by adopting Grounded Theory methodology in a qualitative comparative approach. The theory results from systematic data process as the main outcome: a holistic blended model which is sufficiently flexible to adapt to various setting, and facilitate constructivist learning.

## INTRODUCTION

While the studio environment has been promoted as an ideal educational setting for project-based disciplines, few qualitative studies have been undertaken in a comprehensive way (Bose, 2007). This study responds to this gap by adopting Grounded Theory methodology in a qualitative, comparative approach. The research aims to explore the limitations and benefits of a Face-to-Face design studio in combination with a virtual design studio as experienced by architecture students and educators in order to find the optimal combination for a blended environment to maximise learning.

The main questions driving this study are:

- Presuming that there is a continuing need for on-campus Face-to-Face interaction, what would a blended learning model look like?
- What would be its components and how would they be interrelated?

© KONINKLIJKE BRILL NV, LEIDEN, 2019 | DOI: 10.1163/9789004391598_011

The background begins with characteristics of design studio education and continues with research challenges on blended learning environments and finishes with the introduction of the research and how it covers the gap in the literature. The next section begins with introducing the philosophical position and methodological underpinning of the research approach, continuing with the reasons of choosing Grounded Theory as the methodology. Then, the research design for this case study – including data collection and analysis – is presented through pilot and detailed studies. At the end of this section, the process of organising, transforming, and analysing data are presented accompanied by a number of figures. The next section introduces the blended model, based on the analysed data. The discussion demonstrates some significances of the case study – the blended model – and how it develops learning environment theory.

The main purpose of this paper is to present the process of developing and analysing data based on Grounded Theory. Therefore, comparing the learning environments and characteristics of the blended model are secondary purposes which have been explained in Saghafi (2013) and then have been tested in Saghafi (2015).

## BACKGROUND

The design studio is a problem based learning approach closely aligned to constructivist theory and is suitable for team working, process focused, flexible, practice based, and interdisciplinary learning activities (Eilouti, 2006). Many university activities – including education, research, intellectual criticism and professional training – also exist in the design studio (Hashimshony & Haina, 2006, p. 8). The design studio faces similar challenges to higher education as a whole. Therefore, if a model is able to respond to the problems in design education, it will be applicable in many other fields of higher education.

Although blended courses have been employed in other fields, their application to design education is emerging (Senyapili & Karokaya, 2009, p. 111). Therefore, new and flexible models for design studio education are necessary to respond to changes and unpredictable conditions.

Course design is achieved through organising space, time, and activities together with the consideration of appropriate methods and tools (Sagun, Demirkan, & Goktepe, 2001, pp. 332–333).

Blended learning is still a new topic of practice and research; therefore, more studies are needed to explore and enhance the effectiveness of these environments (Dennis et al., 2006, p. 124).

As noted hereunder, the research literature reveals several deficiencies, limitations and gaps, and subsequent recommendations:

- A lack of attention to student and lecturers' qualitative perceptions of their learning environment can be observed (Fisher, 2003, p. 15). In the future, a more comprehensive approach is needed (Saghafi, Franz, & Crowther, 2010). Creating

IMPLEMENTING GROUNDED THEORY IN RESEARCH ON BLENDED LEARNING

an effective learning environment cannot be achieved without understanding teachers and learners' perceptions, experiences and attitudes (Wang, 2007).

- Holistic research approaches are needed to analyse complex field-like learning environments. Focusing on one or two aspects can result in ignoring the effect of other aspects resulting in inaccurate outcomes.
- Experiencing the components of the blended model by all participants is necessary to compare their perceptions.
- It appears that, generally, blended learning has developed without any research to inform this development or explore its potential.

Therefore, the benefits, limitations and implications of Face-to-Face and virtual learning environments have to be explored comprehensively. This comparative study has shown blended environments to be the most appropriate approach for maximising learning. However, there are several types of blended learning models with a wide range of weaknesses and strengths. This emphasises the importance of comprehensive research into designing effective learning environments, including the design studio model.

Schon (1985, p. 15) believes that well-formed problems result in meticulous practice in professional education and research. Real world problems, however, tend not to be well-formed; they can be disorderly, indeterminate, and problematic (Schon, 1985). Karakaya and Pekta (2007, p. 138) propose that without a systematic method, it is impossible to organise, manage, analyse, and synthesise a study in a complex and interdisciplinary field such as education:

Usually the situations are characterised by uncertainty, complexity, and uniqueness, demanding a framework that enables an integrated approach, understanding and response. (Saghafi et al., 2010, p. 2)

Architectural education cannot progress from the level of experience or description to the level of systematic and critical analysis until it is defined as a problem (Teymur, 2002). Subsequently, to deal with the problem, theories are needed to organise, explain, predict, and make sense of educational practice (Teymur, 2002, p. 1). However, architectural education is full of mysterious and unarticulated assumptions that do not constitute coherent theory. With this lack of theory, in turn, there is little critical evaluation or reflection (Webster, 2001, pp. 2–3).

In the main study, these relate to an understanding of the learning context, particularly in design education in restricted and limited ways, and the use of methodologies that fail to capture and understand the qualitative nature of design pedagogy. Connected to this is the tendency of many studies to make wild generalisations and claims about the emerging generations of learners. Comprehensive qualitative studies such as this are needed to gain a more complete picture of the diverse aspects of learning and the different ways in which learning environments can support such diversity, and respond in a more flexible way to an increasing technological and dynamic world.

## RESEARCH APPROACH

This paper presents the implementation of Grounded Theory as a research methodology in the field of design education. It illustrates how to analyse, organise, and transform data in an inductive approach until a theory is reached. By doing so, different unrelated data will be organised as a tree until a holistic model is formed. The idea is similar to a tree schema, where the tiny roots link to each other, shaping the main stem. Then the main stem is divided into different branches as other findings.

## PHILOSOPHICAL POSITION

This study constitutes a systematic research approach – an approach that is methodologically, ontologically, and epistemologically constructivist. Figure 9.1 presents the philosophical position of Grounded Theory. The triangle, (based on Candy, 1993) highlights the positivist, critical theorist, and interpretive positions, with this study positioned near the interpretive apex.

As indicated previously, this study is concerned with understanding the experiences of students and staff involved in two types of learning environments: a Traditional Face-to-Face design studio and a virtual (online) studio in order to suggest a model that enables an integrated and blended approach. This focus highlights several qualities significant in selecting an appropriate methodology. First, it places emphasis on the perspectives and experiences of the people who are being studied and interpretation of these experiences by the researcher.

Underlying this is an ontological position whereby people and the environment are understood to mutually include and define each other. This position therefore accepts multiple views of reality and sits in contrast to the positivist position that shows that the world and parts of the world have a basic knowable truth about them. While fundamentally interpretivist, critical theorists are driven by a political agenda of making constructions visible and utilising these to effect positive social change.

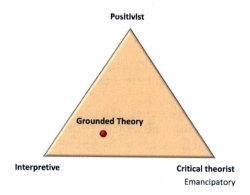

*Figure 9.1. Philosophical position of the grounded theory (philosophical triangle, based on Candy, 1993)*

## IMPLEMENTING GROUNDED THEORY IN RESEARCH ON BLENDED LEARNING

> In Grounded Theory research, the aim is to build theory through construction of categories directly from data. (Birks & Mills, 2011, p. 69)

It is a theory grounded in a particular context. While not intended to be generalisable across contexts, the generated theory or model, in the case of this research, provides a foundation for application and research in other situations.

### METHODOLOGICAL UNDERPINNING

A comparative qualitative approach was undertaken to investigate how essential factors in learning environments influence design studio education. In this respect, the study sought to understand, describe, and explore the experiences of participants in the Face-to-Face and the Virtual Design Studio. This provided a foundation for the generation of theory grounded in the data of participants' perceptions.

Figure 9.2 presents the interrelationship of the research approach, employing Grounded Theory as the methodology to inform exploration of a specially constructed case involving the comparison of student and tutor experiences across a Face-to-Face studio and a virtual design studio.

In this case, the study is situated within the qualitative as opposed to quantitative paradigm. Groat and Wang (2002, pp. 176–179) argue that one of the main features of a qualitative method is its inductive approach where in-depth interviews are analysed in a lengthy interactive process, using a coding scheme to 'induce' meaning from the transcripts.

Qualitative research in blended learning is very productive due to its interpretive and descriptive ability (Gerbic & Stacey, 2009, p. 299). Moreover, the study method can support the complexities of hybrid learning (Gerbic & Stacey, 2009). Overall, the methodology adopts a progressive direction, rather than being pre-determined. It requires both flexibility and rigour (Corbin & Strauss, 2008).

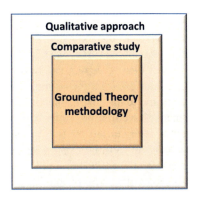

*Figure 9.2. The interrelationship of the components of the research approach*

As indicated, the study employs Grounded Theory as a general methodological framework for the following reasons that have been derived from Groat and Wang (2002, pp. 180–182), Charmaz (2006), Morse et al. (2016), Gray (2009), and Glaser (2014):

- Grounded Theory allows the uniqueness of the situation to emerge. Research does not commence with a preconceived theory. Rather, it begins with the domain of the study.
- In Grounded Theory, the author collects data from a particular setting with theoretical understanding generated through constant comparative analysis.
- A constant comparative approach involves constant comparison of incidents, codes and categories until an integrated theory emerges.
- Grounded Theory provides the tools to synthesise the data, develop concepts, and midrange theory, so far is generalisable to other cases.
- The process of data collection, data analysis and building theory is therefore iterative, open ended and generative because the objects of the study cannot be explained in the first stage.
- The Grounded Theory method also provides flexible guidelines that give direction to the study while at the same time supporting adductive thinking.
- "Grounded abstraction generates implications and possible interventions for application".

Figure 9.3 represents an overall view of the research approach in ten steps. Firstly, a comprehensive literature review has been undertaken in order to: establish the background of the research problem, find the knowledge gaps, determine the objectives, justify the research methodology, and to understand the present knowledge in the research field. This review identifies design education needs and methods, and current models and characteristics of design studios and their future.

Thirdly, Grounded Theory as the methodology configured the research plan as the fourth step. Fifthly, data was collected through both the literature and participants in a pilot study. Pilot data was analysed as the sixth step. A pilot study was carried out as the first step of the field study. An online survey was distributed amongst architecture students and educators to identify their perceptions of the design studio as their learning environment. In this stage, volunteers from the online survey were interviewed. The data was gathered for analysis and to inform the plan of the main study.

As the seventh step, data was collected in the main study. In this stage, an architectural design project was organised for two groups of students studying in the Face-to-Face Design Studio and Virtual Design Studio environments. The data collected from this stage was analysed in the eighth step, using both MAXQDA (Saillard, 2011) and free-hand writing. The blended learning model was produced through theory saturation in the ninth step. Lastly, implications or recommendations of the model were provided and considered in the light of the existing background literature.

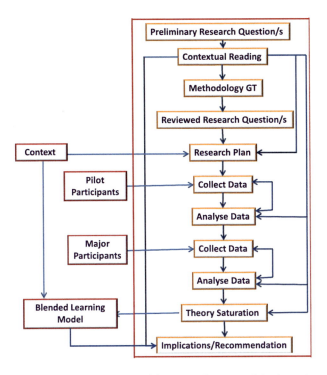

*Figure 9.3. The ten-step process of the research approach in the main study*

The back-connector lines represent when a step is repeated or involves movement from the whole to the details or is a deductive approach instead of inductive one. One dominant example occurred after producing the model. After one month, the model was reviewed critically by the author who benefited from the supervisory team's comments to re-assess the results. During this process, sources of some of the results were reviewed and the coordination and adaption of some inductive results was examined. This approach resulted in a more accurate and comprehensive model.

## RATIONALE FOR RESEARCH APPROACH

The research benefits from a comparative method to compare the benefits and limitations of Face-to-Face and Virtual Design Studio, then optimises these findings in a blended model. It is expected that this study can explain the essential factors of design studio education and their relationships, which can then be used to compare, analyse, and evaluate new settings.

In addition to the reasons given for using Grounded Theory in 'Methodological underpinnings', this method results in managing 'any potential, unforeseen

M. R. SAGHAFI

adverse outcomes' (Birks & Mills, 2011). Also, the iterative process in Grounded Theory provides flexibility to review and re-analyse the data during and after producing the model to ensure originality and an improved outcome. Glaser (1992) suggests that Grounded Theory can be assessed on four criteria: 'relevant to actual problems, fit the data, work in terms of a usual explanation, and be capable of modification by future inquiries' (Merriam, 2002, p. 143). These criteria are applicable in this study.

The pilot study was good practice in designing, implementing, and assessing both survey and interview in the context of QUT (Queensland University of Technology). This stage resulted in producing revisions for the main study. Furthermore, the interview structure was open-ended, thus allowing for fluent and new ideas during the interviews.

## DATA COLLECTION AND ANALYSIS

### Data Collection

The required data in this study has been collected in two stages. Firstly, a pilot study was undertaken based on a questionnaire involving seven students and two tutors, and interviewing four of them including one lecturer and three students. This then informed the main study, involving twenty-two interviews. The data collected from the questionnaires and interviews have been supplemented with data collected through observation and materials produced by participants through the process of learning in the selected studios. The two stages of the process were designed to support each other and so make it possible to enhance the quality and rigor of the study.

### Data Collection in Main Study

In the main study, an architectural design studio was offered within the third-year architecture program and a group was elected to experience both Face-to-Face and Virtual Design Studio in the first semester of 2010. A sub-group comprised an on-campus mode in a conventional Face-to-Face situation in first half of the semester, while a second sub-group participated in an off-campus mode through online learning (Virtual Design Studio) incorporating modern hardware and software for communication and interaction. These sub-groups alternated their situation after mid-semester. Both sub-groups had the same studio time every week.

The author attended all sessions, facilitating the virtual design studio, providing an observation report, and taking some photos from both environments. The Face-to-Face groups usually attended the demonstration studio. Students of virtual group were either off-campus or attending computer labs benefiting from the author's hands-on presence if they were faced with a technical problem, since it was difficult to follow the instructions and solve technical issues at the same time. Therefore, the

184

author had the chance to observe both studios and most of the participants in Face-to-Face or Virtual Design Studios.

The tutor of the Face-to-Face group usually used a data projector, whiteboard and markers for presenting ideas, while the Virtual Design Studio group was dependent on online tools for presentation. Students used their PC or their laptop for synchronous communication through Elluminate Live (Schullo, Hilbelink, Venable, & Barron, 2007).

Twenty-seven people participated in the main study, including one co-coordinator, one lecturer, one tutor, and twenty-four students in two sub-groups. Fourteen people, including three educators and eleven students, participated in interviews. The number of men and women in the interviews was equal: seven for each gender.

The online survey in the main study consisted of multiple choice questions comparing some aspects of Face-to-Face Design Studio and Virtual Design Studio at the end of the semester. The main purpose of designing the survey was to compare different learning activities, design studio aspects, and participants' feelings in both Face-to-Face Design Studio and Virtual Design Studio through three answer choices. Participants were asked to choose between the 'traditional' Design Studio (Face-to-Face), Virtual Design Studio, or both, for each aspect.

According to Candy (1993, p. 101), interviews can better reflect learners' and teachers' perceptions of the learning environment than a multiple choice test such as a questionnaire. The interviews were designed as semi-structured, informal and focused. While the semi-structured interview commences with pre-determined questions the interviewer can change the order of the questions and can build in additional questions if necessary.

*Analysis of Data*

*Data analysis in the pilot study.* After gathering data, coding is necessary to produce a theoretical framework (Charmaz, 2006, p. 46). Data was separated, sorted, and synthesised through qualitative coding that occurred by attaching labels to parts of data (Charmaz, 2006, p. 3). According to Charmaz, coding consists of two phases: initial and focused. In the initial phase, each segment of data takes a code. In the focused phase, the most significant or frequent initial codes are used to sort, organise, integrate and synthesise large amounts of data. Charmaz states that during the first phase, the aim is to remain open to all possible theoretical directions. With the second phase, theoretical integration begins and proceeds through all subsequent analytic steps. This approach has been used for analysing the pilot study.

The approach for analysing the pilot study was relatively different from that used for the main study. In analysing the data collected from the pilot study, the research benefited from the application of NVIVO 8 (Saillard, 2011), qualitative data analysis software to process the information. NVIVO was used to facilitate the archiving, coding, and analysing of data in six steps (Figure 9.4). Transcribed interviews and questionnaires were set in NVIVO, and significant phrases were highlighted. The phrases formed free and tree nodes similar to initial and focused coding in Grounded

M. R. SAGHAFI

Theory. Following this process, different factors in both Face-to-Face and the Virtual Design Studio were compared based on their benefits and limitations. They were analysed again to clarify the advantages and disadvantages of the main factors or concepts and synthesised into a tentative, blended learning model.

*Data analysis in main study.* The method of coding in the data analysis stage followed the approach of Strauss and Corbin (1990) who describe data analysis in a grounded theory perspective as the process of separating, conceptualising, and putting data back together in new ways to evolve a different understanding of phenomena. They believe that for the analysis of data, open, axial, and selective coding should be implemented. According to Strauss and Corbin (2008), the aim of open coding is to begin the process of breaking data down into concepts of objects, events, behavioural actions, thoughts, ideas, and meanings. Strauss and Corbin suggest that the purpose of axial coding is reassembling data dissected during open coding. These are then combined and clarified into categories through a selective coding process. This involves developing various concepts and identifying significant links between concepts for capturing the characteristics of the central phenomena in the field of the study (Strauss, 1987).

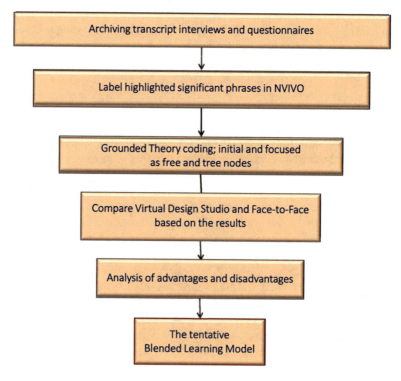

*Figure 9.4. The six step process: Archiving, coding, and analysing data in the pilot study*

186

At the beginning of the data analysis, the author made several maps (Figure 9.5) to briefly depict the individual perceptions of several participants through finding the elements of the related codes. Each individual looks at their environment from a different perspective. Analysing the data from twenty-five participants and inducing outcomes is very difficult, if not impossible. Therefore, data analysis was element-based (essential factors which affect their learning environments), and an appropriate qualitative data analysis tool was employed.

During the analysis of the pilot study, it was realized that NVIVO (8th version) was not sufficiently flexible and user friendly. So, after consultation about and experience with MAXQDA 10, this software replaced NVIVO 8. The data from the main study was managed and subjected to another level of analysis using MAXQDA. From this research, it is apparent that MAXQDA is an appropriate tool with useful features such as selecting coloured codes and setting documents. The high flexibility of this software results in decreasing time spent on analysis and increasing the accuracy of results. This software is used to organise and manage documents, codes, and memos.

Data was classified into different groups and sets. The hierarchical structure of the code system enabled the process of open to selective coding in Grounded Theory. Also, a researcher's ideas can be managed through creating, modifying, selecting and filtering memos. An overview of the coded segments was used to distinguish the advantages and disadvantages of each mode, thus informing the development and evaluation of a blended learning theory.

The data analysis process consisted of eight steps including five steps of coding and three steps of modelling:

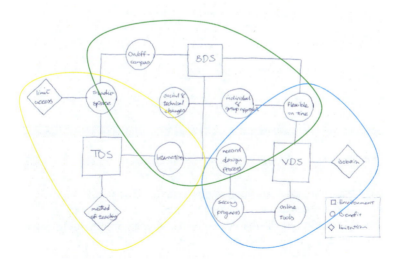

*Figure 9.5. An example of mapping an individual perception of one student*

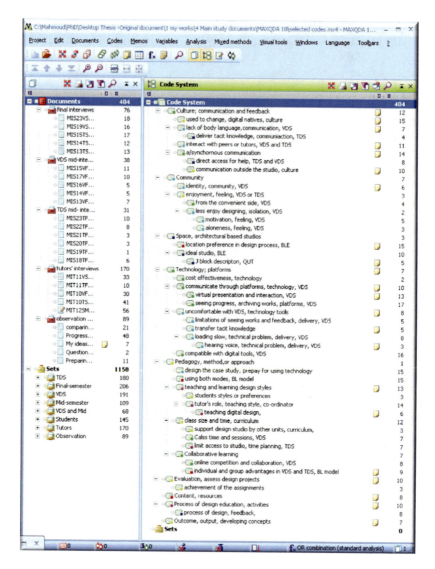

*Figure 9.6. Tree codes: Presenting the hierarchical structure of codes in MAXQDA*

- Open coding produced 646 coded segments in the first step.
- Organising tree codes and decreasing the number of segments to 404
- Classifying coded segments based on the learning environments' elements, type, and positive or negative aspects in nine separated maps (Figure 9.7).
- Combining the above nine maps into a united holistic map (Figures 9.8 and 9.9) and decreasing the number of segments to 231.

IMPLEMENTING GROUNDED THEORY IN RESEARCH ON BLENDED LEARNING

- Classifying 95 coded segments based on the type of learning environments as axial codes (Figure 9.10).
- Finding main characteristics of learning environments (30 coded segments) based on place-time environments (Figure 9.11).
- Establishing the model with 21 selective segments (Figure 9.12).
- Presenting a summary of the main characteristics of the model with 10 selective codes (Figure 9.13).

In the first step of coding, 646 coded segments[1] were realised from the main study data, including transcripts and observations. The process began with creating open codes, but continued with reassembling them into axial codes. Then, related codes were classified in a hierarchical structure and transferred into tree relationships. During the process of analysis, some segments were combined, spilt, or deleted to develop a coding process. The codes were analytically compared, leading to the final structure. This approach provided the opportunity to find the most relevant quotes and to classify them into the appropriate category. Some of these quotes were directly used and some others were paraphrased to form a base for the results.

In the second step of coding, the amount of coded segments[2] decreased to 404. In each step, more dominant codes were sorted from less dominant codes. Figure 9.6 presents the category of elements which formed the first level of tree codes. Each of these nine elements contains several branches that were divided into the third and the fourth levels as sub-branches in some elements. Research data was then classified based on these branches. There are also memos that show the relationship between different branches through their similar components or aspects. According to Birks (2011, p. 106):

> Let loose your creative energy with a rainbow variety of coloured pens of varying thickness in order to differentiate between concepts and illustrate various relationships. (Birks & Mills, 2011, p. 106)

Hence, each code has been identified through different colours. Four colours of dark blue, pink, turquoise, and green were used to show the benefit and limitation of each Face-to-Face Design Studio and Virtual Design Studio respectively. Also, beige and red have been selected to indicate if the related code is neutral or beneficial to both environments. These two steps were achieved using MAXQDA.

In the third step, analysis continued to collect and present element-based maps of selective codes through free-hand writing. From this step, the author attempted to shorten each segment, using a key-phrase or word, and labelling them toward the selected codes. Again, more relevant codes were selected and the number of branches was decreased. Thus, nine maps were provided to separate the benefits and limitations of the Traditional Design Studio (Face-to-Face Design Studio), Virtual Design Studio, and Blended Design Studio for each element. In this step, the number of coded segments was decreased from 404 to 231.[3]

Figure 9.7. presents the related codes for 'Technology' as one of the elements in 'Code System'.

M. R. SAGHAFI

In this arrangement, the position of each code indicates if it is a benefit or limitation by locating it above or below the horizontal line on the map. Also, if the code has been located on the left, connected to the vertical axis, or positioned on the right, it shows whether it belongs to Virtual Design Studio, Blended Design Studio, or Face-to-Face Design Studio respectively.

Then, all of the maps were combined to form a holistic map in the fourth step. The category described in the previous section was considered as a pattern to locate each element. Thus, each group – culture, community, space; technology, pedagogy, evaluation; and content, design process and output – forms a line in the matrix of nine cells as elements of design education (Figure 9.8). Figure 9.8 shows how the three dimensions of nine elements, their related environment (Face-to-Face Design Studio, Virtual Design Studio, and Blended Design Studio), and positive or negative aspect of each segment have been combined into a two-dimensional map. In addition, codes related to each element have been introduced by a specific colour to separate them visually.

Figure 9.9 used the described configuration in Figure 9.8 to allocate all 231 coded segments at this step. Therefore, the location of each branch indicates the related element, environment, and its positive or negative aspect. For instance, dark blue segments located at the central cell are related to the element of pedagogy. The horizontal axis differentiates whether each segment located above or below this line presents positive or negative aspects respectively. Also, the left, right, and middle sides of branches refer to the Face-to-Face Design Studio, Virtual Design Studio,

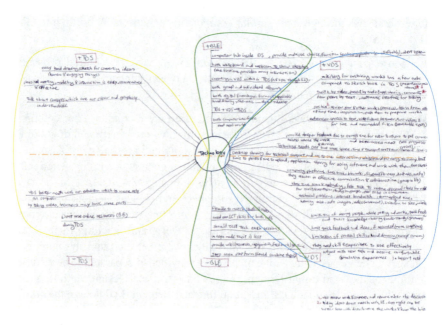

*Figure 9.7. Selected codes for technology as an element of the tree codes*

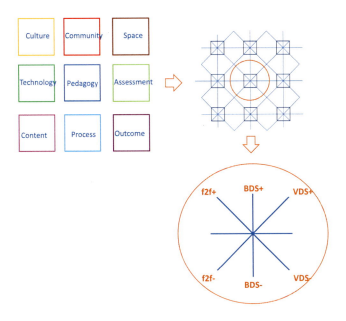

*Figure 9.8. Planning the element based model: Positioning each code to realise its attribute, element, and environment*

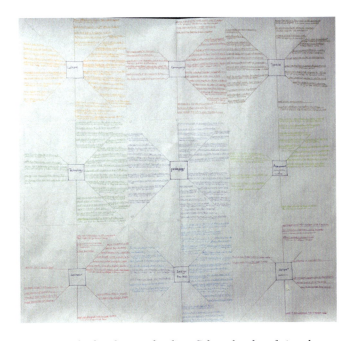

*Figure 9.9. The fourth step of coding: Selected codes of nine elements*

and Blended Design Studio respectively. A higher quality version of this figure (that enables enlargement of the image) is provided in the electronic format.

Continuing the process (on a large A1 sheet with 231 codes) needed a solution to avoid confusion and complexity. Figure 9.10 represents the reordering of the contents of Figure 9.9, decreasing them to mix the selected elements while, at the same time, separating them based on their environment: Traditional Design Studio (Face-to-Face Design Studio), Virtual Design Studio, and Blended Design Studio. Thus, the fifth step was to select the most appropriate segments for designing the proposed model. Consequently, 95 coded segments[4] were positioned in three environments (of Traditional Design Studio, Blended Design Studio, and Virtual Design Studio) containing different colours indicating their element (Figure 9.10). Therefore, the position of each segment not only shows its belonging to each element and environment, but also represents whether it is a benefit or a limitation by locating it above or below the horizontal axis.

In this step, the final selective codes for Traditional Design Studio, Virtual Design Studio, and Blended Design Studio were realised. Considering previous steps, a shift occurred in classifying coded segments from individual-based to element-based to environment-based. In the fourth step, coded segments were categorised based on the main elements and their position to indicate which environment and positive or

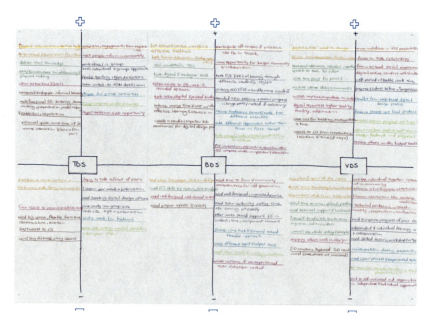

*Figure 9.10. The fifth step of coding: Each code positioned according to its environment and its value*

IMPLEMENTING GROUNDED THEORY IN RESEARCH ON BLENDED LEARNING

negative aspect they belong to; in the fifth step, they were re-organised based on the relevant environment and positive or negative aspect, while their colours present their element.

These results were not accurate enough to determine the attributes of the model. The Virtual Design Studio can refer to both synchronous and asynchronous modes; therefore, mixing these modes as a Virtual Design Studio results in an inaccurate process for producing the proposed model. Likewise, the Traditional Design Studio can refer to both real time mode (live design studio) and asynchronous mode (such as an exhibition of design projects). Thus, the related factors should be separated based on the place-time environments identified during the process of analysis. This new classification resulted in separating these modes and getting a better view of the possibilities. The sixth and final step of selective coding was achieved based on the category of place-time environments (Figure 9.11). In fact, the sixth step of coding can also be considered as a part of the findings to produce the proposed model.

At this point, coding cannot continue since it has reached a sufficient level of saturation. This is the beginning stage of producing the model explained in the next section; related codes and quotes are gathered under each element to compare and analyse. During the process of selective coding, the conceptual framework which impacts the design studio environment is recognised. Research data has been

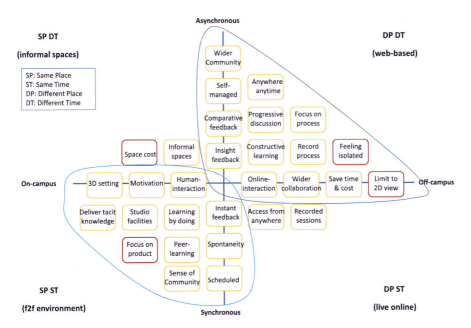

*Figure 9.11. The main attributes of the place-time environments*

193

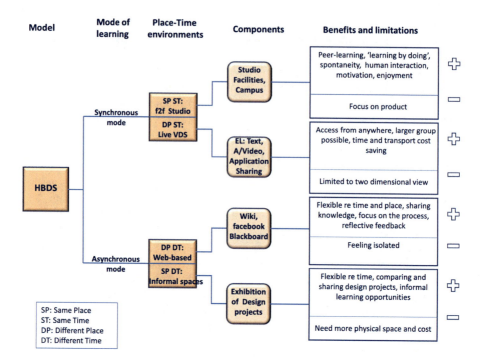

*Figure 9.12. The HBDS model and its attributes*

reviewed and analysed several times from different points of view. This iterative process resulted in improving the model and the framework, controlling the outcome based on the data, and exploring additional outcomes.

*Figure 9.13. The summarised HBDS model complemented by Face-to-Face and web-based education*

## SUMMARY OF RESEARCH APPROACH

The research approach needed to respond to the complexity and context of the design education framework; therefore, a systematic, holistic, and flexible approach was necessary. The grounded theory methodology underpinning the qualitative approach provided flexible, inductive, and in-depth outcomes. Designing and implementing the main study enabled a systematic comparison of the benefits and limitations of the Face-to-Face and Virtual Design Studio through participants' perceptions. This process produced an innovative approach in a holistic study of multidimensional data, transferring the analysis from individual-based to element-based, to environment-based.

The pilot study was a good opportunity to revise the main study questions, tools, and approach, providing a higher quality and rigor of outcome. In each stage, online surveys focused on comparing different aspects of learning environments, while semi-open interviews focused on delivering both educators' and students' experiences of the environments. The roles of the researcher in designing, constructing and facilitating the design studios provided a wider opportunity to be involved in the context and to supplement the data with observation reports.

## FINDINGS

Design studio learning activities and aspects were compared in the pilot study through the surveys. The results indicated that individual perceptions of participants can be varied based on their preferred mode for different activities. An analysis of the data showed that either the Face-to-Face or Virtual Design Studio are not the ideal model for responding to different learners' needs and styles or to different activities in the design studio (Saghafi, Franz, & Crowther, 2012).

A Blended Design Studio, on the other hand, can be appropriate for using one or both environments in response to various learning styles and activities (Saghafi et al., 2012). Participants' perceptions in the study indicated that the Face-to-Face design studio has some dominant advantages which cannot be ignored if replacing it with a Virtual Design Studio. They state that a totally virtual unit cannot respond to their needs. This study confirms that an appropriate model can be blended from the Face-to-Face Design Studio with the Virtual Design Studio, thus optimising the benefits of both environments.

## HOLISTIC BLENDED DESIGN STUDIO (HBDS) MODEL

With respect to the 'place' dimension of the place-time element, what we know as the Traditional Design Studio is referred to as a Face-to-Face learning environment, and the Virtual Design Studio as a web-based learning environment (if used in the context of an asynchronous mode of learning), and as a live online learning environment (if used in relation to the synchronous mode).

195

M. R. SAGHAFI

As revealed in the previous discussion, time is integrally linked with place. In summary, and as already described in part, the category of place-time learning environment has four dimensions:

- SP ST: Same place and time; formal learning spaces such as a physical design studio and a Face-to-Face environment that is restricted by time and place.
- SP DT: Same place but different time; informal spaces such as an exhibition space for design projects, accommodating casual interaction between visitors.
- DP DT: Different time and place; asynchronous virtual learning environments such as web 2, facilitating flexible community-paced learning.
- DP ST: Different place but same time; live online environments, such as Elluminate Live, which are accessible from anywhere.

The most effective codes from the fifth step of the coding process have been re-selected and separated based on the place-time category to form Figure 9.11. Consequently, the sixth step of coding produced 30 selective codes for the related place-time environments. Figure 9.11 provides another way of exploring and describing the qualities of the place-time learning environments. In this figure, various qualities are located along a horizontal on-campus/off-campus axis and a vertical synchronous/asynchronous axis. This diagram is particularly useful in conveying shared qualities or attributes. For instance, both environments of the asynchronous mode can support comparative feedback on student work.

Since the limitations of one environment are counteracted to varying degrees by the positive attributes of other environments, the focus can be on designing learning experiences that are blended to have more benefits than limitations. For instance, Same Place, Same Time as a Face-to-Face environment is restricted to a specific place and time, but Different Place, Different Time as a web-based environment provides access from anywhere at any time.

Therefore, if a blended model combines on-campus synchronous and asynchronous online environments, it will cover most of the attributes presented in the figure and optimise the benefits. For example, in-person interaction and being together in the Face-to-Face Design Studio facilitates experiential learning and the formation of a learning community. Associated with it is a sense of the whole and so it can be equipped and conceptualised to provide access to a range of facilities. Connecting the physical studio space with other on-campus informal learning environments facilitates other forms of interaction such as exhibitions, enabling engagement with the broader community.

In comparison, the web-based design studio facilitates constructive discussion and archiving of students' design processes, therein providing for a focus on the process and a review of progress. Alone, however, these platforms can isolate students in failing to provide the same motivation and enjoyment as the Face-to-Face studio. While the live online studio adds flexibility regarding place and greater possibility for collaboration, it relies on a two-dimensional environment, as opposed to a three-dimensional environment characteristic of the Face-to-Face studio.

196

In the developed HBDS (Hybrid Blended Design Studio) model, Face-to-Face and live online communication delivers scheduled sessions anywhere in real time. When integrated with the asynchronous mode, web 2 and on-campus informal learning spaces this approach can support self-managed learning at different times and in the same places. In this way, various student learning styles can be accommodated. Theoretically, the model offers benefits from all four environments; however, this may not be practically possible owing to different limitations such as available space and resources in some institutions. Figure 9.12 represents the HBDS model (with 21 selective codes) in diagrammatic form. As highlighted, there are four dimensions: mode of teaching and learning; place-time environment; the characteristic components of the environment; and benefits and limitations in terms of teaching and learning activities and experience. With an emphasis on teaching and learning, the model highlights two fundamental modes: the synchronous mode and the asynchronous mode.

Synchronous learning is learning happening at the same time (ST) as teaching Face-to-Face in the designated campus design studio or other campus space. Such real-time learning can be enriched when the Face-to-Face studio is integrated with linked online platforms such as Elluminate Live that connects students and tutors at the same time in different places (DP). Asynchronous learning, on the other hand, is learning happening informally at different times in the one place (such as for student exhibitions that are not part of a scheduled unit time) or in different places, the latter being facilitated through web-based platforms such as Wiki, Facebook and Blackboard. As described hereunder, according to the participants, specific environments or modalities have specific benefits and limitations.

According to the participants' perceptions, integrating online and on-campus education in parallel is valued for providing flexibility in terms of place. So, in the HBDS model, live education is supported through both on-campus and off-campus design studios. More so, participants emphasised the need for implementing a web-based design studio. Therefore, web 2 as an asynchronous mode and Face-to-Face as a synchronous mode of education play the main role in different scenarios, as conveyed in Table 9.1.

Table 9.1 presents four possible scenarios: Scenario 1 utilises benefits from all four environments, as identified in the HBDS model; Scenario 2 is limited by the shortage of physical spaces offering on-campus informal learning opportunities; Scenario 3 omits the live online mode due to possible limitations such as technology and/or group size; and Scenario 4 integrates Face-to-Face with web-based facilities.

The scenarios just described with the secondary components (DP ST and ST DT) options highlights the flexibility of the HBDS model. Increased flexibility can be achieved through multimodality (for example, Face-to-Face with web based learning) and/or through offering a Face-to-Face and the live Virtual Design Studio.

Figure 9.13 simply shows the most important aspects (with 10 codes as an abstract of selective codes) of the blended components in the HBDS model. In the Face-to-Face environment, physical space facilities, motivation, enjoyment and instant feedback have been considered as the most important benefits – while being restricted to time and place – and the focus on the final product are the most important limitations. On the other hand, being flexible with regard to time and place, a focus on the process, and providing progressive feedback have been realised as the most important benefits of web 2. The lack of physical learning spaces and human interaction are the most important limitations of the web-based environments.

This figure represents how the limitations of the web-based learning environment are counteracted by the positive aspects of the Face-to-Face learning environment. For example, lack of human interaction in web-based learning can be counteracted by motivation and enjoyment resulting from Face-to-Face interaction. Therefore, the HBDS model has been produced by balancing and blending individual components in a complementary relationship so as to maximise the contribution of these components. For instance, instant feedback in live communication and insightful feedback in lag time discussion work as complementary components.

*A Conceptual Framework for Design Education*

During the coding process, data collected from the study was classified into the nine elements presented in the previous section. These elements form the core of the final framework. Figure 9.14 represents the final conceptual framework resulting from: realising essential factors, considering the relationship between these factors, and the author's re-configuring of the initial conceptual framework. However, the final conceptual framework was mainly produced through exploring the category of tree codes for realising the main elements and re-shaping the relationship of these elements.

Like the initial framework, the final framework responds to the basic questions of each event: what, why, who, where, and how. Focusing on the pedagogical aspect of the design studio, the learning environment in this version that positions pedagogy at the centre of the framework is different to the first version.

Referring to the tree codes, it is notable that about one quarter of the codes in the first two steps belongs to this field. In this framework, pedagogy is allocated to the central position since decisions made in this field can greatly affect four related cells including technology, community, process, and assessment.

In fact, technology, assessment, and process – as different aspects of 'how' – are mainly determined by pedagogy as the basic 'how'. Overall, pedagogy is identified

*Table 9.1. Different scenarios of the HBDS model*

|  | SP ST | DP ST | DP DT | SP DT | Multimodal | Parallel |
|---|---|---|---|---|---|---|
| Scenario 1 | ✓ | ✓ | ✓ | ✓ | ✓ | ✓ |
| Scenario 2 | ✓ | ✓ | ✓ | – | ✓ | ✓ |
| Scenario 3 | ✓ | – | ✓ | ✓ | ✓ | – |
| Scenario 4 | ✓ | – | ✓ | – | – | – |

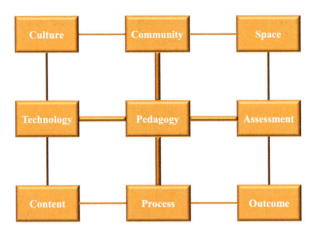

*Figure 9.14. Elements in design studio education: The final conceptual framework*

as the main element because not only does it contains the most number of codes in comparison to other elements, but also has the closest relationship with other elements based on the memos.

The nine elements in Figure 9.14 are connected linearly in two directions to form a matrix. Each three factors forming a horizontal line have a close relationship. The first horizontal line shows the social and physical/virtual environments for the community of learning. The second one presents a diverse 'how' for technology, learning pedagogy, and assessment. The third line describes the story of the design process from input/object/question to output/objective/answer.

## DISCUSSION

*Significance of Findings Discussed in the Context of Existing Knowledge*

Although some of the characteristics of this study can be found in other studies, this study provides a more comprehensive and holistic approach with the following three outcomes considered significant: the study design, the conceptual framework, and the HBDS model as a whole.

*The significance of the study.* The following details eight significant characteristics of the designed study and its implementation.

- Study design: For the main study, the author designed and constructed a Virtual Design Studio at the School of Design (QUT) based on his experience of QUT online modules and his experiences as a lecturer.
- The use of Grounded Theory: The data analysis process which resulted in the research outcomes was unique. This approach explains the presentation and analysis of data within the three dimensions of: nine elements, three environments,

and two positive or negative aspects for each environment in a two-dimensional sheet (Figure 9.8).

- The study: This consisted of two stages: a pilot and a main study. After conducting the pilot study, including the online survey and interviews, the main study was finalised based on the experience gained in both the development of the methodology and the context of the research.
- Main study design: In this main study, all students and tutors had the opportunity to experience both the Face-to-Face and the Virtual Design Studio, and to compare them during the whole semester. The participants in the main study – including the coordinator of the unit, both of the tutors, and many of the students – participated in the surveys and interviews. Many previous case studies were limited to students or educators.
- Data collection: This included survey, interview, and observation. While some studies employ only the questionnaire as a tool for data collection in quantitative research, this study was based on a qualitative approach, benefiting from both survey and interview.
- Research aims: A comprehensive comparison was achieved in this study, differentiating it from the studies that focus on only one or a few specific aspects of learning environments.
- Learning activities: In a live online design studio, these were not limited to lecturing, but included problem-based and project-based learning environments, containing different learning activities such as tutorial, presentation, and critiques.
- Learning environments and their components: All four environments of the place-time category were employed in the study. Exhibition style presentation was used during the final presentation by the second Face-to-Face group. Moreover, the Virtual Design Studio consisted of both synchronous and asynchronous modes using Elluminate Live, Wiki and Facebook.

*The significance of the conceptual framework.* This framework was concerned with capturing and more holistically understanding the complexity and potential of design studio education. The diagram is offered as a basic tool for use in making decisions about the evaluation, comparison, implementation and analysis of various learning environments for design education.

The significance of the comprehensive conceptual framework is its generic identification of factors and their relationships, enabling its application to educational settings including design studios in the contemporary world. Because of its hybrid nature, the framework offers options for each environment. Thus, the conceptual framework has more capacity to represent the blended design studio, and seems to be compatible and flexible enough to respond to different contexts and to a changeable future.

*The significance of the HBDS model as a whole.* This part describes six dominant characteristics of the HBDS model that can be considered significant.[5] These characteristics are mostly different from the benefits of implementing each mode or environment and may be available in similar models. For instance, peer learning as a result of the Face-to-Face design studio approach is not mentioned here. Instead, this discussion focuses on the characteristics of the model that have been derived from considering the model as a whole.

The HBDS model has been constructed based on the perceptions of participants in both the Virtual Design Studio and the Face-to-Face design studio as the first step; then, as the second step, it was designed based on the benefits and limitations of each environment. Therefore, the model has really been constructed based on the best of both environments in the related context.

1. The HBDS is a contextual model since it is applicable in different contexts due to its flexibility. Different scenarios of the HBDS model can be chosen by considering the limitations of each context and through omitting irrelevant components.
2. In the HBDS model (Scenarios 1 and 2) synchronous online environment and Face-to-Face design studio are integrated simultaneously, rather than being on-campus or off-campus learning options in an alternate fashion.
3. The theory elaborated from this study is presented as the HBDS model. Excluding combining different space, time and media, this model supports the following dimensions:
   3.1. Scheduled and community-paced learning for synchronous and asynchronous modes respectively
   3.2. Informal and formal learning through different learning environments
   3.3. Group and individual learning activities
   3.4. Different types of interaction such as one-to-one, one-to-many and many-to-many. Moreover, the HBDS model provides two-directional interaction between on-campus and off-campus participants.
4. The HBDS model extends the boundaries of the blended theory through offering a self-determined, self-managed, and personalised learning environment:
   4.1. Compared to regular blended models, in the HBDS model students have the choice to participate on or off-campus in most of the sessions. Thus, this model benefits from a self-determined learning environment.
   4.2. The HBDS model provides self-managed learning activities due to managing time and place in asynchronous mode. In other words, students and tutors are able to choose when, where, and how to interact during each semester week.
   4.3. The HBDS model provides the opportunity for personalisation of content and activities through sharing knowledge, archiving the process of design, and reflective feedback. Using Facebook as a learning platform allows students to personalise their learning environment. Therefore, the HBDS model is likely to support constructivist learning and address some of the requirements in the learning process which result in increasing students' experience and satisfaction.

5. In the HBDS model, archiving of the design process enables both tutors and students to review, compare, and reflect comprehensively on group and individual progress. Two kinds of archive were provided in the main study, presenting both the process of design and the progressive feedback. While Wiki provides formal and group learning communication, Facebook works as informal and individual learning interaction with both the learning community and the wider virtual communities. The content provided by these platforms presents a constructivist dynamic knowledge produced mostly by participants.

## RELEVANCE AND CONTRIBUTION TO THEORY

Considering the dominant characteristics of this research, its contributions are as follows:

- It provides a design for a comprehensive qualitative comparative study.
- It exemplifies the employment of Grounded Theory as a methodology in design education and the process of analysing the data.
- It informs the improvement of educational settings in design schools.
- Furthermore, since design education is a problem-based and project-based learning model, the outcome can be useful for other fields of these approaches.

## CONCLUSION

This chapter presents the implementation of Grounded Theory as a research methodology in the field of design education. It illustrates how to analyse, organise, and transform data in an inductive approach until a theory is determined. While Grounded Theory and the literature reviews are useful tools in such studies, each study needs innovative approaches to address its particular contextual challenges.

Without a systematic method, it is impossible to organise, manage, analyse, and synthesise a study in a complex and interdisciplinary field such as education. Therefore, a framework was necessary to facilitate the systematic process of research.

The data analysis process consisted of eight steps of describing, interpreting, and analysing, including five steps of coding and three steps of education resulting in the final HBDS model. Innovative approaches in this research lead to a process of transforming multidimensional data from individual perceptions' maps to separated maps of nine elements, and then turning to environment-based model. The iterative process of coding during the data analysis resulted in improving the model and the framework, controlling the outcome based on the data, and exploring additional outcomes. This approach enables the enhancement of the model besides creating a conceptual framework and finding secondary conclusions.

The theory results from a systematic data process as the main outcome: a holistic blended model which is sufficiently flexible to adapt to various settings, and in so doing facilitates a constructivist learning.

IMPLEMENTING GROUNDED THEORY IN RESEARCH ON BLENDED LEARNING

Further research could assess the potential transferability of the outcomes of this study if it covered more disciplines, different institutions, and other learning approaches.

## NOTES

[1] 'Code System' contains 52 different codes and each code, on average, refers to 12.4 segments in this step. Coded segments are text passages which are assigned to a code.
[2] With 50 codes and, on average, 8 segments for each code.
[3] With 33 codes and 7 segments for each code on average.
[4] With 20 codes and an average of 4.7 segments for each code.
[5] Please refer to Saghafi (2013) for more details.

## REFERENCES

Birks, M., & Mills, J. (2011). *Grounded theory: A practical guide*. Los Angeles, CA: Sage Publications.

Bose, M. (2007). The design studio: A site for critical inquiry. In A. Salama & N. Wilkinson (Eds.), *Design studio pedagogy: Horizons for the future* (pp. 131–140). Gateshead: The Urban International Press.

Candy, P. C. (1993). Learning theories in higher education: Reflections on the keynote day, HERDSA 1992. *Higher Education Research and Development, 12*(1), 99–106.

Charmaz, K. (2006). *Constructing grounded theory: A practical guide through qualitative analysis*: London: Sage Publications.

Corbin, J. M., & Strauss, A. L. (2008). *Basics of qualitative research: Techniques and procedures for developing grounded theory* (3rd ed.). Thousand Oaks, CA: Sage Publications.

Dennis, A., Bichelmeyer, B., Henry, D., KCakir, H., Korkmaz, A., Watson, C., & Bunnage, J. (2006). The CISCO networking academy: A model for the study of student success in a blended learning environment. In C. J. Bonk & C. R. Graham (Eds.), *The handbook of blended learning: Global perspectives, local designs* (pp. 120–135). San Francisco, CA: Pfeiffer Publishing.

Eilouti, B. (2006). A problem-based learning project for computer-supported architectural design pedagogy. *Art, Design & Communication in Higher Education, 5*(3), 197–212.

Fisher, K. (2003). Design for learning in the knowledge age. *Educare News, 137*, 15–17.

Gerbic, P., & Stacey, E. (2009). Conclusion. In P. Gerbic & E. Stacey (Eds.), *Effective blended learning practices. Evidence-based perspectives in ICT-facilitated education* (pp. 298–311). New York, NY: Hershey.

Glaser, B., & Strauss, A. (2014). Applying grounded theory. *The Grounded Theory Review, 13*(1), 46–50.

Gray, D. (2009). *Doing research in the real world*. Thousand Oaks, CA: Sage Publications.

Hashimshony, R., & Haina, J. (2006). Designing the university of the future. *Planning for Higher Education, 34*(2), 5–19.

Karakaya, A. F., & Pekta, T. (2007). A framework for web-based education systems supporting interdiciplinary design collaboration. *METU JFA, 2*, 137–148.

Merriam, S. B. (2002). *Qualitative research in practice: Examples for discussion and analysis* (1st ed.). San Francisco, CA: Jossey-Bass.

Morse, J. M., Stern, P. N., Corbin, J., Bowers, B., Charmaz, K., & Clarke, A. E. (2016). *Developing grounded theory: The second generation*. Walnut Creek, CA: Left Coast Press.

Saghafi, M. R. (2013). *A holistic blended design studio model: Exploring and expanding learning opportunities*. Saarbrücken: LAP LAMBERT Academic Publishing.

Saghafi, M. R. (2015). A holistic model for architectural education: Blending face-to-face and web-based learning environments. *Journal of Technology and Education, 9*(4), 253–263.

Saghafi, M. R., Franz, J., & Crowther, P. (2010). *Crossing the cultural divide: A contemporary holistic framework for conceptualising design studio education.* Paper presented at the CONNECTED 2010 – 2nd International Conference on Design Education, Sydney, Australia.

Saghafi, M. R., Franz, J., & Crowther, P. (2012). Perceptions of physical versus virtual design studio education. *IJAR International Journal of Architectural Research, 1*(1), 6–22.

Sagun, A., Demirkan, H., & Goktepe, M. (2001). A framework for the design studio in web-based education. *Journal of Art and Design Education, 20*(3), 332.

Saillard, E. K. (2011). Systematic versus interpretive analysis with two CAQDAS packages: NVivo and MAXQDA. *Forum Qualitative Sozialforschung/Forum: Qualitative Social Research, 12*(1), Article 34.

Schon, D. A. (1985). *The design studio: An exploration of its traditions and potentials.* Intl Specialized Book Service Inc.

Schullo, S., Hilbelink, A., Venable, M., & Barron, A. E. (2007). Selecting a virtual classroom system: Elluminate live vs. Macromedia breeze (adobe acrobat connect professional). *MERLOT Journal of Online Learning and Teaching, 3*(4), 331–345.

Senyapili, B., & Karokaya, A. F. (2009). The future setting of the design studio. *Open House International, 34*(1), 104–112.

Strauss, A. L. (1987). *Qualitative analysis for social scientists.* Cambridge: Cambridge University Press.

Strauss, A. L., & Corbin, J. M. (1990). *Basics of qualitative research: grounded theory procedures and techniques.* Newbury Park, CA: Sage Publications.

Teymur, N. (2002). *Towards a working theory of architectural education.* London: Architectural Papers.

Wang, L. (2007). *Professors and students' perceptions of online learning: A qualitative study.* Paper presented at the Society for Information Technology & Teacher Education International Conference 2007, San Antonio, TX.

Webster, H. (2001). The design diary: Promoting reflective practice in the design studio. In H. Webster (Ed.), *Architectural education exchange* (pp. 3–16). Cardiff: Cardiff University.

JI YU

# 10. MODELLING LEARNING SPACE AND STUDENT LEARNING IN HIGHER EDUCATION

*An Evidence-Based Exploration*

## ABSTRACT

This chapter is part of the author's PhD project that investigates the relationships between learning space and student learning in higher education. The project draws on theories in educational psychology and emphasises the student view and experience. Based on the empirical findings, an integrated model is developed by teasing out the key constructs and depicting the likely relationships between them. The model highlights the integration of physical space into the overall learning context and the complexity of student learning processes. It seeks to provide an insight into the dynamic interplay between learning space and student learning in higher education and contribute to our understanding of the pedagogy-space-learning nexus as a whole.

## INTRODUCTION

There has been increasing interest in learning space research and practice in higher education. Renewed interest in constructivist approaches to education, as well as applications of architectural advances and information and communication technologies (ICTs), have all contributed to the attempts of educators and designers to re-examine how best to design and use learning space for pedagogical activities in higher education. During the past two decades, new types of learning spaces have been established in many countries around the world, termed as 'effective learning spaces', 'inspirational or innovative learning spaces/environments', or 'new generation learning spaces/ environments' (e.g. Fisher, 2005; Harrison & Hutton, 2014; JISC, 2006; Observatory on Borderless Higher Education, 2012; OECD, 2013). Compared with conventional, didactic classrooms, some common features of these new learning spaces include motivating learners and promoting learning as a constructive activity, supporting interdisciplinary, collaborative learning, providing a personalised and inclusive environment, and being flexible in the face of changing needs. Technology also plays a vital part in achieving these aims. In research, current studies fall into three main areas, as summarised by Ellis and Goodyear (2016): (1) pedagogy and curricula and their association with learning space; (2) learning space design; and (3) the development of ICTs and software tools that create virtual spaces in which students can learn.

© KONINKLIJKE BRILL NV, LEIDEN, 2019 | DOI: 10.1163/9789004391598_012

Despite increased recognition of the role of space in pedagogy, the domain is a still relatively new field of study with many issues to be further developed. As Strange and Banning (2001) observe, among the methods employed to foster pedagogical activities, the use of the space is perhaps the least understood and the most neglected. At the theoretical level, researchers (Ellis & Goodyear, 2016; Temple, 2008) have pointed out that fragmented conceptual frameworks impede collective advances in this field. In addition, the majority of learning space studies focus predominantly on the physical features of a space rather than its alignment with desired pedagogical approaches and learning activities. It has thus been argued that there is a great need for rigorous knowledge of the role of learning space in supporting student learning in higher education (Edwards, 2000; Johnson & Lomas, 2005; Mirijamdotter et al., 2006; Temple, 2007).

There have been some attempts to construct general models in order to illuminate the connections between pedagogy, space and learning in higher education (Goodyear & Carvalho, 2014; Lamb & Shraiky, 2009; Radcliffe, 2009). These models are intended to either act as sources to support design and/or evaluation discussion of learning spaces in higher education, or serve to guide future research. They have involved knowledge work of theory-building, hypothesis testing, and modelling. However, as researchers have pointed out (Ellis & Goodyear, 2016), further investigation is warranted through exploratory research – for instance, by talking with students and looking for patterns of covariation in easy-to-operationalise variables that relate to qualities of space and qualities of learning, and identify the likely mechanisms. In other words, if learning space is designed and managed to foster student learning in higher education, it needs to be ensured that such models illuminate the connections in understanding the design and management of space and central dimensions of learning. In addition, efforts are needed to provide more clues on what constitutes a cogent and actionable answer to each concrete question that may arise in the discussions of learning space practice.

This chapter has two major aims: First, by incorporating theoretical notions of student learning research, it hopes to contribute to the bridging of learning space research and student learning research in higher education. Second, by conducting an empirical study on a conventional, lecture based learning space, and a student-centred, innovative learning space, it adds insights into the alignment between well-designed space and high-quality learning, which there is still a lack of empirical evidence.

Below, it starts with a brief outline of the central dimensions of student learning in research, and then introduces the context and method of the empirical work. The model is then presented, followed by the justification and explanation of the constructs.

## STUDENT LEARNING RESEARCH AND THE SAL TRADTITION

Student learning has been an ongoing subject of study in higher education, and includes the following outline frameworks and broad concepts (Entwistle et al., 2002).

- Curriculum frameworks and their influences on learning
- Students' approaches to learning
- The overall teaching-learning context (environment), and students' perceptions of it
- Learning outcomes.

The model presented below mainly draws on the theoretical notions rooted in the research tradition of students' approaches to learning (SAL). It does not target the investigating of the relationships between learning space and direct learning outcomes/performance, which have been studied by some research teams using quasi-experimental methods (e.g. the team at the University of Minnesota – Brooks, 2011, 2012). Exploring the dynamic learning processes within a learning space and students' sense-making is currently lacking but crucially important in gaining a deeper insight into this issue.

The basic distinction between a *deep* and a *surface* approach to learning in the 1970s has exerted a far-reaching influence in studying how to access and improve the quality of teaching and learning in higher education (Biggs, 1987; Entwistle & Ramsden, 1983; Marton & Säljö, 1984; Pask, 1988; Schmeck, 1988). *An approach to learning* is conceptualized in terms of cognitive strategies and motivation. *Surface approaches to learning* refer to students employing surface learning processes (e.g. rote memorisation of course materials) for the purpose of assessment, while *deep approaches to learning* mean that students use deep learning processes (e.g. seeking for meaning, understanding and relating ideas) with an intrinsic interest in learning and understanding. Ramsden (1979) claimed to have identified a third approach to learning/studying, namely, the *strategic approach* whereby students aim to obtain the highest possible grades and seek cues as to how to expend their effort to greatest effect. However, subsequent research has failed to consistently confirm the separate existence of this approach (Kember & Leung, 1998; Richardson, 2000). Some researchers also question the validity of putting the strategic approach as a separate construct as there is no unambiguous evidence for the existence of a separate achieving approach, while there is ample evidence of deep and surface approaches across various studies (Richardson, 1994, 2000). Richardson (2000) then proposed viewing the *strategic approach* as being part of a deep approach to learning. In general, educators aim to foster a rigorous appreciation of the internal structure of a subject and the development of integrative understanding and deep thinking in students.

Over the last few decades, student learning research in higher education have expanded to investigate the ways in which students learn, and have encompassed a wide range of theoretical perspectives that describe individual differences and a variety of ways in which to measure key components of student learning (Biggs, 1993; Entwistle & McCune, 2004; Prosser & Trigwell, 1999; Vermunt, 2005). As different writers may use different concepts for similar or partly overlapping aspects of student learning, to reduce the overlap between categories while maintaining the

J. YU

*Table 10.1. A categorisation of three main dimensions of student learning activities*

| Cognitive | Affective | Regulative |
|---|---|---|
| Relating/structuring | Motivating/expecting | Orienting/planning |
| Analysing | Concentrating/exerting effort | Monitoring/testing/diagnosing |
| Concretising/applying | Attributing/judging oneself | Adjusting |
| Memorising/rehearsing | Appraising | Evaluating/reflecting |
| Critical processing | Dealing with emotions | |
| Selecting | | |

variation at the same time, researchers (Short & Weisberg-Benchell, 1989; Wagner & McCombs, 1995; Vermunt & Verloop, 1999) have compared different taxonomies and categorised them into three main learning components: *cognitive processing activities, affective learning activities,* and *regulative activities.*

*Cognitive processing activities* refer to how students engage in processing subject matter, which leads directly to learning outcomes. *Affective learning activities* are related to the emotions that arise during learning, and the activities that students employ that lead to a mood that may have a positive, neutral or negative effect on the progress of learning processes. *Regulative learning activities* refer to students exerting control over their own cognitive and affective processing activities during learning. See the categorisation of the three dimensions summarised by Vermunt and Verloop (1999) in Table 10.1.

## AN EMPRICAL STUDY

*Method*

The empirical work investigated two contrasting learning spaces in a Chinese university. Space 1 (Figure 10.1) was built in the 1950s and consists of a number of conventional, didactic classrooms. Space 2 (Figure 10.2) is a flexible, innovative learning centre designed through cooperation between the Chinese university and a Finnish university in 2010. Both spaces are designed for all types of student to use in this university.

The investigation was divided into two phases – first, the designers and educators were interviewed about the background of the space's establishment, its embedded pedagogical philosophy and design principles. Documents including archives and course introduction were also collected to supplement the analysis of interviews.

At the second phase, students were recruited to participate in focus group interviews (FGIs), in which they were asked a series of open-ended questions about their learning experience within the two spaces. Participants were selected for each FGI with the aim of capturing as much variation as possible on the following variables: gender, year of study and academic discipline. This was based on the

208

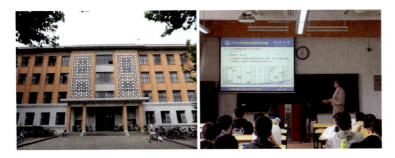

*Figure 10.1. Space 1*

*Figure 10.2. Space 2 (Photo: Sino-Finnish Centre, 2016)*

consideration that both spaces are generic learning spaces, and also because previous student learning research has shown that these variables are closely related to how students go about their learning (Richardson, 2000; Vermunt, 2005). The group size was set at four to six participants after a pilot study. Finally, a total of 28 participants participated in six FGIs, three in Space 1 and three in Space 2.

The questions covered the following aspects: (1) how students understand the concept of 'learning space'; (2) how students learn within the particular space; (3) how students consider the influence of space upon their learning; and (4) students' requirements of, and preferences for learning space, which were often interwoven in responses.

*Data Analysis*

The recordings of all interviews were manually transcribed, resulting in 75 pages of transcripts, consisting of around 35,000 Chinese characters. Content analysis was conducted by the researcher and a second independent researcher in order to improve the inter-rater reliability. The analysis was an iterative process before arriving at stable elements and categories.

## DEPICTING THE MODEL

*Learning Space and the Overall Learning Context*

The model is depicted in Figure 10.3. In the model, there are two types of connecting lines, signifying different natures of the relationships: the '–' represents the elements are linked together and have reciprocal influence upon each other, and the '→' suggests the relationship occurring in a particular direction.

To understand how space is utilised as a pedagogic tool, the model starts with an attempt to demonstrate how the design and organisation of a learning space is associated with the overall learning context. In the domain of student learning research as discussed above, the term 'learning context' describes the circumstances that form the setting for learning, and the broad situation in which something is learned or understood. It has been usually used interchangeably with 'learning environment' in the field of educational psychology (Meyer, 1988; Meyer & Muller, 1990). Given the fact that the term 'learning environment' has been used differently in studies of learning space and those of student learning research, and its use here may cause confusion for readers from the two different fields, this chapter uses 'learning context' instead of 'learning environment' throughout to describe the circumstances that form the setting for learning, and the broad situation in which something is learned or understood.

Through analysing the interviews with the designers and educators of the two spaces, four elements illustrating the connection between learning space and the overall learning context are extracted:

1. conceptions of learning and subsequently the roles of teachers and students;
2. curriculum, course organisation and assessment;
3. institutional and departmental features;
4. impact of local culture.

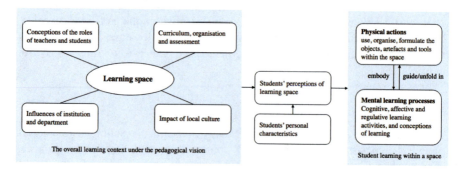

*Figure 10.3. An integrated model of learning space and student learning in higher education based on an empirical study in China*

MODELLING LEARNING SPACE AND STUDENT LEARNING IN HIGHER EDUCATION

Firstly, is learning conceived as the acquisition of knowledge and being stimulated by teachers as in Space 1; or as a constructive, creative process initiated by students like in Space 2? Specifically, Space 1 was built shortly after the foundation of the People's Republic of China in 1949. It was a period when the new country was in urgent need of engineers for large-scale infrastructure construction. This demand had strongly influenced the pedagogical purposes and penetrated the design of campus buildings at that time. According to the archives, the establishment of every building in national owned universities in the 1950s in China required direct approval from the Ministry of Education, in terms of the purpose of the project, the finance budget and the design of space. Thus it was a time when collectivism was given great emphasis while individual value was rarely considered, sometimes even suppressed. The interviewee, who was also an undergraduate student in the university when Space 1 was built, described the pedagogical vision as:

Education in the 1950s was nation-construction driven. Every student of us, is a screw of the country's construction. We were expected to service as engineering and technical support, so we were cultivated in a standardised education mode.

In contrast, Space 2 was built in a period when creative thinking and problem-solving capacity has increasingly been emphasised in higher education, and innovation education has attracted growing interest in educational research and practice around the world. Since the country's reform and opening-up policy in the 1970s, higher education institutions have also achieved more freedom in learning space design. The key pedagogical vision embedded in the design of this space, as highlighted in the archives and by the designer, is to 'create an important hub and engine of international open innovation knowledge' and 'actively contributes to building of creative and sustainable societies of the 21st century through high quality research, education and innovations'. It thus emphasises greatly an innovative and interdisciplinary pedagogical approach.

Secondly, what and how to learn in a space? Space 1 is aligned with a conventional, didactical pedagogical approach, and the assessment mostly relies on an end-of-semester examination. It represents the traditional model that is still dominant in many higher education institutions – the subject matter is determined by the teacher, often in the form of books or chapters the content of which has to be learned. All content is provided through lectures, which the teacher gives to the students by means of PowerPoint presentations, visual aids (e.g. videos and images) and corresponding materials. The teacher normally stands at the front desk and teacher-student interaction also occurs during the formal answer and questions sessions. While in Space 2, most courses employ a project-based learning approach, in which students from different disciplines work on authentic, real-life problems in groups (mostly 4 to 6 students). The role of the teacher is to support students by giving sufficient guidance and feedback. Students attend courses once a week, where they have meetings under the guidance of a teacher, in which progress and difficulties are discussed and the next project phase is previewed. Regarding the type of assessment, each group in a course produces a group product or result, for example, a design, a piece of advice or a plan etc. At the end of courses, the results are presented to the whole class of students in the presence of the teacher and sometimes also the customers. The assessment of individuals is based on their personal development and contribution to the group.

Thirdly, as both cases presented here are generic types of learning spaces that are designed for all university students, we are not able to identify influences of specific disciplines. However, research on student learning has shown that the nature of disciplines differs and sequentially use different teaching and learning approaches (see e.g. Entwsitle, 1983). Therefore, institutional and departmental features need to be considered in designing learning spaces used for specific disciplines (Harrison & Hutton, 2014).

Fourthly, the impact of local culture. The design of both spaces shows the impact of local culture. For instance, there could be many different possibilities in designing a space for teamwork, but Space 2 borrowed the sauna culture specifically from Finland (Figure 10.2, right). Another example is that each divided room in Space 2 has a unique name with a special meaning in Chinese, delivering its message with regard to customs and social behaviour. The multi-purpose lecture room in Figure 10.2 (left) is named 'Stage', saying that 'where the current and future stars appear. If the show gets boring, you can always transform the space into something more interesting and interactive: e.g. ball room, playground etc. Only the ceiling is the limit!' As explained by the designer, these special names not only add the space's distinction but also created 'public connection points' for its users.

*Students' Perceptions of Learning Space*

Researchers (Eley, 1992; Prosser & Trigwell, 1999) have illustrated that students are more influenced by how they perceive a learning context (environment), rather than the objective context itself. In the FGIs with students, it was found that students perceive a learning space differently, which is consequently associated with how they approach their learning within a space and how they evaluate the space. Therefore, *students' perceptions of learning space* represent a crucial mediating element in the model, and plays a central role in students' attitudes, reactions towards a learning space and the way that they learn within the space. Content analysis on students' FGIs reveals that students' perceptions of learning space mainly consist of four aspects:

1. students' perceptions of the engagement within a space;
2. students' perceptions of the flexibility of a space;
3. students' perceptions of the fit between a space and courses;
4. students' perceptions of the fit between a space and their personal preferences.

First, how students perceive engagement within a space – in other words, how do students become aware of how they are expected to learn and behave when they walk into a learning space. As a student explained:

> Space has a guiding effect on the way of your studying. When you walk into two spaces, you will feel the differences of the design, and you will be more likely to adopt certain types of learning in a particular space, because you get more opportunity to do that. Like others said, the 'atmosphere' has an appealing effect.

Second, how students feel about the flexibility of a space and consequently the implied enrichment of learning experiences within a space. Compared to Space 1, most students appreciate the flexibility of Space 2:

> The flexibility of space is quite important. When I learn, for instance, I need to draw something, then I can easily get a small whiteboard here to clear my mind. I feel I can control something by myself, make some adjustment and go back to learning.

Third, how students comprehend the fit between a space and the courses. Most students consider Space 1 is good or necessary for lecturing and unsuitable for team group; while Space 2 is desirable for cooperative learning but too disturbing for self-studying. Therefore, there is no absolutely desirable learning space that fits all types of courses.

And fourth, how students think of the fit between a learning space and their personal preferences. People have their own habitual learning approaches. The uncertainty that in relation to personal traits goes beyond the scope of the study and is inconclusive from the findings themselves due to the lack of evidence in students' own reasoning (for instance, some students expressed that they did not like a particular aspect of a space, without giving any further explanations) – this requires further empirical research to draw more explicit conclusions. These four aspects of students' perceptions of space, to a large extent, resemble the categories proposed by Walker et al. (2011).

*Students' Personal Characteristics*

Research has shown that students' personal characteristics influence how they perceive a learning context and consequently how they go about learning (Baeten et al., 2010; Biggs, 2003; Vanthournout et al., 2014). However, the consideration of students' personal characteristic has been rarely mentioned in current learning space research. This study collected students' demographic information such as age, gender, and academic discipline, which have proved to be significant variables in student learning studies as mentioned above.

In the FGIs, students' opinions varied in terms of which type of learning space is more preferable, reminding us that individual differences need to be taken seriously into account when considering the relationships between learning space and student learning in higher education. In the analysis, students were classified into sub-groups according to their age, gender and subject. The results showed that that academic discipline is the most significant contributor. Natural sciences students considered a conventional space like Space 1 is necessary as most of their courses involve much factual information and less on individual interpretation. Engineering and technology subjects consist of a lot of skills knowledge and practice, therefore students emphasised more on appropriate workplace. Arts and social sciences students experienced more open discussion and idea sharing in their regular learning and thus were more sensitive to cooperative learning space. It can be seen that the subject matter that students are intended to learn and the very nature of knowledge are potentially associated with students' perceptions of a learning space, the way they learn and the actions they take within the space.

Other personal characteristics, such as gender and age seem to be less influential in terms of understanding individual differences in the evidence of this study. Regarding gender, eight out of the total of 16 female students (50%) and seven of the 12 male students (58.3%) preferred Space 2 as a learning space; while other students (six females, 37.5%; four males, 33.3%) considered Space 1 to be a 'preferable, or necessary' space for their learning. There was only a minority percentage of students (two females, 12.5%; one male, 8.3%) who responded that it did not matter where they learn. For age, older students are more likely to prefer an innovative space like Space 2, which is due to the fact that Space 1 resembles the learning space in most senior schools and students need time to adapt to a different type of space after entering colleges.

To arrive at more compelling conclusions regarding these personal factors, further investigation with a larger sample size is needed.

*Student Learning within a Space*

In the model, 'student learning within a space' is comprised of two parts – *students' mental learning processes* and *physical actions during learning*. For mental learning processes, coding was conducted based on the theoretical notions as previously discussed. Four main themes and their specific codes were identified (indicating with; also see Yu, 2017).

1. students' conceptions of learning;
2. cognitive learning activities;
3. affective learning activities;
4. regulative learning activities.

Specifically, for conceptions of learning, students in Space 1 mostly saw learning space simply as a physical site for learning, as they considered learning is 'the increase of knowledge' and 'the acquisition of facts and skills', which can be retained and utilised in practice. In contrast, students in Space 2 discussed more about 'cooperation', 'communication' and 'interpretation' of knowledge' in conceptualizing learning.

MODELLING LEARNING SPACE AND STUDENT LEARNING IN HIGHER EDUCATION

In terms of cognitive learning activities, students described that learning space is related to how they process their subject matter in a particular way: they were more likely to use 'listening/memorizing' processing strategies in a traditional space like Space 1, and more engage in 'relating/ structuring/creating thinking' and 'group discussion' learning activities in an innovative learning environment like Space 2. It means student learning indeed take place as a process of listening to the instruction of the teacher and repeating definitions, formulas, memorizing theories and rehearsing subject matter regularly in the conventional classroom; while a collaborative process of looking for connections between different parts and the merging of new ideas in the innovative environment.

For affective learning activities in a learning space, including their learning motivation', 'emotions' and 'concentration effort'. This means in the FGIs: (1) students described a reason or reasons for acting or behaving in a particular way in a space, especially the reason in deciding where to learn. (2) Students discussed either positive feelings of happiness, ownership, self-confidence when they learned within the space; or negative emotions, such as anxiety, stress, insecurity and helplessness. (3) Students also talked about the action-distracting, task-irrelevant emotions that arise during learning within the space. As a student summarized at the end of one FGI:

If we could divide the composition of a learning space into three levels of factors – some level largely determines whether I will choose to learn or not learn there, the others affect the emotions that arise during my learning, and another is associated with the degree of how effectively I can learn. All these factors of space, through exerting influence on my subjective feeling, willingness, self-initiation and effectiveness of learning, consequently impact upon the attitude, method and outcome of my learning.

Students' mental learning processes within a space also involve how they regulate their learning activities. The FGI data easily distinguished between 'self-regulation' and 'external regulation' – the former refers to students' self-initiated orienting, planning and adjustment of their learning process and activities through their examination of characteristics of the learning task and the situation within the learning space, while the latter is related to the control of teaching, other students and the surrounding events. Most students considered that the flexibility of Space 2 facilitates their self-regulation, while a conventional classroom with fixed seating arrangement like Space 1 provides a feeling of tension and relates to external regulation. Below are two examples:

(A student in Space 1) When I learn here (Space 1), the surrounding people have an effect on me, I guess, it is called 'group effect'. If others around you are playing or doing something irrelevant, I won't have much mood for learning.

(A student in Space 2) When I learn, for instance, I need to draw something, then I can easily get a small whiteboard here to clear my mind. I feel I can control something by myself, make adjustment and go back to learning.

215

In the model, physical actions of student learning refer to how students use and organise the objects, artefacts and tools within a space. At the theoretical level, the existing literature differs in terms of whether physical actions direct mental learning processes, or vice versa (Ellis & Goodyear, 2016; Goodyear et al., 2014; Ingold, 2011). The findings of the present study based on students' self-reported learning experiences did not reveal which perspective is more appropriate as participants' opinions diverge on this issue themselves: some students are more goal-directed, their mental plans of learning precede and direct physical actions; while for other students, their cognitions of space seem to be embodied in physical actions and thus more likely to extended through their own experiences within the space. Thus the argument here is that students' learning processes and their physical actions are actually mutually connected – students interact with spaces both physically and mentally. Physical actions can either enable or impede particular learning activities to take place, thus to some extent embody students' mental processes of learning; and cognition of learning guides and unfolds in students' physical actions.

SUMMARY

As observed in Temple's (2007, 2008) reviews, learning space research has grown mostly by spreading outwards – the literature is very broadly and thinly distributed. Until now research and practice of learning space in higher education, however, are not often well connected with learning theories. The major goal of constructing the above model is to strengthen the theoretical framing that connects space and learning in a more integrated way.

Compared with previous models of learning space, the construction of the above model has three main differences. First, instead of using the 'everyday', general word of 'learning' that may encompass fragmented meaning, the model follows the research tradition of student approaches to learning (SAL) and extracts components illustrating students' mental learning processes from the empirical study: students' conceptions of learning, and their cognitive, affective and regulative learning activities. This categorisation helps to provide a clearer and holistic picture of complex learning processes. But as emphasised by researchers (Vermunt & Verloop, 1999; Wagner & McCombs, 1995), it does not mean the categorisation is exclusive, but rather that it reduces unnecessary, overlapping conceptual meanings and confusions. The specific codes were identified through an exploratory approach, helping to understand what is happening and generate theories from the data. Given the SAL theoretical ground, to some extent, the model bears a resemblance to the general models in studies of student learning and the learning context (environment) (see Biggs, 2003; Vanthournout et al., 2014); however, it expands the scope of context by highlighting the factor of 'space', and connecting students' mental learning activities and their physical actions within a space.

Second, in understanding the interplay between space and learning, the model pays close attention to mediating factors – students' perceptions and students' personal

MODELLING LEARNING SPACE AND STUDENT LEARNING IN HIGHER EDUCATION

characteristics. Although a number of studies have investigated students' perceptions of their academic environment (see e.g. Law & Meyer, 2011; Richardson, 2006), until now little is known about how students perceive a learning space. Exploring this factor contributes to a deeper insight into how students actually learn within a space and the sense they make of what they do. The model also highlights that there are important variations across students in terms of their requirements of and preferences for learning space in higher education. Academic discipline seems to be a most salient factor, which keeps in line with many previous student learning studies (Entwistle & Ramsden, 1983; Entwistle, 2009). Given the trend that learning space is becoming more inclusive across different subjects, more thoughtful design approaches catering for different needs are yet to come in the future.

Third, the model is presented with concrete evidence on two built contrasting learning spaces, allowing the possibility of providing actionable references to the questions in the discussions of how specific aspects of learning space are associated with a certain mode of student learning. Such comparison may also shed light on larger issues regarding the conceptualisation, research and management of contemporary learning spaces in higher education.

In summary, this chapter seeks to contribute to articulate an integrated model of learning space and student learning in higher education, one with a series of connected propositions that specify the key constructs and their interrelationships based on empirical evidence. However, it is worth mentioning that the model does not attempt to combine the perspectives of different stakeholders and find ways for a common good (models with such purposes can be found in other studies, Koning et al., 2005). Nor it can be considered as a single, unifying solution to designing and managing learning spaces – indeed it may never be appropriate and possible to do so. In addition, the investigation of student learning in this model is based on students' self-reported experience, which means that it mainly takes participants' own interpretations of their learning into account, which may not fully reflect the complexity of what actually happens. Future studies could expand on the chapter by including more naturalistic methods, for instance observation and the visual method of making students take photographs of the space (see e.g. the volume edited by Burke et al., 2015).

ACKNOWLEDGEMENTS

The author wishes to thank the staff of the two spaces for their cooperation of the study and permission for accessing and using their materials and records.

REFERENCES

Baeten, M., Kyndt, E., Struyven, K., & Dochy, F. (2010). Using student-centred learning environments to stimulate deep approaches to learning: Factors encouraging or discouraging their effectiveness. *Educational Research Review, 5*(3), 243–260.

Biggs, J. (1987). *Student approaches to learning and studying.* Melbourne: Australian Council for Educational Research.

J. YU

Biggs, J. (1993). What do inventories of students' learning processes really measure? A theoretical review and clarification. *British Journal of Educational Psychology, 63*, 3–19.

Biggs, J. (2003). *Teaching for quality learning at university* (2nd ed.). Buckingham: SRHE & Open University Press.

Boys, J. (2014). *Building better universities: Strategies, spaces, technologies.* London: Routledge.

Brooks, C. (2011). Space matters: The impact of formal learning environments on student learning. *British Journal of Educational Technology, 42*(5), 719–726.

Brooks, C. (2012). Space and consequences: The impact of different formal learning spaces on instructor and student behaviour. *Journal of Learning Spaces, 1*(2), 1–10. Retrieved from http://libjournal.uncg.edu/index.php/jls/article/view/285

Burke, C., Grosvenor, I., & Norlin, B. (Eds.). (2015). *Engaging with educational spaces.* Umea: University of Umea.

Edwards, B. (2000). *University architecture.* London: Spon Press.

Eley, M. G. (1992). Differential adoption of study approaches within individual students. *Higher Education, 23*(3), 231–254.

Ellis, R. A., & Goodyear, P. (2016). Models of learning space: integrating research on space, place, and learning in higher education, *Review of Education, 4*(2), 149–191.

Entwistle, N., & McCune, V. (2004). The conceptual bases of study strategy inventories. *Educational Psychology Review, 16*, 325–345.

Entwistle, N., McCune, V., & Hounsell, D. (2002). *Occasional report 1: Approaches to studying and perceptions of university teaching-learning environments: Concepts, measures and preliminary findings* (ETL Project). Coventry & Durham: Universities of Edinburgh. Retrieved from http://www.ed.ac.uk/etl

Entwistle, N., & Ramsden, P. (1983). *Understanding student learning.* London: Croom Helm.

Fisher, K. (2005). *Linking pedagogy and space: Planning principles for Victorian schools based on the principles of teaching and learning.* Retrieved from http://www.education.vic.gov.au/Documents/school/principals/infrastructure/pedagogyspace.pdf

Goodyear, P., & Carvalho, L. (2014). *The architecture of productive learning networks.* Abingdon: Routledge.

Goodyear, P., Carvalho, L., & Dohn, N. (2014). Design for networked learning: Framing relations between participants' activities and the physical setting. In S. Bayne, C. Jones, M. De Laat, T. Ryberg, & C. Sinclair (Eds.), *Proceedings of the 9th international conference on networked learning.* Edinburgh: Lancaster University.

Harrison, A., & Hutton, L. (2014). *Design for the changing educational landscape: Space, place and learning.* Abingdon: Routledge.

Ingold, T. (2011). *Being alive: Essays on movement, knowledge and description.* Abingdon: Routledge.

Johnson, C., & Lomas, C. (2005). Design of the learning space: Learning and design principles. *EDUCAUSE Review, 40*(4), 16.

Joint Information Systems Committee (JISC). (2006). *Designing spaces for effective learning: A guide to 21st century learning space design.* Bristol: JISC Development Group. Retrieved from http://www.jisc.ac.uk/whatwedo/programmes/elearninginnovation/learningspaces.aspx

Kember, D., & Leung, D. Y. (1998). The dimensionality of approaches to learning: An investigation with confirmatory factor analysis on the structure of the SPQ and LPQ. *British Journal of Educational Psychology, 68*(3), 395–407.

Könings, K. D., Brand-Gruwel, S., & van Merriënboer, J. J. G. (2005). Towards more powerful learning environments through combining the perspectives of designers, teachers, and students. *The British Journal of Educational Psychology, 75*, 645–660.

Lamb, G., & Shraiky, J. (2013). Designing for competence: Spaces that enhance collaboration readiness in healthcare. *Journal of Interprofessional Care, 27*(1), 14–23.

Law, D. C. S., & Meyer, J. H. F. (2011). Relationships between Hong Kong students' perceptions of the learning environment and their learning patterns in post-secondary education. *Higher Education, 62*, 27–47.

Marton, F., & Säljö, R. (1984). Approaches to learning. In F. Marton, D. Hounsell, & N. Entwistle (Eds.), *The experience of learning* (pp. 36–55). Edinburgh: Scottish Academic Press.

MODELLING LEARNING SPACE AND STUDENT LEARNING IN HIGHER EDUCATION

Meyer, J. H. F. (1988). Student perceptions of learning context and approaches to studying. *South African Journal of Higher Education, 2*(1), 73–82.

Meyer, J. H. F., & Muller, M. W. (1990). Evaluating the quality of student learning. An unfolding analysis of the association between perceptions of learning context and approaches to studying at an individual level. *Studies in Higher Education, 15*(2), 131–154.

Mirijamdotter, A., Somerville, M. M., & Holst, M. (2006). An interactive and iterative evaluation approach for creating collaborative learning environments. *The Electronic Journal of Information Systems Evaluation, 9*(2), 83–92.

Observatory on Borderless Higher Education. (2012). *MOOCs and disruptive innovation: The challenge to HE business models.* Retrieved from http://obhe.ac.uk/documents/view_details?id=929

OECD. (2013). *Innovation learning environments: Educational research and innovation.* Paris: OECD. Retrieved from http://www.keepeek.com/Digital-Asset-Management/oecd/education/innovative-learning-environments_9789264203488-en#page1

Pask, G. (1988). Learning strategies, teaching strategies, and conceptual or learning style. In R. R. Schmeck (Ed.), *Learning strategies and learning styles* (pp. 83–100). New York, NY: Plenum Press.

Prosser, M., & Trigwell, K. (1999). *Understanding learning and teaching: The experience in higher education.* Buckingham: The Society for Research in Higher Education.

Radcliffe, D. (2009) A Pedagogy–Space–Technology (PST) framework for designing and evaluating learning places. In D. Radcliffe, H. Wilson, D. Powell, & B. Tibbetts (Eds.), *Proceedings of the next generation learning spaces 2008 colloquium.* Brisbane: University of Queensland.

Ramsden, P. (1979). Student learning and perceptions of the academic environment. *Higher Education, 8*(4), 411–427.

Richardson, J. T. E. (2000). *Researching student learning: Approaches to studying in campus-based and distance education.* Buckingham: Open University Press.

Richardson, J. T. E. (2006). Investigating the relationship between variations in students' perceptions of their academic environment and variations in study behaviour in distance education. *British Journal of Educational Psychology, 76*, 867–893.

Schmeck, R. R. (Ed.). (1988). *Learning strategies and learning styles.* New York, NY: Plenum Press.

Short, E. J., & Weisberg-Benchell, J. A. (1989). The triple alliance for learning: Cognition, metacognition and motivation, In C. B. McCormick, G. E. Miller, & M. Pressley (Eds.), *Cognitive strategy research: From basic research to educational applications* (pp. 33–63). New York, NY: Springer Verlag.

Strange, C., & Banning, J. (2001). *Educating by design: Creating campus learning environments that work.* San Francisco, CA: Jossey-Bass.

Temple, P. (2007). *Learning spaces for the 21st century: A review of the literature.* York: Higher Education Academy.

Temple, P. (2008). Learning spaces in higher education: An under-researched topic. *London Review of Education, 6*(3), 229–241.

Vanthournout, G., Donche, V., Gijbels, D., & Van Petegem, P. (2014). (Dis)similarities in research on learning approaches and learning patterns. In D. Gijbels, V. Donche, J. T. E. Richardson, & J. D. Vermunt (Eds.), *Learning patterns in higher education* (pp. 11–32). London & New York, NY: Routledge.

Vermunt, J. D. (2005). Relations between student learning patterns and personal and contextual factors and academic performance. *Higher Education, 49*, 205–234.

Vermunt, J. D., & Verloop, N. (1999). Congruence and friction between learning and teaching. *Learning and Instruction, 9*(3), 257–280. doi:10.1016/S0959-4752(98)00028-0

Wagner, E. D., & McCombs, B. L. (1995). Learner-centered psychological principles in practice: Designs for distance education. *Educational Technology, 35*(3), 32–35.

Walker, J. D., Christopher, D., Brooks, C., & Baepler, P. (2011). Pedagogy and space: Empirical research on new learning environments. *EDUCAUSE Quarterly, 34*, 4. Retrieved from http://www.educause.edu/erp/article/pedagogy-and-space-empirical-research-new-learning-environments

Yu, J. (2017). The relationships between learning space and student learning in higher education. In W. Imms & M. Mahat (Eds.), *Transitions Australasia: What is needed to help teachers better utilize space as one of their pedagogic tools.* Proceedings of an international symposium for graduate and early career researchers in Melbourne, Australia. Retrieved from http://www.iletc.com.au/publications/proceedings/

MARIAN MAHAT AND MOLLIE DOLLINGER

# 11. MIND THE GAP

*Co-Created Learning Spaces in Higher Education*

### ABSTRACT

Learning does not just take place in the mind of the learner, nor the community in which he or she learns. It also takes place in an environment, whether it is a classroom, a lecture theatre, a maker space, or library. Emerging evidence is beginning to show that the environment in which learning takes place is an important indicator of the quality of students' learning experiences and a building block to support deep, rich learning. Additionally, the evolution in design of learning spaces from a user-centred approach to co-designing is changing the landscape of design practice.

Consequently, the broad aim of this chapter is to explore and understand how co-created physical spaces within universities can facilitate and enhance student engagement and access. This discussion begins by reviewing the literature and evidence base that supports the importance of learning spaces for rich learning and the impact of the design of learning spaces to student success. Drawing on insights globally, the chapter concludes that co-creation of spaces should include the largest user group, that is the students. Such collaboration of the design of learning spaces can benefit students' learning and engagement, as well as the attributes necessary for graduate employability in the 21st century.

### INTRODUCTION

In recent years, there has been a marked increase in the number of new and refurbished building projects in the higher education sector. In Australia alone, public universities, of which there are 40 (TEQSA, 2017), owned $28 billion of building assets, with almost $2 billion being spent on construction in 2015 (Department of Education and Training, 2016). Despite this huge investment, there appears to be a lack of research carried out on the design of buildings, let alone the spaces within them or how these spaces can impact student success. Particularly in a rapidly changing higher education landscape, where key pressures continue to shape higher education, it is surprising that such investment is not commensurate with evidence of the impact of the design of buildings and spaces on teaching, learning and research productivity – key focus areas of universities.

© KONINKLIJKE BRILL NV, LEIDEN, 2019 | DOI: 10.1163/9789004391598_013

Set against a backdrop of global technological and economic transformation, universities internationally are being urged to provide more personalised and responsive education opportunities to students to prepare them for their future. Rapid shifts in information and communication technologies (ICTs), the rise of the knowledge society, and the drive for both individuals and communities to become lifelong learners have prompted the re-imagining of what may constitute optimal conditions for learners to acquire the dispositions, skills and knowledge required for them to thrive in contemporary society (Fullan & Langworthy, 2014).

Specifically, in a higher education landscape where student-centred learning has been touted as key to building 21st century skills, the design of teaching and learning spaces in higher education should focus on the learner and their needs, rather than more traditional forms of education centred around the teacher's input. This student-centred approach has important implications for the design and flexibility of curriculum, course content, interactivity of the learning process, and increasingly the role of 'space'. The narrative suggests that well-designed flexible spaces can more readily accommodate the needs of 21st century learners and therefore contribute to raising student performance and learning outcomes in higher education.

It has been argued that traditional teaching and learning spaces on campuses do not seem to particularly engage or support students in collaborative activities. Herrington (2006) writes that large lectures with students passively listening or taking notes to a teacher discussing some theory or topic is still very common. However, while much research has focused on the pedagogy underpinning this scene, less research has discussed the physical contribution to this picture: the lecture hall. Yet there is growing interest just beginning to emerge on how universities can improve their teaching spaces and meet the needs of the 21st century learners (e.g. Parisio, 2013). While not effectively demonstrated in literature, there are beliefs that physical learning spaces may impact pedagogy and student learning (Mulcahy, Cleveland, & Aberton, 2015). Within the Australian higher education sector there was and continues to be a boom of new major building projects (Jamieson et al., 2000) yet subsequent research following the impact of these projects has not been conducted at scale. Still, to date, many aspects of learning spaces are not even questioned; for example, the continuing separation of student and faculty spaces, and of research and teaching spaces (Jamieson et al., 2000).

Boddington and Boys (2011) argue that there is a need to develop frameworks that can help with the design process of learning environments. However, they also note that the learning spaces literature suffers from a multi-disciplinary interest, causing a mishmash of ideas and terms. Yet perhaps given the cross-disciplinary interest in learning spaces, and the need for more developed frameworks, the process of co-design, which advocates for multiple stakeholder participation, may be of use within the learning spaces research. This is particularly so in higher education, where stakeholders tend to have more say.

The warrant for this chapter flows from broader rationales driving the book, which are documented elsewhere, as well as from several more specific objectives.

The evolution in the design of learning spaces from a teacher-centred approach to co-designing for a student centred experience is changing the landscape of design practice. To understand the impacts of co-design, the analysis hereunder explores how co-created physical spaces within universities can facilitate and enhance student learning. Drawing on insights globally, the chapter concludes that co-creation of spaces should include the largest user group, that is the students. Such collaboration of the design of learning spaces can benefit student learning and engagement, as well as the attributes necessary for graduate employability in the 21st century.

## UNDERPINNINGS OF CO-CREATION AND CO-DESIGN

Wenger (1998) writes that learning is a social process where multiple stakeholders or community partners interact with one another to challenge and develop new knowledge and ideas. In this frame, the process of co-creation, where stakeholders can contribute to the inputs or design of the learning activity or environment in higher education is not particularly novel (Kangas, 2010). Further, as in Wenger's view, learning is not static in co-creation, nor a process of transmission, instead through the social environment, learning is dynamic and, in fact, co-created (Säljö, 2006).

Knowledge co-creation, therefore, is a process that emerges from the interaction and construction of multiple perspectives and/or artefacts (Paavola, Lipponen, & Hakkarainen, 2004). Kangas (2010) additionally writes that knowledge co-creation is not only a social process where new knowledge emerges, but also a process where new knowledge is socially validated through the interaction of multiple stakeholders. Nonaka and Konno (1998) align this to a theory within Japanese culture of knowledge creation known as *ba* (see Figure 11.1) meaning a shared space that serves as the foundation for new knowledge. According to them, awareness of the different characteristic of *ba* can facilitate successful creation of knowledge and when shared, form the knowledge base of organizations (Nonaka & Konno, 1998).

Co-creation and co-design are often entangled and used without distinction from one another. Sanders and Stappers (2008) define co-creation as any "act of collective creativity that is shared by two or more people" (p. 6). Through this definition, Sanders and Stappers (2008) note that co-design can be defined as one act of co-creation, which spans the design process. Therefore, while the aims and objectives of the co-creation process are varied, within the co-design process the aim is limited to a new design of a product or service (Kleinsmann, 2006). In particular, Sanders and Stappers (2008) note that attention is beginning to focus or concentrate towards the 'fuzzy' front end of the design process, as it is chaotic and ambiguous. Arising from the front end of the co-design process are ideas, concepts, and eventually prototypes and products.

Broadly, co-creation as a term rose to prominence famously in the Prahalad and Ramaswamy 2004 book, "The Future of Competition: co-creating unique value with customers". They write that an underutilized resource of many organisations are user perspectives, user knowledge and user experiences. They note further that

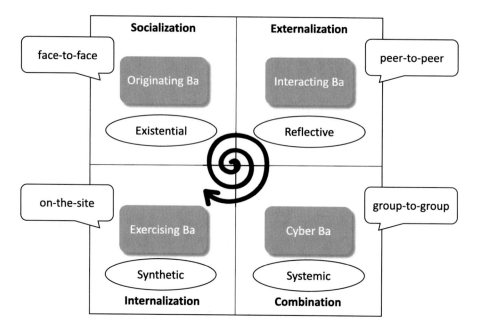

*Figure 11.1. Social construction of knowledge (from Nonaka & Konno, 1998)*

the firm-centric view of an organisation, whereby only the designers are part of value creation process, is changing rapidly as users increasingly express desire to co-create value with the firm, either through a co-design or similar process (Prahalad & Ramaswamy, 2004). Therefore, a process of co-creation, which breaks down the barriers between the organisation and the user, may allow for users to more adequately express their preferences and opinions, and contribute to the value of the products and/or services.

Co-design as a form of co-creation comes from sustained effort in design thinking to create 'user-centric' approaches. Traditionally, this is a break from original design thinking, which was previously conceptualized as situated within only the mind of the designer and their skills (Rowe, 1987). Rowe, for example, writes that design thinking is an interior situational logic of the designer and their subsequent decision-making processes (Rowe, 1987). This idea of design thinking has further been supported by Hebert (1969) who wrote that in contrast to natural sciences, where complex interactions naturally create, the design process is an individually centric and artificial process.

However, more recently, design-thinking literature has begun to question these definitions, with Kimbell (2011) noting that one of the most critical shortcomings of design thinking theory is that it rests on designers as the main agents of design. In contrast, therefore, to traditional views on design thinking, new paradigms emerging more recently reflect that changing shifts in society towards more participatory

MIND THE GAP

designs. Participatory design has its origins in the 1970's, in Nordic countries, as a more democratic approach to designing practices in the workplace (Muller & Druin, 2002).

Participatory design marks a shift in the design process, as users are involved in the process; however, the decision-making remains in the hands of the designers. In the process of participatory design, for example, the researcher (or sometimes the designer) is considered to be the interpreter of what the user may want or need (Sanders, 2002). Yet participatory design does not directly recommend the inclusion of the user in the design process, and instead, participatory design was a force in shaping the co-design thinking literature (Sanders & Stappers, 2008). Thus, while co-design and participatory design have similar foundational theories towards user-centric approaches, they should not be used interchangeably. The key distinction between the two is the distinction between who has the power for decision-making. In participatory design, the researchers and designers have the decision-making authority; whereas in co-design the participants are given equal decision-making power to the designers (Casali, 2013).

EXAMPLES OF CO-DESIGN IN BUILDING PROJECTS

Participatory design and co-design is beginning to be applied to a range of building projects. As noted earlier, sometimes it is difficult to differentiate between examples of participatory design and co-design as much of the literature uses these terms interchangeably, even though a distinction exists. Despite this, the examples of participatory design and co-design have provided an interesting, albeit burgeoning, new direction in design thinking.

For example, in Ljubljana, Slovenia, participatory design was used in an effort to include local residents' opinions on a revitalization project of an estate (Kos & Potocnik, 2005). Before the project began, researchers noted that a large obstacle in the redesign process was the local residents' perception of the estate, and also a general negative feeling towards institutions. Through holding several workshops where residents were allowed to voice their opinions, residents eventually overcame their initial distrust and concerns with the project (Kos & Potocnik, 2005). This case highlights how participatory design can help reduce tensions between user groups and service providers to create greater buy-in for a project.

Another commercial project utilizing co-design was found in a New Zealand based architecture firm called Co-Design Architects, which specializes in co-design for commercial renovations. They have completed a range of projects. One example is the Karori Anglican Church. The process involved a range of meetings, workshops and interviews resulting in a two-phase renovation project (Co-Design Architects, 2017). Users were able to identify specific concerns that resulted in the design solution. For instance, the church members expressed concern over safety for cyclist and pedestrians accessing the site, so they created a perimeter driveway, drop off areas, go slow areas, and additional parking areas (Co-Design Architects, 2017).

225

Within higher education, there are also a few examples of co-design, for example at Monash University in Australia where co-design has been utilized in international development projects in Fiji and Indonesia. The Monash Art Design & Architecture School (MADA) is a leader of co-design events in working with residents in informal settlements on how to integrate nature-based water management into their buildings (Monash University, 2017). The project involved students from the University of South Pacific who undertook the household surveys and co-design activities helping residents design a safer community (Monash University, 2017).

Another example in relation to higher education students can be found in the City of Bandung in Indonesia. A renewal project on a residential rental building was expanded to involve a participatory process with students involved in what kind of space they would like (Nurdini & Harun, 2011). Students were able to voice their opinions to the housing provider and give details to what type of space they would like (Nurdini & Harun, 2011). Yet due to the inexperience of the students in terms of expertise of design and architecture, and the lack of transparency with the students about the budget constraints, some of their requests were unable to be fulfilled given the financial costs or current technology available.

The University of California Berkeley also conducted a co-design exercise for housing in Pinoleville Pomo Nation, a first nations community. Part of the goal of the project was to expose students to first nations culture and lifestyle, as well as to get residents involved in the housing design process (Perez, Shelby, Edmunds, James, & Agogino, 2015). Students as well as the participating architects learned valuable lessons about building users. For instance, tribe members explained how straight corners should not be used in the home because in their culture, their belief is that they invite bad spirits (Perez, Shelby, Edmunds, James, & Agogino, 2015). This example highlights how co-design interventions may be continually applied to minority environments whereby the mainstream ideas may be questioned.

The co-design process has also seen some examples involving youths. For example, the Sorrell Foundation has utilized co-design for youth centres in England. The collaborative process allowed youth to learn about the design process while participating in the project in a meaningful way (The Sorrell Foundation, 2010). The process was used for 15 youth centres. The projects teamed residents up with architectural and branding firms to create concepts for their youth centres. The process involved developing a design brief through workshops, then later refining ideas through further engagement. The end of each project was marked with celebration events (The Sorrell Foundation, 2010).

Similarly, at a primary school in Finland, students participated in a co-design process for renovating their school (Tilassa, 2015). The project involved developing new ideas for furniture and redesigns of some of the spaces. Students participated in a multi-media engagement process that involved a range of techniques including discussions and the creation collages of how they wanted things to look (Tilassa, 2015). Additionally, in another example, architecture students were paired with primary school students to conduct a participatory design exercise. The partnership between Deakin University and Wales Street Primary School, both located in Australia, conducted a four-week project to design a playground (Lozanovska & Xu, 2012). The project culminated in a scale model of the designed playground. Primary students were able to participate in the design of a project where they would be the central users. The success of the project has led Deakin University to pursue collaborations with other primary schools (Lozanovska & Xu, 2012).

These case studies generally present a positive outlook on the potential of co-design, while some help to identify some of the challenges. The common trend appears to be users being able to express their unique needs. Further, the process appears to mitigate some of the power imbalance that can arise between designer and users in many of these projects.

## CO-CREATION IN THE DESIGN OF LEARNING SPACES IN HIGHER EDUCATION

Co-creation has been applied in many areas within higher education, especially areas where student input may serve an ethical purpose. To date, much of this application has been towards the aim of curriculum creation (see examples in Bravenboer, 2016; and Bovill, Cook-Sather, & Felten, 2011). Another area that has gained interest in co-creation is the development of student data and learning analytics (see examples of Dollinger & Lodge, 2018; Slade & Prinsloo, 2013). There are many benefits to co-creation, as discussed above, including low-cost innovation, buy-in and long-term adoption, improved student-staff relationships, and productivity and efficiency gains.

In *Towards Creative Learning Spaces*, the author highlights the importance of the design of learning spaces in shaping learning outcomes (Boys, 2011). She notes that while there is a lack of literature on pedagogical building design, the practice will likely be informed by the available literature on corporate campus design (Hadfield, Kinkead, Peterson, Ray, & Preston, 2003). Theorists have long argued that participation should play an important part in pedagogical design. For instance, in *The Oregon Experiment*, the authors argue that participation is key to the design of educational institutions (Alexander, Silverstein, Angel, Ishikawa, & Abrams, 1975). Further, they use the university context as an example, arguing that the daily users of the building know more about their needs than anyone else (ibid Alexander et al.). They note that participation in the design of the space is important for the students and faculty to feel ownership of their classrooms and labs. Yet Hadfield et al. (2003) also note that the ideas proposed by Alexander and his colleagues are idealistic and do not reflect practice on campuses, where master plans set out development over the long-term, and faculty and students likely cannot even find the offices of the people making these decisions (Hadfield, Kinkead, Peterson, Ray, & Preston, 2003).

However, participatory design and co-design are likely to expand more and within new areas in the higher education context. In his proposal for how classrooms should be renovated to meet the needs of the 21st Century, Owu (1997) recommends getting input from students and faculty through questionnaires and surveys. In his examination of emerging practices for the design of university spaces, Bligh (2014) further argues that involvement from students and faculty should go beyond bounded activities and create long-term relationships with stakeholders through a decentralized process. He further asserts that the design process can be a way of asserting academic values on an institution through an on-going process of discussion, design, and collaboration (Bligh, 2014). This on-going practice of co-design and collaboration can help to shape the culture of an institution.

Several universities do, however, make use of integrated co-design into the development of their campus buildings. For example, co-design was utilized in the planning of 'The Loft' student space at Graz University of Technology in Austria (Tuulos & Kirjavainen, 2016). The study focused on the role of physical space in experimental learning, but offers valuable lessons regarding co-design. It found that students described the space in terms of their practical experience; they talked in terms of what they could do in the space, such as work and relax. Yet on the other hand, faculty spoke about the project in terms of big picture ideas relating to the students' experience, such as creating and identity formation and enforcing the idea of a creative space. The author describes the co-design as a critical component of the creation of an experimental learning space (Tuulos & Kirjavainen, 2016). Further, they note, the space did not have pre-defined norms of how to use it, so the students and faculty were not limited to the experiences expected in a typical classroom (Tuulos & Kirjavainen, 2016).

In another example, at California Polytechnic State University, undergraduate computer and engineering students participated in a co-design discovery process for designing the library's digital interface. The students evaluated a human-computer-interface and provided a report of recommendations to the librarians. This report was also shared with the vendor of the software, who integrated several of the students' recommendations into the interface (Sommerville, 2007). The project later expanded to the design of physical learning spaces. The students' ideas challenged planner perspectives by proposing a blend of formal and informal learning spaces. The project not only created improvement to the library design, but also created relationships between the students and the librarians that lasted beyond the projects (Sommerville, 2007). As technology becomes increasingly integrated in higher education, the digital learning environment will play an equally important role to the physical one.

Additionally, the Australian-based design firm Co Design Construct has utilized co-design for projects with several educational institutions including primary schools and universities (Co Design Construct, n.d.). One project was the remodel of the Student Services Building at the University of Adelaide Waite campus. The process stripped down the centre for a total redesign to create a dynamic student space (Co Design Construct, n.d.). The University of Adelaide has utilized participatory design for several student hub projects. The design of the Hub Central building included 9000 hours of student involvement allowing students to shape their learning environment (Mills, 2011). The number of projects undertaken by the University of Adelaide that utilize co-design exemplifies the incorporation of co-design into organizational culture.

This collection of case studies of co-design is most likely far from exhaustive. Many of the examples of the co-design process in higher education does not make it into the public sphere of knowledge, with perhaps many interventions conducted as part of internal university processes or activities. However, from this list of examples, it can be seen that co-design has been widely applied and is likely to continue to expand. Further co-design may address many of the needs of higher education today including hearing from misaligned or disadvantaged groups, engaging students, and serving the needs of an increasingly diverse student population.

### THE IMPACT OF CO-DESIGN PROCESSES ON STUDENTS

An early study conducted in the UK provides evidence on the links between building design and recruitment, retention and performance of staff and students in the higher education sector. The case study of five higher education buildings found that most students identified structural and functional features, including the quality of the facilities, the library, sports centre, atriums and lecture rooms as key features of buildings that would most influence their decision to study in a particular institution (CABE, 2005). In the same study, students indicated that the features of the buildings they studied in affected their performance in three main ways: by helping motivate them in their work; by facilitating inspiration amongst students; and by providing key facilities critical to the course content (CABE, 2005).

Another study in Finland found that participatory co-design, when a multitude of stakeholders is involved, has positive impact especially on students. The study by Mäkelä, Lundström, and Mikkonen (2015) found that participatory co-design (i.e., collaborative design) of learning spaces can, firstly, support the understanding of users' needs and thus improve both the desirability and adequacy of the design from the user perspective. Second, participatory design is supportive to a democratic organizational culture. Third, increased ownership and dominance of co-designed solutions can lead to their more efficient use in teaching and learning and thereby support obtaining better learning outcomes (Dollinger & Lodge, in press).

Consequently, by involving students in the co-design of buildings, it will not only impact on the structure of the building, but also the students themselves. Dollinger and Lodge (forthcoming) write that three broad areas are likely to be impacted by the co-design process, including students' quality interactions with staff or faculty, student satisfaction and student graduate capabilities. For example, as the co-design process requires a sharing of decision-making responsibilities, students and participating staff may exhibit increased trust and respect for one another, given their ongoing interactions.

This impact may be critical for those working to improve the higher education sector, as building trusting relationships with students often relates to long-term engagement that may improve other student outcomes, including learning (Bowden,

M. MAHAT & M. DOLLINGER

2011). Additionally, given the authentic context of co-design processes and the application of real skills that students perhaps learn in a classroom previously, the co-design process may have the potential to improve students' graduate capabilities, and confidence in themselves when preparing for the workforce.

Participation in the co-design process for students also draws some parallels to work-integrated learning (WIL). WIL courses or opportunities are geared towards helping students apply theories and knowledge they have learned in a more traditional classroom setting in authentic real-world applications. Globally, as many universities are linking their value to their ability to help students transition to the workforce, WIL courses have become increasingly popular (McLennan & Keating, 2008). By creating opportunities for students to gain real world experience, WIL courses have been shown to improve student confidence and gain a clearer understanding of their skills (Coll, Lay, & Zegwaard, 2002). Additionally, Jackson (2015) found that WIL courses positively influenced student perceptions of their peers and students, suggesting that teamwork and collaboration in an authentic setting may help students feel like they belong at a university.

BARRIERS AND IMPLICATIONS

Co-design is a growing area of interest within architecture and building design. Chun (2016) writes that, traditionally, building design users involved in the participatory design method gave feedback but not equal decision-making power. However, in some areas such as the UK, co-design is becoming increasingly common. Yet Chun also warns that co-design, as a mechanism in building design, can be problematic as many architects are not well trained in the co-design process (2016). Further when bringing new stakeholders into the design process, conflict can arise if the architect's opinion or expertise is questioned or challenged.

For example, Chun gives the example of an architect designing something visually beautiful, but perhaps not useful to the users of building, thus the aims of the designer and the user are in conflict and can cause issues in a co-design interaction. However, architectural visual aspirations aside, if the goal of the building is to serve the needs of its users, the co-design process should help, rather than hinder the process. McDonnell (2009), through conducting a study of how designers communicate to building-user/clients, found that designers often espouse their expertise when in conflict with others, thus challenging the balance of power that is typical in a co-design process. Additionally, there may be language barrier in the terminology used on both sides. Thus, the co-design process, without proper support and training for both designers and users, can falter

The inexperience of many users with the design process has encouraged some literature to advocate for the co-design process to work with 'lead users' (e.g. von Hippel, 2005). Lead users are particularly invested users who have shown, perhaps through community forums, their interest in the design process of the products or services they use. However, even still with lead users, there are a select few who

230

are capable of sharing resources that will eventually be useful to the organisation. Further, a downside to using lead users rather than an open inclusive co-design process is that the best ideas or perspectives may still be outside of this community or specific group of users (von Hippel, 2005).

In fact, the uneven distribution of power is not the only problem associated with the co-design process. Time is another often-cited constraint to the co-design process, not only with the time it takes to actually co-design through series of meetings and consultations but also the time the process requires of the users who are participating (Del Gaudio, Franzato, & de Oliveira, 2016; Dollinger & Lodge, 2018). As co-design is often a voluntary process for users, with their time being unrewarded and most likely unpaid, it can be difficult to find willing participants. This is an especially critical point to discuss in relation to equity, as the co-design process should not be restricted to only those who have the pre-existing time and/or resources and funding to share their voice.

By exploring user motivations some of the barriers to co-design, such as finding willing participants, may be resolved. Studies have shown that in certain situations, intrinsic motivation is already present, such as parents who are genuinely interested in to help design toys for children (van Rijn & Stappers, 2008). This may point to the importance of including the right type of users who have a pre-existing interest or concern in the project. They also found that by relinquishing control in the design process, user ownership may increase and users begin to feel they are responsible for the end product or design (van Rijn & Stappers, 2008).

Pirinen (2016) also writes that two issues with the co-design process are the challenges to pre-existing institutional culture and different incentive systems. This relates back to Chun (2016) who wrote that the differing aims and objectives of designers versus users motivates each stakeholder group to act in a unique way. Pirinen's position on the challenge to institutional culture is equally interesting, however, as co-design often faces resistance as a new and unfamiliar idea. Co-design, even organizationally internal co-design, requires coordination across departments and disciplines, which comes with its own suite of challenges. For instance, there may be time constraints on the project delivery date and the resulting conflict with course and assignment timelines of students.

As similarly found with Del Gaudo, Franzato, and de Oliveira (2016), the time required of the co-design process can further limit how employees/designers would adopt the process, as the process can be slow, especially in the beginning when first acquainting oneself with the process. Pirinen (2016) recommends that in order to mitigate these changes, co-design should be implemented originally as part of the institution's culture, rather than just within a single project, as this would allow for a more holistic adoption over a period of time. Similarly, in regard to the design of learning spaces within education towards a shared learning environment has further shown disputes between designers and students, with students feeling the designers' perspectives may negatively impact their learning (Konings, Sidel, & van Merrienboer, 2014). However, the co-design process may help support students' perspectives thereby ensuring that the space suits their needs (Konings, Sidel, & van Merrienboer, 2014).

## CONCLUSIONS

There is constant pressure in the higher education sector to ensure student engagement is achieved to support a positive student experience and consequently high quality learning. Learning, however, does not just take place in the mind of the learner, nor the community in which he or she learns. It also takes place in an environment, whether it is a classroom, a lecture theatre, a maker space, or library. Emerging evidence is beginning to show that the environment in which learning takes place is an important indicator of the quality of students' learning experiences and a building block to support deep, rich learning.

Traditional full-time students spend much of their time on campus, and yet research has only begun to explore the relationship between students' physical environments and their overall student experience. For instance, how does a student centre bring students together with their peers? How does a library facilitate quality of learning? How can a learning space support group work and peer-to-peer learning? These questions and many more linking physical spaces to the overall student experience are important for continued understanding of what constitutes and facilitates student engagement in higher education. In short, research focuses too often on only the pedagogical stakeholder relationships and the outcomes of the student experience without considering a critical foundational element, the environment in which it takes place.

However, for universities to overcome the challenges and issues of designing innovative environments for students, students need to be actively involved in the process. The evolution in the design of learning spaces from a user-centred approach to co-designing is changing the landscape of design practice. Through value co-creation, where students jointly work with designers, faculty and staff, students can integrate their 'voice' in co-designing learning spaces in order to improve the provision and delivery of higher education for the institutions, but also enact improved outcomes and skills required for the 21st century knowledge society.

## REFERENCES

Alexander, C., Silverstein, M., Angel, S., Ishikawa, S., & Abrams, D. (1975). *The Oregon experiment*. New York, NY: The Oxford University Press.

Bligh, B. (2014). Examining new processes in learning space design. In P. Temple (Ed.), *The physical university: Contours of space and place in higher education* (pp. 34–57). New York, NY: Routledge.

Boddington, A., & Boys, J. (2011). *Re-shaping learning: A critical reader*. Rotterdam: Sense Publishers.

Bovill, C., Cook-Sather, A., & Felten, P. (2011). Students as co-creators of teaching approaches, academic developers. *International Journal for Academic Development, 16*(2), 133–145.

Bowden, J. L. H. (2011). Engaging the student as a customer: A relationship marketing approach. *Marketing Education Review, 21*(3), 211–228.

MIND THE GAP

Boys, J. (2011). *Towards creative learning spaces: Re-thinking the architecture of post-compulsory education*. New York, NY: Routledge.

Bravenboer, D. (2016). Why co-design and delivery is "a no brainer" for higher and degree apprenticeship policy. *Higher Education, Skills and Work-Based Learning, 6*(4), 384–400.

Casali, D. (2013, November 28). *Co-design and participatory design: A solid process primer*. Retrieved from https://intenseminimalism.com/2013/co-design-and-participatory-design-a-solid-process-primer/

Chun, M. H. (2016). *Challenges in co-designing a building*. Paper presented at the 2016 Design Research Society 50th Anniversary Conference, Design Research Society, Brighton.

Co-Design Architects. (2017). *About the project*. Retrieved from https://www.codesignarchitects.co.nz/portfolio-item/community-connection-point/

Co Design Construct. (n.d.). *Student hub*. Retrieved from https://www.codesign.net.au/university-of-adelaide-waite-campus-student-hub

Coll, R. K., Lay, M. C., & Zegwaard, K. E. (2002). Enhancing access to experiential learning in a science and technology degree programme. *Journal of Vocational Education and Training, 54*(2), 197–218.

Commission for Architecture and the Built Environment. (2005). *Design for distinction*. Retrieved from http://webarchive.nationalarchives.gov.uk/20110118174721/http://www.cabe.org.uk/files/design-with-distinction.pdf

Del Gaudio, C., Franzato, C., & de Oliveira, A. J. (2016). The challenge of time in community-based participatory design. *Urban Design International, 22*(2), 113–126.

Department of Education and Training. (2016). *Finance publication 2015*. Retrieved from https://docs.education.gov.au/node/42296

Dollinger, M., & Lodge, J. (2018). *Co-creation strategies for learning analytics*. Paper presented at the International Conference on Learning Analytics (LAK), Sydney, Australia.

Dollinger, M., & Lodge, J. (forthcoming). *The Journal of Marketing in Higher Education.*

Dollinger, M., & Lodge, J. (in press). Co-creation in higher education: Towards a conceptual model. *Journal of Marketing for Higher Education, 1*, 1–22.

Fullan, M., & Langworthy, M. (2014). *A rich seam: How new pedagogies find deep learning*. Retrieved from http://www.michaelfullan.ca/wp-content/uploads/2014/01/3897.Rich_Seam_web.pdf

Hadfield, L., Kinkead, J., Peterson, T., Ray, S., & Preston, S. (2003). An ideal writing center: Re-imagining space and design. In M. Pemberton & J. Kinkead (Eds.), *The center will hold* (pp. 166–176). Logan, UT: Utah State University Press.

Herbert, S. (1969). *The science of the artificial*. Cambridge, MA: The Massachusetts Institute of Technology.

Herrington, J. (2006). *Authentic learning environments in higher education*. Hershey, PA: IGI Global.

Jackson, D. (2015). Employability skill development in work-integrated learning: Barriers and best practice. *Studies in Higher Education, 40*(2), 350–367.

Jamieson, P., Fisher, K., Gilding, T., Taylor, P. G., & Trevitt, A. C. F. (2000). Place and space in the design of new learning environments. *Higher Education Research & Development, 19*(2), 221–236.

Kangas, M. (2010). Creative and playful learning: Learning through game co-creation and games in a playful learning environment. *Thinking Skills and Creativity, 5*(1), 1–15.

Kimbell, L. (2011). Rethinking design thinking: Part I. *The Journal of the Design Studies Forum, 3*(3), 285–306.

Kleinsmann, M. S. (2006). *Understanding collaborative design* (PhD doctoral dissertation). Delft University of Technology, Delft.

Konings, K. D., Sidel, T., & van Merrienboer, J. J. (2014). Participatory design of learning environments: Integrating perspectives of students, teachers, and designers. *Instructional Science, 42*(1), 1–9.

Kos, D., & Potocnik, A. J. (2005). Participatory urban renewal. *Urbani Izziv, 16*(2), 141–146.

Lozanovska, M., & Xu, L. (2012). Children and university architecture students working together: A pedagogical model of children's participation in architectural design. *International Journal of Cocreation in Design and the Arts, 9*(4), 209–229.

Mäkelä, T., Lundström, A., & Mikkonen, I. (2015). Co-designing learning spaces: Why, with whom, and how. In S. Nenonen, S. Kärnä, J. Junnonen, S. Tähtinen, N. Sandström, K. Airo, & O. Niemi (Eds.), *How to co-create campus* (pp. 197–211). Tampere: Juvenes Print.

McDonnell, J. (2009). Collaborative negotiation in design: A study of design conversations between architect and building users. *Co Design: International Journal of Co Creation in Design and the Arts, 5*(1), 35–50.

233

M. MAHAT & M. DOLLINGER

McLennan, B., & Keating, S. (2008, June). *Work-Integrated Learning (WIL) in Australian universities: The challenges of mainstreaming WIL*. In ALTC NAGCAS National Symposium, Melbourne.

Mills, N. (2011). Situated learning through social networking communities: The development of joint enterprise, mutual engagement, and a shared repertoire. *Calico Journal, 28*(2), 345–368.

Monash University. (2017, October 24). *MADA travels to Fiji to run co-design workshop with residents*. Retrieved from http://www.artdes.monash.edu.au/news/mada-travels-to-fiji-to-run-co-design-workshop-with-residents.html

Mulcahy, D., Cleveland, B., & Aberton, H. (2015). Learning spaces and pedagogic change: Envisioned, enacted and experienced. *Pedagogy, Culture & Society, 23*(4), 575–595.

Muller, M., & Druin, A. (2002). Participatory design: The third space in HCI. In J. Jacko & A. Sears (Eds.), *The human-computer interaction handbook: Fundamentals, evolving technologies and emerging applications* (pp. 1051–1068). Mahwah, NJ: Lawrence Erlbaum Associates.

Nonaka, I., & Konno, N. (1998). The concept of "BA": Building a foundation for knowledge creation. *California Management Review, 40*(3), 40–54.

Nurdini, A., & Harun, I. B. (2011). Incorporating user for rental housing design case study: City of Bandung, Indonesia. *International Journal of Civil & Environmental Engineering, 11*(2), 40–44.

Owu, M. (1997). Classrooms for the 21st century. In G. Keller (Ed.), *The best of planning for higher education* (pp. 95–103). Ann Arbor, MI: The Society for College and University Planning.

Paavola, S., Lipponen, L., & Hakkarainen, K. (2004). Models of innovative knowledge communities and three metaphors of learning. *Review of Educational Research, 74*(4), 557–576.

Parisio, M. (2013, December 1–4). *Designing learning spaces in higher education for autonomy: Preliminary findings and applications*. In ASCILITE-Australian Society for Computers in Learning in Tertiary Education Annual Conference, Sydney, Australia.

Perez, Y. V., Shelby, R., Edmunds, D., James, A., & Agogino, A. M. (2015). Social factors in the age of social media: Transdiciplinary co-design with the Pinoleville Pomo Nation. In G. Lindsay & L. Morhayim (Eds.), *Revisiting "social factors": Advancing research into people and place* (pp. 166–187). Newcastle: Cambridge Scholars Publishing.

Pirinen, A. (2016). The barriers and enablers of co-design for services. *International Journal of Design, 10*(3), 27–42.

Prahalad, C. K., & Ramaswamy, V. (2004). *The future of competition: Co-creating unique value with customers*. Boston, MA: Harvard Business Press.

Rowe, P. G. (1987). *Design thinking*. Boston, MA: The Massachusetts Institute of Technology.

Säljö, R. (2006, July 4). *Learning and cultural tools: Modelling and the evaluation of a collective memory*. In Presentation at EARLI JURE06 Conference, Tarto, Estonia.

Sanders, E. B. N. (2002). From user-centred to participatory design approaches. In J. Frascara (Ed.), *Design and the social sciences: Making connections* (pp. 1–8). New York, NY: Taylor & Francis.

Sanders, E. B. N., & Stappers, P. J. (2008). Co-creation and the new landscapes of design. *Co-design, 4*(1), 5–18.

Slade, S., & Prinsloo, P. (2013). Learning analytics: Ethical issues and dilemmas. *American Behavioral Scientist, 57*(10), 1510–1529.

Sommerville, M. M. (2007). *Participatory co-design: A relationship building*. World Library and Information Congress, 73rd IFLA General Conference and Council, The International Federation of Library Associations and Institutions, Durban.

TEQSA (Tertiary Education Quality and Standards Agency). (2017). *National register of higher education providers*. Retrieved from https://www.teqsa.gov.au/national-register

The Sorrell Foundation. (2010). *Joined up design for my place*. Retrieved from http://www.thesorrellfoundation.com/wp-content/uploads/2017/06/Joinedupdesign-for-myplace_Engaging-young-people-in-youth-centre-design.pdf

Tilassa. (2015, August 31). *Case: Kaisaniemi primary school co-design*. Retrieved from http://tilassa.fi/en/co-design/case-kaisaniemi-primary-school-co-design/

Tuulos, T., & Kirjavainen, S. (2016, August 10–12). *Creating a home for experimental learning: A case study of an interdisciplinary product development course*. In Proceedings of NordDesign, Trondheim, Norway.

van Rijn, H., & Stappers, P. J. (2008, October). *Expressions of ownership: Motivating users in a co-design process*. In Proceedings of the Tenth Anniversary Conference on Participatory Design 2008, Indiana University Indianapolis, Bloomington, IN.

Von Hippel, E. (2005). *Democratizing innovation*. Cambridge, MA: MIT Press.

Wenger, E. (1998). *Communities of practice: Learning, meaning, and identity*. New York, NY: Cambridge University Press.

# PART 3

# EVALUATING LEARNING SPACE/PLACE PLANNING AND DESIGN, AND THE IMPLICATIONS FOR FUTURE CAMPUS PLANNING AND DESIGN

KENN FISHER

# INTRODUCTION TO PART 3

The final 4 chapters are perhaps the most critical in this book. There is an enormous amount of work that has gone into the first 11 chapters as they are predominantly based on PhD dissertations. But, the key question being asked now in the context of evidence-based policy making is 'do these approaches work and, if so, what it the evidence that they do'. If we are to re-align the 20th C campus estate to a 21st C context, the massive capital expenditure must be responsibly applied to future projects.

So evaluation is critical before we proceed with such innovations in a scaled up format.

Chapter 12 examines the post 2012 literature on the effectiveness of blended mixed technology enhanced active learning environments. A mini meta analysis of over 100 peer reviewed journal research studies was reduced to four scholarly replicable studies. Although these were not large trials they do serve to test and prove post occupancy evaluations of learning spaces and thus the authors draw useful conclusions for ways forward.

Chapter 13 follows on from the previous Part 2 study by Beckers on evaluating the effectiveness of informal learning spaces. This chapter, however, delves quite deeply into the informal learning experience especially for first year university students. The learning commons is their primary experience of university life outside their structured formal teaching and instructor led spatial experiences. Once again we have an analysis and evaluation of how and why these spaces work. The next Chapter 14 examines the concept and role of the library as a whole. It seeks to evaluate student perceptions of the affordances that the 21st C library might offer. Sixteen libraries are studied with aggregated findings presented of the ideal library.

The final Chapter 15 draws together many of the concepts addressed in the other 14 chapters. A blended active formal and informal teaching and learning building is used to develop a model which is prototyped in the new $200 million LTB – learning and teaching building – at Monash University in Melbourne, Australia.

© KONINKLIJKE BRILL NV, LEIDEN, 2019 | DOI: 10.1163/9789004391598_014

KENN FISHER AND ROBERT A. ELLIS

# 12. A CRITICAL REVIEW OF POST 2012 SCHOLARLY LITERATURE ON THE EVIDENCE-BASED DESIGN AND EVALUATION OF NEW GENERATION ACTIVE LEARNING ENVIRONMENTS

## ABSTRACT

Since 2008 – following the Global Financial Crisis – significant funds have been invested in university facilities particularly in Australia. Some of these funds were allocated to teaching and learning spaces and this trend has continued unabated to the time of writing of this article. Increased funding is also being initiated overseas with many of the learning spaces being designed around a next generation learning environment (NGLE) concept, otherwise known as technology enabled active learning (TEAL) environments. Whilst some evaluation of these developments has occurred over the same period it is only since 2011 that any rigorous scholarly studies have begun to emerge, and these are very small in number. Yet significant capital investment in NGLE's continues unabated, and the instigators of these spatial developments still do not know if they actually work. Current debates which are creating tension are holistic definitions of learning environments and what counts as legitimate evidence of effectiveness. This paper reviews evaluation developments since 2011, following a previous article (Fisher & Newton, 2014), which reviewed studies prior to 2011. Five scholarly peer reviewed studies have been examined in relation to the current debates. On the basis of the review, a more holistic approach to evaluation of learning environments is suggested through the use of observational and experiential data with a view to providing an evidence-based approach to inform the burgeoning capital investments required to re-engineer the vast amounts of existing and now very much obsolete university estates learning environments assets.

## INTRODUCTION

The 'traditional' teacher-centred classroom has been extant since the mid-1700's when it evolved during the early stages of the Industrial Revolution. It has transformed in many respects over subsequent decades but only in the 21st Century has there been any sustained significant interest in moving away from a design which promotes a teacher-centred model towards a learner-centred model (Boys et al., 2014; Fisher,

© KONINKLIJKE BRILL NV, LEIDEN, 2019 | DOI: 10.1163/9789004391598_015

2013; Ellis & Goodyear, 2010, 2018). The evaluation of the effectiveness of learner-centred spaces is a work in progress.

It is critical that an evidence-base is established – we need the best possible evidence of how learner-centred classroom designs are more effective than the teacher-centred models to warrant and direct the current investment in learning spaces across the international higher education and school sector (Oblinger, 2006; Boys, 2013). Such evidence is needed not just for those investing in university campus and school development, but also for the teachers who are partners in moving from a teacher-centred model to a contemporary student-focused pedagogical approach and classroom design. In an evaluation of learning space, its indirect relationship to outcomes and its supporting role to pedagogy should not be forgotten.

A comprehensive review of new generation active learning environments literature (Fisher & Newton, 2014) was based largely on material up to 2011 and published in 2014. Since, 2011, there have been further studies in evidence-based approaches to evaluation of learning environments using a range of methodologies which need to be critically reviewed. Many of these studies are appearing without us understanding what dimensions of learning space are being revealed by the use of different categories of data, often because their definitions of learning environments are imprecise. In this study, we look at different categories of data and emphasise the importance of defining New Generation Learning Environments (NGLEs) which acknowledge technologies both in class and online as a key part of the learning space design supporting the student experience across physical and virtual environments.

A renewal of the definition of learning space to routinely include integrated physical and virtual space from a student perspective has significant implications for the types of data chosen as evidence to evaluate NGLEs and brings with it its own challenges. To address these, a research centre was established at the University of Melbourne in 2008 to study evidence around the effectiveness of new generation learning environments (Imms, Fisher, Newton, & Cleveland, 2015) This has proven to be important because since then, considerable financial investment continues to be invested globally in new generation learning environments (NGLEs) and to some degree, these innovations remain largely untested in a scholarly rigorous way.

In examining the effectiveness of New Generation Learning Environments, a number of research domains provide noteworthy contributions. A *first domain* is illustrated by Boys, Melhuish, and Wilson (2014) in exploring the first-year student experience of campus. Her team took the view that students fit into various categories and thus we need to focus on each of those categories individually. To develop this further – in addition to the first-year experience – the second year revolves around the need for decisions around which specialisation(s) students might choose, whilst the third year focuses on specialisation followed by subsequent post graduate programs such as honours and course work masters and finally higher degree research programs.

A *second domain* identifies a link between how, where and why students learn and the associations of these aspects of the student experience with the design of learning spaces (Ellis and Goodyear, in press). Learning space can be understood to be part of a broader education ecology, whose parts all contribute to the quality and innovation of the student experience. In this concept of an ecology, all of its parts are balanced around an idea of, and commitment to, learning. The parts can be conceived of as the micro (e.g. disciplinary knowledge in curricula, material elements and participants) and meso (e.g. approaches, conceptions and perceptions) ecosystems of the student and teacher experience, as well as the exo (e.g. institutional strategy, policy, governance, management and funding) and macro (eg government or sector strategy policy and funding) of the institution being considered (Bronfenbrenner, 1979). To remain in balance and focused on learning, a number of conditions need to be observed. The parts of the ecology require a self-awareness about their role in relation to other parts and how their combined activity can help promote learning. The parts of the ecology also need to routinely seek systematic and cyclical feedback on their activity from stakeholders, to determine if they are fulfilling their function in the ecology effectively. Furthermore, being aware of their role and drawing on feedback, the parts of the ecology need to be capable of continuously self-correcting so that they help to keep the ecology in balance. In this concept of an education ecology, the parts continuously interact to ensure that the main purpose of learning space was to help students learn.

A *third domain* focuses on the instructors, about which much has been considered in the project 'Not a Waste of Space' (de la Harpe et al., 2013), a research project completed for the Australian Ministry of Education's Office of Learning and Teaching. This study sought to develop strategies for professional development for instructors/ teachers/academics to engage with new generation learning environments. There has been a persistent reluctance to take up the affordances offered by these NGLEs, pointing to the need for an evidence-based design approach which may provide the incentive needed to shift instructor behaviours away from the teacher centred model to the blended, active or TEAL oriented student centred model of teaching and learning. Other institutional barriers can also impact on such innovations which also inhibit the scaling up of such progressive approaches to pedagogy (Patterson, 2007).

A *fourth domain* needs to be considered as well – the student demographic. An illustration of this is the development of a learning commons network at the University of Adelaide (Fisher, 2010) where student focus groups representing a range of demographics were consulted over the three-year period of development. Groups included first-year school leavers, adult entry, international students, regional, national, and post-graduate research and coursework students. That is seven student demographic categories in all.

When studies undertaken in the domains above asked students questions such as 'How did you approach your learning?', 'What did you think you were learning?' or 'What did you notice in the environment while you were learning?', the outcomes increasingly tend to involve material elements in the student experience. The growth of tools, technologies and digital equipment in learning and teaching has been exponential and ubiquitous over the last decade.

K. FISHER & R. A. ELLIS

Consequently, a *fifth domain* is relevant to evaluating learning space because it recognises the contribution of sociomaterial aspects of learning environments to the student experience. In this domain, value is given to the entanglement of human and material activity engaged in education and learning (Fenwick & Landri, 2012; Fenwick, 2015). The phenomena under research in this domain is recognised as an assemblage of materials, human activity, ideas and other elements which continuously interact. Sociomaterial approaches to such phenomena as learning space broaden the focus from emphasising the cognitive and social to also include how combinations or assemblages of cognitive, social and *material* elements provide felicitous or infelicitous outcomes for learners and teachers. In an age of big data and analytics which provide access to thousands of research participants and their use of virtual learning space, this combined focus on human activity and material objects can be particularly illuminative. Combined with the experiential data sources described in the previous domains, together these categories of data can provide a more rounded explanation of why some learning space designs are more helpful to students than others.

Given the various perspectives and orientations on sources of data and methodologies that different areas of research use to investigate learning space, a critical review such as the one proposed in this article is thus somewhat fraught. To focus the review, then, it will concentrate primarily on contributing to the debate about evaluating new generation learning environments (NGLEs) such as TEAL (Technology-enabled active learning spaces), ALC (active learning classrooms), blended, 'flipped' and CDIO (conceive, design, implement and operate) learning spaces. Using these as types of case studies, the ensuing discussion will describe the benefits of combining both observational and experiential data from different domains of research in order to more holistically understand the links between student learning outcomes and the design of learning environments.

## EVALUATION AND THE EVIDENCE-BASED CONCEPT

In an attempt to bring a more triangulated, and more robust approach, to the concept of evaluation in the educational space-planning sector, we can benefit by understanding the synergistic relationship between research and practice.

> Between research and practice a new, third discipline must be inserted, one that can translate between the abstractions of research and the practicalities of practice. We need a discipline of *translational development*. Medicine, biology, and the health sciences have been the first to recognise the need for this intermediary step through the funding and development of centres for translational science. This intermediate field is needed in all arenas of research. It is of special importance to our community. We need translational developers who can act as the intermediary, translating research findings into the language of practical development and business while also translating the needs of business into issues that researchers can address. Notice that the need for

244

translation goes in both directions: from research to practice and from practice to research. (Norman, 2010)

This rigorous insight has been adopted by health planners over the last couple of decades in designing healing spaces based on evidence of what works and why (HERD, 2010). In the educational space-planning sector this approach is in its infancy (Fisher, 2013; Fisher & Newton, 2014) and while evaluation methods and tools include qualitative and quantitative data (Denzin & Lincoln, 2011), the field is yet to systematically link variations in the quality of learning experiences to the design of physical and virtual learning environments using observational and experiential data.

*Case Study Evaluations and Findings*

To bring our understanding up to date with the latest research in New Generation Learning Environments (NGLEs) and to suggest how the design of future studies into the effectiveness of NGLEs might benefit from considering how both observational data, revealing how student interact with material elements of the environment, and experiential data, revealing the intent and motivations behind those interactions, can provide a deeper understanding of the key issues involved, the following section of this paper reviews some notable investigations since 2011.

Case study 1: Active learning classroom designs. In this mixed-methods study (Brooks, 2013) explores formal physical learning environments and notes that

research assessing the efficacy of new classroom spaces has lagged considerably, with very few empirical studies offering evidence of their impact on educational outcomes. (op. cit., p. 1)

The study includes a literature review which examines three groupings of research looking at space design: (a) designers and technologists who have largely focussed on learning space innovations; (b) scholars of teaching and learning who have tended to explore the theoretical, normative and philosophical aspects of learning spaces using case studies – note that Brooks argues that these lack empirical evidence and data although he does note that

the tendency has been to report on measures of satisfaction with newly designed spaces, qualitative feedback on student and instructor experiences, and other evaluative metrics;

and (c) evaluations of the Massachusetts Institute of Technology (MIT), Minnesota and North Carolina University TEAL and Scale UP spaces which

demonstrate that the combination of newly designed learning spaces and active learning approaches to teaching contributed to improved student learning outcomes (but) the research designs on which they were based did not provide enough in the way of experimental controls so as to isolate the relative effects of either space or pedagogy. (op. cit., p. 2)

In order to demonstrate that 'space does matter' to the learning experience of students (Whiteside, 2010), Brooks employs a comparative evaluation approach of an active learning classroom design and a traditional teacher-centred space (the latter with rows of desks facing the teacher desk up the front) to investigate both teacher and student behaviour in each space type. He observes an experienced teacher who taught the same lesson in two distinct settings – one an active learning classroom design (see Figure 12.1), and the other a more traditional teacher-centred format – on different days with contiguous curriculum material. Observational coding of teacher and student behaviours at five-minute intervals was carried out. The researchers coded four categories – classroom activities; instructor behaviour; student behaviour; and content delivery – and each of these in turn was analysed.

There were 54 elements of data scored within the evaluation instrument. Key findings included that (a) the instructor lectured more and was at the podium more in the traditional space; (b) students appeared to be on-task at higher and mixed levels in the traditional classroom – it is believed that this could be because the coding model was based around traditional classroom behaviour therefore biasing that format; (c) conversely, classroom discussion and use of the board occurred more frequently in the active learning classroom design, in part because there were more boards and also they were more accessible but also because there was less lecturing; (d) the instructor moved about the room and consulted with students more in the active learning classroom design but did not consult with students significantly more in that design than in the traditional classroom and (e) it was felt that the teacher in the active learning classroom design was still somewhat bonded to the teacher's desk, even though it was not at the 'front' of the space.

The first part of the study seeks to illustrate how formal classroom space is related to the behaviour of instructors and students and the tasks they are engaged in with empirical evidence, Brooks suggests, that the design of space shapes both student and teacher behaviour.

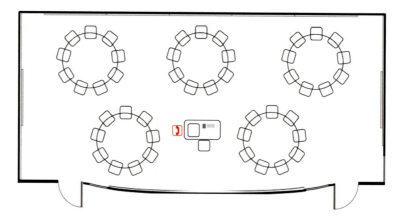

*Figure 12.1. Schematic diagram of an active learning classroom (from Brooks, 2013)*

Brooks then goes into some quantitative detail to validate and qualify these findings. In so doing this quantitative data is qualified noting that the affordance of straight rows of desks and chairs with lineal aisles is quite different from the much more accessible banquet table arrangement where access to all students is readily available. This, plus the types of pedagogy pursued in each type of space, illustrated the following characteristics.

> Traditional classrooms encourage lectures at the expense of active learning techniques, while ALCs marginalise the effectiveness of lectures while punctuating the importance of active learning approaches to instruction, but both are effective at producing high levels of on-task student behaviour. This suggests that different spaces are better suited for different types of activities, but can still achieve similar results. Furthermore, the evidence that active learning techniques do not work well in a lecture classroom and that the lecture does not work in an ALC suggests that instructors should consider adjusting their pedagogy to fit the space in which their course is held. (op. cit., p. 8)

In the new flexible spaces students exceeded final grade projections relative to their American College Test scores. The implication that this study suggests is that if a more active, student-centered pedagogical approach and classroom design is used, student learning outcomes are likely to increase. It should be noted that 'students and faculty had positive perceptions of the new learning environments but also had to adjust to the unusual classroom'.

*Case study 2: Linking learning space development to institutional education missions.* This qualitative ethnographic study, carried out by Boys, Melhuish & Wilson (2014), was supported by SCUP (Society for College and University Planning) via the Perry Chapman Award. It focused on the development of strategies for analysing learning spaces to inform the institutional mission around learning and student engagement. The work focused around new students entering Northumbria University and sought to understand what kinds of data can help in improved design and management of an effective variety of self-directed and informal learning spaces. The study also sought to identify appropriate research methods to evaluate these connections to inform university policy-making citing an evidence-based design approach.

Interestingly both this study and the previous Chapman Prize researchers (Painter, Fournier, Grape, Grummon, Morelli, Whitmer, & Cevetelloet, 2013) chose to focus on informal student-centred learning environments as opposed to formal teacher centred and social food and beverage centred spaces. Whilst there is a dearth of research in this field, and there is increasing pressure for more of this type of space on campus, we suggest that the education space-planning sector needs to understand both categories of space (both formal and informal), how they intersect and leverage off virtual learning space, from the perspective of students who approach their learning successfully in new generation learning environments.

K. FISHER & R. A. ELLIS

Boys, Melhuish, and Wilson (2014) built on the previous Painter et al. (2013) research, and used alternative research methods drawn from anthropology, cultural geography and science & technology studies. The team sought to explore process rather than direct causal evidence as a means of understanding the complexities of campus place-making. They also sought to understand cultural issues around the local (in the classroom), the institutional (university identity) and the wider context (pedagogies, resources, management).

The team developed a grounded theory and mixed-methods approach using the University of Sheffield 'Theory of Change' evaluation process (Hart, Diercks, O'Brien, & Powell, 2009). This model summarises a change initiative (for example, the design of a new learning space; the introduction of new technology into a space, etc.) across a number of distinct areas. It measures outcomes from a change process using: the *current situation* that precedes the intervention; *enabling* factors that define the structures and support which need to be set up or provided to produce the desired outcomes; *process* indicators that define what needs to happen in order to achieve the desired outcomes; *outcome* indicators that define the intermediate or longer-term outcomes and; the overall *impact* desired for the project or programme (op. cit., p. 17). The focus, then, is on how to manage the process towards the desired outcomes (Lefebvre, 1991).

> Through backward mapping a causal narrative or 'theory' is established, e.g. "to achieve the desired impact, the outcomes need to be x, y and z. To achieve these outcomes processes a, b and c need to happen, to carry out a, b and c resources and enabling factors d, e and f are required". Once the Theory of Change and the 'outcome' indicators have been established, evaluation questions are drawn from them and data collection methods are designed. (op. cit., p. 17)

Using this approach, Boys et al. noted that (a) students struggled to match space and activity – both at home, and on campus formally, informally and socially; (b) there were complexities around time and space in negotiating these in the spatial domains with timetable constraints and also distances between spaces; (c) there was a lack of social space and the problem of these being mainly being in the library and; (d) a lack of connectedness and spatial sense of community or home, such as a common room. Table 12.1 illustrates some of these complexities and relationships and the negotiations required to manage learning space occupation.

Key findings from the study suggested that further research might focus on: (a) how the interrelationships of space, belonging and engagement evolve as students progress into senior years; (b) how might these change when experienced in different socio-economic-ethnic backgrounds; and (c) what type of informal learning spaces are appropriate for early 21st Century students? In terms of improving the process leading to new learning space designs, the study suggests that the need to embed learning space research into the space design process, particularly by working towards greater interaction between researchers and campus planners and integrating

A CRITICAL REVIEW OF POST 2012 SCHOLARLY LITERATURE

*Table 12.1. Students' learning: Negotiating space, time and circumstances and institutional space development strategy (adapted from Boys, Melhuish, & Wilson, 2014, p. 17)*

| The Student Experience | Learning Geographies | Student Affect in Learning Spaces |
|---|---|---|
| Student's own 'tools' | Patterns of Formal, Informal and Social learning | Indoor and Outdoor environmental quality |
| Identity development | Synchronous and Asynchronous learning in the Physical and Virtual Campus | Map, evaluate and use data to understand useage of different learning space typologies |
| Cognitively mapping the campus | The educational offering and what is missing | Strive for a seamless experience between students/ peers, instructors, programmes and the university itself |
| Visible Learning | Student Choice to match Student learning styles | Ensure space supports learning and engagement |
| Courses and Instructors are more accessible | Negotiate a Learning Space Typologies to match course requirements | Conduct continuous assessment of the estate using various evaluation tools – strive for continuous improvement |
| Understanding campus culture | Shift the Learning Space Ratio from the present 80:15:5 (Formal: Informal: Social) to map the Virtual ie 50: 30:20 | Ensure differentiated teaching and pedagogies can be supported by differentiated spaces – choice is the key Consider learning space management as a curriculum tool |

more research around how belonging and engagement might relate to retention and achievement, and the role of the campus in this context. A final comment emphasises the 'need [for] more studies of how students perceive and experience these kinds of informal spaces, preferably using the kinds of rich research methods outlined here, so as to develop our understanding of how they work, not just as effective learning environments, but also as centres of engagement' (op. cit., p. 23).

*Case study 3: Linking student engagement data to active learning classroom designs.* This study by Scott-Webber, Strickland, and Kapitula (2013) used measures of student engagement (National Survey of Student Engagement, 2011) as a means of assessing the performance of active learning classrooms. The student engagement measures consider four key aspects – behavioural, psychological, socio-cultural and holistic. In including these factors, Scott-Webber et al. note that this is to a degree inconsistent with a holistic paradigm, as there are many factors which may impact on student behaviours and learning outcomes. Thus, the authors note:

> ... in attempting to establish a relationship between the designed environment and the behavioural factors of student engagement, it is important to develop a body of evidence that establishes a foundation for the idea that the learning environment impacts student behaviours. (Scott-Webber, Strickland, & Kapitula, 2013, p. 2)

The study involved an assessment of student behaviour within the configurations of active learning classroom designs shown in Figure 12.2 and comparing their experiences with those in a traditional classroom design with desks in rows and a teacher position up the front of the classroom.

A number of sources of data were assessed to measure student behaviour in the active learning classroom designs:

- *Demographics and baseline* data included the educational level of the student, type of course, type of active learning classroom design, instructional approach and perceived level of engagement.

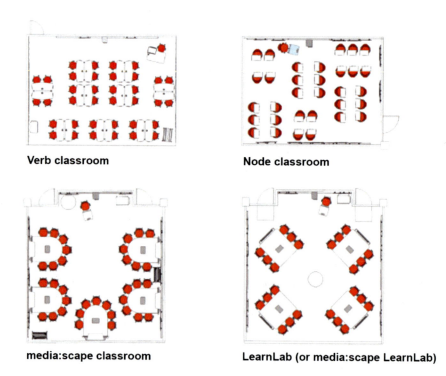

*Figure 12.2. Steelcase 'solutions' for active learning classrooms (from Scott Webber et al., 2013)*

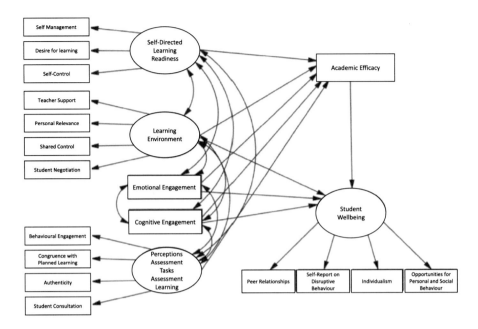

*Figure 12.3. Emergent relational model linking pedagogy, learning environment and student wellbeing (from Waldrip, Cox, & Jin Yu, 2014)*

- *Learning practice* data included the measurement of factors thought to be related to student behaviour such as the students' collaboration and focus, active involvement and engagement, exposure to material and in-class feedback, real-life scenarios, and physical movement within the classroom. Comparisons were made between the traditional and new designs. The study suggests that the measures used provide an 'evaluation of the effect of spatial design on student engagement'.
- *Perception of outcomes* data was collected by asking respondents about their experiences in traditional and new classroom designs, focusing on issues such as engagement in class, ability to achieve a higher grade, motivation to attend class, plus final open-ended comments.

Key findings of the study included the following;

- over 90 percent of students found the active learning classroom designs provided adequate or better engagement and support of classroom practices in comparison to the traditional design.
- a majority of students rated the engagement factors higher or better than the traditional classroom;
- teaching practices were rated as 21.6 in the traditional design and 36.3 out of a possible 48 in the active learning classroom designs. This was interpreted as illustrating improvement in learning practices arising from the new designs;

K. FISHER & R. A. ELLIS

- students believed the new/post classroom layout contributed to 'a moderate to exceptional increase in their engagement in class (90.32 percent), ability to achieve a higher grade (80.65 percent), and increase in motivation to attend class (78.04 percent)' (op. cit., p. 6). The authors acknowledged that there were limitations in the study, not least that the instrument designed to understand the links between engagement and environment had its own limitations and that further research 'employing a greater diversity of data collection methods is needed'.

*Case study 4: Linking qualitatively different student perceptions of learning to the learning environment.* The final case study reviewed here emphasises student perceptions of the learning environment in the research design. While there was some perception data drawn on in case study 3, the design of this study around student perception data and analysis of their experience in learning space is somewhat different to the observational data in the previous case studies such as;

- The coding of teacher and student behaviours in case study 1
- The ethnographic examination of processes in case study 2
- The measures of learning practice of students in situ in case study 3

This fourth project, a quantitative study by Waldrip, Cox, and Jin Yu (2014) examined the effect on personalised learning and well-being in open plan scaled-up learning communities using the Personalised Learning Experience Questionnaire (PLEQ) to evaluate (n=3000) student perceptions of these learning environments. The study also drew on quantitative data on attendance, wellbeing and academic performance in English and mathematics over 3 years of study. In all, 19 factors were included in the model. Whilst it is a school-based study, the rigour and methodology suggest possible use in higher education. The study orientated its research design to get a sense of what students felt it was like to be in an open-plan learning space and how this might be connected to the quality of their learning. The study notes that:

> Historically, research into learning environments has been conceptualised in psycho-social terms, highlighting the origins, causes and/or outcomes of behavior. As the concept of environment, as applied to educational settings in this literature, refers to the atmosphere, ambience, tone, or climate that pervades the particular setting it focuses on the question, "what is it like to be in this environment?" (op. cit., p. 21)

The PLEQ was designed to measure student perceptions such as self-directed learning variables (self-management, learning desire, self-control) teacher support; personal relevance; shared control; student negotiation; emotional engagement; cognitive engagement; behavioural engagement; assessment – congruence with planned learning; assessment – authenticity; assessment – student consultation; assessment – transparency; academic efficacy; emotional tone; peer relationships; affect at school; self-report on disruptive behaviour; individualisation; effective teaching and

252

A CRITICAL REVIEW OF POST 2012 SCHOLARLY LITERATURE

learning; opportunity for personal and social behaviour. The researchers hoped that the relationship between these variables would enable them to develop a sense of how variation in student perceptions of the open-plan learning space might provide some useful evidence to inform the design and use of such spaces.

Paradoxically in some schools the PLEQ results showed a lower impact over the first two years increasing in the third year (Year 9) whereas literacy and numeracy scores increased compared with similar ranked SES schools. As a result, it is thought that open plan learning may impact more favourably on more mature students.

> Students who perceived high levels of student wellbeing also perceive high levels of self-directed learning, assessment, learning environment and engagement and similarly students who perceived low levels of student wellbeing also perceived low levels of the contributing factors. (op. cit., p. 33)

> Students reported experiencing improvement in their engagement and learning when their teachers personalised learning by incorporating opportunities for student voice during and after the learning activities and involved the students in providing peer assessment through a teacher facilitated and scaffolded learning approach. (op. cit., p. 33)

Other key findings included (op. cit., p. 39)

- that self-directed learning readiness, cognitive engagement, and perceptions of assessment tasks/assessment learning were all reciprocally associated with academic efficacy;
- academic efficacy and learning environment were positively associated with student wellbeing;
- it was apparent that students were not seeing emotional engagement as being related to student wellbeing and learning – interviews confirmed this finding in that students perceived emotional engagement as a social rather than a learning dimension and;
- all exogenous variables (i.e., self-directed learning readiness, learning environment, emotional engagement, cognitive engagement, and perceptions of assessment tasks/assessment learning) were positively correlated with one another.
- Perhaps one of the most important outcomes was the development of an emergent relational model which links pedagogy, academic efficacy, the learning environment and student well-being as illustrated.

The authors concluded that the study developed one of the first instruments to explore the complex interactions around the impact on personalisation of learning, academic efficacy and student well-being in the learning environment. In addition, the PLEQ can elicit student perceptions of key elements in optimising a personalised, quality learning environment; enables shared language and understanding for interpretation; facilitates the targeting of differentiated pedagogical interventions; and can track the impact of these over short, medium and long terms.

253

K. FISHER & R. A. ELLIS

## DISCUSSION AND CONCLUSIONS

The field of research into learning space planning in the education sector is diverse and heterogeneous, with little agreement on fundamental definitions, units of research focus, the constituent parts of learning space, how to measure change and improvements, nor a sense of what constitutes evidence which links the design of learning space and student learning behaviour. For the field to move forward more coherently and rapidly, some consensus on fundamental definitions, terminology and units of research are essential. In the light of the studies reviewed, we suggest two propositions should be given serious consideration across the field more generally;

- Concepts of learning space research should increasingly take note of the relational and nested role the virtual learning environment in an elaborated notion of learning space.
- Given the ubiquitous use of material elements (eg technologies, seating configurations) in the student experience, evaluations of learning space should seek to complement the use of experiential data with sociomaterial methodologies and observational data which capture some entangled human and material activity. Carefully done, this will help to shed light on the nature and role of material elements in the student learning experience.

The research case studies reviewed here reveal some of the most recent developments and have highlighted the contribution that different categories of data used in research design can contribute to our understanding of learning space design. Observations of participants in learning space allow us to describe and record how student and teacher behaviour interacts with the design of the space they are in, but that category of data alone does not reveal the intent of the participants. Experiential data, such as the perception data reported in some of the case studies, can reveal what things students and teachers notice in the learning environment and, with carefully designed questions, *why* the participants interacted with elements in the environment in the ways they did. We argue that a fuller understanding of the links between effective student learning and learning space design is more readily achieved if multiple categories of data are used to improve insights into how, and the extent to which, the student experience of learning is related to the physical and virtual environments in which it is situated. However, the understanding that is gleaned from multivariate studies will only feed into workable solutions for practitioners if the outcomes are translated into forms that make sense to students and teachers. Consequently the path of future studies in this area also needs to embrace the principles of a translational development and a closer collaboration between researchers and students and teachers so that the understanding flows in all directions.

In the main, the case studies reviewed sit reasonably coherently within their own terms and definitions, but offer limited homogeneity required to get consensus across the field of learning space planning in the education sector, which is necessary if the field is to move forward more rapidly and coherently. These insights point towards

254

## A CRITICAL REVIEW OF POST 2012 SCHOLARLY LITERATURE

some next steps for the field. As one of the studies suggested, if we are going to design physical learning spaces which improve learning outcomes, then evidence of the links between student behaviour and different configurations of learning space needs to be more fully elaborated with evidence and disciplinary specificity. To develop an effective evidence-base for design, we need evidence of both *how* learners behave in learning space as well as *why*. By understanding how the different categories of data can shed light on different understandings of student and teacher activity, a more holistic basis of evidence will be able to be developed on which the sector can mature.

### REFERENCES

Baudouin, R., Bezanson, L., Borgen, B., Goyer, L., Hiebert, B., Lalande, V., Magnusson, K., Michaud, G., Renald, C., & Turcotte, M. (2007). Demonstrating value: A draft framework for evaluating the effectiveness of career development interventions. *Canadian Journal of Counseling and Psychotherapy, 41*(3), 146–157.

Bower, M., Dalgarno, B., Kennedy, G., Lee, M., & Kenney, J. (2014). *Blended synchronous learning: A handbook for educators.* Canberra: Australian Government Office of Learning & Teaching.

Boyd, D., & Crawford, K. (2012). Critical questions for big data: Provocations for a cultural, technological, and scholarly phenomenon. *Information, Communication, & Society, 15*(5), 662–679.

Boys, J., Melhuish, C., & Wilson, A. (2014, May). *Developing research methods for analysing learning spaces that can inform institutional missions of learning and engagement.* Ann Arbor, MI: Society for College and University Planning.

Bronfenbrenner, U. (1979). *The ecology of human development.* Cambridge, MA: Harvard University Press.

Brooks, C. (2012). Space and consequences: The impact of different formal learning spaces on instructor and student behavior. *Journal of Learning Spaces, 1*(2), 1–10.

Brown, M., Dugdale, S., Felix, E., Holeton, R., & Myers, C. (2013). Learning space rating system. *Educause*, p. 56.

CDIO. (2015). *Conceive, design, implement & operate.* Retrieved June 21, 2015, from http://www.cdio.org

Churches, A. (2001). *Bloom's digital taxonomy.* Retrieved November 22, 2018, from http://burtonslifelearning.pbworks.com/f/BloomDigitalTaxonomy2001.pdf

Cleveland, B. (2013). *Development and pilot testing of the School Spaces Evaluation Instrument (SSEI) module 3: Alignment of pedagogy and learning environments.* Melbourne: LEARN (Learning Environments Applied Research Network) Universtiy of Melbourne.

Coffield, D., Hall, E., & Ecclestone, K. (2004). *Learning styles and pedagogy in post-16 learning: A systematic and critical review.* London: The Learning and Skills Research Centre.

de la Harpe, B., Mason, T., Mcpherson, M., Fisher, K., & Imms, W. (2014). *Not a waste of space: Professional development for staff teaching in new generation learning spaces.* Canberra: Australian Government Office of Learning and Teaching.

Denzin, N., & Lincoln, Y. (Eds.). (2011). *The Sage handbook of qualitative research* (4th ed.). Los Angeles, CA: Sage Publications.

Dovey, K., & Fisher, K. (2014). Plans and pedagogies. *Journal of Architecture.*

Ellis, R. A., & Goodyear, P. (2018). *Spaces of teaching and learning: Integrating perspectives on research and practice.* Berlin: Springer.

Ellis, R. A., & Goodyear, P. (in press). *The education ecology of universities: Integrating strategy, learning and the academy.* London: Routledge/SRHE.

Ellis, R. A, Goodyer, P., Fisher, K., & Marmot, A. (2014). *Modelling the complex learning spaces.* Canberra: Australian Research Council Discovery Grant Award.

Erlauer, L. (2003). *The brain compatible classroom: Using what we know about learning to improve teaching.* Alexandria, VA: Association for Supervision and Curriculum Development.

255

Fenwick, T. (2015). Sociomateriality and learning: A critical approach. In D. Scott & A. Hargreaves (Eds.), *The Sage handbook of learning* (pp. 83–93). London: Sage Publishers.

Fenwick, T., & Landri, P. (2012). Materialities, textures and pedagogies: Socio-material assemblages in education. *Pedagogy, Culture & Society, 20*(1), 1–7.

Ferguson, R. (2012). Learning analytics: Drivers, developments and challenges. *International Journal of Technology Enhanced Learning, 4*(5–6), 304–317.

Fisher, K. (2005). *The campus as thirdspace*. Educause Conference Proceedings, Melbourne, Australia.

Fisher, K. (2010). *A strategy for a distributed precint hub and spoke learning commons framework for the university of Adelaide* (Report to the Infrastructure Committee). Adelaide: University of Adelaide.

Fisher, K. (2013). *Transforming design thinking through the translational design of learning and knowledge environments.* HERSDA (Higher Education Research and Development Society of Australia) Conference Proceedings, Auckland, New Zealand.

Fisher, K., & Newton, C. (2014). Evaluating 21st C learning environments. *HERDSA Journal.*

Freeman, S., Eddy, S., Mcdonough, M., Smith, M., Okoroafor, N., Jordt, H., & Wenderoth, M. (2014). Active learning increases student performance in science, engineering, and mathematics. *PNAS, 111*(23), 8410–8415.

Gadermann, A., Guhn, M., & Zumbo, B. (2012). Estimating ordinal reliability for likert-type and ordinal item response data: A conceptual, empirical, and practical guide. *Practical Assessment, Research and Evaluation, 17*(3). Retrieved October 9, 2013, from http://pareonline.net/pdf/v17n3.pdf

Geertz, C. (1973). Thick description: Toward an interpretive theory of culture. In C. Geetz (Ed.), *The Interpretation of cultures: Selected essays* (pp. 3–30). New York, NY: Basic Books.

Hart, D., Diercks-O'brien, G., & Powell, A. (2009). Exploring stakeholder engagement in impact evaluation planning in educational development work. *Evaluation, 15*(3), 285–306.

HERD. (2015). *Health environments research and design journal.* Retrieved June 21, 2015, from http://her.sagepub.com

Hiebert, B. (2012). *Post-pre assessment: An innovative way for documenting client change. Guidance perspectives around the world.* Retrieved October 9, 2013, from http://iaevg.org/crc/resources.cfm? subcat=200,202&lang=en

Imms, W., Fisher, K., Newton, C., & Cleveland, B. (2015). Retrieved June 21, 2015, from http://www.learnetwork.edu.au & www.e21le.com

Jankowska, M., & Atlay, M. (2007). Use of creative space in enhancing students' engagement. *Innovations in Education and Teaching International, 45*(3), 271–279.

Johnson, L., Adams Becker, S., Estrada, V., & Freeman, A. (2015). *NMC horizon report: 2015 higher education edition.* Austin, TX: The New Media Consortium.

Masie, E. (2011). *Classroom of the future & classroom of 2011 survey.* Saratoga Springs, NY: The MASIE Center and The Learning Consortium.

Norman, D. (2010). *The research practice gap.* Retrieved June 21, 2015, from http://www.jnd.org/dn.mss/essays.html

Painter, S., Fournier, J., Grape, C., Grummon, P., Morelli, J., Whitmer, S., & Cevetelloet, J. (2013). *Research on learning space design: Present state, future directions.* Ann Arbor, MI: Society for College and University Planning.

Patterson, T. (2007). The rise and fall of innovative education: An Australian university case study. *Innovative Higher Education, 32*(2), 71–84.

Pearson, K. (1901). On lines and planes of closest fit to systems of points in space. *Philosophical Magazine, 2*, 559–572. Retrieved from http://pbil.univ-lyon1.fr/R/pearson1901.pdf

Prensky, M. (2006). Listen to the natives. *Educational Leadership, 63*, 5.

Prensky, M. (2012). *Bain gain: Technology and the quest for digital wisdom.* New York, NY: Palgrave Macmillan.

Radcliffe, D., Powell, D., & Tibbets, B. (2007). *Learning spaces in higher eudcation: positive outcomes by design.* Canberra: Australian Government Office of Learnng and Teaching.

Riddle, M., & Souter, J. (2012). Designing informal learning spaces using student perspectives. *Journal of Learning Spaces, 1*, 6.

Scott-Webber, L., Strickland, A., Kapitula, L. R. (2014). *How classroom design affects student engagement*. Grand Rapids, MI: Steelcase.

Silva, P., & Gouveia, L. (2013). *The impact of digital in learning spaces: An analysis on the perspective of teachers in higher education*. Proceedings of Informing Science & IT Education Conference (InSITE) 2013, Porto.

Smith, S. (2014). The study of undergraduate student and information technology. *Educause*.

von Ahelefeld, H. (Ed.). (2014). *Position paper on evaluating school learning spaces*. Paris: OECD.

Waldrip, P., Cox, P., & Jin Yu, J. (2014). Quantitative research on personalising learning and wellbeing in open-plan up-scaled learning communities. In V. Prain, P. Cox, C. Deed, D. Edwards, C. Farrelly, M. Keeffe, V. Lovejoy, L. Mow, P. Sellings, B. Waldrip, & Z. Yager (Eds.), *Chapter in adapting to teaching and learning in open-plan schools*. Rotterdam, The Netherlands: Sense Publishers.

Walker, J., Brooks, D., & Baepler, P. (2011). Pedagogy and space: Empirical research on new learning environments. *EDUCAUSE Quarterly, 34*, 24.

Zogby, J., & Zogby, J. (2014). *The 2014 survey of students*. Baltimore, MD: Laureate University.

JACQUELINE PIZZUTI-ASHBY

# 13. DESIGNING FOR THE FUTURE

*A Post-Occupancy Evaluation of the Peter Jones Learning Centre*

ABTSRACT

This exploratory study examines the Peter Jones Learning Centre's (PJLC) transition from a quiet, autonomous interior to a learning commons model that encourages collaboration and socialization.

Located at University of the Fraser Valley (UFV) in British Columbia, the PJLC has been revitalized to support new learning theories and provides a hub for students' involvement and engagement on campus. Research in the planning, function, and utilization of non-formal learning environments is limited, therefore the study's purpose is threefold: first, to gain insight as to administrators' perceptions and observations of student learning in non-formal learning space; second, to understand how administrators implement their understanding of learning into the planning, design, and operation of the PJLC; and third, to examine the transactional relationship between the learning environment and learner.

Using the post-occupancy evaluation, ten semi-structured interviews were conducted, including five administrators influential in the PJLC design and space programming, and five learners who had utilized the facility over the course of their studies. The space performance evaluations conducted assessed the PJLC's technical, functional, and behavioural features. This was followed by structured observational sweeps that included the documentation of 1,943 campus members' location, activities, gender, and sociological grouping preference. Administrators' describe student learning in non-formal learning space as technologically supported, socially driven, and multitask-oriented, and explained that they integrated their understanding of student learning in the PJLC's space programming, physical design, policies, services, and resources provided.

The space performance evaluations demonstrated how the PJLC's setting functioned and identified structural and environmental features that supported and hindered students' use. Learners interviewed described that the PJLC's physical design, operation, services, and resources provided were influential in their use of the facility. The observations conducted of campus members' utilization of the PJLC document a series of social and activity patterns within the building.

The study's findings suggest further research in areas such as gender, preference of learning space, integrated planning and research, environmental assessment, and inclusive learning environments that accommodate students with special needs.

© KONINKLIJKE BRILL NV, LEIDEN, 2019 | DOI: 10.1163/9789004391598_016

## BACKGROUND OF THE STUDY

The university campus is a distinct ecology in that its intensions are to provide a place for people to gather and learn. The environment is designed and comprised of both symbolic and functional features that convey to members the institution's culture and pedagogical values (Chapman, 2006; Kenney, Dumont, & Kenney, 2005; Oblinger, 2005; Riddle & Souter, 2012; Strange & Banning, 2001). The relationship between students and their physical setting informs and influences the development and design of members' learning experiences (Kenney et al., 2005; Lippman, 2010; Strange & Banning, 2001). Greater interest in this transactional relationship is emerging as campus administrators recognise the importance of the built environment in student engagement, learning outcomes, and first-year retention (Chapman, 2006; Kuh, Kinzie, Schuh, & Whitt, 2005; Reynolds, 2007; Walton & Galea, 2005).

Scholars agree that our understanding of student learning within the context of post-secondary education has changed primarily due to a shift in learning paradigms and advancements in technology (Brown & Long, 2006; Prince, 2004). Learning paradigms on the delivery of content are incorporating a more student-centred approach (Diaz, Brown, & Salmons, 2010; Johnson & Lomas, 2005).

In addition, research indicates that active learning, i.e., students participating and engaged in their learning process, experience greater gains in retaining content (Prince, 2004). Providing formal and non-formal spaces that support active learning exercises – such as collaborative, cooperative, and problem-based approaches – have become increasingly important as studies suggest that involvement in these activities positively influences student learning outcomes and success (Astin, 1999a; Jamieson, 2009; Kuh, Cruce, Shoup, Kinzie, & Gonyea, 2008).

Technological advancements have also influenced environmental design (Brown & Long, 2006; Cunningham & Tabur, 2012; Jamieson, 2009; Oblinger, 2006b). Current technology has mobilised instructional content and lectures, providing the opportunity for learning and collaboration from any desired geographical location (Oblinger, 2005). As a result, the campus environment, in its entirety, is being redefined as having the potential to accommodate for learning at any time or in any space, and as such being altered to support this digital age (Brown & Long, 2006; Oblinger, 2006a).

Learning environment researchers have focused primarily on formal learning space (e.g., the classroom and laboratory), due to the perceptions that this is where education happens and that the formal learning process is superior as compared to students' learning experience outside of the classroom (Smith, 2008). There are multiple advantages in investigating formal learning settings. These advantages include having greater research controls and data availability (e.g., access to grades, attendance, retention, persistence, and teaching evaluations) to assess the relationship between students and their environment (Blackmore, Bateman, O'Mara, & Loughlin, 2011).

Furthermore, the classroom's physical setting, designed and utilised for the delivery of content, supports instruction and designated learning activities. This allows the researcher to assess the instructor-student dynamic in addition to

DESIGNING FOR THE FUTURE

observing the instructor's behavioural expectations and student learning outcomes (Fraser, 2001; Moos, 1979; Veltri, Banning, & Davies, 2006; Villar & Alegre, 2007).

The dominance of formal learning space in the literature has resulted in a narrow perspective of the role that the surrounding campus environment has on students' learning experience. In the academy, learning has been traditionally evaluated in the classroom and defined as an acquisition of knowledge products.

Given the recent advancements in understanding how people learn and the mobility of learning content, researchers are now considering the influence that non-formal learning environments, including the library, the campus green, the cafeteria, and campus residences, have on student learning, involvement, and engagement (Hussain & Adeeb, 2009; Kuh & Gonyea, 2003; Kenney et al., 2005; Oblinger, 2005, 2006a). Research indicates non-formal learning environments play a vital role in contributing to what an individual "knows, believes, feels, or is capable of doing" (Falk & Dierking, 2000, p. 12). Given the unstructured nature of these places, researchers are challenged by how to define, measure, and assess learning in a self-directed context.

Astin's (1984) Theory of Involvement proposes that students experience greater gains in learning and personal development if they are both academically engaged and socially connected with members of the campus milieu (Astin, 1975, 1984). These activities include interaction with faculty and peers, participation in student groups, and academic involvement outside of the class (Astin, 1993). Astin (1999b) further explains that a student's degree of learning and development is dependent upon the quality and quantity of time and effort devoted to these academic and social activities (Astin, 1999b).

For the purposes of this study, learning is defined by the academic and social activities that students are engaged in. These activities are measured by observing students' behaviours exhibited within a non-formal learning space (Matthews, Andrews, & Adams, 2011).

Campus buildings provide the structure and atmosphere for students to engage in activities supportive of their learning experience (Kenney et al., 2005; Oblinger, 2005, 2006b). As campus space is built and renovated to support and nurture learning, the library, in concept and design, is experiencing the greatest transformation. For many campuses, the library serves as a centre for non-formal learning and "the physical manifestation of the core values and activities of academic life" (Kuh & Gonyea, 2003, p. 256). Historically, the layout has been planned to accommodate and organise information for the purposes of individual research and exploration (Larsen, 2010).

Recently, libraries have expanded into learning commons that are designed to offer greater functionality in terms of accommodating for collaboration, content creation, and technology use (Accardi, Cordova, & Leeder, 2010; McCarthy & Nitecki, 2010; Webster, 2010). Revitalising the library as a learning commons involves incorporating a variety of hubs designed to support group and individual use, student services, tech labs, retail shops, and faculty offices (Accardi et al., 2010; Cox, 2011). Learning commons have become a place for the campus to nurture the diversity of human contact and to build a learning community beyond the classroom (McCarthy & Nitecki, 2010, p. 2). The learning commons' hubs serve as optimal

261

sites to observe students actively engaged in the learning process, in that these facilities often comprise the largest space dedicated to supporting both formal and non-formal learning activities.

## PURPOSE OF THE STUDY

Lewin's (1936) research on the person-environment-behaviour dynamic provides a theoretical foundation to explore the influence that learning environments have on students and the administrators that govern them. Lewin's Field Theory (1936) suggests, "to understand or to predict behaviour, the person and his environment have to be considered as one constellation of interdependent factors" (p. 338). This study utilises Lewin's Field Theory to examine the relationship between the planning and design of space and its resulting function and utilisation.

Lippman (2010) asserts that the examination of learning environments is necessary in order to "understand how they function" and the behavioural patterns that they create (p. 4). The purpose of this study is to observe student use of non-formal space and to understand how the technical and functional aspects of the building's design support or discourage students' activities that contribute to their learning experience. Further, Temple (2007) states "literature throws almost no light on managerial decision-making about space issues affecting students or staff" (p. 8). Therefore, this investigation also explores the planning and design process of a non-formal learning environment in order to better understand how this multi-functional facility is informed and shaped to reinforce students' educational objectives.

## RESEARCH QUESTIONS

Learning environment research is an avenue to inform the planning process and design of future spaces that are supportive and conductive to learning (Bennett, 2009; Lippman, 2010; Moore & Wells, 2009; Nixon, 2009; Stark & Samson, 2010). The assessment of space and understanding its utilisation are key in meeting current and future educational objectives (Oblinger, 2005; Temple, 2007). Therefore, the study explores three main areas of inquiry: design, function, and user experience.

### Design

Modifying and adapting campus space is a complex process which requires those responsible in space planning to understand users' learning needs as well as the physical infrastructure necessary to support the intended activities. Research indicates that administrators' perceptions and observations of students' learning outside the classroom play an integral role in informing the design of these spaces (Barber & Armacost, 2006; Davis & Shorey, 2006; Lombardi & Wall, 2006; Neame & Lomas, 2006; Potter & King, 2006). This study's first question asks:

What are administrators' perceptions and observations of student learning in a non-formal learning context?

*Function*

Emphasised by Veitch and Arkklen (1995), "The efficiency with which humans' function is determined in large part by the limitations and proscriptions of the designed environment" (p. 316). Learning commons are unique, multi-functional environments planned to serve a variety of user groups and intentions. Furnished with cafés, computer labs, book reserves, research stations, study carrels, and group rooms, these buildings intersect spaces to foster academically and socially dynamic settings. The second and third questions of this study address the transition from conceptualising to contextualising student learning by inquiring:

How do administrators implement their understanding of student learning into the planning, design, and operation of the Peter Jones Learning Commons (PJLC)?

How does the PJLC perform as a learning environment?

*User Experience*

Campus members' experience in non-formal learning environments is vitally important in how the university is perceived in supporting students' learning objectives. In addition, information regarding students' usage of facilities helps to inform the current and future transitions of campus facilities. To understand the features of the PJLC that influence students' learning activities and to gain insight into their use, the final questions are:

What are learners' perceptions, observations, and experience using the PJLC?

What are the patterns of student space usage in the PJLC?

## METHODS OF ASSESSMENT

The literature describing the assessment of learning space design, its physical implementation, and subsequent usage, is limited (Hunley & Schaller, 2006). Developing a standardised and accepted method is difficult due to the challenges in identifying measurable variables coupled with the transient nature of the space and its occupants. Furthermore, institutions tend to rely on staff observations to determine and define the success of the space (Barber & Armacost, 2006; Davis & Shorey, 2006; Lombardi & Wall, 2006; Neame & Lomas, 2006; Potter & King, 2006).

For formal learning spaces, variables identified often include learning outcomes, as demonstrated by grades, and students' attendance and retention (Herzog, 2007). Student activities and person-environment interactions are variables frequently measured in non-formal learning space (Hunley & Schaller, 2006; Palomba &

Banta, 1999). Although no formal evaluative process has been established within the discipline of education, qualitative, quantitative, mixed, and multiple methodologies have been exercised in assessing learning space.

The review of the literature also identifies that the planning, implementation, and assessment of learning spaces has not been thoroughly investigated and therefore not well understood. Watt (2007) indicates that, "In both the management literature and the physical plant literature, little attention has been paid to how research facilities are used" (p. 6). She further emphasises that no empirically tested metric is available for administration to determine the extent in which campus members utilise the space allocated to them.

Blackmore et al. (2011) identify that there are several physical features of the built environment that factor into students' achievement, performance, and learning outcomes. However, the authors cite that the studies conducted on the design, implementation, and evaluation of learning environments are limited and contain significant gaps such as failing to acknowledge the contextual uniqueness of the school's setting (Blackmore et al., 2011, p. 8). Blackmore et al. point out that the design phase of learning space is primarily informed by the philosophical posturing of the group as opposed to empirical evidence. The authors also indicate that designers frequently fail to elicit users' input as to their perceptions and use of the space.

As post-secondary institutions invest in the design and construction of educational facilities, consideration should be given to including students in the planning phase while evaluating how the setting will accommodate their present and future learning needs (Oblinger, 2006a). The literature highlights that digital technology will continue to be a driving force in students' acquisition of information and the design of learning space. Research suggests that building in an assessment process for these unique non-formal settings is essential in understanding how the environment is functioning and meeting students' and administrators' learning objectives.

*Research Design*

This exploratory study is a qualitative inquiry into both the design of non-formal learning space and the relationship between students and their learning environment at the PJLC. The methodology selected for this study is the post-occupancy evaluation (POE). This study's POE incorporates semi-structured interviews, casual and structured observations, place-centred activity mapping, photography, and institutional archives to describe the planning, design, function, and utilisation of the built environment following its renovations.

The POE is a systematic process of assessment that examines a building's performance as defined by several factors, including meeting occupant expectations and satisfaction (Cole, Robinson, Brown, & O'Shea, 2008; Preiser, 1995; Zeisel, 2006; Zimring, Rashid, & Kampschroer, 2010). The feedback obtained is used in the design, planning, and development of facilities to provide insight as to how inhabitants of the built environment perceive and behave within it (Preiser,

DESIGNING FOR THE FUTURE

1995; Zeisel, 2006). The literature also refers to the POE as a facility performance evaluation (FPE) or building performance evaluation (BPE) (Federal Facilities Coucil, 2001; Preiser, 1995; Zimring, Rashid, & Kampschroer, 2010).

The POE was developed by the building sciences in the early 1960s as a way of determining occupants' needs and satisfaction in subsidised housing (Federal Facilities Coucil, 2001). The use of POE then expanded to include additional facilities such as hospitals and prisons. By the 1980s, the POE was being applied to commercial buildings and offices. Now, and increasingly, the POE is being applied to the university campus as a way to better understand the relationship between students and facilities designed for learning (Ornstein, 2005).

The POE integrates multiple methods including surveys, observations, and interviews to assess the functioning of a building and inform stakeholders of the changes necessary to improve its intended use (Preiser, 1995; Zeisel, 2006). The POE process is thus utilised to contribute ideas on future design and development as it concerns academic space and its intended occupants (Zeisel, 2006). Over the past forty years, this methodology has gained increased attention and further use in the campus environment as a method to better understand the use of campus space, and to provide valuable feedback to help inform the development of future learning environments (Li, Locke, Nair, & Bunting, 2005; Lippman, 2010; Spooner, 2008).

*Setting and Study Site*

The facility selected for this single case study is the Peter Jones Learning Commons (PJLC) located at the University of the Fraser Valley (UFV) campus. The University of the Fraser Valley's Abbotsford campus is located on a 64-acre parcel located in Abbotsford, British Columbia, Canada. Depicted in Figure 13.1, the PJLC was selected because of my prior research conducted on UFV's campus environment as well as my existing knowledge of the historical evolution of the PJLC.

Founded as Fraser Valley College (FVC) in 1974, this two-year vocational school provided public access to post-secondary vocational training in British Columbia's Fraser Valley (Woodroff, 1983). As a commuter college, it served adult learners through its Chilliwack campus, in addition to holding classes in churches, restaurants, offices and basements throughout the region (Woodroff, 1983). To accommodate the college's growth and further provide residents with access to post-secondary education, FVC built a second campus located in the city of Abbotsford and continued its physical expansion from 1987 to 1997. FVC's Abbotsford campus constructed five new buildings during this time period, including the one under investigation, the Peter Jones Learning Centre. In 1991, the government granted FVC university-college status and renamed the school University College of the Fraser Valley (UCFV).

The formal designation of "university-college" and the addition of baccalaureate programming altered not only the organisational mission and behavioural norms but also introduced the staff, faculty, administration, and students to a new paradigm

265

*Figure 13.1. Peter Jones Learning Commons. Exterior view of west entrance*

(Gaber, 2003; Henkel, 2002; Henkel, 2005; Jones, 1994; Levin, 2003). The direction of the institution changed from a community focus to that of teaching and research excellence. Internally, the administrators' attitudes, behaviours, and values adopted this new mission (Stensaker, 2005; Stensaker & Norgard, 2001). Organisationally, UCFV transitioned its structure, policies, and purpose in order to accommodate its additional mandate and younger student demographic. Campus members interpreted the university-college designation as a transitional step towards one day receiving full university status (Jones, 1994; Levin, 2003; Levin, 2004).

From 2007 to 2009, the campus underwent another series of major renovations to lobby for full university status. Revitalisations to the PJLC were undertaken as well as the construction of new facilities such as Baker House student residence and the Envision Athletic Centre. The PJLC's refurbishment included its name change to the Peter Jones Learning Commons. In 2008, UCFV attained full university status as the University of the Fraser Valley serving local high school students and community members residing the region.

The PJLC is the largest facility dedicated to non-formal learning space at UFV. Conceived and built in 1995, the intention of the PJLC was to physically, culturally, and academically facilitate the institution's paradigm shift from a two-year vocational college to a four-year university-college (P. Jones, personal communication, January 28, 2011). Although UFV had an existing library, there were concerns that the space could not physically accommodate the learning resources needed to serve baccalaureate students. This transition required the addition of infrastructure and space

DESIGNING FOR THE FUTURE

to support educational and technological resources and to encourage self-directed and autonomous learning activities (P. Jones, personal communication, January 28, 2011).

James K. M. Cheng Architects Inc. designed the PJLC in 1994 (J. Smith, personal communication, January 18, 2011). James Cheng is a prominent Canadian architect who established himself in the early 1990s as a leader in condominium design and is credited with the architectural style known as Vancouverism (Cheng, 2011). Influenced by his mentor Arthur Erickson, architect of Simon Fraser University and the University of Lethbridge, James K. M. Cheng is also known for his use of concrete and glass façades in his buildings' design (Cheng, 2011).

The PJLC is a concrete and brick constructed building consisting of two stories, with a convex outer wall, glass atrium, and a series of windowed walls allowing for natural light and access to surrounding views of Mount Baker. The colour scheme used at the time of construction consisted of white, greys, taupe, rose and rosewood. The building measured 5,745 square metres in size and the cost of construction amounted to $10.6 million dollars (J. Smith, personal communication, January 18, 2011).

Promoted as a 'one-stop shop' for students to access learning resources, the PJLC opened in October 1995 housing the college's main Library (see Figure 13.2), in addition to a series of student services including the Writing Centre, Math Centre, First Heritage Computer Access Centre, Staff Development Lab, two seminar rooms that also served as classrooms, and a satellite/teleconferencing room (J. Smith, personal communication, January 18, 2011). Over the course of its history, the PJLC has experienced a series of minor remodels to accommodate the changing needs of

*Figure 13.2. Library first floor (G170). Entrance of library*

267

the institution. However, in 2007 administration and faculty collectively discussed avenues and ideas to better support teaching and learning within the PJLC thus encouraging the most significant renovation from 2007 to 2009 (Landolfi, 2007).

In 2008, a series of renovations to the PJLC were undertaken and included the addition of a café, alterations to the library's first floor to encourage group work, and reconfiguration of the Writing Centre layout and inclusion of an anteroom. The Rotunda's study bar was further furnished with flexible seating and couches have been added to create a lounge area. Furthermore, the PJLC's programming was modified to include two new services including the Assessment Centre and Teaching & Learning Centre. Additional services housed in the PJLC include the Library, Math Centre, Writing Centre, Instructional Media Services, and Envision Computer Lab.

*Subjects*

UFV's Institutional Accountability Report Plan (2011) indicates that from 2010 to 2011, UFV consisted of 15,783 students with 83.7% registered as undergraduates. Of those students enrolled, 60% were female and 40% were male. Students' average age was 24.1 years. Fifty-one percent (51%) of students attended UFV full-time and 43% of all students were enrolled in a bachelor's degree program. Two-thirds of UFV students reside locally in Abbotsford or its surrounding communities. In 2011, the institution employed a total of 710 faculty, 30 non-teaching faculty, and 689 staff including management.

*Sampling Strategy, Sample Size, and Subject Recruitment Procedure*

All interviewed participants in the study were recruited by purposive sampling and selected based on their expertise in the planning, design, and usage of the PJLC. Tongco (2007) describes that, "Purposive sampling, when used appropriately, is more efficient than random sampling in practical field circumstances because the random member of a community may not be as knowledgeable and observant as an expert informant" (p. 154).

Furthermore, the POE method relies on expert opinion when attempting to understand the managerial design decisions and users' experience post-renovation (Carthey, 2006). To ensure greater dependability in the information gathered, a total of 5 administrative and 5 student experts were chosen to interview. Five administrators were purposively selected based on their expertise and experience in the planning and design of the PJLC. Their selection was based on these criteria: (a) a current or former employee of UFV, (b) influential and knowledgeable in the design process of the PJLC, and (c) willing to share information regarding their perceptions of student learning and the design process of the PJLC.

Five students were also purposively selected to interview based on their expertise in using the PJLC pre- and post-renovation. The selection of these students was based on the following requisites: (a) experience using the PJLC as a non-formal learning environment, (b) exposure to the PJLC pre- and post-renovations, (c) willingness to share information regarding their learning preferences and use of the PJLC. The student participants were also employees of the institution, and four of the five worked directly in the PJLC.

As students and staff, these participants offered both a depth and breadth of understanding as to how the PJLC functioned pre- and post-renovations. No new UFV students were recruited for the interview portion of this study as they lacked this vital knowledge of the PJLC's refurbishment in 2008. However, the observations evaluating students' use of the PJLC accounted for all new and existing members that utilised the facility.

*Variables and Measures*

In the context of a qualitative paradigm, data dependability and transferability are key measures in determining the internal reliability and external validity of the study (Joppe, 2000; Lincoln & Guba, 1985; Shenton, 2004). Lincoln and Guba (1985) describe the dependability of qualitative data as based on two factors: the consistency of the product and the process that the data is obtained through. To determine the dependability of qualitative data, the researcher should account for and describe the environmental changes that occur during the execution of the study, and explain how these changes influenced the research approach (Lincoln & Guba, 1985).

The transferability of data pertains to "demonstrating that the results of the work at hand can be applied to wider population" (Shenton, 2004, p. 69). The data collected for this study is intended to highlight and identify the specific environmental features and participant behaviour unique to the physical milieu of the PJLC; therefore, the transferability of this data to other learning commons is limited in most respects. Dependability of the data gathered in this study was verified through the following measures:

- Environmental evaluation and direct observations conducted in the PJLC's naturalistic setting, as opposed to through a secondary source such as video surveillance;
- Participant interviews provide a first-hand account on the perceptions and use of the PJLC's learning environment;
- Multiple methods and triangulation were used in verifying the data collected;
- Photographs illustrate the environmental and in-situ observations conducted; and
- Several interview participants responded similarly to questions regarding their observations of campus members' behaviour and use of the PJLC, in addition to identifying similar features pertaining to the PJLC's design weaknesses and strengths.

*Data Collection: Instruments and Protocols*

The study uses multiple data collection methods to gain a comprehensive perspective on the planning, design, and use of the PJLC. Ten (10) semi-structured

J. PIZZUTI-ASHBY

interviews with administrators and students were conducted. Eighty-five hours of direct observations including casual and structured were performed. The structured observations consisted of creating 50 place-centred maps documenting users' activities, location, day and time, grouping preference, and gender during each hour of operation (7:00 a.m.–11:30 p.m.) and each day of operation (Monday through Sunday).

The casual observations included 35 space performance evaluations assessing the PJLC's technical, functional, and behavioural features during all operational hours and days. The performance evaluations were complemented with 178 still images selected to analyse the space. In addition, institutional archives were used to provide greater context to the planning and design of the PJLC. To understand both the complexity of students' behaviour in non-formal learning space and administration's design decisions, the use of multiple methods provided for the triangulation of data that helped to establish the dependability and transferability of the information gathered.

## Data Preparation and Analysis

Following data collection, a qualitative analysis was conducted. The methods for analysis consist of:

- Transcribing, coding, conceptualising, and categorising the content derived from the semi-structured interviews with administration and students;
- Entering structured observations into an Excel database and graphing the results for further interpretation;
- Synthesising the place-centred activity maps of each zone to illustrate patterns in usage, space, and behaviour;
- Aggregating the observation evaluations conducted on each space and summarising the results to create a building performance summary for each zone; and
- Analysing the photographic documentation of the PJLC and categorising the content in an Excel spreadsheet to supplement the observation evaluations conducted.

## RESULTS AND FINDINGS

### Paradigm Shift: Autonomous Learning to Student Engagement

This study reveals that several unanticipated challenges were experienced while altering the PJLC's original built intentions and reprogramming the space to adopt a new set of objectives. The transition of a building that supports autonomous learning activities to one that encourages socialization and collaboration was, at certain junctures, difficult to realize. Issues pertaining to a library's transformation as an information repository to a socially dynamic space are not uncommon (Hussong-Christian, Rempel, & Deitering, 2010; Lippincott, 2008).

270

Bennett (2009) describes that the influence of information technology has been instrumental in the library's paradigm shift from a place where information is sought to an environment that is learner-centred. He explains that library space has had to academically and physically accommodate for this new digital age and forge new relationships with information technologists. For many libraries, areas once dedicated to books and reserves have now been replaced with computers, group study rooms, and cafés (Bennett, 2009, p. 9).

Libraries, as Bennett (2009) continues, are at a pivotal point in their transition and now need to be focused on encouraging intentional learning. However, he highlights that the culture of learning within library space is not well known or understood by those responsible for the planning and design of library spaces. Bennett (2009) describes:

> If we want to make learning happen in libraries, then understanding learning processes and applying that understanding systematically to our planning and design work is the key to further advance. To do this, we must think more like educators and less like service providers. We must build an understanding of how people learn, consider the pivotal role of intentional learning in that process, and – most critically – choose to enact the learning mission of our institutions rather than simply support it. (p. 11)

Understanding the institution's culture of student learning is critical in providing an environment that supports and encourages behaviours that result in the acquisition of knowledge, however just as vital is our comprehension as to how these educational structures evolve and respond to physical changes. In his book, *How Buildings Learn*, Brand (1995) stresses that the adaptability of a building is critical in its sustainability and ability to continue to serve the changing needs of its occupants. Universities undergoing a revitalization process to encourage new learning behaviours need to consider assessing the space pre-design and determine how the environment is being used, the activities it supports, and the stakeholders that may be impacted by its changes (Hussong-Christian et al., 2010; Shen, Shen, & Xiaoling, 2012).

Furthermore, establishing a series of measurable learning objectives for the proposed setting helps to guide the space programming, planning, and design of the facility (Bennett, 2009; Warger & Dobbin, 2009). These objectives would also support the post-analysis of the space in order to determine if the environment is achieving its learning intentions (Warger & Dobbin, 2009). Developing a design cycle of evaluation provides campus administration with information regarding their unique student demographic and the structures that best support students' learning activities.

*A Multi-Faceted Approach*

The interview and observational data gathered in this study indicate that the design of non-formal learning space requires a multi-faceted approach to appeal to its users. Interviews with UFV Administrators and students intersect on issues such as the importance of implementing flexible spaces for users to adapt to their learning needs and preferences; in addition to suggesting that the space should provide comfort. Supplying students with the most current forms of technology in their learning space was also stressed.

Students and administrators converged on the need for implementing spaces that support greater collaboration and student engagement. The literature and research conducted in the development and design of non-formal learning environments also promote these ideas of flexibility; comfort and aesthetics; technological resources and support; and collaboration as trends in the design of learning spaces (Hunley & Schaller, 2006; Jamieson, 2009; Reynolds, 2007; Temple, 2007). The importance of environmental factors in learning is emphasized in Zandvliet and Straker's (2001) assessment of physical and psychosocial features of IT classrooms. As the authors explain:

> The provision of adequate working environments for students is more than a comfort or safety issue but rather also a learning issue in that an inadequate physical learning environment might affect psychosocial disharmony perhaps disrupting or distracting the intended learning goals. (Zandvliet & Straker, 2001, p. 9)

*Flexibility*

During administrator-interviews, the word *flexibility* was used repeatedly. Monahan (2002) subdivides the *flexibility* of educational space as *versatility, scaleability, fluidity, convertibility*, and *modifiability*. Learning environment research defines the *versatility* of a space as one that can easily transform to changing pedagogical and learning needs (Chism, 2006; Jamieson, 2009; Temple, 2007). Administrator-interviews also used flexibility in reference to the PJLC's *scaleability* in that the recent renovation required the expansion and contraction of certain student services and study space (Monahan, 2002).

Administrator-interviews also applied the term *flexibility* when discussing the fluidity of these newly created spaces in the PJLC issues with the flow of individuals and sound into other surrounding spaces. The convertibility of the PJLC was also highlighted by administrators as the facility was originally built to provide campus planning with the future option of building a third floor. Student-interviews describe flexibility as the agility of their space, permitting them to reconfigure their surroundings to engage with each other and to accommodate their learning preferences (Chism, 2006; Jamieson, 2009; Monahan, 2002; Temple, 2007).

*Comfort*

Comfort was paramount for students and UFV administrators interviewed. During this study, participants indicated that comfort embodied the physiological aspects of the space, such as thermal, visual, and acoustic features; however, they also described comfort in relation to the behavioural, contextual, psychological, and social atmosphere of the setting (Cole et al., 2008). Learning environment research

DESIGNING FOR THE FUTURE

primarily defines comfort as physiological and identifies issues such temperature, illumination, and level of distractions as influential in students' comfort and their use of learning space (Chism, 2006; Jamieson, 2009; Temple, 2007). Chism (2006) notes that the discomfort experienced by a student "makes a compelling distraction to learning". UFV administrators and students also described comfort in the context of the PJLC's furnishings.

Chism (2006) describes that providing students with furniture, particularly chairs, that are comfortable and adjustable to varying body types is important in encouraging student use of the environment (Chism, 2006). As was indicated during the interviews with administrators, providing non-formal learning spaces reflective of a student's home environment with couches, natural light, and neutral wall colours were intended to encourage use and comfort. Administrators ease of food and beverage consumption in learning spaces was another strategy to accommodate students' needs and support longer use of the setting.

*Technological Resources and Support*

Cox and Jantti's (2012) recent study found that students who spent up to one hour a year accessing the library's electronic resources had higher marks as opposed to those students who never used the library's system. It is through these types of studies that we are learning about the impact students' use of technology is having on students' learning outcomes and success.

As found in this study, UFV students stated that their ability to complete assignments, conduct research, gather learning resources, and communicate with faculty was heavily influenced by their access to technology. Furthermore, the structured observations indicated that students heavily utilized the PJLC's zones dedicated to computer use and designated for assignments and research.

The use of technology and the ability to access learning resources online has increased the demands on the physical space to provide and support the latest technology (Chism, 2006; Jamieson, 2009; Oblinger, 2006a; Temple, 2007). Rooms outfitted with technology, often referred to as "smart rooms", are in demand by students, as they provide instantaneous access to information, learning materials, and virtual connections with others (Cunningham & Tabur, 2012).

The successful delivery of technology to learning environments relies on resources and support, such as access to experts knowledgeable in setup and implementation and equipment, such as electrical outlets, projector screens, and monitors. Furnishings in these spaces also require mobility and flexibility in order to adapt and physically position learners to utilize these resources.

As witnessed during the observations of this study, electrical outlets behaved like black holes attracting students and furniture to them. This resulted in furniture disrupting members' circulation and access of the space. Chism (2006) recommends "Rather than cumbersome rack systems and fixed ceiling-mounted projectors, learning spaces of the future will need more flexible plug-and-play capabilities" (p. 2.7).

273

J. PIZZUTI-ASHBY

*Collaborative and Individual Study Space*

To encourage greater collaboration in the PJLC and support the pedagogical swing towards group work, UFV administrators modified the PJLC Library's first floor from quiet, individual study to group study. Administrator-interviews explained that they observed students' inclination to want to work around one another even in silent spaces. As a result, study carrels were replaced with group tables outfitted with electrical outlets and mobile seating. Soft lounge seating and couches were also provided.

Space and furnishings can enhance collaboration and communication and are important components in encouraging the flow and exchange of dialogue (Chism, 2006; Jamieson, 2009; Oblinger, 2006a; Temple, 2007). Furthermore, the style of furnishings and their layout also influence students' ability to work with one another and to connect visually with others in the space (Herman Miller, 2005, 2007).

*Table 13.1. Campus members' location and sociological grouping preference*

| Location | Individual | Pair | Group |
|---|---|---|---|
| Group Study Rooms | 5% | 22% | 73% |
| Library 1st floor | 54% | 22% | 24% |
| Library 2nd floor | 90% | 8% | 2% |
| Rotunda/Writing Centre Anteroom | 39% | 30% | 31% |
| Clickz Café | 31% | 28% | 41% |

Cunningham and Tabur (2012) also support this finding of students' inclination to want to study around others but cite that administration is overemphasizing this trend to convert individual learning space to group study space. The authors explain that, "Students consistently design ideal spaces with quiet areas and indicate noise dampening features".

The desire for quiet, contemplative study is as strong as ever and a common student complaint often involved "the lack of quiet space within the library" (Cunningham & Tabur, 2012, p. 2). The need to maintain and preserve silent study space was also evident in the interviews conducted with UFV students. Students emphasized the importance of having access to an environment void of audible distractions. In addition, administrators stated that they had noticed an increase in usage of the Library's 2nd floor space that is dedicated to silent study. Furthermore, the structured observations documented the Library's 2nd floor as the space most utilized by students for studying purposes.

*Student Usage, Environmental Factors, and Gender Preference*

Administrators' perceptions of student learning in non-formal learning space as social, technologically supported, and multitask-oriented are not uncommon (Cunningham

DESIGNING FOR THE FUTURE

& Tabur, 2012). Cunningham and Tabur's (2012) review of the literature on the design of library space, found that this current generation of students are noted for their "ability to multitask" (p. 2). UFV students' perceptions of the pedagogical shift from individual to collaborative work was also supported by the authors who describe students' increasing need to locate spaces to support group assignments (Cunningham & Tabur, 2012).

In his study evaluating student activities in library space, Suarez (2007) also found "socializing behaviours" as "very prevalent" and commented that students were often engaged in utilizing technology and involved in multiple activities including studying, socializing, and consuming food and beverages while utilizing the space.

*Table 13.2. Campus members' location and observed activity*

| Location | Studying | Socializing | Researching | Reading | Eating |
|---|---|---|---|---|---|
| Group Study Rooms | 28% | 71% | 0% | 0% | 1% |
| Library 1st floor | 39% | 28% | 26% | 5% | 0% |
| Library 2nd floor | 89% | 9% | 1% | 0% | 0% |
| Rotunda/Writing Centre Anteroom | 43% | 44% | 0% | 2% | 2% |
| Clickz Café | 45% | 50% | 0% | 0% | 3% |

Environmental factors that appeared to influence usage of the PJLC, such as lighting, noise, and temperature, are supported in the research (Cunningham & Tabur, 2012). The authors indicate that, "Student preference is for abundant natural light with a decided aversion to fluorescent lighting" (Cunningham & Tabur, 2012, p. 4). Similarly, Suarez (2007) also found that lighting, noise, and temperature impacted students' use of non-formal learning space. In his study on library space, Suarez (2007) notes that the brighter lit spaces appeared to have more alert students utilizing them as opposed to the dimly lit spaces that were observed with students napping.

Suarez (2007) also describes that ambient noise was tolerated in library space though loud and disruptive noise was not. Students were observed departing the space when noise began distracting them from their tasks. Temperature was another factor that Suarez (2007) identifies as influencing students' comfort in the usage of library space. Students characterized spaces that were perceived as too warm or fluctuated in temperature as uncomfortable (Suarez, 2007).

During the observational period of this study it was noted that the PJLC was a well-utilized facility that equally attracted and retained both genders. This was an interesting finding, given that at the time of this study UFV's current student population consisted of 60% female and 40% male. The overrepresentation of males in library usage was also noted in Applegate's (2009) study evaluating student usage of library space at Indiana University Purdue University Indianapolis. She also

J. PIZZUTI-ASHBY

found that "men were distinctly overrepresented as library users, relative to their presence on campus" as they comprised "42% of the students on campus but 53% of University Library users" (Applegate, 2009, p. 343).

Male campus members were documented utilizing the PJLC spaces that were primarily designed for quiet, individual use. These areas also were noted for their fixed furnishings, access to natural light, and elevation on the second floor of the PJLC. Although Applegate (2009) cites that there was no notable gender pattern of usage in her study on library space, she did identify that males outnumbered females in their utilization of the "soft chair" area that was described as secluded and individually oriented (p. 343).

Understanding gender preferences and their selection and use of non-formal learning spaces is not widely discussed or investigated in learning environment research even though differences in gender perceptions of facilities have been identified in the literature. Bennett and Benton's (2001) study assessed the perceptions of students regarding campus architecture. Participants (n=301) were questioned on a series of pictures depicting a variety of campus buildings located throughout the United States. The authors found that students assigned individual success with modern architecture versus traditional architecture and that, overall, males' perceptions of individual success were not as influenced by the architectural styles as opposed to female participants (Bennett & Benton, 2001).

Furthermore, Reynolds (2007) surveyed 46 US and Canadian private and public post-secondary institutions on the influence campus facilities had on student recruitment and retention. With 16,153 student responses, results of his survey revealed significant differences between genders and how influential the condition and state of facilities were in students' decision to attend the institution. Women were identified as rejecting an institution more frequently than men due to poor maintenance or inadequate facilities and open spaces. Men indicated a higher rejection towards institutions that did not have adequate support for technology, computer lab facilities, and research labs. It was also noted that the top three facilities specified as the most influential in students' decision to attend an institution were facilities in their major, the library, and technology.

During the planning and development of educational structures, administration should consider the impact that environmental characteristics and building design have in students' perceptions, preferences, and selection of learning space. Designing facilities that encourage and engage both genders is vital given the current challenges Canadian and U.S. universities face regarding the decline of enrolment, retention, persistence, and completion of male college students (Sax, 2008; Statistics Canada, 2009).

*Inclusive Learning Environments*

During this study, I observed physical challenges and barriers that appeared to hinder disabled campus members' utilization of the PJLC's non-formal learning space.

Learning environment research and literature interprets, defines, and illustrates the accessibility and flexibility of educational space primarily through the lens of an able-bodied user. It was observed that the PJLC's furnishings and layout were problematic for physically disabled students even though administrators perceived their design as flexible for users. For example, tables and chairs on wheels may be perceived as flexible and modifiable to the able-bodied user but fixed from the perspective of someone who has limited use of their arms or body's leverage. Fixed furniture environments may actually provide greater safety and comfort for disabled students as the furniture is not mobile and their circulation and movement about the space is not subject to change while they are using it.

Technologically, access to electrical outlets appeared limited for those wheelchair-disabled campus members. Outlets located in the Group Study Rooms, Writing Centre Anteroom, and the café were near ground level. The majority of the Rotunda's outlets were located on the study bar. However, the Library's first floor and second floor did provide study carrels and group tables that were equipped with outlets for those seated there.

The lack of physically supportive spaces for disabled students is also identified in the literature (Oblinger, 2006a; Strange & Banning, 2001). One of the assumptions made when designing space for learners includes that they are able-bodied students. Oblinger (2006a) notes that these assumptions regarding who is utilizing the space need to change in order to provide learning environments that are supportive and inclusive for all students wanting to engage in learning activities.

Fichten, Asuncion, Barile, Robillard, Fossey, AND Lamb (2003) cite that in Canada, "11% of Canadians with disabilities graduated from university. The comparable figure for nondisabled Canadians is 20%, almost double the rate for Canadians with disabilities" (p. 74). Oblinger (2005) identifies in "The National Learning Infrastructure Initiative" "that approximately 10% of college and university students have some form of disability". In response, she suggests implementing policies that emphasize physical accessibility for disabled students and emphasizes their importance in the design of learning spaces.

## DISCUSSION: LIMITATIONS & FUTURE RESEARCH

*Limitations*

Limitations are those conditions of the study that the researcher has no influence over. The limitations of the study are as follows:

- As the study only assesses one building located at a single university in Canada, limited assumptions or extrapolations should be made toward the assessment of similar facilities; furthermore, the uniqueness of this specific context makes it difficult to replicate in another environment (Creswell, 2003).
- A total of ten interviews were conducted. Five current and former University of the Fraser Valley administrators were purposively selected based on their

expertise in the design and planning of the PJLC. Five current students, who concurrently served as University of the Fraser Valley staff, were also interviewed based on their expertise in using the PJLC before and after renovations to the facility. Due to the small and unique interview sample, results of the interviews should not be generalized.

- The interview questions were developed based on a review of the literature and expert opinions. Focus groups with administrators or students were not conducted.
- As a former employee of University of the Fraser Valley, my relationship with the interview participants may have influenced their responses or I may have exhibited my own bias.
- Due to time constraints, I may not have observed all students using the PJLC during the course of my observations. This inability to account for all activities conducted in the space may have skewed my results.
- As the sole researcher conducting the structured observations, there was no external validating source employed to confirm the behaviours that I coded. This may have resulted in inaccuracies or discrepancies in the observational data that I collected.

*Future Research*

Those interested in pursuing research in learning environments should consider investigating gender preferences of learning space; integrated planning and research; environmental assessments as part of the design process; and the development of inclusive learning environments. The findings presented in this study indicate that there may be gender preferences as to the design and usage of the various learning spaces studied.

In addition, several universities are transitioning towards an integrated planning approach and are requiring new ways to manipulate and intersect their facilities and student data. Although the post-occupancy evaluation has been in existence for at least fifty years, it has not been widely implemented as part of the assessment in the design process. Furthermore, the design and implementation of inclusive learning spaces and the environmental needs of impaired users is not well understood. This segment describes these areas of interest in greater detail.

*Gender Preferences*

The data gathered and literature reviewed during this study suggests that gender may influence the preference for certain environmental and design characteristics of learning spaces. As institutions and their academic departments create programs designed for particular demographics, they may want to consider designing a context that takes into consideration the particular environmental needs of the demographic and discipline that they are serving.

It was observed during this study that gender may also influence the type of learning space desired. Results indicated that males utilized learning space primarily designed for individual use. These areas also were noted for their fixed furnishings, access to windows and natural light, and elevation and views of the surrounding campus milieu. Females were observed utilizing areas of the PJLC that were supportive of social and collaborative learning activities.

These spaces were also described as providing a flexible furniture arrangement, accommodating for both individual and group study. Investigating the factors that influence male and female students in their selection and usage of learning environments is an area worthy of further inquiry. Designing facilities that encourage and engage both genders is vital given the current challenges Canadian and U.S. universities face regarding the decline of enrolment, retention, persistence, and completion of male college students (Sax, 2008; Statistics Canada, 2009).

*Integrated Planning and Research*

Advancements in technology have allowed researchers and practitioners in the disciplines of education, campus planning, and environmental design access to powerful tools and instruments that are able to gather, track, analyse, and visualize the mass of data being collected and housed within university departments such as Institutional Research, Campus Planning, and Facilities Management. However, for many institutions, the databases that house facilities and student-related data are not integrated (Watt, 2007). Developing a database that provides a rich description of room characteristics correlated with student attendance, grades, and course completion may lead to a greater understanding between the physical features of a space and academic achievement.

In addition, overlapping this information with budgetary data on campus facilities may also provide further insight regarding the relationship between where resources are being invested in the campus's infrastructure and users' behavioural outcomes associated with facility's renewal projects. Furthermore, this information may also help to identify the physical areas on campus that are under-resourced, neglected, and inadequately used as well as inform facility projects in development. I would also suggest that university administrations and campus planning departments consider developing an audit trail of their campus's physical changes.

An audit trail includes the data, rationale, objectives, meeting minutes, negotiations, and plans regarding space change. Creating an audit trail benefits those interested in assessing the performance of the setting and its intended goals. In addition, the process of modifying a space often includes a series of negotiations and transactions between those wanting to repurpose the environment and those invested in the setting's current state. The audit trail can serve as reference to the bargaining that occurred during the physical shift and the agreements made between each party. This record also assists administration in its consistent communication and response to the campus community regarding concerns over space modifications.

*Building in Assessment*

The literature review and research conducted in this study indicates that campus administrations use a variety of informal and formal instruments to assess campus facilities and their perceived success in meeting the user's needs and university objectives. However, administrators interviewed during this study revealed that the renovations conducted on the PJLC were done without an evaluative component built into the process.

As described by this study's literature review, evaluation of a facility's performance post-renovation is not commonly addressed. Further research as to why pre- and post-occupancy evaluation has not become a standard in campus renewal and development projects should be investigated and better understood. Conducting interviews with campus planners at a variety of universities may offer insight as to how to approach, budget for, and integrate tools such as the post-occupancy evaluation, as well as a more discrete space performance evaluation, into campus planning process.

Also, implementing an impact assessment to screen and scope the environmental, social, financial, and policy impact of a proposed project may help to clarify potential issues with a facility's design. This is particularly important in light of the efforts made to reduce buildings' costs and bolster campus sustainability and energy efficiency.

*Inclusive Learning Environments*

Building inclusive learning environments that support both able and disabled users is an important but often overlooked feature confronting the design of non-formal learning spaces. Including campus members with disabilities as part of the space planning dialogue is essential in understanding the perspective and physical vantage point that these learners experience the environment.

However, limited research has been conducted in this area to better understand the perceptions, behaviours, and unique physical needs of students utilizing the campus (Haller, 2006). Therefore, it is recommended that inclusive learning environments be further explored in order to spearhead the dialogue on how to best support the diversity of students attending and learning on campuses.

In addition, this may also help to inform and educate campus planning as to how they interpret and define the flexibility and versatility of a space. Furthermore, space performance evaluations should incorporate guidelines in assessing disabled members' access to environmental control features, safety elements such as emergency phones and access to exits, layout of furniture, and circulation of the space.

## CONCLUSION

The aim of this study is to understand the cycle of design beginning with administrators' observations of student learning in a non-formal learning context

DESIGNING FOR THE FUTURE

and then to determine how those perceptions have translated into the PJLC's environmental design. The cycle concludes with students' feedback as to their preferences, experience, and usage of the PJLC post-renovation. As was indicated in the study, the PJLC has experienced a series of transformations since its inception in 1995.

The dynamics of a younger demographic, the infusion of technology, and a paradigm shift in institutional mission have influenced the design and programming of the PJLC. Administrators involved in the recent revitalization of the PJLC cite the challenges of meeting the changing needs and environmental expectations of today's students.

Results indicate that there are social and behavioural patterns students have established in using the PJLC. These patterns appear to be influenced by time of day, environmental design, and the operational hours of services. Additionally, these patterns raise questions regarding gender and age preferences pertaining to the types of learning environments that are most supportive during their studies.

Major changes to the facility, including the addition of a popular retail vendor to the building, has increased campus member's usage of the space and consequently altered the dynamics of the PJLC. Administration voiced several challenges regarding the PJLC's increasingly social atmosphere and the concerns expressed by university staff attempting to deliver learning services and work in the environment without disruption. When space on campus is at a premium, questions regarding how to best align space planning with academic and learning objectives naturally arise.

Universities undergoing the renewal and development of their campuses need to consider the influences that these changes may have on both the immediate space and the surrounding areas. Architect Christopher Alexander poignantly states, "When you build a thing you can not build that thing in isolation, but must also repair the world around it, and within it, so that the larger world at that one place becomes more coherent, and more whole" (Alexander, Ishikawa, Silverstein, Jacobson, Fiksdahl-King, & Angel, 1977, p. xiii).

Designing, implementing, and sustaining the campus's learning environment requires institutions to examine formal and non-formal space as not merely something static, and maintained, but as dynamic and evolving, requiring systematic review and adaptation in order to continue to optimally serve its intended purpose (Stigall, 2007).

## REFERENCES

Accardi, M. T., Cordova, M., & Leeder, K. (2010). Reviewing the library learning commons: History, models, and perspectives. *College & Undergraduate Libraries, 17*(2–3), 310–329. Retrieved from http://dx.doi.org/10.1080/10691316.2010.481595

Alexander, C., Ishikawa, S., Silverstein, M., Jacobson, M., Fiksdahl-King, I., & Angel, S. (1977). *A pattern language.* New York, NY: Oxford University Press.

Applegate, R. (2009). The library is for studying: Student preferences for study space. *The Journal of Academic Librarianship, 35*(4), 341–346.

Astin, A. W. (1975). *Preventing students from dropping out.* San Francisco, CA: Jossey-Bass.

Astin, A. W. (1984). Student involvement: A developmental theory for higher education. *Journal of College Student Personnel, 25,* 297–308.

Astin, A. W. (1993). *What matters in college? Four critical years revisited.* San Francisco, CA: Jossey-Bass.

Astin, A. W. (1999a). Involvement in learning revisited: Lessons we have learned. *Journal of College Student Development, 40*(5), 587–598.

Astin, A. W. (1999b). Student involvement: A developmental theory for higher education. *Journal of College Student Development, 40*(5), 518–529.

Barber, J. M., & Armacost, P. H. (2006). Peter H. Armacost library: Eckerd college. In D. G. Oblinger (Ed.), *Learning spaces* (pp. 18.1–18.6). Retrieved from http://www.net.educause.edu/ir/library/pdf/P7102cs5.pdf

Bennett, M., & Benton, S. (2001). What are the buildings saying? A study of first-year undergraduate students' attributions about college campus architecture. *NASPA Journal, 38*(2), 159–177.

Bennett, S. (2009). Libraries and learning: A history of paradigm change. *Libraries and the Academy, 9,* 181–197.

Blackmore, J., Bateman, D., Loughlin, J., O'Mara, J., & Aranda, G. (2011, June). *Research into the connection between built spaces learning spaces student outcomes.* Melbourne: Education Policy and Research Division, Department of Education and Early Childhood Development. Retrieved from http://www.eduweb.vic.gov.au/edulibrary/public/publ/research/publ/blackmore_le arning_spaces.pdf

Brown, M. (2005, July–August). Learning space design theory and practice. *EDUCAUSE Review Online.* Retrieved from http://net.educause.edu/ir/library/pdf/erm0544.pdf

Brown, M., & Long, P. (2006). Trends in learning space design. In D. G. Oblinger (Ed.), *Learning spaces* (pp. 9.1–9.11). Retrieved from http://net.educause.edu/ir/library/pdf/PUB7102i.pdf

Carthey, J. (2006). Post-occupancy evaluation: Development of a standardised methodology for Australian health projects. *The International Journal of Construction Management, 6*(1), 57–74. Retrieved from http://www.sykehusplan.no/data/061114_khb_poejc_ijcm_poe_jul06.pdf

Chapman, P. M. (2006). *American places: In search of the twenty-first century campus.* Westport, CT: Praeger Publishers.

Cheng, J. K. (2011, March 20). *Architect James Cheng on studio 4 with Fanny Kiefer* [video]. Retrieved from http://www.youtube.com/watch?v=GXqfs34tnUM&feature=relmfu

Chism, N. (2006). Challenging traditional assumptions and rethinking learning spaces. In D. G. Oblinger (Ed.), *Learning spaces* (pp. 2.1–2.12). Retrieved from http://www.educause.edu/learningspaces

Cole, R. J., Robinson, J., Brown, Z., & O'Shea, M. (2008). Re-contextualizing the notion of comfort. *Building Research & Information, 36*(4), 323–336. Retrieved from http://www.geog.ubc.ca/courses/geog446/readings/Comfort%20paper.pdf

Cox, A. M. (2011). Students experience of university space: An exploratory study. *International Journal of Teaching and Learning in Higher Education, 23*(2), 197–207. Retrieved from http://www.isetl.org/ijtlhe/pdf/IJTLHE953.pdf

Cox, B., & Jantti, M. (2012). Discovering the impact of library use and student performance. *EDUCAUSE Review Online.* Retrieved from http://www.educause.edu/ero/article/discovering-impact-library-use-and-student-performance

Creswell, J. W. (2003). *Research design: Qualitative, quantitative and mixed methods approaches.* Thousand Oaks, CA: Sage Publications.

Cunningham, H. V., & Tabur, S. (2012). Learning space attributes: Reflections on academic library design and its use. *Journal of Learning Spaces, 1*(2), 1–6.

Davis, B., & Shorey, D. (2006). The information commons northwestern university. In D. G. Oblinger (Ed.), *Learning spaces* (pp. 30.1–30.7). Retrieved from http://www.net.educause.edu/ir /library/pdf/PUB7102.pdf

Diaz, V., Brown, M., & Salmons, J. (2010). Unit 3: Collaborative learning spaces. In V. Diaz J. & J. S. Strickland (Eds.), *EDUCAUSE learning initiative discovery tool: Collaborative learning workshop guide.* Retrieved from net.educause.edu/ir/library/pdf/ELI80083.pdf

Falk, J., & Dierking, L. (2000). *Learning from museums: Visitors experiences and the making of meaning.* Walnut Creek, CA: AltaMira Press.

DESIGNING FOR THE FUTURE

Federal Facilities Council, Board on Infrastructure and the Constructed Environment, & National Research Council. (2001). *Learning from our buildings: A state-of-the-practice summary of post-occupancy evaluation* (Technical Report No. 145). Washington, DC: National Academy Press.

Fichten, C. S., Asuncion, J. V., Barile, M., Robillard, C., Fossey, M. E., & Lamb, D. (2003). Canadian postsecondary students with disabilities: Where are they? *The Canadian Journal of Higher Education, 33*(3), 71–114.

Fraser, B. J. (2001). Twenty thousand hours: Editor's introduction. *Learning Environment Research, 4*(1), 1–5.

Gaber, D. (2003). Building a system of autonomous institutions: Coordination and collaboration in British Columbia's community college, university college, and institute system. *Community College Review, 31*(2), 47–73.

Haller, B. A. (2006). Promoting disability-friendly campuses to prospective students: An analysis of university recruitment materials. *Disability Studies Quarterly, 26*(2), 1–19. Retrieved from http://dsq-sds.org/article/view/673/850

Henkel, M. (2002). Academic identity in transformation? The case of the United Kingdom. *Higher Education Management and Policy, 14*(3), 137–145.

Henkel, M. (2005). Academic identity and autonomy in a changing policy environment. *Higher Education, 49*, 155–176.

Herman Miller. (2005). *Importance of informal space for learning, collaboration, and socialization.* Retrieved from http://net.educause.edu/ir/library/pdf/ELI0535.pdf

Herman Miller. (2007). *Rethinking the classroom: Spaces designed for active and engaged learning and teaching.* Zeeland, MI: Herman Miller. Retrieved from http://www.hermanmiller.com/content/dam/hermanmiller/documents/solution_ess ays/se_Rethinking_the_Classroom.pdf

Herzog, S. (2007). The ecology of learning: The impact of classroom features and utilization on student academic success. *New Directions for Institutional Research, 2007*(135), 81–106.

Hunley, S. A., & Schaller, M. (2006). Assessing learning spaces. In D. G. Oblinger (Ed.), *Learning spaces* (pp. 13.1–13.11). Retrieved from http://www.educause.edu/learningspaces

Hussain, I., & Adeeb, M. A. (2009, July). Role of mobile technology in promoting campus-wide learning environment. *The Turkish Online Journal of Educational Technology, 8*(3), 48–56.

Hussong-Christian, U., Rempel, H. G., & Deitering, A. M. (2010). The library as learning commons: Rethink, reuse, recycle. *College & Undergraduate Libraries, 17*(2–3), 273–286. Retrieved from http://dx.doi.org/10.1080/10691316.2010.481951

Jamieson, P. (2009). The serious matter of informal learning. *Planning for Higher Education, 37*(2), 18–25.

Johnson, C., & Lomas, C. (2005). Design of the learning space: Learning & design principles. *EDUCAUSE Review Online, 40*(4), 16–28.

Jones, P. (1994, October). *The university college in BC: A new paradigm in higher education?* Paper presented at The Canadian University in the 21st Century Conference, Manitoba, Canada.

Joppe, M. (2000). *The research process.* Retrieved from http://www.ryerson.ca/~mjoppe/rp.htm

Kenney, D., Dumont, R., & Kenney, G. (2005). *Mission and place.* Westport, CT: Praeger Publishers.

Kuh, G. D., Cruce, T., Shoup, R., Kinzie, J., & Gonyea, R. (2008). Unmasking the effects of student engagement on first-year college grades and persistence. *The Journal of Higher Education, 79*(5), 540–563.

Kuh, G. D., & Gonyea, R. M. (2003). The role of the academic library in promoting student engagement in learning. *College and Research Libraries, 64*, 256–282.

Kuh, G. D., Kinzie, J., Schuh, J., & Whitt, E. (2005). *Assessing conditions to enhance educational effectiveness: The inventory for student engagement and success.* San Francisco, CA: Jossey-Bass.

Landolfi, E. (2007, September). *Post-secondary centres for teaching and learning: A Canadian perspective.* Retrieved from http://www.ufv.ca/assets/tlc/brown+bags/landolfi.pdf

Larsen, S. (2010, December). From reference area to learning common: Modernising university library space. *BFP, 34*, 337–341.

Levin, J. (2003). Organizational paradigm shift and the university colleges of British Columbia. *Higher Education, 46*(4), 447–467.

283

J. PIZZUTI-ASHBY

Levin, J. (2004). *Two British Columbia university colleges and the process of economic globalization.* Retrieved from http://www4.ncsu.edu/~jslevin2/UNIVER1June04.DOC.175

Lewin, K. (1936). *Principles of topological psychology.* New York, NY: McGraw-Hill Book Company.

Li, P. P., Locke, J., Nair, P., & Bunting, A. (2005). *Creating 21st century learning environments.* Retrieved from http://dx.doi.org/10.1787/558676471016

Lincoln, Y. S., & Guba, E. G. (1985). *Naturalistic inquiry.* Beverly Hills, CA: Sage Publications.

Lippincott, J. K. (2008). Information commons: Surveying the landscape. In C. Forrest & M. Halbert (Eds.), *A field guide to the information commons* (pp. 18–30). Lanham, MD: The Scarecrow Press.

Lippman, P. C. (2010). *Can the physical environment have an impact on the learning environment?* doi:10.1787/5km4g21wpwr1-en

Lombardi, M. M., & Wall, T. B. (2006). Perkins library Duke university. In D. G. Oblinger (Ed.), *Learning spaces* (pp. 9.1–9.11). Retrieved from http://www.net.educause.edu/ir/library/pdf/PUB7102i.pdf

Matthews, K. E., Andrews, V., & Adams, P. (2011). Social learning spaces and student engagement. *Higher Education Research & Development, 30*(2), 105–120.

McCarthy, C. A., & Nitecki, D. A. (2010). *An assessment of the bass library as a learning commons environment.* Retrieved from http://libraryassessment.org/bm~doc/mccarthy_cheryl.pdf

Monahan, T. (2002). Flexible space & built pedagogy: Emerging IT embodiments. *Inventio, 4*(1), 1–19. Retrieved from http://www.torinmonahan.com/papers/Inventio.html

Moore, A., & Wells, K. (2009). Connecting 24/5 to millennials: Providing academic support services from a learning commons. *Journal of Academic Librarianship, 35,* 75–85.

Moos, R. H. (1979). *Evaluating educational environments.* San Francisco, CA: Jossey-Bass.

Neame, S., & Lomas, C. (2006). The Irving K. Barber learning centre: University of British Columbia. In D. G. Oblinger (Ed.), *Learning spaces* (pp. 38.1–38.8). Retrieved from http://www.net.educause.edu/ir/library/pdf/P7102cs25.pdf

Nixon, A. L. (2009, March). Aligning learning space design and student work: Research implications for design processes and elements. *EDUCAUSE Review Online.* Retrieved from http://www.educause.edu/ero/article/aligning-learning-space-design-and-student-work-research-implications-design-processes-and-elements

Oblinger, D. G. (2005). Leading the transition from classrooms to learning spaces. *EDUCAUSE Quarterly, 28*(1), 14–18.

Oblinger, D. G. (2006a). Learning how to see. In D. G. Oblinger (Ed.), *Learning spaces* (pp. 14.1–14.11). Retrieved from http://www.educause.edu/learningspaces

Oblinger, D. G. (2006b). Space as a change agent. In D. G. Oblinger (Ed.), *Learning spaces* (pp. 13.1–13.11). Retrieved from http://www.educause.edu/learningspaces

Ornstein, S. W. (2005). *Post-occupancy evaluation in Brazil: Evaluating quality in educational facilities* (pp. 135–143). Retrieved from http://www.oecd.org/dataoecd/26/49/37905357.pdf

Palomba, C., & Banta, T. (1999). *Assessment essentials: Planning, implementing and improving assessment in higher education.* San Francisco, CA: Jossey-Bass.

Potter, W. G., & King, F. E. (2006). The student learning center the university of Georgia. In D. G. Oblinger (Ed.), *Learning spaces* (pp. 41.1–41.7). Retrieved from http://www.net.educause.edu/ir/library/pdf/P7102cs28.pdf

Preiser, W. F. E. (1995). Post-occupancy evaluation: How to make buildings work better. *Facilities, 13*(11), 19–28.

Prince, M. (2004). Does active learning work? A review of the research. *Journal of Engineering Education, 93*(3), 223–231.

Reynolds, G. L. (2007). The impact of facilities on recruitment and retention of students. *New Directions for Institutional Research, 2007*(135), 63–80.

Riddle, M. D., & Souter, K. (2012). Designing informal learning spaces using student perspectives. *Journal of Learning Spaces, 1*(2), 1–6.

Smith, M. K. (2008). *Informal learning.* Retrieved from http://www.infed.org/biblio/inf-lrn.htm

Spooner, D. (2008). Assessing the learning value of campus open spaces through post-occupancy evaluations. *Planning for Higher Education, 36*(3), 44–55.

Stark, M., & Samson, S. (2010). Organized spontaneity: The learning commons. *College & Undergraduate Libraries, 17*(2–3), 260–272.

284

Stensaker, B. (2005, December). *Strategy, identity, and branding: Re-inventing higher education institutions*. Paper presented at the City Higher Education Seminar Series (CHESS), London, United.

Stensaker, B., & Norgard, J. (2001). Innovation and isomorphism: A case-study of university identity struggle 1969–1999. *Higher Education, 42*, 473–492.

Strange, C. C., & Banning, J. H. (2001). *Educating by design: Creating campus environments that work*. San Francisco, CA: Jossey-Bass.

Suarez, D. (2007). What students do when they study in the library: Using ethnographic methods to observe student behavior. *Electronic Journal of Academic and Special Librarianship, 8*(3). Retrieved from http://southernlibrarianship.icaap.org/content/v08n03/suarez_d01.html

Temple, P. (2007). *Learning spaces for the 21st century: A review of the literature*. Retrieved from http://www.heacademy.ac.uk/assets/documents/.../Learning_spaces_v3.pdf

Tongco, M. D. C. (2007). Purposive sampling as a tool for informant selection. *Ethnobotany Research & Applications, 5*, 147–158. Retrieved from http://scholarspace.manoa.hawaii.edu/bitstream/handle/10125/227/i1547-3465-05-147.pdf?sequence=4

Veitch, R., & Arkkelin, D. (1995). *Environmental psychology: An interdisciplinary approach*. Englewood Cliffs, NJ: Prentice Hall.

Veltri, S., Banning, J., & Davies, T. (2006). The community college classroom environment: Student perceptions. *College Student Journal, 40*(3), 1–7.

Villar, L. M., & Alegre, O. M. (2007). *Student perceptions of classroom environment and instructors' reflections*.

Walton, S., & Galea, C. (2005). Some considerations for applying business sustainability practices to campus environmental challenges. *International Journal of Sustainability in Higher Education, 6*(2), 147–160.

Watt, C. (2007). Introduction: Why are data on facilities important? *New Directions for Institutional Research, 135*, 5–10.

Webster, K. (2010, November–December). The library space as learning space. *EDUCAUSE Review Online, 45*(6), 10–11. Retrieved from http://www.educause.edu/ero/article/library-space-learning-space

Woodroff, E. (1983). *The founding of Fraser Valley college*. Abbotsford: University of the Fraser Valley.

Zandvliet, D.B. and Straker L. (2001). Physical and psychosocial ergonomic aspects of the learning environment in information technology rich classrooms. Ergonomics. London: Taylor and Francis.

Zimring, C., Rashid, M., & Kampschroer, K. (2010). *Facility Performance Evaluation (FPE)*. Retrieved from http://www.wbdg.org/resources/fpe.php

NEDA ABBASI AND KENN FISHER

# 14. DEFINING QUALITY IN ACADEMIC LIBRARY SPACES

*Criteria to Guide Space Planning and Ongoing Evaluation*

### ABSTRACT

The chapter addresses the key question of "what defines quality in academic library spaces?" Drawing upon a review of existing literature on planning, design and post-occupancy evaluation of libraries, a framework is proposed which includes six key factors to be considered in the planning and design of academic library spaces: (1) functionality; (2) being learner-centred; (3) sustainability; (4) social inclusiveness; (5) being technology-infused; and (6) a sense of inspiration.

Development of this framework was followed by a series of site visits from sixteen academic libraries in Australia in order to better understand the practical implications of the criteria of quality included in the proposed framework and to examine different ways of translating them into the language of space design. Each of the libraries visited had responded to a certain context, specific challenges, and a set of requirements in a unique way. Different design features and responses in these library spaces were linked to the six key factors and their corresponding criteria of quality and measures and helped in mapping out the current trends and issues in planning, design, and evaluation of academic library spaces.

The chapter concludes with addressing the importance of refining the definition of quality of library spaces according to the social, cultural, pedagogical and technology-related contexts of an institution and highlighting the need for ongoing evaluation of library spaces quality.

### INTRODUCTION

This chapter addresses the key question of what defines quality in academic library spaces? Drawing upon a review of existing literature on planning, design, and post-occupancy evaluation of libraries, a framework is proposed which includes six key qualities to be considered in the planning and design of academic library spaces: (1) functionality; (2) being learner-centred; (3) sustainability; (4) social inclusiveness; (5) being technology-infused; and (6) a sense of inspiration. A series of site visits from sixteen academic libraries in Australia also assisted in understanding the

© KONINKLIJKE BRILL NV, LEIDEN, 2019 | DOI: 10.1163/9789004391598_017

N. ABBASI & K. FISHER

practical implications of the proposed qualities and different ways of translating them into the language of space design.

Each of the libraries visited had responded to a certain context, specific challenges, and a set of requirements in a unique way. Different design features and responses in these library spaces were linked to the six key qualities and their corresponding criteria or measures of quality. The chapter concludes with mapping out an image of the current trends and issues in planning, design, and evaluation of academic library spaces; addressing the importance of refining the definition of quality of library spaces according to the social, cultural, pedagogical, and technology-related contexts of an institution; and highlighting the need for ongoing evaluation of library spaces quality.

## CONTEXT & BACKGROUNDS

Academic libraries have been facing with the significant challenge of keeping pace with changes in relation to students' demographics, pedagogy, and technology (Latimer, 2011; Schmidt, 2006). Pedagogical changes, for example, had considerable implications for the ways that degree programs are structured, the subjects are delivered, and student learning is assessed. For learning spaces, this has meant a move away from the focus on accommodating didactic teaching approaches towards facilitating more student-centred approaches e.g. collaborative and project-based learning. Libraries as the heart of the university life then need to offer a variety spaces for independent research, access to information, teamwork, discussion, and collaboration as well as social and informal learning. According to Latimer (2010) the key drivers of a changing approach to the design of academic libraries include: the increasing availability of e-resources or virtual collections; technological advances in technology such as self-check machines, sorting robots, compact shelving, and RFID technology; social networking and the role of the library as a meeting place; and increased competition with other information providers highlighting the need for marketing strategies.

For library spaces to keep pace with changes, understanding the evolving patterns of student learning behaviours, space uses, needs, and preferences is of paramount importance which brings to the fore the need for an ongoing evaluation of library spaces. The very first step in any evaluation is to develop a set of standards or criteria against which the subject can be assessed. In order to perform ongoing evaluation of academic library spaces, it is necessary to define what constitutes ideal library spaces which are responsive to the needs and characteristics of students, faculty, library staff, and visitors. In another words, it is necessary to define quality in academic library spaces.

## DEFINING QUALITY IN ACADEMIC LIBRARY SPACES

A review of literature was carried out to: better understand some of the planning and design principles identified for library spaces; achieve insights into characteristics of good library spaces; and identify a number of qualities for academic library spaces (e.g. Antell & Engel, 2006; S. Bennett, 2003; Scott Bennett, 2009; Building

288

Futures, 2004; Cunningham & Tabur, 2012; Dewe, 2016; Edwards, 2009; Faulkner-Brown, 1979; Freeman, 2005; Gayton, 2008; Gotsch & Holliday, 2007; Jordan & Ziebell, 2009; McDonald, 2008; Shill & Tonner, 2003, 2004; Wand, Harbur, & Scotti, 2005; Webb, Schaller, & Hunley, 2008; Worpole, 2013).

In particular, some major studies and reports on qualities of effective and responsive libraries were reviewed and a summary of the qualities and factors addressed in these publications were created. For example, in a report developed for Library Council of New South Wales (2005), a number of qualities were addressed for library spaces: functionality; flexibility and adaptability; accessibility; comfort; technology integration; identity; and marketing strategies. With regard to functionality, the importance of a simple plan and layout with clear and logical relationships, access between spaces, clear routes, unobstructed sightlines, visual markers, and colour coding or art works to promote legibility, wayfinding, and a sense of orientation is highlighted. Incorporating flexibility and adaptability to ensure optimising the use of spaces over time and accommodating changes are also addressed.

In addition, the issue of accessibility to the whole community and people with special needs is considered in terms of layout, entry, signage, and indicators as well as shelving height. Environmental comfort in relation to lighting, acoustics, heating, ventilation, and integration of technology as a part of a "Technology Plan" determining the level of usage and the type of services to be provided are also addressed. Another factor which is more or less relevant to the context of public libraries is "image and identity". Libraries are considered as "a focal point for the community", "a place to meet, discuss, listen and learn", "a place with civic function", and "expressive of its community" relating to the people it serves in an "inviting, non-institutional and welcoming way" (Library Council of New South Wales, 2005, p. 50). Finally, marketing strategies are addressed in order to "encourage community use of the library and increase visits and borrowings". For the physical design of the library this may mean "consideration of internal and external colour schemes to create ambience or themes", "provision of separate quiet areas and noisy areas to attract different types of users for different types of library activities", "creative design and use of shelving to display new books, promote genre collections, or to link to a particular community issue/theme", and "consideration of customer flows to ensure that areas of heavy usage are well-located and large enough to minimise disruption of other activities" (Library Council of New South Wales, 2005, pp. 52–53).

In the context of academic libraries, McDonald (2008) defines ten criteria for good library space: (1) functional; (2) adaptable; (3) accessible; (4) varied; (5) interactive; (6) conducive; (7) environmentally suitable; (8) safe and secure; (9) efficient; and (10) suitable for ICT. He states that library spaces should work well, look good, and last well while fulfilling missions of an institution and ensuring a blend of traditional and electronic services. The area provided should be appropriate enabling a balance among teaching, learning, and research spaces as well as a balance among people, books, IT, and services. Library spaces should be flexible allowing for the easy and quick change of use. The issue of flexibility is particularly important due

N. ABBASI & K. FISHER

to the diversity of learners and learning styles coupled with current and emerging pedagogies.

He calls for social spaces within libraries which are inviting, accessible, and promote independence. There should be different space types including quiet, private and formal learning spaces, social, casual and interactive spaces, collaborative and group study spaces, presentation and IT spaces, and rooms dedicated to teaching and training. It is also essential that library spaces are well organised enhancing contacts between users and services. A sense of place should be invested in library spaces motivating and inspiring learners. Library spaces should be environmentally sustainable for readers, books, and computers. They should be safe and secure spaces for people, collections, equipment, data, and the building (McDonald, 2008).

McDonald (2008, p. 15) suggests focusing on "congruence among people, place and behaviour" in library design, an approach which recognises the complex and dynamic interrelationships among people, collection, and technologies. In the context of academic libraries, this means working towards achievement of a balance between the needs of the teaching, learning, and research communities. Similarly, drawing upon Barker's (1968) theory of "Behaviour Setting", Schneekloth and Keable (1991) highlight the importance of working toward achievement of a fit between people, the behaviour setting they occupy, and the behaviours and activities that they are engaged in.

## A FRAMEWORK OF QUALITY FOR ACADEMIC LIBRARY SPACES

Literature review helped in identifying the qualities with high degree of importance which appeared repeatedly in many studies. A framework was then developed which outlined six qualities in academic library spaces: (1) functionality; (2) being learner-centred; (3) sustainability; (4) social inclusiveness; (5) being technology-infused; and (6) a sense of inspiration. Figure 14.1 presents these six qualities in planning, design, and evaluation of academic libraries.

These qualities were considered in a hierarchy of importance with functionality being the first priority and most essential quality and a sense of inspiration coming to the fore once other five qualities are addressed. Each of the six qualities was then linked to a number of measures or quality indicators in order to facilitate the planning and evaluation processes. Table 14.1 lists quality indicators or measures linked to the six key qualities.

Development of the framework was followed by sixteen site visits to achieve insights into the practical implications of the library space planning and design qualities and elaborate on measures or quality indicators (Table 14.2).

### Functional

The design quality of 'functionality' has to do with library spaces fulfilling a number of goals including: supporting the delivery of services and programs;

290

# DEFINING QUALITY IN ACADEMIC LIBRARY SPACES

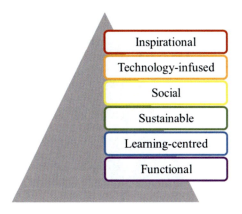

*Figure 14.1. Six key qualities of academic library spaces*

*Table 14.1. Key qualities of academic library spaces linked to their corresponding measures or quality indicators*

| Qualities | Measures of Quality |
|---|---|
| *Functional* | • Size, area & adjacencies |
| | • Materials |
| | • Lighting & acoustics |
| | • Wayfinding strategies |
| | • Access & egress |
| | • Furniture & storage |
| *Learning-cantred* | • Variety of spaces |
| | • Flexibility in use, service, and organisation |
| *Sustainable* | • Natural light |
| | • Thermal comfort |
| | • Natural ventilation |
| | • Sustainable design principles |
| | • Space management |
| *Social* | • Welcoming entry |
| | • Place-making |
| | • Interactive spaces |
| | • Social spaces of different scales |
| | • Staff workspaces |
| *Technology-infused* | • Flexible furniture design |
| | • Dedicated spaces |
| | • Services and infrastructure |
| *Inspirational* | • Views and vistas |
| | • Architectural design features |
| | • Exhibition & display spaces |
| | • Visual connection |

*Table 14.2. List of academic libraries visited in Australia*

| | | |
|---|---|---|
| VIC | *Deakin University* | • Waurn Ponds Campus Library |
| | | • Burwood Campus Library |
| | *University of Ballarat* | • Mt Helen Campus Library |
| | *La Trobe University* | • Bundoora Campus Library |
| | *University of Melbourne* | • Eastern Resource Centre (ERC) |
| | | • Baillieu Library (Ground Level Refurbishment) |
| | | • Barry Street Library |
| | | • Brownless Biomedical Library |
| NSW | *Macquarie University* | • Macquarie Park Campus Library |
| QLD | *Queensland University of Technology* | • Kelvin Grove Campus Library |
| | | • Gardens Point Library |
| | *University of Queensland* | • Ipswich Campus Library |
| | | • Biological Sciences Library at St Lucia Campus |
| | | • Social Sciences Library at St Lucia Campus |
| | | • Walter Harrison Law Library |
| ACT | *University of Canberra* | • Bruce Campus Library |

accommodating the collection efficiently; and responding to users' needs and characteristics. Dimensions of functionality of spaces include the size, layout, adjacencies, materials, lighting, acoustics, wayfinding strategies, access and emergency, furniture, and storage provisions.

With regard to the size of different library spaces, there are standards and guidelines which can be used to work out the required areas. Space planning and making decisions about space allocation should start with a close examination of specific social, cultural, and pedagogical contexts of an academic library. The layout and relationship of spaces or space adjacencies need to be closely examined so that spaces can be used effectively while accommodating multiple functions of academic libraries. The materials used in indoor and outdoor spaces should last and be easy and economical to maintain.

In relation to natural lighting, considerations need to be given to the issues of glare and excess heat. Given individual students' different preferences and requirements, one key consideration which applies to both natural and artificial lighting is users' degree of control over lighting. Task lighting can be provided for tables and individual study desks which allows students to adjust the level of lighting according to their needs and preferences (Figure 14.2).

Among the strategies which can be applied to address acoustic comfort through reducing the negative impacts of indoor noise within library spaces are: (1) zoning i.e. defining and colour coding quiet, noisy, interactive, and collaborative zones; and (2) using sound absorbing materials on floors, walls or dividing screens, and ceilings (Figure 14.3).

Another functional dimension of library spaces has to do with wayfinding strategies that to assist students and visitors in finding their way around spaces. Architectural

DEFINING QUALITY IN ACADEMIC LIBRARY SPACES

*Figure 14.2.* Barry Street Library of the University of Melbourne, Australia: *Showcases some good examples of the use of artificial lighting in study areas with the feature of students' ability to control the desired level lighting*

*Figure 14.3. In order to control the noise created from student groups working together, in* La Trobe University Library at Bundoora Campus, Melbourne, *sound absorbing materials were used for the screens dividing the space and defining the group study areas*

design or spatial attributes and objects are tools through which wayfinding strategies can be implemented. When it comes to the architectural design, main axes may be defined to: maintain sightlines and the ability to observe or have a glimpse of the activities in different spaces; provide clues on the location and sequence of

293

N. ABBASI & K. FISHER

library settings; and increase readability of spaces for users. Atriums are another good example of design-related strategies to facilitate wayfinding by providing vertical visual and physical connections. Spatial attributes including lighting design and colour themes may also be considered to encourage readability of spaces and facilitate movement and wayfinding across spaces. Wayfinding objects include all written information, maps, signs, symbols, and landmarks i.e. sculpture, art works, and natural elements. In relation to the application of objects and particularly signs, it is essential to examine the proper size, location, and orientation. Landmarks can also be created to act as orientation cues, position markers, and a focal point around which a number of learning settings are organised.

Design functionality has also to do with access for all different individuals with different abilities and special needs and quick evacuation in emergency situations. Functionality of academic library spaces also include provisions for security and safety. A design response to the issue of safety is maintaining visual links and visibility throughout spaces: a passive surveillance approach. Another strategy suggested to support safety and security is defining zones based on who can access which spaces e.g. public, private, and privileged zones. Schneekloth and Keable (1991, p. 5) refer to this approach as "resolution of public, private, and interface functions" highlighting the importance of delineating "areas for public access to library services and materials, areas for staff processing of materials and information that are secure and separate from public access, and areas for staff and user interactions such as reference and service desks".

Finally, the functional quality of library spaces has to do with furniture design i.e. ergonomic considerations and storage provision i.e. library staff workplace storage and short-term lockers for students to store personal belonging or charge electronic devices. Design also needs to address solutions and integrate systems that facilitate library staff work. Examples of these supportive elements and systems are automatic doors i.e. facilitating the library staff moving book trolleys and automated sorting technologies systems.

*Learner-Centered*

The second quality of academic library spaces is being learner-centred. Planning and design of academic library spaces should focus on learners i.e. how they learn, study, seek information, collaborate, and socialise with each other, and interact with spaces. The paradigm shift in higher education from a teaching-centred approach to an approach that is centred on learning requires a parallel paradigm shift in libraries from a service culture to a learning culture (Bennett, 2005). As Bennett (2005) suggests, "the success of the academic library is best measured not by the frequency and ease of library use but by the learning that results from that use". In addition, accommodating the wide range of activities students are engaged in, along with their different characteristics, abilities, skills, learning needs, styles, and preferences require a learner-centred approach to design of library spaces.

294

Offering 'choice' to students to make decisions about when, where, and how to learn is at the core of such a student-centred approach to design. Two basic approaches to generating choices may be adopted including: (1) creating a variety of library settings; and (2) maximising flexibility to accommodate multiple functions and leave room for changes.

*Creating a Variety of Library Settings*

An alternative view of "library" as a "logical extension of the classroom" for students means that libraries should accommodate functions and activities which go beyond quiet individual study and information seeking (Freeman, 2005). The concept of "hybrid learning spaces" in libraries highlights the importance of serving "a far broader purpose than simply accommodating information" (Bryant, Matthews et al., 2009). Different terms and categories were considered for space types in academic libraries. While every institution needs to define and determine these categories according to its missions and contexts i.e. social, cultural, curricular, and pedagogical contexts, some main library space types can be considered: (1) individual study spaces; (2) collaborative spaces; (3) dedicated group spaces; (4) formal teaching and training spaces; and (5) research support spaces.

Despite the increasing emphasis on collaboration and group spaces, the individual quiet study space, as "an important aspect of any place of scholarship", continues to maintain its place in academic libraries (Freeman, 2005, p. 5). Traditionally, study carrels were common examples of provisions for quiet individual study and the spaces allocated to them tended to be dull and institutional. This traditional approach has been challenged in new libraries and refurbishment projects. Individual study spaces have therefore evolved to respond to two seemingly conflicting demands: (1) meeting the requirements of a distraction free space i.e. provision of a degree of visual and acoustic privacy; and (2) creating an open environment with pleasant and vibrant ambience (Figure 14.4). With this regard, transparency, arrangement of study carrels or desks, height of separating elements, lighting, and colour themes are important factors to consider. Existing research provides insights into characteristics of study spaces which are important for students including freedom from distractions and noise, good lighting, personal control of temperature and ventilation, comfortable chairs and adequate desk space, plain décor, and furnishings (Stoke et al., 1960).

Collaborative spaces or learning commons form another category of important functional spaces which are now becoming an integral part of libraries in many institutions across the world. Collaborative spaces are generally open-plan environments which include different learning settings with access to desktop computers, data and power points, and wireless technologies. Basically, collaborative spaces accommodate unstructured and casual group study along with a range of multiple modes of learning and interactions. In collaborative space, learners may be engaged in conversation with each other while working on their own, collaborate in

*Figure 14.4. Study spaces created along two sides of an internal garden in* University of Queensland Ipswich Library, Ipswich, *accommodate quiet individual study, offer a pleasant well-lit ambient and view of the rainforest garden and water features, and are not completely secluded or isolated*

pairs or in large groups, and work with multiple digital devices and technologies. In a study of the use of collaborative spaces in an academic library in New England, Silver (2007) found these spaces as the primary location on the campus for supporting both curriculum-initiated and student-driven collaborative learning which were heavily used and highly valued by the students. Among the characteristics found to influence students' selection of collaborative spaces are: comfort; control over features of the spaces; facilitating interpersonal communication; and "integration of basic human needs and desires (such as eating, drinking, and enjoyment) with learning activities" (Webb et al., 2008, p. 407). An overarching design attributes of collaborative spaces is flexibility: students are able create a setting within the collaborative space on an ad-hoc basis by simply rearranging furniture.

Another category of functional spaces in academic libraries includes dedicated group spaces which accommodate the formal group work and may require a certain level of acoustic privacy and access to specific equipment e.g. data projectors, smart boards, and projection screens. Examples of dedicated group spaces are project rooms, quiet study rooms, and seminar spaces (Figure 14.4).

Two other categories of functional spaces in academic libraries include formal teaching and training rooms and research support spaces. Given the emergent role of academic libraries in supporting learning and teaching, formal teaching and training rooms as well as large group presentation spaces i.e. tutorial rooms and lecture halls

# DEFINING QUALITY IN ACADEMIC LIBRARY SPACES

*Figure 14.5. In Deakin University Library at Waurn Ponds Campus, Geelong, project and study rooms are defined as separate enclosed spaces while maintaining visual connections. These spaces are also equipped with technologies and furniture to support students' collaborative learning needs*

have been largely incorporated into library buildings. With regard to research support spaces i.e. quiet study spaces for postgraduate research students, students' research behaviours and needs should be closely examined to determine design principles and requirements.

In addition to the main categories referred earlier, academic libraries should provide two key categories of spaces with common attributes regardless of their contexts: (1) spaces to enrich social and personal experiences of students i.e. lounges, break-out areas, gathering spaces for social and community events, and quiet nooks and crannies; and (2) spaces to promote inclusiveness and access of individuals with special needs. In the section on 'social inclusiveness' quality of academic library spaces, these spaces will be closely examined.

With regard to creating a variety of spaces in academic libraries, there are a number of elements which can be used to define a space and communicate clues to the library users that certain behaviours and activities are expected and accepted in the spaces. Some of these space defining elements include: (1) furniture, dividing walls, and screening element; (2) colour schemes; (3) lighting; and (4) technologies and equipment. Built-in furniture can be used to provide a degree of visual and acoustic privacy and communicate certain messages to library users about accepted uses and activities in specific library spaces (Figure 14.6). Semi-private or group study settings may be created within open plan spaces by simply designing appropriate furniture such as learning pods, screens, and canopies (Watson, 2006). In a study of the

*Figure 14.6. Refurbishment of* Brownless Biomedical Library of University of Melbourne *showcases some good examples of using furniture and colours to define a range of spaces where a formerly dull rectangular space was broken down into a number of smaller spaces that accommodate a variety of functions. Built-in furniture helps in defining areas for small group collaboration and study*

relationship between the kind and placement of furniture with students' patterns of use and behaviour, Young (2003) suggested that "anecdotal evidence lead to inferences that carrels promote independent, quiet study, while group tables invite noise".

In relation to the impacts of colours on individuals' moods, behaviours, motivation, and nature of uses and activities, diverse views exist on the most appropriate colours conducive to expected activities for specific spaces (Figure 14.7). Nevertheless, some general rules may be considered e.g. 'hot colours' may be the right choice for "lively interactive areas" and 'cool colours' may be appropriate for "quiet contemplative study" (McDonald, 2008, p. 19).

*Maximising Flexibility*

Another dimension of the learning- and learner-centred libraries has to do with flexibility and adaptability. Changes and differences are inevitable including changing collection, different needs of student cohorts, and various faculty's teaching practices. Emerging pedagogical trends, development of new programs, and advances in technologies mean that library spaces need to accommodate short-term reconfigurations and long-term developments. Even during a typical academic semester, student's needs and learning styles may change e.g. higher demands for quiet individual study spaces during the exam periods.

DEFINING QUALITY IN ACADEMIC LIBRARY SPACES

*Figure 14.7. In* Queensland University of Technology at Kelvin Grove Campus, Brisbane, *a range of colour palettes are used in different library spaces corresponding to specific activities that students are engaged in*

Given this, "flexibility of function" is necessary "to allow spaces to change and adapt to different uses dependent on the time of the semester or group that was using the space" (Graves & Berg, 2009, p. 68). Social, economic, cultural, and environmental changes also face the universities with the challenge to revisit their educational philosophies and shift their pedagogical focuses. Libraries as "learning laboratories" require spaces which can be easily repurposed in response to changing philosophies and shifting pedagogical trends. To remain dynamic and play an active role in a campus life, spaces that define academic libraries and the services they offer must "continually stimulate users to create new ways of searching and synthesizing materials" (Freeman, 2005, p. 8).

In relation to maximising flexibility and adaptability, there are a number of factors to be considered including: (1) building structure i.e. location of columns and load-bearing elements; (2) openness of spaces or open plan layout; (3) provision of power and data connections in appropriate locations to allow flexible arrangements of spaces and accommodate multiple functions in the same space; and (4) furniture, screening, and dividing elements (Figure 14.8). The size and shape of furniture along with features such as moveability and modularity are important design considerations to support a range of activities and arrangements (Figure 14.9). Simple and modular furniture, for example, can be configured in many ways to suit different numbers of participants, tasks, and functions (Anders, Calder, Elder, & Logan, 2009; Huon & Sharp, 2009).

It is important to note that maximising flexibility and adaptability of academic library spaces does not solely depend upon the application of design-related strategies

*Figure 14.8. A variety of learning spaces is created in* Biological Science Library of University of Queensland, Brisbane, *to accommodate a range of individual and group activities. Sliding panels also installed to open up adjacent spaces and create bigger space when necessary*

and spatial features. Processes and policies implemented by academic libraries and institutions including management of collection as well as technologies integrated i.e. wireless networks and laptop loan policies may maximise the potentials of library spaces to be used for multiple purposes.

*Sustainable*

This quality has to do with environmental factors and relevant considerations to make students and library staff feel comfortable while performing their tasks. Among the key design-related consideration in this regard are considerations related to the provision of natural light and thermal comfort.

DEFINING QUALITY IN ACADEMIC LIBRARY SPACES

*Figure 14.9. Dividing elements installed on the tables in* Macquarie University Library at Macquarie Park Campus, Sydney, *have the flexibility to be taken out and create different learning settings*

The amount and quality of natural light provided in library spaces should be adequate with little or no need to supplement it with artificial light during the day. It is also necessary to consider strategies to minimise glare and excessive heat associated with the natural light i.e. provision of shades and shutters to control the natural light. Library spaces should also provide thermal comfort for students and library staff during the winter and summer. In relation to the indoor air quality and ventilation, the library spaces should not be too humid or too dry and the fresh air needs to circulate in these spaces.

An increasing emphasis on sustainability also suggests incorporating sustainable design features and principle into library spaces. Academic libraries should consider implementation of passive ventilation and solar panels in order to minimise the need for air-conditioning. Adopting sustainable design principles in library spaces has also to do with taking into consideration environmental impacts of building materials. In recent years, organisations and groups were established which aim at increasing the awareness about environmental issues and encouraging libraries to incorporate sustainability into their buildings and practices. A great deal of discussion has evolved on this topic using terms such as green or greening libraries (Antonelli & McCullough, 2012; Jankowska & Marcum, 2010). Cases in point are the publications and programs initiated by IFLA's Environmental Sustainability and Libraries Special Interest Group (Hauke, Latimer, & Werner, 2013).

N. ABBASI & K. FISHER

*Figure 14.10.* Macquarie University Library, Sydney, *showcases efforts to create a sustainable learning environment by implementing a range of sustainable design solutions i.e. reusing and recycling demolition and construction wastes, using recycled materials, maximising the use of natural light from courtyards and skylights and controlling glare by shading and double facades, and using Automated Storage & Retrieval System (ASRS)*

Another dimension of the quality of sustainability in academic libraries has to do with sustainable practices and collection (Antonelli, 2008; Aulisio, 2013). One of the innovative solutions in this regard is the use of Automated Storage and Retrieval System (ASRS) to address sustainable growth in relation to both built spaces and energy consumption as observed in the case study of Macquarie University library. This innovation allowed almost double the physical items (2.3m items) to be kept onsite and doubled the library seats. It is expected to reduce the projected greenhouse gas emissions by 817 tonnes per year while also allowing to the savings in ongoing electricity consumption (Brodie, 2012).

*Socially Inclusive*

This quality was defined to address two functions of academic libraries as places which (1) are open and welcoming to a wide range of users; and (2) foster a sense of community and place-identity. The role of libraries as a social place to meet or a "third place" to be engaged in independent study, collaboration, or socialisation away from both the workplace and home environments has been well documented (Banning, Clemons, McKelfresh, & Waxman, 2006; Oldenburg, 2001; Waxman, Clemons, Banning, & McKelfresh, 2007).

## DEFINING QUALITY IN ACADEMIC LIBRARY SPACES

Generally, a library that is open and welcoming to a wide range of users has an entry area that act as a comfortable space between outside and inside and accommodates a range of functions from waiting and informal meeting to providing display and information for students and visitors. Among the considerations to support these functions of a library entry are: (1) proper size, form, and layout to accommodate multiple functions e.g. waiting and informal social interactions without compromising the easy flow of people's movement in and out of library spaces; (2) lounge type furniture with attractive design and vibrant colours; (3) a cafe or food and drink vending machines; (4) a gallery or exhibition spaces; and (5) transparency i.e. use of glass walls.

The image or identity set by libraries is another dimension of social inclusiveness. Some of the planning and design principals which promote a positive image and a sense of place-identity include: (1) highlighting the library as the "intellectual heart" and "focal point" of a university campus "both symbolically and in terms of its physical placement" i.e. being placed in a prominent site and developed with significant scale and character (Freeman, 2005) (Figure 14.11); (2) impressive external skin of a library building/facade architecture; (3) creative design of outdoor spaces adjacent to the entry (Figure 14.12); and (4) using elements borrowed from the context of a library i.e. social, cultural, natural, and historical contexts (Figure 14.13).

With the advent of ICTs which allow access to information almost anywhere anytime, the role of academic libraries as places to collaborate and become engaged in social interactions are emphasized more than ever before. Freeman (2005, p. 3) argues "whereas the Internet has tended to isolate people, the library, as a physical place, has done just the opposite" acting as "the centrepiece for establishing the intellectual community and scholarly enterprise".

*Figure 14.11. In* La Trobe University Library at Bundoora Campus, Melbourne, *one of the main entrances is located along one side of the Agora, the central hub of the campus accommodating a range of student services and amenities i.e. ATM, coffee shops, and stores; a strategy that highlights the role of library as the 'focal point' of the university campus*

*Figure 14.12. A number of design features is included in* Deakin University Library at Waurn Ponds Campus, Geelong, *to turn the library into the heart of the campus. An outdoor area is being designed in front of the library. The library is also in close proximity to student centre building and a natural open area including a pond*

The essence of social inclusiveness is the value placed on "people" by libraries, and higher education institutions in a broad sense. Design responses to such a people-centred approach to library design may include: opportunities to find and make meaningful places; interactive library service desk; social spaces of different sizes and scales; high quality and efficient workspace for library staff; and collaborative planning and design processes.

It is important that the design leaves room for people to not only find but also make their own 'place'. Provision of nooks and crannies may be one design response in this regard. In addition, fixed features and furniture may be avoided or kept to minimum so that students have the ability to move and rearrange them (Figure 14.14). Library service desk should support interactions of the library staff and students. Related design strategies may include having a service desk that is visible and accessible and integrating multiple service desks into one single service point.

A library that places value on people also includes small pockets of social spaces with special attention given to the choice of furniture, lighting, and provision of proper level of acoustic and visual privacy. In addition to spaces to accommodate social interaction

*Figure 14.13. Inside* Deakin University Library at Waurn Ponds Campus, Geelong, *the design creatively incorporates some of the carrels of the old library in the ceiling defining a space below and adding a style to the interior architecture. Staircase walls were also made using old and outdated books from the old library which contributes to the identity and historical backgrounds of the library*

*Figure 14.14.* Deakin University Library at Burwood Campus, Melbourne, *presents some good examples of providing opportunities for students to not only find their spaces in the library but also create their "own" places among the library spaces*

of small groups, spaces may be provided to accommodate large group gatherings and events. These community gathering spaces may be incorporated into circulation spaces e.g. entrance lobbies and stairs. Another dimension of a people-centred approach to designing libraries has to do with the provision of quality workspaces for library staff.

Finally, a people-centred library is the library developed out of collaborative processes. Issues and challenges of today's academic libraries as the intellectual hub of a university campus and centre of active learning are far more complicated than those of traditional libraries as book warehouses. Traditionally, libraries were developed based on standards specified for the number of collections and seatings required. While these standards should be considered in the development of academic libraries, it is essential to actively engage different stakeholders i.e. students and library staff in planning, design, and evaluation processes to achieve comprehensive insights into the space requirements and uses.

*Technology-infused*

This quality has to do with the integration of technologies into spaces. Brucker (2009) suggests maintaining and maximising "connectivity" as the key to the integration of technologies into library spaces. In other words, while it is important to invest into ways to update technological systems and add different types of technologies, considerations need to be given to mobile electronic devices i.e. laptops, phones, and tablets that students bring to libraries with themselves and ways to support their use.

With regard to the effective ways of incorporating technologies into physical spaces of learning, a general principle is maximising flexibility and adaptability of physical environments. Advances in technologies happen in a fast pace and spaces need to keep up with these technological changes. In addition, some of the factors which were addressed in sections on functional and flexible qualities of library spaces have close relevance to effective integration of technologies including: (1) provision of adequate number of power and data points in required locations; (2) implementing creative cabling systems; and (3) furniture considerations i.e. design, size, and form to support students' flexible use of technologies e.g. accommodating both individual work and collaboration.

*Inspirational*

In addition to responding to functional requirements, academic library spaces should be inspirational spaces where a sense of place is fostered. The quality has to do with aesthetics of spaces and their affective influences on users. According to Latimer (2011, p. 126), "the creation of exciting and attractive library space has been shown to bring people into the physical library to use the virtual resources".

In addition to physical attributes of spaces, human factors play an important mediating role in enhancing the inspirational quality of an academic library. Webb et al. (2008) highlight these human factors when suggesting that academic libraries

*Figure 14.15. In the refurbishment of level 2 of* Walter Harrison Law Library of University of Queensland, Brisbane, *design solutions were incorporated to address requirements of technology use i.e. provision of power points on the partitions next to desks and creating a range of spaces to accommodate different functions and activities*

provide a place where people can come together and feel that they belong to a community of learners. Similarly, Sommer (1966, p. 40) describes this as social increment, that is, "the ways in which the presence of other people stimulated a person to greater activity". In another study, Sommer (1970) also reports library readers' preference for open areas and suggest that these individuals found the presence of others to be beneficial to their motivation.

Among design factors which foster a sense of place and create inspiring spaces in academic libraries are: (1) exhibition spaces and display surfaces; (2) views to outside or inside spaces i.e. indoor garden and landscaped spaces; (3) visual connections i.e. horizontal or across a floor level and vertical or across different levels through voids and atriums; and (3) innovative and inspirational design features i.e. forms and shapes, furniture design i.e. soft furniture (Webb et al., 2008), colour schemes, and lighting.

## EMERGING TRENDS IN ACADEMIC LIBRARY SPACES IN AUSTRALIAN INSTITUTIONS

Academic libraries are increasingly being required to provide a range of services and this has critical implications for their physical spaces. More and more, these new "hybrid learning spaces" in libraries are developed to serve "a far broader purpose than simply accommodating information" (Bryant, Matthews, & Walton, 2009).

*Figure 14.16. Refurbishment of* Baillieu Library of University of Melbourne, Melbourne, *presents a number of design strategies to create inspirational spaces i.e. maintaining openness and creative incorporation of built-in display spaces*

N. ABBASI & K. FISHER

Studies provide evidence for the success of integrating this variety of spaces within libraries in attracting students. A survey carried out by Shill and Tonner (2004, p. 149) found that the libraries which had developed their physical spaces showed "sustained increases in usage of the physical facility following project completion". Following the library visits in Australia and review of international examples, a number of common trends could be identified.

Incorporating a cafe in close proximity of the library entrance is one of these trends which was observed in one way or another in all the libraries visited. A cafe can significantly mitigate the institutional feel of the library building and create an informal and friendly environment. Another common design approach was the focus on furniture design and maximising flexibility in their use. While this trend was quite evident in newly built or refurbished spaces, the effort to update existing spaces by placing new furniture could be observed in libraries which had not yet acquired enough funds to carry out major renovations to their spaces. This resonates the study findings by Webb et al. (2008) which showed a preference for soft furniture.

The literature review and site visits assisted in identifying a number of quality indicators to measure the success of addressing each of the six criteria of quality in design of academic library spaces and guide post occupancy evaluation of these spaces (Table 14.3). The criteria of quality and their indicators may as well be used early in the programming and planning phases and considered to refine the design solutions throughout the design phase.

*Table 14.3. Criteria of qualities in academic library spaces and their corresponding quality indicators*

| Qualities of library spaces | Quality indicators |
|---|---|
| Functional | The size and area provided for different library spaces are appropriate. Adjacencies/Relationships of Spaces work well and support the various functions of the library spaces. The materials used are endurable and maintainable. An efficient combination of natural and artificial lighting supports students' needs and activities. The issue of acoustics was addressed properly. Strategies are applied to facilitate wayfinding in the library spaces. The library spaces can be safely and quickly evacuated in an emergency situation. The library spaces can be accessed easily. The design takes into consideration issues around access for people with special needs. Visual link is maintained across library spaces and among bookshelves. Lockers are provided for students' valuable personal belonging. The storage provided in the staff and administrative areas is adequate. The design incorporates elements and systems facilitating staff work. |

*(cont.)*

# DEFINING QUALITY IN ACADEMIC LIBRARY SPACES

*Table 14.3. Criteria of qualities in academic library spaces and their corresponding quality indicators (cont.)*

| Qualities of library spaces | Quality indicators |
| --- | --- |
| | There are spaces which effectively support research activities. |
| | The number of research support spaces provided is adequate. |
| | There are spaces which effectively accommodate teaching and formal training. |
| | The number of teaching spaces and formal training provided is adequate. |
| | Adequate numbers of phone, power, and data connections are provided throughout the library spaces. |
| | The building structure does not impose significant limitations on short- and long-term changes. |
| | The design of furniture supports different activities and arrangement of the library spaces. |
| | The screening and dividing elements used in spaces contribute to flexibility in use, service, and organisation. |
| | The openness of spaces or open plan layouts are maximised to support flexibility. |
| *Sustainable* | The design makes the most of natural light. |
| | Thermal comfort is provided in library spaces during the winter and summer. |
| | The indoor air quality and ventilation is properly addressed in library spaces. |
| | The library spaces are not too humid or too dry and fresh air circulates in them. |
| | The library incorporates sustainable design principles. |
| | The implementation of sustainable design features has reduced the need to use air-conditioning in the library spaces. |
| | The environmental impact was a key consideration in the choice of materials used in the library spaces. |
| | Integration of environmental sustainability in physical spaces works alongside sustainable practices and collection management. |
| *Social* | An entry or intermediary space is created in the interface of inside and outside of the library building. |
| | Appropriate seating and waiting area is provided in the entry space. |
| | Transparency promotes the link between the intermediary space and inside the library building. |
| | The intermediary space includes food and drink vending machines and may incorporate or be adjacent to a cafe. |
| | The design of the library spaces leaves room for people to not only find but also make their own places. |
| | The library service desk supports interactions of the library staff and students. |
| | Small pockets of social spaces are created throughout the library. |

*(cont.)*

*Table 14.3. Criteria of qualities in academic library spaces and their corresponding quality indicators (cont.)*

| Qualities of library spaces | Quality indicators |
| --- | --- |
| | Library spaces are provided to accommodate large group gatherings and major social events. |
| | The library building is the focal point of the university campus. |
| | The facade of the library impresses the users and fosters a sense of place-identity. |
| | The natural and landscaped outdoor areas near the library entries project an attractive image. |
| | The design includes elements borrowed from the context of the library. |
| *Technology-infused* | Furniture design supports students' flexible use of technologies. |
| | Power points are easily available on desks and tables or in close proximity of them. |
| | There are spaces for students' quick access to information. |
| | The location of power points and creative cabling systems promote flexibility. |
| *Inspirational* | The design makes the most of views. |
| | Library spaces include innovative and inspirational architectural design features. |
| | The lighting and architectural forms promote a sense of place. The choice of colour schemes and furniture design foster inspiration. |
| | There are exhibition spaces and surfaces throughout the library. |
| | The design promotes visual connection throughout the library spaces. |

## CONCLUSION

It is clear that all libraries are seeing a Renaissance in this new century. Clearly this is brought about by the emergence of wireless mobile broadband. Students can now learn any time anywhere anyplace so why go to the library? The rapid destocking of books, many of which are now available online, is seeing the spaces released for student study and collaboration. The library as the focal space on a campus is also reinforcing the idea of social capital. The library remains the principal place for cross faculty collaboration and interaction. Otherwise, it is food and beverage outlets which reign supreme.

Universities are now also exploring learning hubs, student centres, and other facilities to enhance the student experience and provide learning support services. Students are voting with their feet in the sense that they very much prefer to 'learn independently together' or learn collaboratively with their peers.

Increasingly courses are being delivered online through the flipped classroom sometimes with MOOCs and sometimes MOCCs (massive online open/campus courseware). Certainly, the evidence is showing that there needs to be a face-to-face component for online learning to be at its most effective.

DEFINING QUALITY IN ACADEMIC LIBRARY SPACES

Predominantly, the central library is being inhabited by younger first year undergraduate students who use the library as their 'home base' whilst they negotiate all the opportunities on campus. In the second and third years, as students move into their major studies, they tend to migrate to satellite learning hubs which are based in schools and faculties or campus precincts. These learning hubs have help desks and other resources which tend to be allied to the subject discipline in which they are based.

Across the globe, there is a rapid transformation of university thirdspaces to accommodate uncertain futures . This is associated with a reengineering of the teacher centred formal learning spaces into collaborative learner centred informal learning spaces which may or may not have an instructor present. However, the evidence to illustrate these spaces actually work is minimal. Studies such as these illustrated in this Chapter - which is based on a sequence of evaluations of university campus libraries and learning - is gradually building a body of evidence to illustrate the validity and effectiveness of these typologies.

The rate of change in online learning has accelerated exponentially over the past five to ten years and is now seriously impacting on university campuses. Indeed, some universities such as the Western Sydney University are expanding their campuses through vertical distributed city centred campus in a sense bringing the campus to the student. These campuses are largely 'course agnostic' as demands wax and wane over time. Thus, the learning commons and learning spaces are agile and adaptive to to cater for unknown future teaching and learning models. Many are framed around 21st Century library planning and design principles.

Further development of this work is likely to 'morph' into the effectiveness of these spaces for student health and well-being examining and measuring how we inhabit spaces and places in these typologies. We also need to ideally attract students to the campus so they have a 'rite of passage' from their schooling studies through to graduating to the workplace whether it be through research, industry, NGOs, service or other commercial endeavours.

What remains valid, however, is that evidence based planning and design is the most reliable and viable method of insuring that scarce capital works funding in the current higher education sector climate is fundamental to prudent expenditure. We believe that these evaluations must continue as new projects are conceived, designed, constructed, and occupied as an essential factor in continuous improvement.

## REFERENCES

Anders, D., Calder, A., Elder, K., & Logan, A. (2009). Investigating the dynamics of an integrated learning space at James Cook university. In D. Radcliffe, H. Wilson, D. Powell, & B. Tibbetts (Eds.), *Learning spaces in higher education: Positive outcomes by design* (pp. 39–44). Brisbane: University of Queensland.

Antell, K., & Engel, D. (2006). Conduciveness to scholarship: The essence of academic library as place. *College & Research Libraries, 67*(6), 536–560.

Antonelli, M. (2008). The green library movement: An overview and beyond. *Electronic Green Journal, 1*(27), 1–11.

N. ABBASI & K. FISHER

Antonelli, M., & McCullough, M. (2012). *Greening libraries*. Sacramento, CA: Library Juice Press, LLC.

Aulisio, G. J. (2013). Green libraries are more than just buildings. *Electronic Green Journal, 1*(35), 1–10.

Banning, J. H., Clemons, S., McKelfresh, D., & Waxman, L. K. (2006). Designing the third place: A concept for campus auxiliaries. *College Services, 6*(3), 46–50.

Barker, R. G. (1968). *Ecological psychology: Concepts and methods for studying the environment of human behavior*. Stanford, CA: Stanford University Press.

Bennett, S. (2003). *Libraries designed for learning*. Retrieved from http://www.clir.org/pubs/reports/pub122/pub122web.pdf

Bennett, S. (2005). Righting the balance. In *Library as place: Rethinking roles, rethinking space*. Washington, DC: Council on Library and Information Resources.

Bennett, S. (2009). Libraries and learning: A history of paradigm change. *Libraries and the Academy, 9*(2), 181–197.

Brodie, M. (2012). Building the sustainable library at Macquarie university. *Australian Academic & Research Libraries, 43*(1), 4–16.

Brucker, J. (2009). *Small-scale, high-impact renovations: Redesigning library spaces on a budget*. Chicago, IL: The Galter Health Sciences Library, The University of Chicago. Retrieved from http://www.youtube.com/watch?v=ags7nFk4b6Q

Bryant, J., Matthews, G., & Walton, G. (2009). Academic libraries and social and learning space: A case study of Loughborough university library, UK. *Journal of Librarianship and Information Science, 41*(1), 7–18.

Building Futures. (2004). *21st century libraries: Changing forms, changing futures*. Retrieved from http://webarchive.nationalarchives.gov.uk/20110118095356/http:/www.cabe.org.uk/files/21st-century-libraries.pdf

Cunningham, H. V., & Tabur, S. (2012). Learning space attributes: Reflections on academic library design and its use. *Journal of Learning Spaces, 1*(2). Retrieved from https://libjournal.uncg.edu/index.php/jls/article/view/392/287

Dewe, M. (2016). *Planning public library buildings: Concepts and issues for the librarian*. London: Routledge.

Edwards, B. (2009). *Libraries and learning resource centres*. London: Routledge.

Faulkner-Brown, H. (1979). The open plan and flexibility. *Proceedings of International Association of Technological University Libraries, 11*(3), 3–9.

Freeman, G. T. (2005). *The library as place: Changes in learning patterns, collections, technology, and use*. Retrieved from http://www.clir.org/pubs/reports/pub129/pub129.pdf

Gayton, J. T. (2008). Academic libraries: 'Social' or communal? The nature and future of academic libraries. *Journal of Academic Librarianship, 34*(1), 60–66.

Gotsch, J., & Holliday, D. (2007, March 29–April 1). *Designing a library environment that promotes learning*. Paper presented at the ACRL Thirteenth National Conference, Baltimore, MD.

Graves, C., & Berg, E. (2009). Supporting teaching and learning through the intelligent design of learning support spaces: A Griffith university example. In D. Radcliffe, H. Wilson, D. Powell, & B. Tibbetts (Eds.), *Learning spaces in higher education: Positive outcomes by design*. Brisbane: The University of Queensland and the Australian Learning and Teaching Council.

Hauke, P., Latimer, K., & Werner, K. U. (2013). *The green library-die Grüne Bibliothek: The challenge of environmental sustainability-Ökologische Nachhaltigkeit in der praxis* (Vol. 161). Berlin: Walter de Gruyter.

Huon, G., & Sharp, H. (2009). Centre for teaching and learning seminar room. In D. Radcliffe, H. Wilson, D. Powell, & B. Tibbetts (Eds.), *Learning spaces in higher education: Positive outcomes by design*. Brisbane: The University of Queensland and the Australian Learning and Teaching Council.

Jankowska, M. A., & Marcum, J. W. (2010). Sustainability challenge for academic libraries: Planning for the future. *College & Research Libraries, 71*(2), 160–170. doi:10.5860/0710160

Jordan, E., & Ziebell, T. (2009). Learning in the spaces: A comparative study of the use of traditional and 'new generation' library learning spaces by various disciplinary cohorts. In D. Radcliffe, H. Wilson, D. Powell, & B. Tibbetts (Eds.), *Learning spaces in higher education: Positive outcomes by design*.

312

DEFINING QUALITY IN ACADEMIC LIBRARY SPACES

Latimer, K. (2010). Redefining the library: Current trends in library design. *Art Libraries Journal, 35*(1), 28–34.

Latimer, K. (2011). Collections to connections: Changing spaces and new challenges in academic library buildings. *Library Trends, 60*(1), 112–133.

Library Council of New South Wales. (2005). *People places: A guide for public library buildings in New South Wales.* Sydney: Library Council of New South Wales. Retrieved from http://www.sl.nsw.gov.au/services/public_libraries/library_mgt/lib_management_docs/peopleplaces_2ndedition.pdf

McDonald, A. (2008). The top ten qualities of good library space. In K. Latimer & H. Niegaard (Eds.), *IFLA library building guidelines: Development & reflections* (pp. 13–29). Berlin: K. G. Saur.

Oldenburg, R. (2001). *Celebrating the third place.* New York, NY: Marlowe & Company.

Schmidt, J. (Ed.). (2006). *From library to cybrary: Changing the focus of library design and service delivery.* Hove: Psychology Press.

Schneekloth, L. H., & Keable, E. B. (1991). *Evaluation of library facilities: A tool for managing change.* Champaign, IL: University of Illinois Graduate School of Library and Information Science.

Shill, H. B., & Tonner, S. (2003). Creating a better place: Physical improvements in academic libraries, 1995–2002. *College & Research Libraries, 64*(6), 431–466.

Shill, H. B., & Tonner, S. (2004). Does the building still matter? Usage patterns in new, expanded, and renovated libraries, 1995–2002. *College & Research Libraries, 65*(2), 123–150.

Silver, H. (2007). *Use of collaborative spaces in an academic library.* Library Research Seminar IV, London, Ontario. Retrieved from http://lrs4.fims.uwo.ca/abstracts/lrsiv_silver.pdf

Sommer, R. (1966). The ecology of privacy. *Library Quarterly, 36*(3), 234–248.

Sommer, R. (1970). The ecology of study areas. *Environment and Behavior, 2*, 271–280.

Wand, P. A., Harbur, A., & Scotti, J. (2005). *The academic library in 2010: A vision report of symposium 2010.* Retrieved from http://connect.ala.org/files/16943/academic_libraries_in_2010_pdf_33440.pdf

Watson, L. (2006). The saltire centre at Glasgow Caledonian university. *SCONUL Focus, 37*, 4–11.

Waxman, L., Clemons, S., Banning, J., & McKelfresh, D. (2007). The library as place: Providing students with opportunities for socialization, relaxation, and restoration. *New Library World, 108*(9–10), 424–434.

Webb, K. M., Schaller, M. A., & Hunley, S. A. (2008). Measuring library space use and preferences: Charting a path toward increased engagement. *Libraries and the Academy, 8*(4), 407–422.

Worpole, K. (2013). *Contemporary library architecture: A planning and design guide.* London: Routledge.

Young, V. E. (2003). *Can we encourage learning by shaping environment? Patterns of seating behavior in undergraduates.* ACRL Eleventh National Conference Proceedings. Retrieved from http://www.ala.org/ala/mgrps/divs/acrl/events/pdf/young.PDF

LEANNE ROSE-MUNRO AND SAADIA MAJEED

# 15. AT-SCALE INNOVATIVE UNIVERSITY LEARNING SPACES OF THE FUTURE

*An Approach to Evidencing and Evaluating What Works*

### ABSTRACT

This chapter explores a concept and an emerging methodological approach being used to inform the design development and evaluation of next generation university learning spaces. The methods of evaluation aim to capture evidence of the physical design affordances that facilitate student-centred collaborative learning experiences. The underpinning concept model provides justification for the mixed methods interdisciplinary approach, which includes the use of prototyping to interrogate the learning space design from the perspective of the interrelationships between pedagogy, spatial affordances and technology (Radcliffe, 2009; Finklestien, Weston, Ferris, & Winer, 2016).

During the design development phase, informed student voice is used to cultivate the design affordances. Informed student voice is once again used during the post occupancy evaluation phase to determine the success of inhabiting the next-gen learning space.

Next generation learning spaces (NGLS) are associated with physical spaces that are augmented with technology, aiming to enhance the learning opportunities for students (Brooks, 2012). NGLS's can be described as innovative spaces that promote the mixing of the physical and virtual, with both individual and group learning, and a blended mobile presence that facilitates the personal engagement of each student with the learning process (Crisp, 2014).

The intersection of the pedagogical approach, spatial design and technology attributes in NGLS's in primary and secondary schools aim to invite participation in personalised learning experiences through the use of differentiated teaching and learning practices and tools, thus enabling student-centred learning (Rose-Munro in Imms et al., 2015; Radcliffe, 2008; Blackmore et al., 2011). At this time, little is known about NGLS's in higher education.

Commentators however report that transformational change in Universities are driven in part by an employability skills gap, with critics reporting that higher education institutions have failed to impart the necessary business and soft skills for graduate employment in economies that are increasingly complex and competitive (Collet, Hine, & du Plessis, 2014). It is imperative that all university stakeholders

© KONINKLIJKE BRILL NV, LEIDEN, 2019 | DOI: 10.1163/9789004391598_018

L. ROSE-MUNRO & S. MAJEED

respond to transformational change and the development of innovative learning spaces with a clear vision of the expected return on investment, and build campus infrastructure with the confidence that the physical design affordances will have a significant impact upon enabling student success.

INTRODUCTION

Globally it is a disruptive time of change as innovative technologies are distilled into workplaces, education and communities far and wide. However, out of uncertain times can emerge creative new ideas, new opportunities and ways of doing. As such, there is increasing recognition that new knowledge can come from many directions as the ubiquitous nature of technology enables 'unlikely' entrepreneurs; that is, students who perhaps in the past had the *will but not the wares*. This proposition poses some of the greatest challenges and opportunities for universities, in particular, how to harness and nurture *all* students as emerging multifaceted-entrepreneurs who are forward thinking and future ready.

There currently exists a lack of empirical data regarding the relationship between skills and employment, and a lack of shared meaning across and between stakeholder groups (academics, industry and students) in their understanding of skills (Collett, Hine, & du Plessis, 2014). In addition, at the curriculum level academics are uncomfortable teaching skills beyond their discipline-specific experience (Barrie et al., 2009; Da La Harpe et al., 2009 cited in Collett et al., 2014).

Compounding this, it is a reality that some university courses are preparing students for jobs that potentially will not exist by the time they graduate because of the sophisticated automation of tasks racing ahead of sector-wide transformational change (New Horizons, 2016; OECD, 2011; P21CS, 2009). At this critical junction, we would like to pose the question:

What is the value proposition of coming to campus to learn?

And against this backdrop, we propose a new concept model and methodological approach that curates the employability skills gap in learning space design attributes with informed student voice. The key position here is that learning spaces are a physical platform where, in a safe and creative environment, students can put into practice the skills required for employment in future job markets. Further to this proposition, the notion that NGLS design affordances prompt curiosity in students and academics.

In addition, engagement with the spatial attributes of NGLS enable greater opportunity for collaboration, communication, critical-thinking and complex problem solving and creativity (P21CS, 2009; Fisher, 2016; OECD, 2011). In support of this notion, Chiu and Cheng (2017) found varying levels of students' academic ability is not a factor in an overall positive effect on creativity and innovation with innovative learning environments supporting active learning pedagogies such as co-operative, collaborative and team-based learning. Creativity is a process in which anyone can

316

engage, it is an innate human ability to generate ideas, solve difficult problems and exploit new ideas; thus, it can be thought of as the fuel for innovation (Kelley, 2001; Florida, 2014). Creativity involves an ebb and flow between behaviours associated with convergent and divergent thinking, with strong links made between creative cognition and the affordances of the physical environment (Chan & Nokes-Malach, 2005; Lipnicki & Byrne, 2005).

Finally, '*informed* student voice' relates to the notion that as a key inhabitant of higher education NGLSs, students are well positioned to provide feedback on the spatial attributes and affordances that enrich their learning journey, providing informed comment on the elements that enable the acquisition of skills that lead to student success (Van Lier, 2008; Gibson, 1977; Pruyn, 1999, Freire, 1970).

## METHOD AND CONCEPT

The concept model proposed here is underpinned by a mixed methods interdisciplinary approach that uses tools of evaluation with origins in the social sciences such as semi-structured interviews, photo elicitation, surveys; and methods originating from the sciences such as acoustic measurement, thermal comfort, indoor air and lighting quality as well as emergent methods such as thermal counters that track human occupancy levels and spatial movement patterns (Creswell & Plano Clark, 2011; Moss, 2003).

The underpinning theoretical stance is rooted in constructivism and theories of person-environment interaction (Barker, 1968; Walsh, 1973). Recent advances in neuroscience inform the behaviours and needs of people involved in creative pursuits and the process of learning (Carson, 2013).

### University Next-Generation Learning Spaces (NGLS)

On-campus learning spaces are a platform where people come together to access experts, and in so doing form face-to-face learning communities in a myriad learning space types that enable differing small and large-scale learning activity. In face-to-face learning sessions students are increasingly required to construct complex responses based on their learned strategies to problem solving and creativity (Crisp, 2014). Walsh in 1973 stated that there is growing belief that the physical environment does profoundly influence psychological states and social behaviour.

Nearly a half a century on in 2017, redeveloping and designing innovative university learning spaces is high stakes because of the iterative nature of technology in education, which infiltrates the fabric of the built learning environment, impacting learning and teaching behaviours in ways that are yet to be fully realised or understood. Adding to the intensity of decision-making regarding innovative space design, educational researchers are now describing the '21st C learner' based upon forecasting the attributes required to be successful in a globally connected world (Griffen & Care, 2012; Belanca & Brandt, 2011).

While technology is broadly reported to have an impact on learner efficacy and engagement, researchers continue to explore student social-transactional behaviours, where knowledge transmission, sharing and co-creation are just some of the drivers, behind engagement with technology in educational settings (Griffen & Care, 2012; Molye, 2008; New Horizons Report, 2016; Abbott, 2007).

However, technology solutions in education alone cannot close the employability skills gap of the 21st C learner, which requires students to not only be creative, but also have a growth mind-set to be relevant and sustainable in professions of the future (Hattie, 2014; OECD, 2011; P21CS, 2009). Here, there is an opportunity to develop NGLSs that are safe places for students to participate in the development of such skill sets, curated by academics who engage in student-centred pedagogies the sum of which, for the purpose of this chapter, are referred to as 'active learning'.

Student-centered active learning involves student agency which defined as the power of the student to act and take control of their own learning journey (Van Lier, 2008) Such agency directs students towards a growth mind-set that ultimately addresses the employability skills gap. Hattie (2012) and Dweck (2007) assert that a growth mind-set, for example, is when a student does not know an answer and, when they make an error they experience failure and are anxious. They resiliently and methodically keep trying different learning strategies until they experience a level of success.

Critical to a growth mind-set, a deep-seated belief that one can learn and attain new knowledge and errors are a normal function of the learning journey. Bloom's taxonomy of metacognitive activity (Bloom, 1953), and approaches such as Student Observations of Learning Outcomes (SOLO) align in principle to active learning. As a result of the combination above, active learning and teaching aim to elicit particular student and academic behaviours, and the NGLS are the platform on which the active learning behaviours are performed.

The term NGLS refers specifically to the next iteration of physical learning spaces in times of change (Dori et al., 2003; Heppell, Chapman, Millwood, Constable, & Furness, 2004; Van Note Chism, 2002). The concept of a changing learning landscape is not new, however evidencing the connection between learning space and learning principles is relatively emergent in the research literature.

Van Note Chism (2002) was one of the first researchers to link learning principles with learning space design. Using the American Association of Higher Education 'Learning Principles and Collaborative Action' (1998), she argued that to facilitate connected, active learning in a social context, we need to develop a range of spaces:

- where small groups could meet to work on projects;
- for whole-class dialogue;
- where technology can be accessed easily;
- for displaying ideas and working documents;
- that can accommodate movement and noise; and
- include spill-over spaces in corridors and lobbies (Van Note Chism, 2002).

AT-SCALE INNOVATIVE UNIVERSITY LEARNING SPACES OF THE FUTURE

These design principles align to more recent thinking around the affordances of physical spaces that facilitate creative behaviours and needs, and foster different modes of work, states of mind and perspectives of the inhabitants (Lipnicki & Byrne 200; Steelcase, 2017).

*Model*

Designing and delivering a scaled-up university-wide NGLS is a high-risk proposition because of the sheer size of the operation, however, a fundamental risk mitigation strategy is evidence-based decision-making. In the absence of evidence-based design principles for higher education NGLS, a concept model has been proposed to ground further rigorous research.

The Higher Education Learning Space Evaluation Model Rose-Munro and Majeed (2017), depicted in Figures 15.1 and 15.2, evolved from design thinking, a methodology that is solution focussed and action oriented. This approach seeks to articulate guiding principles and a set of success criteria prior to the commencement of the design development journey of NGLS. The construct of the model is informed by Brinkerhoff's (2008) success case methodology, which is an approach that aims to quickly uncover 'what works' in order to frame lines of inquiry.

The HE evaluation model is inspired in part by Hattie (2008), who states educators should 'know thy impact' and shift practice iteratively and collectively with the students, as they identify what enables them to have the greatest impact on student achievement and progression. Furthermore, the model is informed by space planning standards developed by the Australian Tertiary Education Facilities

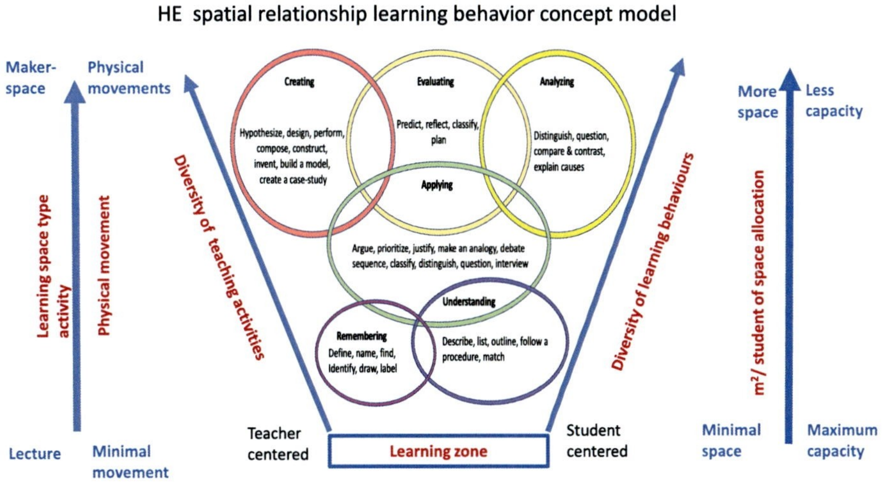

*Figure 15.1. Higher education learning space evaluation concept model 1 (from Rose-Munro & Majeed, 2017)*

319

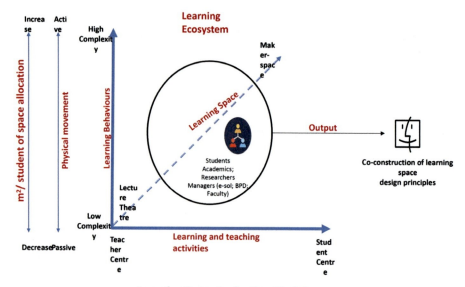

*Figure 15.2. Higher education learning space evaluation model concept 1a (from Rose-Munro & Majeed, 2017)*

Management Association (TEFMA, 2009) that align with the Australian government funding model for higher education facility management.

Thus, the higher education learning space evaluation model is based upon four main elements associated with the 'learning zone' which operates in the physical learning space:

- Square meterage of space allocation per student
- Physical movement in the space
- Diversity of teaching activities
- Diversity of learning behaviours

In Figure 15.2 the 'learning zone' is expressed as metacognitive learning activities curated by the academic, and learner behaviours enacted by the student in a physical learning space. The larger circles represent more desirable complex active learning pursuits. The Y axis demonstrates variables such as space types, physical space size relational to generalised impact upon number of students (capacity).

In terms of determining space type, a percentage-of-fit is associated with a weighting towards the ease at which a particular activity can be administered in a space due to its design affordances. For example; a maker-space (a large adaptable flat-floor learning space) enables variable learning activities associated with collaboratively creating, analysing and evaluating. A maker-space can facilitate model making and design-construct type activity. This space type requires a greater square meter area per student to operationalise and support student circulation, physical movement and kinaesthetic learning that employs the use of various learning tools and materials. As such, maker-spaces accommodate less students and take up more space than lecture halls with rows of seats and minimal student circulation.

Nevertheless, research shows that physical movement influences attention, organization, vision, speech, balance, and coordination; it also enhances focus, memory and cognitive flexibility required for improved academic performance (Fisher & Dovey, 2014; Flexer, Smaldino, & Crandell, 2005; Lipnicki & Byrne, 2005). Traditional pedagogy in the learning zone design for activities such as remembering and understanding requires students to quietly sit for long periods and focus on teacher-led lessons.

Hence, learning spaces were rigidly arranged with rows of desks and uncomfortable chairs. To meet the global standards of a high-tech 21st century economy, the framework for learning behaviours in the 21st century begins with a set of building block skills known as the "5 Cs": collaboration, creativity, critical thinking, communication and character building and, in response, NGLS are evolving to facilitate such skill development.

Structured rows of desks are being replaced with more adaptive informal spaces that encourage student interaction and collaboration. Teacher-led activities are being replaced with opportunities for "hands-on", student-driven active learning involving self-reflection, testing, challenging and the socialisation of new ideas. Such learning behaviours require movement of students between areas for individual, small group and large group learning.

This has impacted on the design of NGLS that now have mobile desks, various table and chair sizes and heights and wireless technology allowing space to be flexibility reconfigured in minutes therefore enabling a myriad of modes of work and learning. Hence the stage is set for redesigning learning spaces that prompt creativity which is considered an important dimension of productivity (Kelley, 2001), student success and future employability.

*Case study: Prototyping the Learning and Teaching Building (LTB)*

A new University Learning and Teaching Building (LTB) was in the early phases of construction when it was decided to prototype all of the proposed learning spaces in order to check the alignment of the pedagogical brief and the design brief. During the design development phase of the LTB, key success criteria were derived from the University mission statement, campus master plan, academic agenda and informed student voice.

The prototyping project fundamentally tested the furniture and technology layouts and the pedagogic intent of all the learning spaces. The LTB was completed in November 2017 and aims to create transformational change in learning and teaching and enhance students on campus learning experiences. The LTB has some of the most innovative at-scale *fit-for-active-learning-purpose* spaces that the university has encountered.

To begin with, between 2015–2017, a University-wide educational agenda articulated a desire to move towards active learning pedagogies in order to inspire transformational change in the way learning and teaching was traditionally curated. This approach was in line with reviews and a critique of the type of learning activities that take place in NGLS, and whether these activities can effectively deliver on the community expectations for a 21st C higher education (Keppell, Souter, & Riddle, 2012).

As a result of the University-wide agenda, numerous Units *or subjects* began 'flipping', defined as placing some curriculum content online in order to reduce the amount of time spent on didactic teacher-centred lecturing, while increasing the amount of student-centered learning activity in face-to-face sessions. Simultaneously, numerous NGLS's to be used by multiple faculties were in development mode. The pedagogical brief for the NGLS's had clear aspirational targets of activating student agency with objectives grounded in enhancing student learning experiences and success, building capacity through academic teacher up-lift enabling the up-take of active learning pedagogy.

The spatial design attributes of the NGLS had to align with the brief, providing a platform for students to participate in an environment that enabled the development of skills such as creative and critical thinking, collaboration, communication, complex problem solving, empathy and inclusiveness. Beichner (2014) notes that consistently well-designed learning spaces can facilitate active learning even though the implementing pedagogies may vary. Similarly, attempts to create a pedagogic framework for learning spaces highlights the need for rich learning environments that reflect the real world, are interactive and collaborative, offer networking opportunities, and incorporate active learning strategies like problem-based learning (Ling & Fraser, 2014).

Throughout the LTB prototype project, the Higher Education Learning Space Evaluation concept model was tested. An interdisciplinary team of stakeholders including students set about replicating, testing, rating, re-creating and re-testing *all* the proposed learning space types in the early stages of construction of the LTB. All of the participant stakeholders had an invested interest in the performance standards of innovative learning spaces. Prior exploration of the interrelationships between pedagogy, spatial design and technology informed the construction of a prototype evaluation tool (Radcliffe, 2008; Finklestien, Westin, Ferris, & Winter, 2016).

Using the tool, participants rated on a Likert scale the affordances of the mock space as they participated in a mock active learning session. The criteria for the successful habitation of the prototype space was underpinned by the notion of testing the alignment between an active learning lesson plan and the proposed design attributes and affordances of the learning space, with student agency given a high rating on the scale of success.

## AT-SCALE INNOVATIVE UNIVERSITY LEARNING SPACES OF THE FUTURE

*Table 15.1. Success evaluation criteria, 1 indicates not achieved,*
*5 indicates successfully achieved*

| Prototype Learning Space Success Indicator | 1 | 2 | 3 | 4 | 5 |
|---|---|---|---|---|---|
| Invite active participation/physical movement | | | | | |
| Supports movement towards writable surfaces | | | | | |
| Explicit teaching zone supports a central focal point | | | | | |
| Some smaller furniture pieces have mobility | | | | | |
| Larger furniture pieces anchor the design | | | | | |
| Students can sit in a variety of group sizes | | | | | |
| Students can formulate groups of 6 for standard assessment tasks | | | | | |
| Space can be readily flexibly rearranged for a variety of delivery modalities | | | | | |
| Everyone can see and access the technology | | | | | |
| Table size and shape are fit-for-purpose and proportional to the space | | | | | |

The test parameters listed in Table 15.1 represent the interrelated nature of pedagogy, spatial design and technology, overlaid with the intentionality of active learning activity. In addition, a judgement was made on the basis that the space supports the use of various learning objects and tools other than simply 'technology'. For the purpose of the prototype activity this was deemed *BYO small objects-based learning* and, as such, table size and function became another test parameter.

When a proposed space type rated low on a parameter(s) on the success criteria scale, the students and other stakeholders collaboratively set about re-creating an alternative AV and furniture layout. The space was then re-tested until all participants were satisfied the space had reached its maximum potential and the alignment of the lesson plan and learning space design matched.

The value-add of the collaborative interdisciplinary prototype project was highlighted when various table shapes and sizes were tested. For example, large round tables of the same height were found to lower the success of a space as students found objects hard to access when they were in the middle of the table. Also noise became an issue as students raised their voice to be heard across the breadth of the diameter of the table, causing the phenomena known as the 'Lombard effect', where voices are continuously raised to be heard over the next person(s). Further, there was a sense of disconnect between students on opposing sides of the circle.

Oversized round tables took up floor real-estate thus diminishing circulation potential. Students found they lost visual connection across the spaces effectively looking at the back of many heads. While in this case study post-occupancy evaluation is yet to commence, an emerging interdisciplinary mixed method approach to evaluating learning space occupation and habitation is planned. Such an approach aims to test the outcomes of attempts to align pedagogy-spatial affordances and technology in a university next-generation learning environment.

323

## CONCLUSIONS

While the post-occupancy evaluation success criteria was still in development mode at the time of writing, it is envisaged that student progress and achievement (Hattie, 2012), graduate attributes and skills (Collett et al., 2014; OECD, 2011; UK CES, 2014) and student perceptions of the learning space's 'usefulness for learning' will be fundamental to the evaluation process. In addition, there is also an opportunity to closely track student behavior and creativity in the NGLS. In practice, too often data obtained from these parameters is overlooked in the early design stages of University learning spaces, resulting in important lessons from student experiences being overlooked.

It is hoped that a future community of practice will emerge that enables prototyping and post-occupancy evaluation of University learning spaces, promoting the development of learning space design principles that foster employability and future ready students. Those involved in the evaluation of learning spaces might consider this approch as a way forward in developing further research and policy guidelines for the next generation of university learning spaces.

## REFERENCES

Abualrub, I., & Stensaker, B. (2017). How are universities responding to demands for an improved learning environment? *Journal of Further and Higher Education, 42*(5), 721–732. doi:10.1080/0309877X.2017.1311991

Barker, R. G. (1968). *Ecological psychology: Concepts and methods for studying the environment of human behaviour*. Stanford, CA: Stanford University Press.

Beichner, R. J. (2014). History and evolution of active learning spaces. *New Directions for Teaching and Learning, 2014*(137), 9–16. doi:10.1002/tl.20081

Binkley, M., Erstad, O., Herman, J., Raizen, S., Ripley, M., Miller-Ricci, M., & Rumble, M. (2012). Defining twenty-first century skills. In P. Griffin, B. McGaw, & E. Care (Eds.), *Assessment and teaching of 21st century skills* (pp. 17–66). Dordrecht: Springer.

Blackmore, J., Bateman, D., Loughlin, J., O'Mara, J., & Aranda, G. (2011). *Research into the connection between the built learning spaces and student outcomes* (p. 22). Melbourne: Department of Education and Early Childhood Development.

Bloom, B. (1956). *Taxonomy of educational objectives*. New York, NY: David McKay.

Bower, M., Dalgarno, B., Kennedy, G. E., Lee, M. J. W., & Kenney, J. (2015). Design and implementation factors in blended synchronous learning environments: Outcomes from a cross-case analysis. *Computers & Education, 86*, 1–17. doi:http://dx.doi.org/10.1016/j.compedu.2015.03.006

Bridgstock, R. (2016). Educating for digital futures: What the learning strategies of digital media professionals can teach higher education. *Innovations in Education and Teaching International, 53*(3), 306–315. doi:10.1080/14703297.2014.956779

Brooks, D. C. (2011). Space matters: The impact of formal learning environments on student learning. *British Journal of Educational Technology, 42*(5), 719–726. doi:10.1111/j.1467-8535.2010.01098.x

Brooks, D. C., & Solheim, C. A. (2014). Pedagogy matters, too: The impact of adapting teaching approaches to formal learning environments on student learning. *New Directions for Teaching and Learning, 2014*(137), 53–61. doi:10.1002/tl.20085

Byers, T. (2016). A quasi-experimental and single-subject research approach as an alternative to traditional post-occupancy evaluation of learning environments. In W. Imms, B. Cleveland, & K. Fisher (Eds.), *Evaluating learning environments: Snapshots of emerging issues, methods and knowledge* (pp. 117–130). Rotterdam, The Netherlands: Sense Publishers.

Carson, S. (2013). *Your creative brain: Seven steps to maximize imagination, productivity and innovation in your life.* San Francisco, CA. Jossey-Bass.

Chan, J., & Nokes-Malach, T. (2016). Situative creativity: Larger physical spaces facilitating novel uses for everyday objects. *Journal of Problem Solving, 9*(1), 29–45.

Charlton, D. (2015, July 9). The rise of the gig worker in the sharing economy. *Tech Crunch.*

Chiu, P. H. P., & Cheng, S. H. (2017). Effects of active learning classrooms on student learning: A two-year empirical investigation on student perceptions and academic performance. *Higher Education Research & Development, 36*(2), 269–279. doi:10.1080/07294360.2016.1196475

Dweck, C. (2007). *Mindset: The new psychology of success* (Ph.D.). New York, NY; Ballatine Books.

Elliot, F., & Malcolm, B. (2011). The case for a learning space performance rating system. *Journal of Learning Spaces, 1*(1).

Ellis, R. A., & Goodyear, P. (2016). Models of learning space: Integrating research on space, place and learning in higher education. *Review of Education, 4*(2), 149–191. doi:10.1002/rev3.3056

Fisher, K. (2016). *The translational design of schools: An evidence-based approach to aligning pedagogy and learning environments*: Rotterdam, The Netherlands: Sense Publishers.

Florida, R. (2014). *The rise of the creative class.* Cambridge, MA: Basic Books.

Gibson, J. (1977). The theory of affordances. In R. Shaw & J. Bransford (Eds.), *Perceiving, acting and knowing: Toward an ecological psychology.* Oxford: Oxford University Press.

Imms, W., Cleveland, B., & Fisher, K. (2016). *Evaluating learning environments: Snapshots of emerging issues, methods and knowledge/edited by Wesley Imms, Benjamin Cleveland, Kenn Fisher.* Rotterdam, The Netherlands: Sense Publishers.

Imms, W., Mahat, M., Byers, T., & Murphy, D. (2017). *Type and use of innovative learning environments in Australasian Schools: ILETC survey 1.* Retrieved from http://www.iletc.com.au/publications/reports

Johnson, L., Adams Becker, S., Cummins, M., Estrada, V., Freeman, A., & Hall, C. (2016). *NMC horizon report: 2016 higher education edition.* Austin, TX: The New Media Consortium.

Kelley, T. (2001). *The art of innovation: Lessons in creativity from IDEO, America's leading design firm.* New York, NY: Random House.

Kersh, N. (2015). Rethinking the learning space at work and beyond: The achievement of agency across the boundaries of work-related spaces and environments. *International Review of Education, 61*(6), 835–851. doi:10.1007/s11159-015-9529-2

Knight, P. T., & Yorke, M. (2006). *Employability: Judging and communicating achievements.* York: Higher Education Academy.

Lamb, G., & Shraiky, J. (2013). Designing for competence: spaces that enhance collaboration readiness in healthcare. *Journal of Interprofessional Care, 27*(S2), 14–23. doi:10.3109/13561820.2013.791671

Lee, N., & Tan, S. (2011). *A Comprehensive learning space evaluation model.* Retrieved from http://www.olt.gov.au/project-comprehensive-learning-space-swinburne-2008

Ling, P., & Fraser, K. (2014). Pedagogies for next generation learning spaces: Theory, context, action. *International Perspectives on Higher Education Research, 12*, 65–84. doi:10.1108/S1479-362820140000012008

Lipnicki, D., &Byrne, D. (2005). Thinking on your back. *Cognitive Brain Research, 24*, 719–722.

Martinez, R., Gonzalez, C., Campoy, P., Garcia-Sanchez, A., & Ortega-Mier, M. (2014). Do classes in cooperative classrooms have a positive influence on creativity and teamwork skills for engineering students? *International Journal of Engineering Education, 30*(6), 1729–1740.

Oblinger, D. G. (Ed.). (2006). *Learning spaces.* Washington, DC & Boulder, CO: Educause.

Oliver, B. (2015). Redefining graduate employability and work-integrated learning: Proposals for effective higher education in disrupted economies. *Journal of Teaching and Learning for Graduate Employability, 6*(1), 56. doi:10.21153/jtlge2015vol6no1art573

Park, E. L., & Choi, B. K. (2014). Transformation of classroom spaces: Traditional versus active learning classroom in colleges. *Higher Education, 68*(5), 749–771. doi:10.1007/s10734-014-9742-0

PISA 2015 Collaborative Problem-Solving Framework. (2017). Retrieved from https://www.oecd.org/pisa/pisaproducts/Draft%20PISA%202015%20Collaborative%20Problem%20Solving%20Framework%20.pdf

Pruyn, M. (1999). *Discourse wars in gotham-west: A latino immigrant urban tale of resistance & agency. The edge: Critical studies in educational theory*. Boulder, CO: Westview Press.
Radcliffe, D., Wilson, H., Powell, D., & Tibbetts, B. (Eds.). (2009). *Learning spaces in higher education: Positive outcomes by design*. St Lucia Qld: The University of Queensland.
Research and Development Div.
TEFMA (Tertiary Education Facilities Management Association). (2009). *Space planning guidelines* (3rd ed.). Sydney: TEFMA Publication.
The Future of Jobs: Employment, Skills and Workforce Strategy for the Fourth Industrial Revolution. (2016). Retrieved from http://reports.weforum.org/future-of-jobs-2016/chapter-1-the-future-of-jobs-and-skills/
The New Work Smarts. (2017). *Horizon report: 2017 higher education edition*. Sydney: NMC. Retrieved from https://www.nmc.org/publication/nmc-horizon-report-2017-higher-education-edition
Walsh, B. (1973). *Theories of person-environment interaction: Implications for the college student*. Iowa City, IA: American College Testing Program.
Wright, S., & Parchoma, G. (2011). Technologies for learning? An actor-network theory critique of 'affordances' in research on mobile learning. *Research in Learning Technology, 19*(3), 247–258.

KENN FISHER

# 16. AFTERWORD

*21st C learner modalities*

This book has been an evidence-based journey from city through campus to library to thirdspaces and finally the 'classroom'. It has been the utmost pleasure to draw the authors' specialised doctoral dissertation evaluations together all in the one place for the critical reader to use as a resource. The chapters combine theory with practice, in keeping with the translational design ethos of this collection. But what is missing is an examination of how students learn in the digital world of the 21st C, and how should planners and designers cater for these learning modalities on the campus and in the learning environments?

In a related vein, over the 12 months or so it took to curate this book, a client engaged the editor as an educational planner to assist in a major transformation of a 7000-student foundation school which covered years 12 and 13 as a transition year to post-secondary educational futures.

The process involved linking pedagogy to space using the strategic documents of the organisation as a guide and as an audit trail to ensure that all of the recommendations had a sound base. However, through the fact-finding stage of the study it became apparent that, whilst the organisation was ready for significant transformation, it had a significant gap in its strategy. It did have a teaching excellence framework, but it didn't have a 'learning theory' to drive its overarching philosophy. It was still focussed on a 20th C learning paradigm in that it was largely teacher centred. And that form of teaching was not really technology enabled active learning but was rather passive and teacher led in nature.

Reading Bolton (2008) on learning theories, there are three categories he (and others) have identified as the principal models of learning, with all having a part to play depending on the context. The three included behaviourist, cognivist and humanist. Bolton spoke himself of not succeeding in secondary school, where the cognitive approach predominated and, when he joined the army, he managed to survive the combined behaviourist/cognitive model they used. He doesn't mention the humanist in his own earlier learning years, but I suspect that is where he was at after secondary school and the army, as illustrated in the figure.

As this book came together in parallel with the foundation school project, with the book chapters exploring learner centred spatial models in response to self-directed learning, it became apparent that there needed to be developed a learning theory for the client organisation. Working with their e-Learning team the following key themes evolved as pivot points for the move to the new campus and, in so doing, provided an evidence-base for the kinds of spaces that would be needed for these learning modalities.

© KONINKLIJKE BRILL NV, LEIDEN, 2019 | DOI: 10.1163/9789004391598_019

K. FISHER

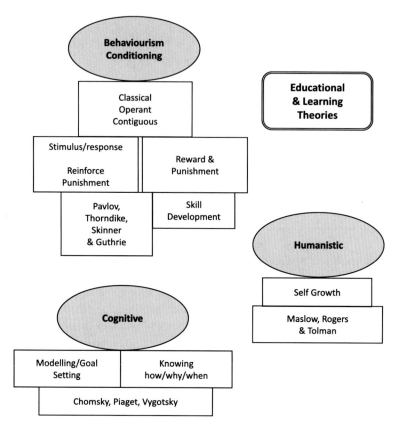

*Figure 16.1. The three over-arching modes of learning theory (Bolton, 2005)*

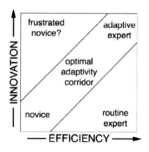

*Figure 16.2. Adaptive teaching framework (Bolton, 2005)*

Bransford (2005) speaks about the notion of 'adaptive expertise', where the teacher moves over all domains in context of the material being taught and to whom and in what setting.

AFTERWORD

For this particular client, five pedagogies were suggested as fundamental to a 21st C teaching and learning model – blended and collaborative learning; self-directed personalised learning; integrated curriculum; differentiated teaching; and deep learning. Of themselves, they do not make a 'learning theory', but they may tempt the client organisation to piece one together from the myriad theories that exist in the literature. For those readers wanting an expose of the majority of extant theories, Schunk (2012) is recommended.

*Blended Learning & Collaborative Learning*

'Blended learning' – also referred to as 'hybrid learning' – combines traditional face-to-face classroom instruction with online learning (Educause, 2018). Evidence as to its effectiveness has been emerging incrementally over the past 5–10 years. One such meta-analysis noted that:

> The corpus of 50 effect sizes extracted from 45 studies meeting meta-analysis inclusion criteria was sufficient to demonstrate that, in recent applications, purely online learning has been equivalent to face-to-face instruction in effectiveness, and blended approaches have been more effective than instruction offered entirely in face-to-face mode. (Means, Toyama, Murphy, & Baki, 2013)

Another study of the Australian Science and Mathematics School noted that in excess of 90% graduate students progress to university. The ASMS is a problem- and project-based school which uses exclusively blended and collaborative learning. (ASMS, 2018). Further, the entire Faculty of Engineering at the University of Melbourne converted all years to blended and collaborative learning over the period 2007 to 2012 following an evaluation after the first-year prototype (Chang, R., Stern, L., Sondergaard, H., & Hardgraft, R., 2009). Another meta-study – a predecessor to the Fisher and Ellis (2019) study which is a Chapter in this book, was undertaken by Fisher and Newton (2012) with four studies showing improved learning outcomes from blended learning.

More recently Monash and Queensland Universities have joined up to offer blended courses online. This is most likely a first-of-its-kind agreement to jointly develop online course material to use on both campuses. Initially focusing on two subjects, one in business and one in science, both will be delivered at both institutions. Professor Wright noted that:

> We aim to have about 80 courses in a very high quality, blended learning environment. Both Monash and UQ have an expectation we can develop this into other courses and other subject areas, and ultimately into more advanced courses where we can get best use of the respective strengths of two great institutions. Even though the course material being developed is online, it will be used for students attending campus, using what universities call blended learning. After

K. FISHER

absorbing the online content, students attend group sessions where they deepen their learning with tutorials, practicals or other active learning experiences. It's very important to stress this is not about taking teaching away from students; it's about enriching their learning experiences. (Dodd, 2018)

In piloting a project not previously tested is was noted that this was an 'ambitions project', but it was based on a survey of students 70% of whom advised that they wanted a blended approach to learning. Thus, there was a form of evidence to underpin this pilot and, indeed, it is expected that the pilot study will be further evaluated for the two subjects before launching the approach across many subjects.

*Self-Directed Learning (Also a Component of Personalised Learning)*

This is defined as:

In its broadest meaning, self-directed learning describes a process in which individuals take the initiative, with or without the help of others, in diagnosing their learning needs, formulating learning goals, identifying human and material resources for learning, choosing and implementing appropriate learning strategies, and evaluating learning outcomes. (Knowles, 1975, p. 18)

Polk College has undertaken deep research on this. They have developed the motivational strategies for learning questionnaire (MSLQ) which examines: *motivational constructs*: (1) intrinsic goal orientation (2) extrinsic goal orientation (3) task value (4) control of learning beliefs (5) self-efficacy for learning and performance (6) task anxiety and the *learning strategies construct*: (1) rehearsal, (2) elaboration, (3) organisation, (4) critical thinking, (5) metacognitive self-regulation, (6) time/study environmental management, (7) effort regulation, (8) peer learning, and (9) help seeking. (Boyer & Usinger, 2015). The Malcolm Knowles Award (acknowledged as the world renowned and recognised expert in adult learning) is part of the International Society of Self Directed Learning. Knowles work leads the research effort on the efficacy of self-directed learning (SDL Global, 2018). The Australian Science and Mathematics School practices this form of learning (ASMS, 2018).

*Interdisciplinary Curriculum*

One definition for this is:

Interdisciplinary/cross-curricular teaching involves a conscious effort to apply knowledge, principles, and/or values to more than one academic discipline simultaneously. The disciplines may be related through a central theme, issue, problem, process, topic, or experience. (Jacobs, 1989)

The nomenclature for inter-disciplinary and cross-curricular teaching includes theme and thematic unit. The structure has goals and outcomes that postulate student learning outcomes resulting from this form of pedagogy. The process works in two stages. Firstly, within language there is integration of listening, speaking, reading, writing, thinking. The second phase involves including all subject areas. Interdisciplinary and cross-curricular pedagogy is a means of reducing fragmentation and isolated skill instruction in siloed subjects.

It also enables transferability of skills of learning – especially in thinking and reasoning – but also supports a more authentic model of learning as students study such questions as water security, food security, resources, transport and so on, making connections between subject areas to support an argument related to a theme. Most countries integrate the development of 21st century skills and competencies in a cross-curricular way, i.e. across subject areas. ICT-related skills are often the exception to this, i.e. they are taught in some countries as a separate subject. (Ananiadou & Claro, 2009). In particular, for cross curricular teaching and learning in bilingual classes:

'the findings show that students in classes where cross-curricular collaboration was practised demonstrated a better understanding of the targeted grammatical items. This could be attributed to enhanced teacher awareness of students' needs, a more suitable curriculum and changes in teachers' pedagogical foci in lessons'. (Yuen, 2014)

The ASMS rigorously follows an interdisciplinary model for STEM programmes. This program uses the:

Principles of inquiry, collaboration, and co-design to ensure that the learning is authentic, meaningful, and connected to real world problems. The program explores a range of social, political, economic, and ethical issues that impact on the Health industry. Strong connections are made with industry partners and students design solutions to complex problems faced by industry. As they work, they match the disciplinary knowledge into interdisciplinary themes ready for the construction of task design. Following this process, the learning and assessment activities and rubrics are structured, written and ready for student learning and teacher's work. (ASMS, 2018b)

*Differentiated Instruction*

Differentiated instruction (DI) is made up of three key components (1) the teacher acts a facilitator and guide with students working peer-peer and teacher working teacher-student; (2) group arrangements and assessment are interdependent and, (3) curriculum content, activities and outputs are adapted so that students have entry points that match their learning readiness, interests and profiles (PLS Classes, 2018). The U.S. Department of Education has a framework for differentiated teaching which forms a part of personalized learning. Thus, students learning plans are design to meet the 'individual learning needs, preferences, and interests' Sparks, D. (2015).

This approach is grounded in Tomlinson's (2003) model, although Rock et al. (2008) suggest there is a need to 'determine students' readiness, interests, preferences, strengths, and needs ... whilst teachers might consider students' styles of thinking, they should not confuse this with learning styles. In fact, we urge resisting the temptation to try to match instructional methods with students' preferred modalities because research does not support such a practice' (cited from Landrum & McDuffie, 2010, p. 35).

> Beyond experiential evidence that pervasive uniformity in teaching fails many learners, there is reason in both theory and research to support movement toward classrooms attentive to student variance that is manifest in at least three areas: student readiness, interest, and learning profile. (Tomlinson et al., 2003)

A D.Ed. study of six secondary schools found that results from focus groups identified four themes: (1) limited knowledge of teachers of differentiated instruction, (2) lack of professional development, (3) teachers value 'collaborative education, peer education, learning communities, mentoring, and collegiality' as a means of professional development, and (4) valuing teaching methods that are supported by data (Kiley, 2011). Whilst it seems that this form of instruction struggles to be sustainable, the D.Ed. study above notes that those teachers that believe in it can achieve it. Furthermore, the 2010 National Education Technology Plan framework notes that "Results suggest that differentiation of instruction and assessment are complex endeavours requiring extended time and concentrated effort to master. Add to this complex reality of schooling, such as large class sizes, limited resource materials, lack of planning time, lack of structures in place to allow collaboration with colleagues, and ever-increasing numbers of teacher responsibilities, and the tasks become even more daunting".

However, since that time there is a much greater range of online learning as used in a blended 'flipped' format, enabling a more the learning can be personalised and thus differentiated.

*Deep Learning*

Fullan et al. (2014) suggest that deep learning:

> Increases self and others' expectations for more learning and achievement by providing a process; increases student engagement in the learning through personalization and ownership; connects students to the "real world", which is often more reflective of their own reality and cultural identity, which can be particularly important for students from other cultures; resonates with

AFTERWORD

spiritual values that link to vast numbers of the population whether secular or religious; builds skills, knowledge, self-confidence, and self-efficacy through inquiry; builds new relationships with and between the learner, their family, their communities, and their teachers; and deepens human desire to connect with others to do good.

One of the best resources for deep learning is the new pedagogies for deep learning project http://npdl.global/. It is led by Michael Fullan so has high level credibility. Their 6 Cs mantra is a good access point for schools. There is a Vic DET program behind the NDPL entitled FUSE (DET, 2018). (Source: Graeme Oliver, former Deputy Head, Australian Science & Mathematics School). Successful deep learning requires cross faculty support and professional development, and active learning classrooms. Two programs (a) the University of Iowa (Iowa) Transform, Interact, Learn, Engage (TILE) program and (b) the Indiana University (Indiana) Mosaic Initiative have taking this route. The "Mosaic Active Learning Initiative" has a mosaic – or variety – of alternatives designs in contrast to the SCALE-UP model. With flexible, mobile furniture and a technology rich environment the affordances were such that a wide variety of pedagogies – simultaneously face-to-face and online – are possible. 'As such, students could think deeply about the history via digital methods not previously possible through the traditional classroom structure'. (Morrone, Flaming, Birdwell, Russell, Roman, & Jesse, 2017).

An AIR (2014) study observed that in New York network schools: (1) OECD PISA-Based Test for Schools (PBTS) resulted in higher scores on content knowledge and problem solving, (2) had more positive interpersonal and intrapersonal attributes, (3) graduated on time (in 4 years of Grade 9), (4) were more likely to enroll in 4-year post-secondary programmes, (5) effects varied across paired schools, and (6) were beneficial for students entering with low achievement, and also improved achievement results for high achievers. However, post-secondary enrolments for lower achievers did not increase.

The evaluation of, and resulting evidence-base, for these technology-enabled active blended learning (TEAL) classrooms are compelling and provide significant arguments as to how designers, planners, teachers and academics alike should consider what a 21st C campus and learning environment might look like. Perhaps my final word is that the 21st C campus will look like a library – i.e. the whole campus will look like a library, as students vote with their feet to choose spaces and places for learning that support their self-directed personalised learning needs and modalities. The virtual and the technology will lead, not follow.

Finally, I would like to thank the co-authors of this publication for, without their patience, passion and scholarly efforts, we would still be learning and teaching in the once innovative Industrial Age 19th & 20th C classroom cell.

K. FISHER

## REFERENCES

AIR (American Institute for Research). (2014). *Findings from the study of deeper learning: Opportunities and outcomes.* Washington, DC: American Institutes for Research.

Ananiadou, K., & Claro, M. (2009). *21st century skills and competences for new millennium learners in OECD countries* (EDU Working Paper No. 4). Paris: OECD. Retrieved from http://repositorio.minedu.gob.pe/bitstream/handle/123456789/2529/21st%20Century%20Skills%20and%20Competences%20for%20New%20Millennium%20Learners%20in%20OECD%20Countries.pdf?sequence=1&isAllowed=y

ASMS. (2018). *Personal communication with principal of ASMS.* Retrieved from https://research.unimelb.edu.au/learnetwork/home

ASMS. (2018a). Retrieved from https://www.asms.sa.edu.au/student-learning/

ASMS. (2018b). Retrieved from https://www.asms.sa.edu.au/portfolio/health-sciences/

Bolton, J., Abbots, R., Brown, K., Fox, J., Hawkes, L., Jones, C., Joyce, K., McGimpsey, H., Sharman, R., Stepney, M., Thacker, S., Tunicliffe, P., & Watts, S. (2008). *Making waves in education: Learning theories.* Retrieved from http://escalate.ac.uk/downloads/5811.pdf

Boyer, N., & Usinger, P. (2015). Tracking pathways to success: Triangulating learning success factors. *International Journal of Self-Directed Learning, 12*(2), 22–48.

Bransford, J., Vye, N., Stevens, R., Kuhl, P., Schwartz, D., Bell, P., Meltzoff, A., Barron, B., Pea, R., Reeves, B., Roschelle, J., & Sabelli, N. (2005). Learning theories and education: Toward a decade of synergy. In P. Alexander & P. Winne (Eds.), *Handbook of educational psychology* (2nd ed., p. 95). Mahwah, NJ: Lawrence Erlbaum Associates.

Chang, R., Stern, L., Sondergaard, H., & Hardgraft, R. (2009). *Places for learning engineering: A preliminary report on informal learning spaces.* Proceedings of the Research in Engineering Education Symposium, Palm Cove, Queensland.

DET Victoria. (2018). Retrieved from http://fuse.education.vic.gov.au/Resource/ByPin?Pin=9KWMRK&SearchScope=All

Dodd, T. (2018, May 2). Blended courses online. *The Australian.* Retrieved from https://www.theaustralian.com.au/higher-education/monash-uq-firs...nded-courses-online/news-story/6e6a69bc0bec1ee1be92a9f10df7e724

Educause. (2018). Retrieved from https://library.educause.edu/topics/teaching-and-learning/blended-learning

Fisher, K., & Newton, C. (2012). Transforming the twenty-first-century campus to enhance the net-generation student learning experience: Using evidence-based design to determine what works and why in virtual/physical teaching spaces. *Higher Education Research & Development, 33*(5), 903–920. doi:10.1080/07294360.2014.890566

Fullan, M., & Langworthy, M. (2013). *Towards a new end: New pedagogies for deep learning.* Seattle, WA: Collaborative Impact.

Jacobs, H. (Ed.). (1989). *Interdisciplinary curriculum: Design and implementation.* Alexandria, VA: Association for Supervision and Curriculum Development.

Kiley, D. (2011). *Differentiated instruction in the secondary classroom: Analysis of the level of implementation and factors that influence practice.* Kalamazoo, MI: Western Michigan University.

Knowles, M. (1975). *Self-directed learning: A guide for learners and teachers.* New York, NY: Cambridge Books.

Landrum, T. J., & McDuffie, K. A. (2010). Learning styles in the age of differentiated instruction. *Exceptionality, 18,* 6–17.

Means, B., Toyama, Y., Murphy, R., & Baki, M. (2013). The effectiveness of online and blended learning: A meta-analysis of the empirical literature. *Teachers College Record Volume, 115,* 1–47.

Morrone, A., Flaming, A., Birdwell, T., Russell, J., Roman, T., & Jesse, M. (2017). *Creating active learning classrooms is not enough: Lessons from two case studies.* Retrieved from https://er.educause.edu/articles/2017/12/creating-active-learning-classrooms-is-not-enough-lessons-from-two-case-studies

PLS Classes. (2018). *Differentiated instruction for today's classroom®.* Retrieved from https://plsclasses.com/browse-enroll/classes/differentiated-instruction-for-todays-classroom-online/

334

Rock, M., Gregg, M., Ellis, E., & Gable, R. (2008). REACH: A framework for differentiating classroom instruction. *Preventing School Failure, 52*(2), 31–47.

Schunk, D. H. (2012). *Learning theories: An educational perspective.* Boston, MA: Allyn & Bacon.

SDL Global. (2018). Retrieved from https://www.sdlglobal.com/knowles-award

Sparks, D. (2015). *Differentiated instruction: A primer.* Retrieved from https://www.edweek.org/ew/articles/2015/01/28/differentiated-instruction-a-primer.html

Tomlinson, C. A., Brighton, C., Hertberg, H., Callahan, C., Moon, T., Brimijoin, K., Conover, L., & Reynolds, T. (2003). Differentiating instruction in response to student readiness, interest, and learning profile in academically diverse classrooms: A review of literature. *Journal for the Education of the Gifted, 27*(2–3), 119–145.

Yuen, Y. L. (2014). A glimpse into the effectiveness of L2-content cross-curricular collaboration in content-based instruction programmes. *International Journal of Bilingual Education and Bilingualism, 18*(4), 443–462.